D1091026

THE GYPSY-BACHELOR OF MANCHESTER
The Life of Mrs. Gaskell's Demon

VICTORIAN LITERATURE AND CULTURE SERIES
Karen Chase, Jerome J. McGann, *and* Herbert Tucker, *General Editors*

DANIEL ALBRIGHT
  Tennyson: *The Muses' Tug-of-War*
DAVID G. RIEDE
  Matthew Arnold and the Betrayal of Language
ANTHONY WINNER
  Culture and Irony: *Studies in Joseph Conrad's Major Novels*
JAMES RICHARDSON
  Vanishing Lives: *Style and Self in Tennyson, D. G. Rossetti, Swinburne, and Yeats*
JEROME J. MCGANN, Editor
  Victorian Connections
ANTONY H. HARRISON
  Victorian Poets and Romantic Poems: *Intertextuality and Ideology*
E. WARWICK SLINN
  The Discourse of Self in Victorian Poetry
LINDA K. HUGHES and MICHAEL LUND
  The Victorian Serial
ANNA LEONOWENS, Edited and with an Introduction by Susan Morgan
  The Romance of the Harem
ALAN FISCHLER
  Modified Rapture: *Comedy in W. S. Gilbert's Savoy Operas*
BARBARA TIMM GATES, Editor
  Journal of Emily Shore, with a new Introduction by the Editor
RICHARD MAXWELL
  The Mysteries of Paris and London
FELICIA BONAPARTE
  The Gypsy-Bachelor of Manchester: *The Life of Mrs. Gaskell's Demon*
PETER L. SHILLINGSBURG
  Pegasus in Harness: *Victorian Publishing and W. M. Thackeray*
ALLAN C. DOOLEY
  Author and Printer in Victorian England

THE
GYPSY-BACHELOR
OF MANCHESTER
The Life of
Mrs. Gaskell's Demon

Felicia Bonaparte

University Press of Virginia
Charlottesville and London

PR
4711
B6
1992

FLORIDA STATE
UNIVERSITY LIBRARIES

JUN 29 1993

TALLAHASSEE, FLORIDA

THE UNIVERSITY PRESS OF VIRGINIA
Copyright © 1992 by the Rector and Visitors
of the University of Virginia

First published 1992

Library of Congress Cataloging-in-Publication Data

Bonaparte, Felicia.
    The gypsy-bachelor of Manchester : the life of Mrs. Gaskell's
demon / Felicia Bonaparte.
        p.   cm. — (Victorian literature and culture series)
    Includes bibliographical references and index.
    ISBN 0-8139-1390-X (cloth)
    1. Gaskell, Elizabeth Cleghorn, 1810–1865.   2. Gaskell, Elizabeth
Cleghorn, 1810–1865—Political and social views.   3. Women and
literature—England—History—19th century.   4. Novelists,
English—19th century—Biography.   I. Title.   II. Series.
PR4711.B6   1992
823'.8—dc20   92-292
[B]   CIP

Printed in the United States of America

FOR

Ruth Zabriskie Temple
Friend and Scholar
With Admiration and Affection

Contents

Acknowledgments

I began this book a long time ago and I have, in the writing of it, incurred many debts and obligations that I here acknowledge with pleasure.

I could not have begun this work had not The City College of New York granted me a sabbatical leave, and I could not have taken that leave had I not, during that year, received a fellowship as well from The American Council of Learned Societies and a summer stipend from the National Endowment for the Humanities. I am profoundly grateful to all for their generous support.

I spent that year as a Fellow of the Radcliffe Institute (now the Bunting Institute) at Harvard University and I am deeply indebted to it for more things than I can mention. In every conceivable way, it provided me with a room of my own. I shared that year at the Radcliffe Institute with an exceptional group of Fellows, and I am most thankful to them for their interest and encouragement. For their friendship and good counsel, I wish especially to express my gratitude to Carolyn Heilbrun and Grace A. Mojtabai. I thank the university too for its cordial hospitality and for giving me free access to its many splendid libraries. I am particularly grateful to the Houghton for allowing me to read what is now its very rare copy of Elizabeth Gaskell's "Diary."

During my year at the Radcliffe Institute I was fortunate, moreover, to be affiliated with Adams House. I thank all the members of the House, especially Joanne and Richard Kronauer, the Acting Masters for that year, for a great many happy memories.

And I wish also to thank the members of the Harvard Victorians for inviting me that year to be associated with their group.

Over the years, I have had the pleasure of reading a number of papers on Gaskell, and I am grateful to all of those who helped me to work out my thoughts through their questions and suggestions. But I wish to thank particularly the

Fellows of the Radcliffe Institute who heard the paper that
became in essence the argument of this book; the members of
the English Institute who, by inviting me to speak at a session
on biography, allowed me to develop further my ideas on the
relationship between literature and life; and the students and
faculty both of the Bread Loaf School of English who, by
asking me to give one of the annual Elizabeth Drew Lectures,
offered me a chance to explore some of the theoretical
questions involved in the writing of biography.

I am enormously grateful too to those who helped me put
this manuscript into its final shape. I wish to thank my very
good friend Elizabeth J. Hodge for reading the manuscript in
several of its progressive stages and for offering invaluable
suggestions on its substance and its style. I wish to thank the
anonymous reader to whom the University Press of Virginia
sent it for evaluation and Victorian Series editor Karen Chase. I
am deeply indebted to them for their sympathetic reading and
for recommending revisions which have improved it in every
way. And I wish to thank the editors at the university press,
Cathie Brettschneider and Cynthia H. Foote, for their kindness
and their help.

I should like to thank as well those who made available to
me copies of letters in their possession and who allowed me to
quote from them: the Brotherton Collection, Leeds University
Library, The Huntington Library, San Marino, California, the
Trustees of the National Library of Scotland, and Mr. J. G.
Sharps, for whose help and generosity I am additionally
grateful. To The National Portrait Gallery and to the Director
and University Librarian, the John Rylands University Library
of Manchester, I am grateful for permission to use the portraits
of Elizabeth Gaskell by George Richmond and W. J. Thomson
which appear on the cover of this book.

Finally, I should like to thank those whose liberal help and
kindness made it possible for me to use the materials at these
libraries: at the Huntington, Kathy Schneberger; at the
National Library of Scotland, I. C. Cunningham; at the
National Portrait Gallery, Deborah Samson; and, at the John
Rylands University Library, John Tuck. Most especially, I wish
to thank Christopher Sheppard at the Brotherton Collection. I
could not have proceeded without him.

THE GYPSY-BACHELOR OF MANCHESTER
The Life of Mrs. Gaskell's Demon

I

·····⊷∞⊶·····

Introduction

I PROPOSE IN THIS STUDY to examine Elizabeth Gaskell's life and fiction as one continuous metaphoric text. My interest will be biographical but my method will be critical. I shall not, therefore, be concerned with Gaskell's fiction as works of literature, but neither shall I be concerned, except as they touch other things, with the facts of Gaskell's life. The facts, indeed, or what we have of them, are, for the most part, established already. In her superb and definitive study of the record of Gaskell's life, to which all subsequent work on Gaskell must be, as I am, deeply indebted, Winifred Gérin has not only gathered most of the available data, she has gone as far as one can go in interpreting Gaskell's history purely on the basis of facts.[1] My intention is to explore Elizabeth Gaskell's inner existence. In that existence lies the key to a very different woman, one, however, inaccessible by the usual biographical means. Only by "reading" Elizabeth Gaskell as though she were a poetic text can we enter the private world that the inner woman inhabits.

The facts alone of Gaskell's life can be and often have been misleading. While many other women novelists escaped, at least in bare essentials, becoming models of "femininity," Gaskell appears to have been the epitome of the ideal Victorian woman. Jane Austen, for instance, never married. Neither did Emily Brontë. Emily's sister Charlotte did marry, but not until she was thirty-eight, by which time she had secured her reputation as a novelist. George Eliot too, although she had not yet turned her hand to the writing of fiction when she moved in with George Henry Lewes, had already made a name for herself with her essays, translations, and reviews. And none of these women ever had children. The record, however, of Gaskell's life seems to paint a different picture. Born Elizabeth Cleghorn Stevenson, Gaskell, before she turned twenty-two, married the Rev. Mr. William Gaskell, a clergyman who was to become the minister of the Cross Street Chapel in Manchester, undoubtedly the most prestigious Unitarian chapel in England. His work involved him in many enterprises, and through him Gaskell herself became an active member of her community. She bore six children, four of whom lived, and they, along with her husband and home, appear to have been, until she died at the age of fifty-five, the center of her whole existence. Except for the fact that she wrote fiction, Gaskell seems thus to have lived, in Coventry Patmore's now infamous words, the life of "the angel in the house."

There are some instances in which Gaskell did not conform to the ideal, and feminist readers—Aina Rubenius and Elaine Showalter, for example, both in pioneering works[2]—have rightly drawn attention to them. Gaskell did not surrender her income, like other Victorian women, for instance, to her husband to dispose of. She liked to travel, and she often, unlike most women of her day, did not take her husband along. And she appeared, at the end of her life, to show an unusual independence for a nineteenth-century woman when she purchased and furnished a house without consulting or telling her husband. But these are small and rare exceptions in a life that cannot be, on the facts alone at least, seen as anything but conventional in the most extreme degree.

And it is in conventional terms that most of her readers have seen Gaskell. In his assessment of her work, published in 1874, G. B. Smith, for example, began by remarking that Gaskell's "life was one of those which furnish the best evidence that woman is frequently fitted to accomplish greater work than that which is usually assigned to her sex" but ended by saying that, nonetheless, "Mrs. Gaskell lacked none of those virtues which make home 'the earthly paradise.'" In his reevaluation of the nineteenth-century novel written in 1935, David Cecil likewise observed that the "outstanding fact about Mrs. Gaskell is her femininity." "Charlotte Brontë's admirers do not think of her as Mrs. Nicholls; George Eliot's admirers would wonder whom one meant if one referred to her as Mrs. Cross. But Elizabeth Cleghorn Stevenson is known to the world as Mrs. Gaskell" and "that," he continued, "is just as it should be." For "in an age whose ideal of women emphasized the feminine qualities at the expense of all others, she was all a woman was expected to be: gentle, domestic, tactful, unintellectual, prone to tears, easily shocked. So far from chafing at the limits imposed on her activities, she accepted them with serene satisfaction." And in 1965, Arthur Pollard, in an account written on the centenary of her death, suggested that Gaskell, in addition to being the ideal Victorian woman, was the very incarnation of "a Victorian Dissenting minister's wife."[3]

And yet there is a reason to doubt that Gaskell was the kind of woman that is suggested by such a life. It is simply that the facts on which our conclusions are based are, when we examine them closely, wholly inadequate as evidence. Many details are available for some aspects of Gaskell's life, but for others very few. And for some—the very items in which we might hope to read something of her inner thoughts—there are virtually none at all. Thus, although there appears to be ample information on Gaskell, the truth is that we know very little.

For this, to a very large extent, Gaskell is herself responsible. She took extraordinary pains to keep her private life a secret. When she became a public figure, she was often asked to provide information about herself, but she always refused to do so. "I disapprove," she writes, for instance, replying to one such request, "so entirely of the plan of writing 'notices' or 'memoirs' of living people, that I must send you on the answer I have already sent to many others: namely an entire refusal to sanction what is to me an objectionable & indelicate practice, by furnishing a single fact with regard to myself. I do not see why the public have any more to do with me than to buy or reject the wares I supply them."[4] In a more humorous vein to Anne Robson—one of two sisters of her husband, both of whom became her friends—Gaskell writes that she so much disapproves of "biographies of living people" that she is willing to allow whoever asks to "invent mine, & have often learnt some curious particulars about myself from what they choose to say" (*L* 570).

But it was not just while she lived that Gaskell wanted to avoid being the subject of public comment. She herself was one day to write a biography of Charlotte Brontë but, from her very earliest days, she did her best to see that no one would ever be able to write hers. It may be, as G. A. Payne reports on the strength of a story he heard, that Gaskell, on being told that Thackeray had on his deathbed asked his daughters not to let anyone write his biography, made the same request of hers.[5] But long before 1863, which was the year of Thackeray's death, Gaskell had begun to ask her correspondents to burn her letters. Once or twice a letter's contents make such a request intelligible. Thus, in a letter to John Forster, one of the friends she shared with Dickens, Gaskell speaks ill of Effie Grey, Mrs. John Ruskin, whom, as it happened, she had known as a girl at school. Effie had recently left her husband, and rumor had it he had been cruel to her. Gaskell, however, who admired Ruskin, could not believe he had been responsible for their quarrel and separation. In her letter, she blames Effie, who had always, she explains, been a vain and flighty girl. The letter is long, and by the end Gaskell regrets her words about Effie, which seem to her now excessively harsh. "Oh! Mr. Forster," she bursts out suddenly, "if you don't burn my letters as you read them I will never forgive you!" (*L* 195). But most of the letters Gaskell wants burned have nothing in them even she could consider reprehensible. What, for example, could Gaskell have feared from the survival of a letter she writes to her daughter Marianne in which she reports that the piano needs tuning, being flat by more than half a note, laments that the little black kitten is lost, and, in answer to a question, explains the nature of "scripture readers"? Yet Gaskell suddenly stops in the middle to write "Pray burn any letters. I am always afraid of writing much to you, you are so careless about letters," and ends by repeating *"Burn this"* (L 185). She even devises a secret code that she explains to George Smith, her publisher: a star at the beginning of a letter indicates that it may be kept; otherwise, it must be burned (L 324).

Perhaps such requests ought to be honored, great as the loss of such letters must be. Gaskell's second daughter did honor the request her mother made. Before she died, Margaret Emily, known to the family as Meta, burned all the letters in her possession. This may very well have been a case of life imitating art, for Gaskell had already in *Cranford* described precisely such a bonfire, and Meta had certainly read the book. In *Cranford,* it is the heroine, Matty, who, feeling she has reached an age at which death is a possibility, gathers all the family letters and, reading them over for the last time, commits them one by one to the flames. The reason she gives might well have been the reason Gaskell gave her daughters for asking them to burn her letters. They must " 'not be allowed,' " she says, " 'to fall into the hands of strangers' " (2:51).[6]

Florence and Julia, the younger daughters, held, it is possible, similar bonfires, for only a handful of the letters Gaskell wrote to them survives. William may have burned letters too. Gaskell must have written to him on her many trips abroad, but not a single letter remains. Marianne alone of all the family kept the letters Gaskell sent her, proving that her mother was right to think that on this she could not be trusted. Whatever Gaskell had to say to William and her other daughters has been, thus, irretrievably lost.

Lost as well are many letters Gaskell wrote to her various friends. A few are left, like those, for instance, Gaskell wrote to Catherine Winkworth. Catherine was one of the many young people Gaskell befriended throughout her life. She seems to have liked the young especially and to have sought out their company. Perhaps she herself provided the reason when she wrote, in "A Dark Night's Work"—a story published in *All the Year Round* from January through March of 1863[7]—about the heroine's father, Edward, that he liked "the joyous, thoughtless company of the young better than that of the old—given the same amount of refinement and education in both" (7:416). The young beguiled him out of himself. Perhaps they beguiled Gaskell as well. Catherine was one of seven children of a Manchester silk manufacturer whom, along with her brothers and sisters, Gaskell had met when some of the girls had become pupils of her husband's. Although the others—Susanna, Emily, Selina, Alice, William, and Stephen—are all mentioned, either specifically by name or simply under the family rubric, in a number of her letters, the only letters that exist to any member of that family are the few to Catherine Winkworth. Another of Gaskell's younger friends was the painter Eliza Fox, "Tottie," as Gaskell often called her. The daughter of William Johnson Fox, a liberal, unconventional man, and herself a successful artist mingling in bohemian circles, Eliza was independent, free. Writing to her, Gaskell often seems more open in expression, even bolder in the thoughts she allows herself to think. A good collection of the letters Gaskell wrote to her are left. Still another younger friend was Parthenope Nightingale, the sister of the famous Florence. Gaskell knew the entire family. She even wrote a part of one novel, *North and South,* at the Nightingale house. Florence had impressed her enormously but it was the quiet Parthenope with whom she had developed a friendship. Of the letters she wrote to her, nearly a dozen are in existence. And nearly a dozen remain of the letters to Lady Kay-Shuttleworth, another, although not a younger, friend. Lady Kay-Shuttleworth, an heiress, had married a prominent physician, and both had taken up the hobby of pursuing the literati, whom they liked to invite for visits. Charlotte Brontë was one of their guests, and it was at their home in Windermere that Elizabeth Gaskell met her.

But many of the letters she wrote to her friends have disappeared. None, for instance, has been preserved of Gaskell's letters to Mary Mohl. An Englishwoman who lived in France, Mary Mohl (born Mary Anne Clark), had become part of the circle, as a young girl, of Chateaubriand. Later, she had married Julius Mohl, the well-known German Orientalist. Their home was almost a salon, welcoming many famous people both from England and from the Continent. Whenever Gaskell went to Paris, she always stopped at Mary Mohl's. On many occasions she stayed with her, sometimes for extended visits. She must have written to her frequently when she was at home in Manchester. But not a single letter is left. Although she burned no letters herself, by an ironic twist of fate, the letters Mohl received from Gaskell were set ablaze by an incendiary bomb that dropped on the warehouse in which they were stored in Berlin during World War II. A second bomb, hitting the office of the Gaskell family solicitor, destroyed, in another ironic turn, all the papers stored in Manchester, possibly some letters too (*L,* pp. xii–xiii). Thus, in one way or another, fire consumed very large portions of the record of Gaskell's life.

It is certainly tempting to speculate that in the ashes of those flames lie the answers to our questions. To some the answers undoubtedly do, but not to a multitude of others. For Gaskell did not object to having a biography written about her simply because she cherished her privacy, although like most Victorians she did. She would have appreciated the obituary written for her by David Masson who, after discussing her fiction, remarks that of her "private life" it would be "unfitting to speak."[8] Nor did she shy away from notice merely because she felt a woman should not be talked about in public, although that was the Victorian view and Gaskell very clearly shared it. In *Wives and Daughters,* which was published serially in the *Cornhill Magazine* from August 1864 to January 1866, Mr. Gibson, backing away from a fight that touches on the honor of his daughter, says, and Gaskell seems to agree, that " 'A quarrel between two men which drags a woman's name into notice is to be avoided at all costs' " (8:604). She took such enormous pains to conceal herself because she did not want to be known. The proof is that in the letters we have, and these are considerable in number, Gaskell hardly ever reveals anything of her inner life. The letters are full of information, but mostly of external details. Most concern affairs of the household. We learn what her husband and children are doing. We hear of the running of the house. Gaskell is often planting flowers or tending livestock in the yard. Cooking is always going on, and sometimes we actually get a recipe. And there are even helpful hints on how to cut down the time required for household chores like washing and ironing. Sometimes, although she does not like to make a point of her good deeds, Gaskell reports on the work she is doing for the needy, sick, and poor. Not too often but occasionally she makes a comment about a friend, although it is seldom a personal comment and hardly ever betrays the nature of her interest or attachment. Only rarely do we encounter any kind of general discussion. Abstract ideas are seldom alluded to, and public issues seldom brought up. Even her work tends to elicit little more than the business matters that she must settle with her publishers. All this factual information would make most letters dull and dry, but Gaskell's are nothing of the sort. Quite the contrary. All the way through, there is such a play of charm and humor, so much exuberance and good cheer, along with such sad and tender moments and so many flashes of insight, that, as we read, we are thoroughly taken with her delightful personality. But that is precisely what prevents us, at least initially, from realizing that Gaskell has given nothing away about her inner thoughts and feelings. And this is just what she intended. Gaskell creates such a swarm of detail, such a clutter of events, and covers it all with so much spirit, because she wants to disguise the fact that she has kept her real self hidden.

This is by no means to suggest that Gaskell is not utterly candid. Candor has always been considered one of Gaskell's greatest virtues, and unquestionably it is. But candor is not the same as truth. While her deception is deliberate, it is entirely unconscious. As Gaskell writes in *Sylvia's Lovers* about her heroine at one point, "No one knew much of what was passing in Sylvia; she did not know herself" (6:442). Gaskell herself is the first and last of those from whom she conceals the truth. Most of us have an inner life that we keep secret to an extent, both from others and from ourselves. But seldom is there as great a difference between the outer and inner existence as there was in Gaskell's case. And while it was her inner identity that shaped the choices of her life, Gaskell herself was not aware there was a secret self within her.

This self, however, that she conceals so carefully in her life and letters Gaskell fully reveals in her work. Gaskell's fiction has been receiving a reassessment in recent years. A major novelist in her day, Gaskell, like many other Victorians, began to suffer from neglect at the end of the nineteenth century and it has taken many decades to bring her to our attention again. The centenary of her death, the publication of her letters, and the revival of interest in the fiction of the Victorians combined with the recent feminist movement are reponsible, each in part, for a rekindled interest in Gaskell. And many studies of her art, centering on every issue from the exploration of form to the interpretation of substance, have established her again as an important and serious novelist.

But in one significant way Gaskell's fiction is very different from the fiction, for example, of a novelist like George Eliot. Gaskell's friend Anne Thackeray Ritchie, the daughter of William Makepeace Thackeray and a novelist herself, once compared the two by saying that "Some writers create their characters and rule over this dream-world of theirs as Prospero did in his island; others seem to be rather the servants of their imaginations, and to be governed by their own fantasies." Eliot, she thought, belonged in the first class. Gaskell, she thought, belonged in the second.[9] The fact that Gaskell cannot dissociate herself fully from her imagined world often leads her to make mistakes in the creation of her fictions. But it also allows us to gain access to her through her art.

To many readers, Gaskell's fiction has seemed as "feminine" as her life. But there have always been a few who have seen glimmers of other things. David Masson, for example, Miriam Allott, and John McVeagh have intuited inner conflicts. Margaret Ganz, in an excellent study, has pointed out that Gaskell's humor is the result of her effort to reconcile opposing tensions in her thought.[10] And feminist readers, although a few continue to call her "Mrs. Gaskell," perpetuating the feminine image,[11] have begun both to explore feminist issues in Gaskell's fiction—as, for example, Patsy Stoneman in her study of class and gender—and to detect resistance in it to the feminine ideal. Jenni Calder, for instance, has shown that Gaskell's heroines seek to find strategies to survive in a paternalistic society; Nina Auerbach has suggested that Gaskell uses the women of *Cranford* to create a "holy community" in which women are empowered; Maureen Reddy has remarked on the "feminist rage" contained in the story "The Grey Woman"; and Coral Lansbury, in two works, has argued that on social issues Gaskell did not always hold the "feminine" views attributed to her.[12]

Critical studies such as these have taken us in the right direction. But Gaskell's fiction will, I think, not be fully understood until we realize that these moments of rebellion in her work are not individual moments of occasional insurrection in an otherwise conventional text. They are not part of the text at all. The text, as we have indeed suspected, is almost always ideally "feminine." They are a part, its visible signs, of what we must come to recognize as a subtext in her thought, one that runs under her work as its unified antithesis, one that challenges and subverts everything the text asserts. It is in this subversive subtext that Elizabeth Gaskell conceals the secrets that explain her fiction. And it is here that she encodes the secrets that explain her life.

Gaskell draws heavily in her fiction on people and incidents in her life, so much so that one of her readers, John G. Sharps, has so far found, in a most impressive study, some seven hundred pages of parallels.[13] But Gaskell deals with her experiences less historically than poetically. She never merely transmits a fact. Facts, in truth, do not really interest her. She lives within herself far more than in the external world. It is as though there were in her mind—and in a very real sense there is—an ongoing drama for which she appropriates externals only when she needs them to work out some inner thought. Thus, although they are recognizable as events she has experienced or as people she has known, these externals, by the time Gaskell has turned them into fiction, are entirely transformed. They are no longer recollections but symbolic representations. And these representations become a part of a poetic language in which Gaskell "writes" herself into the structures of her books. Parallels are not always, therefore—although they sometimes help to fill gaps in our knowledge of her history—accurate transcripts of her life. But, as a metaphoric vocabulary, they are always true enactments of the drama in her mind.

To Gaskell this drama is more important than the reality that engendered it or the fiction it creates. Edna Lyall quotes Marianne as saying the girls would occasionally mention that one or another character was just like someone they all knew, only to have their mother reply " 'So he is, but I never meant it for him.' "[14] Gaskell was unaware of her source because what mattered was the image into which she had transformed it. The image also mattered more than the fictional form it took. This is perhaps most amusingly obvious in the curious fact that Gaskell found it hard to think of names for the characters of her fiction or to remember the names she picked. Her stock of names is very small. Margarets, Marys, Smiths, and Browns are among her very favorites. There is an Alice in *Mary Barton* and another in *Sylvia's Lovers*. In *Mary Barton* there is a family that figures prominently named Wilson. Another family named Wilson figures in "The Manchester Marriage." Dixons weave in and out of her fiction, appearing in "Half a Lifetime Ago," "Libbie Marsh's Three Eras," and, as servants in both cases, in the story "A Dark Night's Work" and the novel *North and South*. Now and then, to the reader's confusion, names are repeated within a work. In *Sylvia's Lovers,* for example, there are two unrelated Donkins, one a lawyer and one a tailor. Once in a while, Gaskell repeats not just first or second names but identical combinations. A minor character in *Mary Barton* shares the name of Molly Gibson with the heroine of *Wives and Daughters*. It is not unusual for Gaskell to call the same character by different names. Miss Browning, thus, in *Wives and Daughters,* is given several names in the manuscript.[15] In "Lois the Witch" the heroine's lover begins his fictional life as Ralph but is suddenly renamed Hugh, Ralph becoming then the name of the heroine's uncle instead. Even for animals in her fiction Gaskell can only think of clichés. The dog, for instance, in "Cousin Phillis" is predictably named "Rover" (7:48). And, the most amazing thing, sometimes Gaskell cannot remember the names of her characters at all. Having, for instance, been interrupted by domestic obligations in the writing of *Wives and Daughters,* Gaskell returned to the book to find that she had "forgotten all the names" (*L* 557). Yvonne ffrench suggests that Gaskell reuses names so much in her fiction because she has a pedestrian mind.[16] But Gaskell's mind is not pedestrian, and even if it were, that would not explain why she cannot think of names—names are everywhere around her—or forgets them when she does. The reason, rather, is that to Gaskell her characters are not independent entities with identities of their own. They are momentary embodiments of the images in her mind. That is also the reason Gaskell seldom describes how her characters look. Coral Lansbury suggests that Gaskell fails to give descriptions because she is not by nature visual.[17] But that is actually not the case.

Gaskell is extremely visual and she depicts in vivid detail whatever she imagines seeing as something in the external world. She does not, however, imagine her characters as having an external existence. All her characters are within her. They are projections of herself.

Much of what Gaskell invents in her fiction becomes metaphoric in the same way and so do the conventional signs and the traditional symbols she uses. Whatever meets a need in her mind becomes an image in her quarry. This is not to say that Gaskell has no purpose in her work beyond the expression of her self. There is a real artist in Gaskell, and that artist is concerned with the fictional recreation of the world that she observes. Generally Gaskell is able to balance the private meaning of her images against the fictional purpose they serve. But there are times when the inner drama becomes so much more intense in her mind than her conscious artistic intentions that there is a disproportion, a disruption, in the text. An incident is, for example, reported with a passion that is not warranted by the details of the narrative. Or for no apparent reason, there is a shift in the narrator's tone. Often Gaskell becomes ambivalent in her attitude to her material. Not infrequently she contradicts herself or negates what she has said. And on occasion, as she develops an image to its necessary conclusion without giving sufficient thought to the artistic point of her story, she creates an event or a character that has nothing whatever to do with her subject or her theme. These are moments in which Gaskell fails most visibly as an artist. But they are also moments in which, by detaching it from the narrative, Gaskell holds her subtextual meaning in high relief against her text.

The images that Gaskell creates take many different forms in her fiction. Sometimes they function as figures of speech, sometimes, embodied, they become characters, sometimes, dramatized, they become plots, and often, localized, they become settings. Even the weather is, in Gaskell, usually generated by a metaphor. But it is not in her fiction alone that Gaskell thus enacts her images. The very same imagistic vocabulary is to be found in most of her letters and, even more to the point, in her life. Just as she embodies and dramatizes images into characters and plots, so she realizes them in her life in her relationships and her actions. That is why it is important to "read" the whole of Elizabeth Gaskell—her life, her letters, and her fiction—as one continuous metaphoric text. Often it is only an image which appears in one of her stories that can explicate an action or a relationship in her life.

Gaskell conceived herself in images not only because her imagination tended, as I believe most do in fact, to apprehend the world imagistically, but because it was only through images that she could tell the world those truths she wanted not to know herself. Kathleen Tillotson has remarked that Gaskell combined the innocence of the dove with the wisdom of the serpent.[18] In fiction Gaskell found a way to practice her serpentine wisdom on others but to remain innocent of the fact that she had discovered it in herself. Gaskell herself was aware in some way that she had to her fiction confided secrets she had confessed nowhere else. There were, she wrote once to a friend, things that she could write in a book that she could neither say in person nor put down in a letter. "It may seem strange," she added naïvely, "and I can't myself account for it,—but it is so" (*L* 171).

To know the story of Gaskell's life we need to decode what she encoded. We need to come to know her vocabulary, recognize how her syntax works, and decipher her secret language. We need, using critical methods to answer biographical questions, to "read" Elizabeth Gaskell as though she were a poetic text.

That is what I propose to do here. I have not, in my "reading" of Gaskell, been committed to any school, either critical or psychological. Like Derrida and the deconstructionists, I do focus on language here and extend the methods of criticism beyond the immediate boundaries of literature. My interest, however, is not in language or the ideas it subverts. While I might be said to wish to "deconstruct" the ideal Mrs. Gaskell, my real intention is to "construct" the inner Gaskell I see revealed. Up to a point I share as well, with Jacques Lacan and Roman Jakobson, the Freudean view that the unconscious is structured like a symbolic language. A passage in *The Interpretation of Dreams* seems, in fact, especially pertinent to my analysis of Gaskell. For sometimes reading Gaskell's fiction is like having a front seat at a performance of her dreams, and a remark that Sigmund Freud makes on the manner in which "dream-thoughts" are transformed into "dream-content" offers a relevant analogy to the manner in which I see Gaskell turning her own life into the matter of her art. "The dream-thoughts and the dream-content are presented to us," Freud writes, "like two versions of the same subject-matter in two different languages. Or, more properly, the dream-content seems like a transcript of the dream-thoughts into another mode of expression, whose characters and syntactic laws it is our business to discover."[19] But, unlike Lacan and Jakobson, I am not as much concerned with the contents of the unconscious or with the character of that language as I am with the way in which Gaskell, in her imagination, uses metaphors and symbols to conceive her own identity. And I obviously share assumptions with some recent feminist thought. My effort, however, has been from the first, rather than to impose a theory, to follow as far as I can the lead of Gaskell's images and structures and to avoid, as much as possible, forcing them into any extraneous definition or design.

I realize that this kind of biography is of necessity an interpretation, psychological inference being at best only an inspired guess. And an interpretation, of course, takes us, as we have increasingly recognized in the past few decades or so, across the subtle line that divides the worlds of history and fiction.[20] But every biography, it seems to me, is fictional to a great degree. Although the biographer cannot invent the factual evidence like the novelist, in the handling of that evidence he is engaged in making fictions. For evidence does not speak for itself. We speak through it, hence interpret it. Except perhaps for simple records, as of births and deaths and marriages, nearly every kind of testimony needs in some way to be construed. What, for example, did Emily Dickinson mean when she observed in a letter "My mother does not care for thought"? Was she suggesting that her mother, as one of her biographers claims, had a capacity for thought although she did not care to exercise it,[21] or was she, as it seems to me, rather expressing her contempt for the intelligence of her parent? Although the evidence is historical in the sense that we have the words written on a piece of paper in a hand we think is Dickinson's, the documentation requires a "reading" and can support what we must call, since we can never know the truth—and would not necessarily know it even if Dickinson had told us, for there is no reason to trust her under-standing of her intention—two entirely different "fictions."

Nor can we hope to escape these difficulties in a purely factual life. Although an account that tried to restrict itself to a recording of the events might come closer in some ways to our ideal of objective truth, the fact that even here the evidence, if it indeed has all come to light—for if there were still some missing pieces we would obviously have a fiction perpe-trated by pure chance—would require to be selected, organized, put in perspective. And the notion on the basis of which we would do all this would, being a picture we had already formed of the subject in our minds, be an a priori fiction.

Even if this were not the case, even if a book of facts could be somehow put together, it would still not, in itself, offer a portrait we could call true. "What a wee little part of a person's life," wrote Mark Twain in the Preface to his *Autobiography,* "are his acts and his words! His real life is led in his head, and is known to none but himself. All day long, and every day, the mill of his brain is grinding, and his thoughts, not those other things, are his history." Without an account of the inner life, a biography is false. With it, since that inner life must be reached by interpretation, a biography is fiction.

Thus, a biographical study is a Heisenbergian enterprise, a work in which it is not possible to achieve truth and certainty both. Both are important, and I would argue that everyone who deserves a biography should be the subject of at least two, one that stays as close as possible to the collection of the data and another that seeks to pass beyond it to some fictional truth. Where inner and outer lives agree, the two will often overlap. Where they do not, as in Gaskell's case, the factual and the fictional stories will be very different tales. In either case, neither the evidence nor the method will be the same. The factual record will be established by the kind of scholarly research that we have generally accepted as appropriate for a life. The fiction, however, must be "read" in whatever revelations can be found of the inner self.

There is no question that the biographer who is engaged in making fictions can make serious errors too. The errors that he risks, however, are those we all risk every day. It is by a process not very different—through speculations that we base on clues we find in words and deeds—that we know our friends, our spouses, and, to a degree, ourselves. About ourselves we have, it is true, certain privileged information, but we have a blindness too, and it is often only by inferences founded on what we do and say that we are able to arrive at a self-interpretation. Thus, however truthful its author, an autobiography that attempts to pass beyond mere external data is of necessity a fiction too. All we can hope, in writing biographies, whether of ourselves or others, is that, instead of "writing" a portrait into the evidence we have, we have tried to "read" it out. I have tried to do so here.

One last word on my procedure. The final and in some respects the hardest problem I faced here was to find a way to convey the portrait I had perceived of Gaskell. Gaskell's images were, for one thing, so entirely interrelated that the meaning of each depended on its connection to the rest. A true account of each individually and of the whole that they created would, ideally, have required all to be discussed at once. This, of course, being impossible, I decided to let them fall into a sequence that suggested the progression of an argument. I do not mean to imply, however, that they existed in this order or that they were, in Gaskell's mind, arranged in such a logical way. The human mind is not an argument, and Gaskell's psyche was, like most, not the neat and coherent thesis that, in my effort to elucidate, I have tried to make it here. And yet I believe there is a logic on which every psyche hangs, and I shall be altogether satisfied if, although in this linear way, I can suggest the frame on which Gaskell's inner existence depended.

To trace this logic, I have had to ignore the chronology of Gaskell's works. Gaskell did not develop in time. Although I believe that in her death she acted out the end of the argument, during her life she did not progress logically from image to image. Her mind far more resembled a wheel turning around and around continually. Every incident in her life and every work of fiction she wrote was the product of an instant at which the wheel had briefly stopped. Sometimes there was an external reason for the wheel to stop at that point. But just as often there was not. And the place at which it stopped might be progressive or regressive. Some of Gaskell's early stories take us to the end of her argument and some of her very latest tales return us to an earlier spot. Although it would certainly thus represent the actual state of her history better, marking as well her steps forward and back, reading her fiction chronologically would make her argument unintelligible.

Finally, just as Gaskell herself said, in *The Life of Charlotte Brontë,* that she would allow her subject to speak as much as she could for herself, I have attempted to let Gaskell here tell her own tale as much as possible. Not only have I quoted the letters and the fiction whenever I could, I have tried, in my discussion, to write about her in her own images.

II

Alone! Alone!

ALTHOUGH SHE WAS ONLY the outer shell of the woman who lived within, there really was a "Mrs. Gaskell," someone who, to all appearances, embodied the "feminine" ideal. She was the product of the experiences of Elizabeth Gaskell's childhood. Gaskell herself, beginning to work on her biography of Charlotte Brontë, wrote to Brontë's friend Ellen Nussey that in her view it had been the "domestic peculiarities of her childhood" that had "(as in all cases) contributed so much to make" Charlotte Brontë "what she was" (*L* 294). Gaskell was thinking perhaps of herself when she inserted those parentheses, for, in that way she had of knowing without knowing that she knew, Gaskell was keenly aware that her life had been forever after shaped by the events of her first eighteen years.

These are years she hardly ever mentions in her correspondence but to which—like many characters she herself creates in her narratives who, especially in their dreams, keep reliving their childhood memories—in her fiction she returns over and over again. What Gaskell suffered during these years would have had a traumatic effect even on a less sensitive child. On Gaskell the effect was devastating. No one had as acute a capacity as Gaskell to remember pain, not only its cause but its very sensation, and in her fiction it is clear that time was never able to soothe or distance to diminish the sorrow that she experienced as a child.

As she was to remember them later, her childhood years were marked repeatedly by the deaths of those she loved and by her own abandonment and exile. Six of her brothers and sisters had died when Elizabeth Cleghorn Stevenson was born on September 29, 1810. Her mother, Elizabeth Holland Stevenson, had given birth to eight children in little more than a dozen years, and of those eight only the first, Gaskell's beloved brother John, and the last, herself, survived. The six in-between all died in infancy or in the first few years of their lives. Gaskell was haunted by these deaths. It is hard for her to construct a story that does not contain the death of a sibling, although, in the typical way she works, the fact is not reproduced as it happened but rather as it affected her. Thus, although she was not alive at the time her siblings died, Gaskell often imagines herself as the one who bears the loss. In "A Dark Night's Work," for instance, it is Ellinor, the heroine, who, as Gaskell's surrogate self, mourns the loss of a younger sibling. "Ellinor's grief," the narrator writes, "was something alarming, from its quietness and concealment. She waited till she was left—as she thought—alone at nights, and then sobbed and cried her passionate cry for 'Baby, baby, come back to me—come back'; till every one feared for the health of the frail little girl, whose childish affections had had to stand" such a shock (7:413). Sometimes Gaskell feels the loss not as a sister but as a mother. Gaskell identified with her mother, perhaps especially because she had been given her mother's name. Many women in her fiction are made to relive Mrs. Stevenson's history, and Gaskell often describes their grief as though she were recording her own. In *Cranford,* for instance, a novel that Dickens published serially in *Household Words* from December 1851 through May of 1853, a character who is named Mrs. Brown announces suddenly—although in the story there is no reason for her to do so—that she has " 'lost six children.' " As she speaks, she looks at the narrator, who notices that she has "those strange eyes that I've never noticed but in mothers of dead children—with a kind of wild look in them, as if seeking for what they never more might find" (2:131).

Gaskell identified so much with her mother in her loss that she lived in apprehension, when she became a mother herself, that her own children would die. Her first child was, in fact, stillborn, and in a diary she began shortly after the birth of her second, Gaskell not only expresses her gratitude to God for letting her baby live, she also prepares herself for the loss that she seems to believe inevitable. "Oh!" she writes, "may I try not to fasten and centre my affections too strongly on such a frail little treasure; but all my anxiety, though it renders me so aware of her fragility of life, makes me cling daily more and more to her."[1] "May I," Gaskell writes again, this time when her daughter is ill, try not to "make her into an idol, but strive to prepare both her and myself for the change that may come any day" (p. 11). "Lord," she writes yet once more, "unto thee do I commit this darling precious treasure; thou knowest how I love her; I pray I may not make her too much my idol" (p. 17).

The first thirteen months of Gaskell's childhood passed, as far as we know, without incident, but it was to be the last untroubled period of her life. Just as she entered her second year, a chain of events that was to determine not only the course of Gaskell's history but the patterns of her identity was precipitated by the death of Elizabeth Holland Stevenson. Gaskell may have felt responsible, in afteryears, for her mother's death. It is indeed entirely possible that Mrs. Stevenson, never strong, was finally, after so many pregnancies, simply exhausted by her last. Gaskell may have heard such thoughts expressed by the members of her family. Most of the daughters in her fiction, although the reasons are vague and general, feel guilty when their mothers die. Thus, in "Half a Lifetime Ago," a story published in *Household Words* in October of 1855—but which Gaskell had reworked from her earlier "Martha Preston," which had appeared in 1850 in *Sartain's Magazine*—Susan Dixon suddenly thinks, as her mother lies dying, of all the things she might have done for her but had neglected over the years (5:282). Sylvia too in *Sylvia's Lovers,* published in 1863, experiences guilt when her mother falls ill because she feels she should have been a better daughter than she was (6:137). Often the dead blame the living in Gaskell. Falling into one of the many comparisons that we find in her fiction that have nothing to do with the plot but everything to do with her history, Gaskell, in *Sylvia's Lovers* again, describes the heroine as looking at one of her lovers "with the mute reproach which some of us see (God help us!) in the eyes of the dead, as they come before our sad memories in the night-season" (6:374).

The death of Elizabeth Holland Stevenson brought her sister, Hannah Lumb, from Knutsford to London to stay with her brother-in-law. What her initial plan might have been, or indeed whether she had one, we have no way of knowing now. We know, however, that once there she received a letter from her daughter, Mary Anne, who offered to care for her uncle's infant child. Whether she merely wanted to help during William Stevenson's mourning or whether she wanted Elizabeth permanently Mary Anne does not make clear. Widowers did, in the nineteenth century, sometimes parcel their children out. She was herself at the time just twenty, but crippled in a childhood accident, she may have thought she would never marry and have a child of her own to care for. Elizabeth might have seemed to her her only chance to become a mother. The letter she sent speaks very well for her. It reveals an intelligent young woman, sensitive, thoughtful, warm, and kind, who had a genuine affection for her little infant cousin. Imagining there will be objections, Mary Anne tries to anticipate and to answer them one by one. Assuring her mother she is capable of taking care of a small child, she promises to do everything necessary, everything possible, for the baby, even to pay out of her own allowance for everything the infant might need. What little she has will give her, she says, "double pleasure" when "I shall have little Elizabeth to share a part with me."[2] The letter seems to have been persuasive, and Mrs. Lumb returned from London bringing the infant Elizabeth with her. Fictional portraits of Mary Anne, chiefly Mr. Benson in *Ruth,* a novel that appeared in January of 1853—Gaskell as we shall later see is never inhibited in her fiction by the sex of her originals—suggest that Gaskell recalled Mary Anne with enormous affection and gratitude. It was her name she chose to give to her first surviving daughter. In her imagination, and to some extent in fact, Mary Anne had become her second mother. But before a year had passed, quite unexpectedly, Mary Anne died. Gaskell, by the age of two, had, thus, lost her mother twice.

In Gaskell's fiction, Mary Anne's death is seldom enacted as a separate event. It seems in her memory to have fused rather with her mother's passing. And for her mother, it would appear, Gaskell never ceased to mourn. When, for example, she received, in February of 1849, some letters written by her mother from a family friend, George Hope, she wrote in reply "I will not let an hour pass, my dear sir, without acknowledging your kindness in sending me my mother's letters, the only relics of her that I have, and of more value to me than I can express, for I have so often longed for some little thing that had once been hers or touched by her. I think no one but one so unfortunate as to be early motherless can enter into the craving one has after the lost mother" (*L* 614). The fact that she uses a word like "relics" to describe her mother's letters tells us that she had, in her mind, sanctified her mother's memory. The word appears in just this way in the story "Crowley Castle," which Gaskell published in *All the Year Round* in December of 1863. Here, the heroine, Theresa, speaks of her dead mother's jewels as "relics" (7:698).

It is unlikely that Gaskell actually remembered her mother's death, but, as she places herself in her fiction as the witness of dying siblings, so she imagines the death of a mother over and over again. Sometimes she writes a quiet death scene, poignant in its sense of loss. Susan in "Half a Lifetime Ago" sits with her dying mother, for instance, looking in sorrow on her "dear face," treasuring each of "those precious moments, while yet the eyes could look out with love and intelligence" (5:283). More often, however, the death scene is wild with unbearable grief and sorrow. Ellinor in "A Dark Night's Work" is an example once again. The death of her mother nearly kills her, it leaves her in such a state of despair. " 'Mamma! mamma,' " Gaskell writes, "cried the child, in shapeless terror. . . . Undeterred by deadly cold or stony immobility, she kissed the lips and stroked the glossy raven hair, murmuring sweet words of wild love, such as had passed between the mother and child, often and often, when no witnesses were by, and altogether seemed so nearly beside herself in an agony of love and terror, that" her father "arose and, softly taking her in his arms, bore her away, lying back like one dead" (7:412). Similarly, in "The Heart of John Middleton," which Gaskell published in *Household*

Words in December of 1850, Grace, the daughter of the protagonist, witnesses her mother's death. The "wild knowledge," Gaskell writes, "of death shot through her young heart, and she screamed aloud" (2:408). That scream is echoed throughout Gaskell's fiction. Leonard, the heroine's son in *Ruth*, utters, when his mother dies, "a cry" that is "heard through the house." It is the cry, Gaskell explains, "of one refusing to be comforted" (3:445).

Daughters like Susan Dixon, above, often quarrel with their mothers. Yet even when they are locked in conflict, something greater binds them together. Thus, for example, in "The Poor Clare," a story published in *Household Words* in December of 1856, Mary and Bridget are always in conflict. "There were," Gaskell writes, "wild quarrels between them, and wilder reconciliations. There were times when, in the heat of passion, they could have stabbed each other. At all other times they both—Bridget especially—would have willingly laid down their lives for one another" (5:334).

It is not difficult to see what Gaskell imagines a mother to be. A mother is, very simply, love. To be deprived of a mother in Gaskell is to be deprived of love. In "The Well of Pen Morfa," which appeared in *Household Words* in November of 1850, Gaskell states so very explicitly. Nest, the heroine, losing her mother, says " 'my mother is dead. No one loves me now' " (2:259). It happens in "The Well of Pen Morfa" that Nest has, in fact, no other family, but for Gaskell a mother's love has no rival in the world. In *North and South,* another novel Dickens serialized in *Household Words,* this one appearing from September of 1854 through January of 1855, Mrs. Thornton, the hero's mother, compares her love to that of the girl whom her son wishes to marry. " 'A girl's love is like a puff of smoke—it changes with every wind,' " she says. A mother's love " 'is given by God, John. It holds fast for ever and ever' " (4:249). A mother's love outlasts the grave. The heroine of *Mary Barton,* Gaskell's first novel, which appeared in October of 1848, is another motherless child. One night she feels that her mother's spirit has returned to visit her. At first she is frightened. But soon she realizes that "If her mother had conscious being, her love for her child endured" (1:269).

This love is an indispensible necessity to the welfare of a child. When Owen, the hero of "The Doom of the Griffiths," a story Gaskell had begun when Marianne was a baby (*L* 384) but which she only finished later and published in *Harper's New Monthly Magazine* in January of 1858, recalls the death of his mother, he apostrophizes her in this way: " 'dear, precious mother who brought me forth, and then left me—with no refuge in a mother's heart—to struggle on through life alone' " (5:260). Life is painful, as Elizabeth Gaskell had better reason than most to know, and a mother's love for her child is, as Gaskell conceives it, a refuge.

The thought that she herself might die and leave her own children motherless preyed continually on Gaskell's mind. She did not, she said, fear death for herself. "As for death," she writes, for instance, to her sister-in-law Anne Robson, "I have I think remarkably little constitutional dread of it—I often fear I do not look forward to it with sufficient awe, considering the futurity which *must* follow." It is for her children she worries. To die would be to leave them unloved. She tries to comfort herself with the thought that God will care for them. "I do often pray for trust in God, complete trust in him—with regard to what becomes of my children." But it is "difficult," she continues—wondering perhaps why God had not taken better care of her—"to have the right trust in God almost when thinking about one's children" (*L* 16). This is why she writes the letter. Having no "sister or near relation whom" she could entreat "to watch over" the children, she asks Anne Robson—as she may have imagined her mother asking her sister Hannah Lumb—to care for her daughters if she dies. Many women in Gaskell's fiction make a similar request. In *North and South,* the heroine's mother, Mrs. Hale, for instance, feels "a tender craving" as she lies dying "to bespeak the kindness of some woman towards the daughter that might soon be left motherless" (4:280). The daughter, Margaret, is an adult, but there is no age at which a child ceases to be, in Gaskell's view, the object of a mother's concern. It is significant that Gaskell began her "Diary" because, she said, she wanted to leave it for Marianne as "a token of her Mother's love" (p. 5).

For Gaskell there is no aberration of which a child may not be capable once deprived of maternal love, no sin, no crime it may not commit. The fact that a child has lost its mother is the universal defense for wrongdoing in Gaskell's fiction. When Ruth is about, in the novel *Ruth,* to yield, for instance, to her seducer, Gaskell simply pleads her case by asking the reader to remember "how young, and innocent, and motherless she was!" (3:56). Similarly, in "The Doom of the Griffiths," the narrator defends one of the girls who seems a little lax in her morals by saying "it is enough to say that Nest was very giddy, and that she was motherless" (5:253). In "The Heart of John Middleton," Grace's father is, like his daughter, a motherless child, and this for Gaskell is sufficient to account for his brooding soul and for the fact that he is planning a murder. " 'I never remember my mother,' " he says. " 'I should have been a better man than I have been, if I had only had a notion of the sound of her voice, or the look of her face'" (2:384). In "A Dark Night's Work" the heroine's father is, again, like his daughter, motherless, and he not only contemplates murder but eventually commits it (7:406).

Nothing could have replaced for Gaskell the love of the mother she had lost, but a kind and sensitive father might have made her loss more bearable. This she was not, however, to have. Although he certainly meant no harm, William Stevenson, had he intended deliberately to destroy his daughter, could not have attempted to do so more effectively than by taking precisely the course of action he did. We need not concern ourselves with his story, interesting though it is in itself, but certain details need to be mentioned because they affected Gaskell's life and are often recalled in her fiction.

William Stevenson was born in 1772 in the town of Berwick-on-Tweed. He was a bright and gifted man but also, if his life is a clue, a restless and erratic one. He was, it would seem, a great idealist, a sincere humanitarian, and he determined, as a young man wishing to do some good in the world, to prepare himself for the ministry. An excellent scholar, he had no difficulty finding not only a position as a Unitarian minister when he had completed his studies but another teaching the classics. It was on the strength of his expectations that William Stevenson, no doubt, proposed to Elizabeth Holland. But she had no sooner accepted than he resigned from both his posts, claiming that he had come to believe it was wrong to be paid for preaching and that he had, at the same time, lost his faith in the utility of a classical education. His integrity is commendable. Gaskell does commend it, in fact, in her novel *North and South,* in which the heroine's father, Mr. Hale, although he continues teaching the classics, gives up his ministry when he develops what Gaskell describes as scruples of conscience. It is, however, revealing that Gaskell does not explain what those scruples are, focusing all our attention instead on the very serious consequences of his decision to his family.

Having no income at this point, William allowed himself to be persuaded by his very good friend James Cleghorn, whom he was later to remember in his daughter's middle name, to try his hand for a while at farming. Cleghorn had a farm himself and was putting into practice many experimental methods that had just come into vogue, and William, after spending a period working for Cleghorn to learn those methods, bought himself a farm in Scotland. He could not, however, make a success of it. Within four years his farm had failed. Gaskell often in her fiction recalls these years in her father's life. Sometimes she recalls them humorously, as, for example, in "My French Master," a story she published in *Household*

Words in December of 1853. The narrator, a delightful young woman, opens the story with an autobiography that centers chiefly on her father, a man who had once "set himself up as an amateur farmer on a very small scale." "My mother," the narrator continues, "rejoiced over the very small scale of his operations; and when my father regretted, as he did very often, that no more land was to be purchased in the neighbourhood, I could see her setting herself a sum in her head, 'If on twelve acres he manages to lose a hundred pounds a year, what would be our loss on a hundred and fifty?' " (2:506). The loss is amusing here because the narrator's parents have the income to sustain it, as it happens. But this was not the case with the Stevensons, and a more accurate account of the severity of the consequences of Mr. Stevenson's failure as a farmer is to be found in the novel *Ruth*. Here, when the heroine's father fails, the effect on his daughter is catastrophic, leading, in fact, at last to her death. And Gaskell, although not overly harsh, is not entirely sympathetic. If "he had been," the narrator writes, "in any way a remarkable character, one might have supposed him to be the object of an avenging fate, so successive were the evils which pursued him; but, as he was only a somewhat commonplace farmer, I believe we must attribute his calamities to some want in his character of the one quality required to act as keystone to many excellences" (3:36). Gaskell never names that quality, but from the discussion that follows, it seems to have something to do with effort. Perhaps to Gaskell it seemed her father had simply not tried hard enough.

Mr. Hale in *North and South,* having once resigned his ministry, decides he must give private lessons in order to support his family. This is what William Stevenson did. When, however, he moved to Edinburgh in the hope of finding more pupils, he discovered a new career. Contributing a number of essays to the periodicals of the day, he realized he could make a living by becoming a professional writer. He had, it is clear, a gift for words that he may have inherited from his mother, a cousin of the poet James Thomson, and that he was to bequeath to his daughter. Soon he had made quite a name for himself, so much so that he attracted the attention of Lord Lauderdale. Lauderdale had just been named a candidate for the governor-generalship of India, and William seemed to him exactly the kind of man he wanted as a secretary. Unfortunately, he made his offer before he had been confirmed in his post, and by the time it had become obvious that he was not to be appointed, William had already, precipitously, brought his family to London so as to be ready to sail. Lauderdale, luckily, felt responsible and was able to find William a position at the

Treasury as the Keeper of the Records, a position William kept for the remainder of his life.

Whether by choice or by necessity, William had settled down at last. And yet, in important ways, he had not, apparently, altered much at all. His daughter, although she had been born after he had ceased his wanderings, seems to have suffered more than anyone from her father's uncertain temper. In her fiction Gaskell always imagined herself, on her mother's death, clinging desperately to her father. Ellinor in "A Dark Night's Work" finds it hard to love again after she has lost her mother. Her love, Gaskell writes, is completely "dammed up." In time, however, it "burst its banks," and when it did so, it predictably "overflowed on her father" (7:413).

That was the moment Gaskell's father should have lavished his love on her. Instead he sent her to live with the Lumbs. Gaskell spent the rest of her life trying to understand why. For us it is hard to understand too. His situation was, grantedly, difficult, but not extraordinarily so. His wife had died leaving two children, Elizabeth and her brother, John. But John, if he was still at home (and no one actually knows his whereabouts at this period of his life), was already thirteen. He did not need to be taken care of, not at least in practical ways. Elizabeth was the only burden. To be sure, at thirteen months, she still needed the kind of care Victorian men were not trained to give. And William had his work, of course, which took him out of the house all day. But he could have hired someone. Many Victorian households did. Rather than send his daughter to Knutsford, he might perhaps have asked Mary Anne to come to take care of her in London. Hannah Lumb herself would have stayed, very probably, had he asked her, for an indefinite time to help. But, as Gaskell was to suggest of the heroine's father in *Ruth,* he simply did not try very hard. We do not know what he would have done had Mary Anne not made the offer to take Elizabeth off his hands, but once she did he did not hesitate.

In Gaskell's mind it was bad enough that her father had sent her away. But it was infinitely worse that he never took her back. Mary Anne's death a year later must have raised the question again of what was to be done with Elizabeth. But, although enough time had passed for William to adjust to his circumstances, it did not occur to him, it appears, that he might reclaim his daughter. For we have to assume that had he wanted her, she would have been returned immediately. Since she was not, we have to believe that he never asked for her back.

Gaskell instead, when Mary Anne died, remained in the house with her Aunt Lumb. There is no doubt she loved Aunt Lumb, and, it would seem, for very good reason. Hannah Lumb was kind and generous and she appears to have loved Elizabeth. "My dearest Aunt Lumb, my more than mother," Gaskell wrote in her "Diary" in 1837 on the day of Hannah Lumb's death. "On May 1st," she continued, "I lost my best friend. May God reward her for all her kindness to me!" (p. 28). In her fiction, Gaskell remembered her dearest Aunt Lumb with affection and gratitude in the many portraits she drew of women who act as surrogate mothers. In "The Moorland Cottage," for instance, a long short story Gaskell published in 1850 as a Christmas book, the heroine, Maggie, finds a surrogate mother in Mrs. Buxton, a wonderful woman whose goodness and warmth recall Aunt Lumb. The end of the story sees the wedding of Maggie and Mrs. Buxton's son, so that, in a very real way, Maggie becomes Mrs. Buxton's daughter. Gaskell's last novel, *Wives and Daughters,* draws heavily on "The Moorland Cottage," as a number of readers have noted,[3] and Molly, a girl who has lost her mother, finds in the neighboring Mrs. Hamley, as Maggie does in Mrs. Buxton, a surrogate mother just like Aunt Lumb. Since Mrs. Hamley often, in fact, calls her by the name of a daughter she had lost years ago as an infant, Molly seems a reincarnation of Mrs. Hamley's actual child. And, as in "The Moorland Cottage," Molly at the end of the novel marries her surrogate mother's son.

Women like these are wonderful tributes to the memory of Aunt Lumb. Also tributes to Aunt Lumb are the dowagers of Gaskell's fiction, a group of characters just as warm and just as affectionate, but—since they are generally sharper, wittier, more assertive, grittier—on the whole a more interesting lot. Of these, by far the most delightful is the title character of "My Lady Ludlow," a long short story Gaskell published in *Household Words* from June to September of 1858. The story's narrator, a young woman whose father has died and whose mother can no longer afford to keep her, is living now with Lady Ludlow, a distant relative of means who, in a sense, takes the place of her mother. Lady Ludlow is magnificent, both as a character and as a person. She could have ruled empires, we have no doubt, without in the least disturbing her lace. Deprived, however, of the majesty that is unquestionably her due, she rules with an iron hand instead her house, her estate, and most of the village that, in an almost feudal way, still depends on her goodwill. Haughty in temper, fixed in her views, and generally crusty in her de-meanor, she is, however, so deeply generous and so genuinely good that, although she alienates many and intimidates not a few, she comes eventually to be loved and admired by nearly everyone.

Most accounts of Gaskell's childhood picture her happy at Aunt Lumb's. But Anne Thackeray Ritchie reports that she was told something quite different. "I have heard," Ritchie remarks, "that Mrs. Gaskell was not always happy in these days,—imaginative children go through many phases and trials of their own,—in her hours of childish sorrow and trouble she used to run away from her aunt's house across the Heath and hide herself in one of its many green hollows, finding comfort in the silence, and in the company of birds and insects and natural things."[4] And Gaskell in her fiction suggests that it is Ritchie who is right. Along with the surrogate mothers, for instance, who are tributes to Aunt Lumb, we often find in Gaskell's stories aunts who are harsh, unkind, ungenerous, sometimes even actively wicked. The situation, for example, in "The Half-Brothers"—which Gaskell published in 1859 in a collection of short stories entitled *Round the Sofa*—parallels Gaskell's history almost exactly. The aunt in the story, however, is cruel. So is the aunt in "Lois the Witch," published in *All the Year Round* in October of the same year, in which Gaskell once again reproduces her own history. Gaskell does not, in either character, intend to criticize Aunt Lumb. The aunts in these stories only project Gaskell's unhappiness in her circumstances. Aunt Lumb was wonderful, Knutsford was fine. She, however, was utterly miserable. Even when the aunt is kindly, as is Aunt Shaw in *North and South,* the heroine, longing to go home, is, like Margaret, sad and troubled.

Having left her with Hannah Lumb, William Stevenson appears virtually to have forgotten his daughter. In the next eleven years he seems not to have bothered to visit her or to have asked her to visit him. What could have passed through Elizabeth's mind as she waited, year after year, for her father to remember her? In her fiction, it is clear, Gaskell felt she had been rejected and abandoned by her father. Three years after the death of his wife, William Stevenson remarried and very soon had two more children. Still, it did not seem to occur to him that he should take Elizabeth back. But it must have occurred to Elizabeth. Gaskell was later in her fiction to repeat again and again that love makes us selfish and cruel. Mrs. Thornton in *North and South,* trying to claim her son's attention when his thoughts have turned to Margaret, who is the woman that he loves, prompts the narrator to remark on her behalf that "love is selfish" (4:224). When Philip asks Hester, in *Sylvia's Lovers,* to look at the house he has found for Sylvia, he is so happy that he forgets Hester herself is in love with him (6:356). The title character of *Mary Barton* is actually overjoyed at the thought of sharing with the man she loves a vigil over a sick friend. Her love has made her forget her friend is in pain and may be dying (1:251). To

Gaskell William Stevenson too must have appeared to have been made, by his love for his new family, cruel in his treatment of her.

It was for this reason too perhaps that Gaskell felt love could not be explained. Generally it is sexual love that Gaskell tends to find inexplicable, but, as Françoise Basch has observed, "there is" in all of Victorian fiction "an almost systematic confusion between different sorts of love—filial, fraternal, parental, passionate"[5]—and this is especially true in Gaskell. The narrator of "Six Weeks at Heppenheim," a story published in the *Cornhill Magazine* in May of 1862, speaks for a great many others in Gaskell when he concludes that love " 'goes by fancy' " (7:391). And no one ever knows in Gaskell, since Gaskell did not know herself, what accounts for the ways in which fancy settles on its preferences.

The fact that her father did not recall her when he remarried must have made Gaskell, who was only four at the time, feel that there was something wrong with her. Until he remarried and had new children, she could believe he had sent her away simply because he could not take care of her. She could blame circumstances, not herself. But once he remarried and had more children, she had not only to admit that he was able to care for children but that he actually wanted to have them. It was her he did not want. It had, then, to be that he did not love her. And if her father did not love her, did it not mean she was unlovable? Gaskell all her life felt certain that she was unworthy of love.

It was not until she was twelve years old that her father asked her to visit. The reason, as Gaskell must have known, was probably not that he wished to see her but that he thought she might want to say good-bye to her brother, John. John had joined the Merchant Navy and was about to set sail for India on his first long voyage at sea. Thus, in 1822, Elizabeth found herself going to London to see a father she had not seen since the early days of her childhood and to meet for the very first time her stepmother, Catherine Thomson Stevenson, her half brother, William, who was now seven, and her half sister, Catherine, now six.

Gaskell repeated this visit apparently annually for the next five years. During those years she was also a pupil at the Miss Byerleys' School in Warwickshire. The school was good, as such schools go, and, as she later told Mary Howitt, Gaskell was fairly "happy" there (*L* 12). She was not, however, happy in London during her visits to her father. "Long ago," she wrote in a letter, "I lived in Chelsea occasionally with my father and stepmother, and *very, very* unhappy I used to be; and if it had not been for the beautiful, grand river, which was an inexplicable comfort to me, and a family of the name of Kennett, I think my child's heart would have broken" (*L* 616).

We do not know what happened there to make Elizabeth so unhappy, but in a letter Mrs. Stevenson wrote after her husband's death we find perhaps an important clue. Gaskell had spent some time in London at the end of her father's life, and on his death Mrs. Stevenson wrote to tell Aunt Lumb that she and her husband had found Elizabeth much improved in her behavior on this last visit. This time, Mrs. Stevenson wrote, her father had not been even once "hurt or vexed about her." This time, her conduct had been "very beautiful."[6] What, we are compelled to ask, had been Elizabeth's conduct before? How had she "hurt" and "vexed" her father? In *Wives and Daughters,* the heroine, Molly, reliving much of Gaskell's history, is, although the sweetest child, described as being "naughty and passionate" and given to bursts of "violent temper" (8:363). It is not difficult to imagine that Elizabeth too had outbursts, coming, as she was, as a guest to a house that in her mind was the home in which she belonged, but from which she had been exiled. She must have been pained, she must have been angry, to find Mrs. Stevenson's son and daughter installed as the children of the house, while she, no less her father's child, was only a visitor, a stranger. It is easy to picture her as she remembered herself, sitting obviously by a window looking for solace in the river, wondering what it was she had done for her father to reject her. It may be she had arrived in London seeking to be reassured. Secretly she must have hoped that she could win her father back. Perhaps she did not behave very well when she realized that her father did not intend to ask her to stay. A word of affection might have calmed her. Instead, however, he had been vexed. There is no record that Mrs. Lumb ever showed Gaskell her stepmother's letter. But it seems likely that she did. For the word *vex,* as we shall see, tends to appear whenever Gaskell describes a conflict between a character who is clearly a surrogate self and another who is obviously meant to stand in the place of her father.

Gaskell found it very difficult to put the blame where she knew it should fall. Much of the anger she felt toward her father she spent on her stepmother instead. Stepmothers fare in Gaskell's fiction even worse than in fairy tales. Her greatest fear with regard to her children was that her husband, if she died, would marry again and so submit them to the tyranny of a stepmother (*L* 16). We do not know whether Catherine Stevenson deserved to be recalled in this way. The fact that Gaskell, who would have thrived on the smallest show of affection, was unhappy in her house makes us suspect that she did not do all that she could have for her stepdaughter. In her letter to Aunt Lumb, Catherine Stevenson writes that, because of her good behavior during her last visit to London, "I shall ever love Elizabeth as my own child." Whether or not she meant what she said, she seems to be confessing here that she had not so loved her before. Gaskell always, in her fiction, blamed the second Mrs. Stevenson for keeping her an exile in Knutsford. She might have been right to an extent. Had Mrs. Stevenson wanted Elizabeth, Mr. Stevenson would have probably, even if he had not thought of bringing her to London himself, asked Elizabeth to live with them. This does not exonerate him. But it adds her to the list of the culpable.

William and Catherine, her half siblings—who might have been, had things turned out differently, a brother and a sister to her—remained in Gaskell's imagination forever the rivals for her father's love. How very deeply she felt that rivalry we can guess by a poem she wrote on the third anniversary of the birth of her first, her stillborn, child.

> On Visiting the Grave of my Stillborn Little Girl
> Sunday, July 4, 1836
>
> I made a vow within my soul, O child,
> When thou wert laid beside my weary heart,
> With marks of death on every tender part,
> That, if in time a living infant smiled,
> Winning my ear with gentle sounds of love
> In sunshine of such joy, I still would save
> A green rest for thy memory, O Dove!
> And oftimes visit thy small, nameless grave.
> Thee have I not forgot, my firstborn, thou
> Whose eyes ne'er opened to my wistful gaze,
> Whose sufferings stamped with pain thy little brow;
> I think of thee in these far happier days,
> And thou, my child, from thy bright heaven see
> How well I keep my faithful vow to thee.

(1:xxvi–xxvii)

This is not a very good poem, although its sincerity makes it moving. Nevertheless, it is important. By the time she wrote this sonnet, Gaskell had had a second child, and, although it commemorates loss, the poem's theme is really fidelity. Gaskell is thinking of her father. He had allowed his new children to drive from his mind all thought of the old. Gaskell promises in the poem that she will never do as he did. Much as she loves her second daughter, she will not let the "living infant" displace her love for her dead child.

In her letter, Mrs. Stevenson had ended by saying that she hoped "nothing" now would "break that friendship which I trust is between us at this time, and also the love that she and her brother and sister have for each other." But after Mr. Stevenson's death, Mrs. Stevenson, it appears, did not keep in touch with Elizabeth. In a letter to a cousin, Gaskell writes in 1855 that she is planning a trip to Glasgow, where she intends to stop for a visit with Catherine and Mrs. Stevenson. Neither has she seen, she adds, in the past twenty-five years (*L* 254). Her half brother, who had died in the meantime, she had never seen again (*L* 267a).

The last important events of the years that were to shape the rest of her life occurred when Gaskell was eighteen. Her brother, still in the Merchant Navy, had sailed to India once again. This time, however, he did not return. Late in 1828, or possibly early in 1829, word came to London that he had been lost, although the circumstances were not known and were never to be discovered. On hearing the news, Elizabeth came, or was asked to come, to London. The disappearance of her brother must have touched her very deeply. They had not spent much time together but what they felt for each other was genuine. Part of it was the bond they shared as the survivors of the first marriage. John, when in England, unlike their father, seems to have stopped whenever he could to see his little sister in Knutsford. And he appears to have written his sister whenever possible from abroad. Only a few of his letters survive, but they are full of warmth and affection. John, moreover, seems to have been aware of his sister's literary talent and to have encouraged her to use it. "I am very glad," he writes on June 8, probably in 1827, "to hear that you have begun a Journal & have no doubt it will be a very amusing as well as interesting one—at least I know you can if you like, make it so—I shall hope to have good long extracts from it."[7] Gaskell was obviously in the habit of sending him samples of her work, and John must have been the first to recognize that she had a gift for humor.

Gaskell recalled her brother John in the sailors of her fiction. Sometimes sailors are major characters, like Charles Kinraid in *Sylvia's Lovers*. Sometimes they are the supporting cast, like William Wilson in *Mary Barton*. Often they are lost at sea. Gaskell was haunted by lost sailors. She was haunted by disappearances. In a work called "Disappearances," which she published in *Household Words* in June of 1851, she gathered many cases of people who had disappeared mysteriously. The work is not particularly good, but it is interesting in style, being in part a fictional narrative and in part documentary journalism. Gaskell did not invent the genre—the combination of fact and fiction, journalism and storytelling, having appeared over the centuries in a variety of forms—but she used it in many works and developed it so well that there are times she seems to anticipate, although in a less self-conscious way, modern experiments in this vein. Many sailors in her fiction disappear but return miraculously, as Gaskell must have wished it possible for her brother John to do. Many of Gaskell's sailors have sisters—Peter Jenkyns in *Cranford,* for instance, and Frederick Hale in *North and South.* Always the sailors of her fiction are enormously appealing.

But John is also recalled perhaps in another set of brothers who act the part of surrogate fathers. The fact that John was considerably older, that he was fond of her, and that he seemed, unlike her father, concerned for her welfare, must have made him appear to Gaskell as much a father as a brother. Maggie in "The Moorland Cottage" sees her brother in this way. Their father is dead, and "from a child" Maggie "had always," Gaskell writes, "pictured" her brother "to herself as taking her father's place" (2:302). When her brother was lost at sea, Elizabeth must have felt she had lost the only real father she had had.

Her actual father too, however, was very soon to be taken from her. Not long after John disappeared, William Stevenson suffered a stroke that was shortly to prove fatal. He died in March of 1829, Elizabeth, still at the time in London, helping to care for him in his last days. Whatever Gaskell had felt about him, and it had been and was to remain always something extremely complex, her father's death now left Elizabeth unconnected in the world. Aunt Lumb was still alive in Knutsford but—having lost her father and mother, her brother John, and the six siblings whom, although she had never known, she had grieved for in her mind—Gaskell felt desperately alone. This is how characters in her fiction always feel in similar circumstances. When Mary Barton loses her father, having already lost her mother, she cries " 'Oh, he's gone—he's dead—all gone—all dead, and I am left alone!' " (1:439). Margaret Hale in *North and South* also loses her mother first. Later, when her father dies, she feels—as Gaskell underscores by using her words as the chapter's title—utterly "Alone! Alone!" (4:421). Margaret is not, any more than was Gaskell, without relations at this point. She has, in fact, an aunt, like Gaskell, with whom she has lived for many years. She has, like Gaskell also, cousins. She even has a sailor brother, although he is living far away, just as Gaskell must have sometimes thought her brother John might be. But all of this is unimportant. To Gaskell, Margaret is "alone" because she is the child no longer of a loving father and mother. All her life she had been forsaken. Now she had been forsaken again, but this time wholly and irrevocably. Gaskell must have imagined often what life with her parents might have been, and that picture in her mind must have sometimes been more real to her than her actual existence. Many characters in her fiction, wiping entire lifetimes away, return in old age to live in memory as children with their parents again. When, in "Half a Lifetime Ago," William Dixon falls ill, for instance, in his mind he returns to his childhood, to live once more with the parents he loved. When he awakens the next morning, he has forgotten everything since (5:294).

Thus, by the time she was eighteen, Gaskell had not only been unloved, rejected, exiled, and abandoned; she had lost nearly every person with whom she had had a real connection. Ellinor in "A Dark Night's Work," losing her parents, is afraid to love anyone again since, as Gaskell goes on to explain, every one of "her strong attachments" had found "a sudden end in death" (7:413). Gaskell never let go of her dead. She always saw their empty places. And she was always in some sense trying to reach them beyond the grave. In her review of Claude Fauriel's *Chants populaires de la Grèce moderne,* which she published in *Household Words* under the title "Modern Greek Songs" in February of 1854, Gaskell comments with particular sympathy—although she is taken with all the old customs recorded in these modern songs—on the ancient custom in Greece of asking those who are being buried to take a message to the dead, whom they will be joining soon (3:478). To Gaskell the dead never die utterly. Somehow, they people the world still. In "Curious if True," a story she published in the *Cornhill Magazine* in February of 1860, the narrator fancies he hears the dead. For him the "voices of generations . . . yet echoed and eddied in the silent air" (7:262). Gaskell recalls her dead in her stories. Her father, her mother, her sisters, her brothers, her surrogate parents, her surrogate siblings, all return to live again on the pages of her fiction.

It is this history that determined the remainder of Gaskell's life. In *Mary Barton* Gaskell observes, reflecting on the passengers Mary sees around her on a train, that "we are all of us in the same predicament through life. Each with a fear and a hope from childhood to death" (1:327). The hopes and fears of Gaskell's life were born in these traumatic experiences.

III

Undine

IN HER OWN WAY, Elizabeth Gaskell knew she had been scarred by her past. One recurring type in her fiction is the child who is made to pay for the sin of its father. Frequently Gaskell embodies this theme in a supernatural story. Thus, in "The Old Nurse's Story," for instance, a story published in *Household Words* at Christmas in 1852, a wicked old man is the source of a curse that destroys his daughters and granddaughters. In "The Doom of the Griffiths," an ancestral curse dooms five generations in turn. Another curse that blights the children of a number of generations is to be found in "Morton Hall," one more story Dickens published, the following year, in *Household Words*. Sometimes Gaskell handles the theme in a more realistic manner. Ellinor in "A Dark Night's Work" suffers all her life because her father has committed a crime. So does the hero in "Right at Last," a story that, when it appeared in *Household Words* in 1858, was published as "The Sin of a Father."

Gaskell felt she had been deprived of the love that was her due. She thought of this love as her lost birthright, as she implies in the many times that she returns to the story of Esau. As one of the children of her father's first marriage, she was, like Esau, a first-born. Like Jacob, her half brother and half sister had stolen the blessing that belonged to her. She alludes to this blessing in "The Moorland Cottage," in which the roles of the biblical pair are enacted—Gaskell, as always, changes the story to suit her ends— by Maggie and her brother, Edward. As Isaac does in the biblical story, Mrs. Browne prefers one child, and it happens to be Edward. And, as she prepares to leave for America with her brother, Maggie waits patiently as her mother says a long good-bye to Edward. Then "with something of Esau's craving for a blessing, she came to bid her mother 'good-bye,' and received the warm caress she had longed for for years" (2:369). But the most moving allusion to Esau occurs in "Modern Greek Songs." Gaskell pauses here to retell a story told by Fauriel in which a young man leaves his home because his mother does not love him. The leave-taking, a wonderful ritual, takes place in an echoing dale. The "most doleful farewell songs" are sung at this parting, and finally the young man mounts a rock and improvises "a poem on the sufferings he had experienced from the indifference of his mother." "He cried to her to bless him once," Gaskell concludes with great passion, "before he went away for ever, with something of the wild entreaty of Esau when he adjured Isaac to 'Bless me, also, O my father!' " (3:474).

Gaskell needed to be loved. Writing, for instance, about Ruth in the novel of that name, the narrator says: "Love was very precious to Ruth now, as of old time. It was one of the faults of her nature to be ready to make any sacrifices for those who loved her, and to value affection almost above its price; . . . lonely as the impressionable years of her youth had been—without parents, without brother or sister—it was, perhaps, no wonder that she clung tenaciously to every symptom of regard, and could not relinquish the love of any one without a pang" (3:246). Gaskell too valued affection almost above its price. She too was ready to make any sacrifice, not only, in fact, *for* those who loved her but *so that* she would be loved. She was even willing to steal, if she had to, her father's affection. This is made clear in "The Crooked Branch," a story she published in *All The Year Round* in 1859 under the title "The Ghost in the Garden Room." The story concerns a young man named Benjamin who leaves his home but returns one night to rob his parents with a band of burglars. Money is one of Gaskell's images. It functions in a number of ways, but all have something to do with love. Gaskell often, for example, writes about love in the language of money. Thus, at the end of "The Moorland Cottage," Gaskell writes that Maggie Browne, having wrested love from the world, at last died "*rich* in the love of many" (2:382; italics mine). Buying and selling too are images associated with the loss of love or the need to repossess it. In the passage above from *Ruth,* Ruth is said to *value* affection almost above its *price*. The acquisition of money, similarly, especially through illicit means, is the acquisition of love. When Benjamin, therefore, steals from his parents, it is not their money he takes. Metaphorically, it is their love.

Gaskell was willing to steal love too. Her need for love was so compelling that she was willing to become whatever anyone wished her to be. And what that was was only too obvious. Wretched on her visits to London, she had "hurt" and "vexed" her father by the expression of her misery. He had not wanted to know what pained her. He had not wanted to hear her rage. What he had wanted she finally learned to give him when she returned at eighteen and earned the praise of Mrs. Stevenson in her letter to Aunt Lumb for behavior that was "beautiful." Maggie in "The Moorland Cottage" feels that she must try to earn the love her mother has denied her, and she does so by attempting to become ideally good. In her own unconscious way, Gaskell too must have decided sometime before she turned eighteen that to earn the love she needed she would try to become "good."

Gaskell did not need to invent the ideal that she became. It had been invented already by the society in which she lived, in the Victorian ideal of woman. It is true, as Lansbury says, that Gaskell, as a Unitarian, was one of the few Victorian women not brought up to see herself in the image of that ideal.[1] Always among the avant-garde, the Unitarians held opinions that were, for the time, advanced on most social and political questions, including the place and condition of women. But a distinction must be made between convictions in the mind and patterns in the imagination. Gaskell believed what she had been taught. And she had been shaped in part by the Unitarian attitude. Many of her special virtues were the product of this upbringing. She was straightforward, simple, honest. She was not coy. She did not flirt. In some ways, she was very courageous and in others independent. And, as feminist critics have seen, she even continued, on some questions, to hold the avant-garde opinions of the Unitarian world. Passing her character on to her heroines, Gaskell created many young women who, even when their lives are conventional, are not wholly stereotypical. But in her imagination it was not what she believed but the need to win the love of which she had been deprived that determined what she saw, how she felt, and in what patterns both her fiction and her life would be required to be conceived.

Thus, although she never heard such platitudes in her family certainly, and although she did know better at some level of her thought, in her imagination Gaskell not only believed in the ideal of Victorian femininity, she believed in it so completely that her views are all clichés. But Gaskell had to be simple-minded and inflexible in these views. To admit reservations and complexities would have opened the door to questions that might have led the way to doubts. And Gaskell could not afford to doubt the image by which she had determined she would win the love she needed.

In the simplest possible way, a woman to Gaskell was an adornment. Often a woman was a flower. One young man in *Wives and Daughters* likes to visit a neighboring house—and Gaskell does not say his views are mistaken or unacceptable—because there is in it the "feminine presence" of "flowers" and other "pretty things" (8:358). Similarly, in *Sylvia's Lovers* it is the "sweet scent of dried lavender and rose-leaves" issuing from her oak chest that is the mark of Sylvia's femininity (6:87). In *North and South* the heroine, Margaret, in one of the novel's major images, is identified as a rose. Nor are these concessions merely to the popular idea. Gaskell associates women with flowers as much in her letters as in her fiction. Describing a weaver's wife, for instance, whom she has met by chance one day, she writes to John Forster she is "so womanly" that "she makes one think of hawthorn blossom" (*L* 59). Gaskell was fond of flowers herself and, it was said, a splendid gardner.

A woman, to Gaskell, should be graceful, a pleasure to the eye to behold. One of the scenes in *Sylvia's Lovers* is revealing in this respect because it happens to be a contrast to a scene in Ibsen's *A Doll's House*. Gaskell's scene is a description of the heroine at her spinning wheel:

> People speak of the way in which harp-playing sets off a graceful figure; spinning is almost as becoming an employment. A woman stands at the great wool-wheel, one arm extended, the other holding the thread, her head thrown back to take in all the scope of her occupation; or if it is the lesser spinning-wheel for flax,—and it was this that Sylvia moved forwards tonight—the pretty sound of the buzzing, whirring motion, the attitude of the spinner, foot and hand alike engaged in the business-the bunch of gay coloured ribbon that ties the bundle of flax on the rock—all make it into a picturesque piece of domestic business that may rival harp-playing any day for the amount of softness and grace which it calls out.

(4:44)

In Ibsen's play it is Nora's husband, Torvald, who holds the parallel view. Kristin, Nora's friend, is visiting, and she happens to be knitting when Torvald returns from work one day. She seems, as she knits, ungraceful to him. Her arms are too close, he thinks, to her sides, her hands make quick and choppy movements. He suggests she take up embroidery. A woman embroidering can allow one arm to rest softly in her lap while with the other, lifting the thread, she can make long and graceful gestures.

The difference is that Ibsen here is satirizing Torvald's attitude. Gaskell is entirely serious. Ibsen, of course, was ahead of his time, although only sixteen years divide the first performance of *A Doll's House* from the appearance of *Sylvia's Lovers*. But the play itself explains why Gaskell holds the views she does. Gaskell has, as Nora does, internalized the social prejudice and has come to see herself just as her society does. Gaskell was an adornment herself. The marble bust by David Dunbar, done when Elizabeth was about twenty, shows a beautiful young woman, classic in feature, self-possessed, warm and apparently open in character, and, if one looks long enough perhaps at the curl of her lip, ready, as soon as we turn away, to break into a playful smile.

Women have, in Gaskell's view, no intellectual ability. As far as any Victorian did, Unitarians believed that women should be educated as men were. Theoretically Gaskell did too. Many young women in her stories are given, as a matter of course, instruction in subjects that were considered by the Victorian world appropriate only in the education of men. Thus, in *Ruth,* Mr. Benson teaches Ruth mathematics and Latin, which, when she becomes their governess, Ruth teaches the Bradshaw girls. Similarly, in "Cousin Phillis," published serially in the *Cornhill Magazine* from November of 1863 to February of 1864, the heroine, who is taught by her father, learns Italian, Latin, and Greek. We often find her in the kitchen reading Dante as she peels apples. And yet, while commenting on the plan, which was then much in the news, to establish the Nightingale Fund to support a school for women to be trained to become nurses, Gaskell writes to one correspondent "I would not trust a mouse to a woman if a man's judgment was to be had. Women have no judgment" (*L* 316).

Gaskell had had, at the Miss Byerleys', a fairly good eduation herself. And she was bright, as is only too evident in her shrewd remarks in her fiction. Many are such as could have been the basis of philosophical positions and would have become so in the hands of a more intellectual novelist. Gaskell, however, does not develop them. She seldom makes much of her perceptions. Often she almost throws them away, tucking them into subordinate clauses or hiding them between parentheses. And the reason is that she does not consider thinking a woman's task. She does not believe she does it well, and she does not object to saying so. "I know," she writes in one of her letters, "I'm easily imposed upon in the metaphysical line" (*L* 91). Being a woman, she naturally has, as she admits in another letter, "a very runaway kind of mind" (*L* 384). Her "thoughts," as she concedes in a third, are entirely "bewildered" (*L* 72).

Knowledge and analytic ability are not entailed in her self-image. Her grammar and spelling tell us something of how Gaskell saw herself. She took both grammar and spelling seriously, but she had trouble getting them right. Although she is never incoherent, sometimes her sentences run wild and clauses tumble over each other as she flits from thought to thought. Subjects and verbs do not always agree. And always she has trouble with spelling. She can never, for example, distinguish *its* from *it's*. Possessive plurals are likely to have apostrophes placed before the *s*. And double consonants are a mystery to her. Where, she asks of one correspondent, do double consonants go in "parallels" (*L* 544). She is well aware of her difficulties and sometimes attributes them to hurry. "I write," she explains in one letter, "all sorts of grammar, & all sorts of spelling, & all sorts of papers, for I am in a great hurry" (*L* 182). It "is hard," she explains in another, "to me to write a proper letter; with Dear Sir in the right place, & verbs agreeing with their nominatives, & {agreeing with} governing— their accusatives; and it is letters of that kind I dread receiving, because of the knowledge of grammar, & good pens required to answer them. . . . you will not mind grammar or spelling or penmanship in my answers, will you, so I shan't dread having to reply" (*L* 384).

Whenever, in a similar manner, she handles intellectual topics, as in her fiction she sometimes does, she does not hold herself responsible for knowing or understanding the issues in a theoretic way. Thus, she opens *Mary Barton,* which deals with the condition of workers in the new industrial age, by writing, in the very Preface, "I know nothing of Political Economy, or the theories of trade." Since the questions of the novel cannot be answered except by appealing to political ideas and to economic theories, this is an extraordinary admission. It does not bother Gaskell, however. She can imagine, she writes in a letter, a book on this subject that might approach the problems politically and economically. But it would have to be written by a man (*L* 73).

Perhaps being "Alone! Alone!" she had a greater interest in people than in knowledge or ideas. Abandoned as she always felt, perhaps she wanted, more than anything, to establish human connections. But it may also be that Gaskell was afraid to think too much. She always avoided introspection. To one young novelist, Herbert Grey, who had written to ask advice, Gaskell remarks that just as "it is always an unhealthy sign when we are too conscious of any of the physical processes that go on within us," so "we ought not to be too cognizant of our mental proceedings, only taking note of the results" (*L* 420). Introspection was too threatening. It might lead her to self-knowledge. Thinking in general was dangerous. Who could tell where it might end? While she was writing *Wives and Daughters* and struggling still with her inner conflicts just nine months before her death, Gaskell at one point wrote to her publisher that she was "tired of spinning my brain." "I hate intellect," she continued, "and literature, and fine arts, and mathematics! I begin to think Heaven will be a place where all books & newspapers will be prohibited by St Peter: and the amusement will be driving in an open carriage to Harrow, and eating strawberries & cream for ever" (*L* 561). She was coming very close in this novel to the truth about herself and she did not want to know it. But she could always just stop thinking, since the result could be called "feminine."

In the letter in which she had said she would not trust a mouse to a woman if a man's judgment was to be had, Gaskell had continued to state that women were endowed instead with "hundreds of fine and lovely qualities" and had concluded by naming three: "tact, and sensitiveness and genius" (*L* 316). The three make a sequence in a sense. Genius, by which Gaskell means the ability to intuit, allows a woman to understand things that are neither shown nor spoken. A woman who uses her intuition is sensitive to what others feel. And a woman who behaves in a sensitive way to others is a woman who is tactful. Gaskell often makes it a point to let us know that her fictional women are in full measure endowed with all three. One particularly touching moment is to be found in a scene in *Ruth*. The Reverend Mr. Benson in this scene is walking with his sister, Faith. They happen to be climbing a hill, and Benson, who suffered a childhood accident because of which he is now crippled—Gaskell is obviously re-calling the accident that crippled Mary Anne Lumb—finds it hard to climb alone. His sister, therefore, supports his arm, but seeing a crowd of people ahead as they near the crest of the hill, Faith intuits that her brother will be embarrassed to be seen in so helpless a condition. Instantly she shifts her position in such a way as to make it seem that it is she who is leaning on him (3:112).

Gaskell herself was known for her tact, and a wonderful story is told in Manchester intended to illustrate it. At one of the sewing schools to which Gaskell devoted much of her time, there appear once to have been young women whose behavior was very rough. Whenever the bell rang to dismiss them, they always rushed out in such a stampede that, as they descended the stairs, there were always a number of injuries. The woman who headed the sewing school had tried every remedy she could think of, but not a one had met with success. She had even hired a retired soldier to keep order on the stairs, but he had not only failed in his efforts, he had found himself engaged in so many physical scuffles that, afraid he would lose a limb, he had resigned in utter defeat. Just when the woman gave up all hope of dealing with her unruly pupils, Gaskell volunteered to help. Instead of lecturing the young women, as the head of the school had done, instead of using force like the soldier, Gaskell positioned herself at the door and, when the bell rang, offered her hand to each young woman as she passed, bidding each a good afternoon. The women, who had never apparently been treated by anyone before as civilized human beings, responded instantly in kind. Taking her hand and returning the greeting, they walked quietly down the stairs with the utmost of decorum.[2]

Tact, intuition, and sensitivity were essential tools for someone who at an early age had learned, as Gaskell had, that she must bend to those who would not bend to her. Bending itself was a feminine virtue. Gaskell suggests the adaptability that is required of a woman in a verse she writes to head chapter 5 of *North and South:*

> I ask thee for a thoughtful love
> Through constant watching wise,
> To meet the glad with joyful smiles,
> And to wipe the weeping eyes;
> And a heart at leisure from itself
> To soothe and sympathise.

What she is describing here is nothing less than a chameleon. Her "heart at leisure from itself," a woman must change as those change around her— sad with the sad and glad with the happy. Psychologically, she is pro- hibited from having a distinctive form herself.

One of the images in which Gaskell embodies her sense of the feminine ideal is the image of the hostess. Woman as hostess was an idea popular in the nineteenth century. In one of her many delightful essays, this one entitled "Company Manners"—which was published in *House- hold Words* in May of 1854—Gaskell, inspired by Victor Cousin's essay on Mme. de Sable, and armed, as she adds in a tongue-in-cheek way, with information she has gathered from talking to the French, for whom the "art of Sableing" is "traditional," undertakes to provide for the English guidelines for duplicating the French salon (3:491). On first reading about Mme. de Sable, she was, Gaskell confesses, "inclined to laugh" at this talent for which alone Victor Cousin praises the Frenchwoman. But "when I thought of my experience in English society—of the evenings dreaded before they came, and sighed over in recollection, because they were so ineffably dull—I saw that, to Sable well, did require, as M. Cousin implied, the union of many excellent qualities and not-to-be-disputed little graces" (3:493).

Gaskell had spent many dull evenings as a hostess in her home. The Gaskells often entertained friends as well as professional acquaintances. In one of her letters to Catherine Winkworth, Gaskell dreads the arrival of a group made up chiefly of the latter. "The Derbishires are coming," she writes, "with 'Zoe' "—this is Geraldine Jewsbury, whom Gaskell here satirically calls by the title of her first novel—"Dr. Hodgson, Mr Green (shan't we be intellectual, that's all?) and a few others. I wish myself well thro'it" (*L* 32). In her essay Gaskell describes just such an intellectual evening. "I have visited," she writes, "a good deal among a set of people who prided themselves on being rational. We have talked what they called sense, but what I call platitudes, till I have longed, like Southey, in the 'Doctor,' to come out with some interminable nonsensical word (Ava-llibogibouganorribo was his, I think) as a relief for my despair at not being able to think of anything more that was sensible" (3:507). She does not object to serious subjects. Those who visited Mme. de Sable came pre-pared, she continues, for either wit or serious conversation (3:597). It is the pretension she dislikes. She goes on to describe one gathering at which the guests were all very solemn, but which suddenly became lively when someone suggested they play a game. "Making fools of ourselves was better," she concludes, "than making owls" (3:509).

None but the grave would disagree. But Gaskell's point is to extol the virtues of the ideal hostess, and these, as Gaskell one by one names them in the course of the essay, are virtues of the ideal woman: charm, a cheerful disposition, a graceful manner, a thoughtful concern for the welfare of each guest, an intuitive understanding of the unspoken needs of each, and the emotional sensitivity to draw the very best from everyone. It does not surprise us to learn that Gaskell was a famous hostess herself.

The art of Sableing gives feminine virtues a particularly glamorous form, but Gaskell embodied these in her fiction in another image as well. Even more than that of the hostess, this image was a Victorian cliché, and a discussion of it appears in one of the essays of W. R. Greg. Greg was a very interesting man. A member of Gaskell's set in Manchester, he was a well-known Unitarian and a very important industrialist. Gaskell once, in one of her letters, refers to him as "a friend of mine" (*L* 311). Greg was also a reviewer and an essayist of note. His views are very seldom original, but that is precisely why he is useful as a background source for Gaskell. Although more advanced in some respects than many of his English contemporaries, his positions are almost always typical of the Manchester creed. To measure Gaskell against Greg is, on virtually every topic, to measure the extent to which Gaskell holds to what for her are the ortho-doxies of her world. In one of his essays, "Why Are Women Redundant?" Greg takes up a good many questions concerning the status of women in England, and he concludes that a woman's virtues are the virtues of a servant. Servants, he explains, fulfill "both essentials of a woman's being: they are supported by, and minister to, men."[3]

There are a great many servants in Gaskell, and while they appear in many forms—male and female, sweet and sour—we do not have to study them long to realize that, although with some overlap, they come essen-tially in two types. The second I shall deal with later. The first is a group whose characteristics are, for Gaskell as for Greg, the attributes of the ideal woman. Servants who belong to this class are devoted and loyal in everything, but Gaskell makes them pass a test to prove how faithful they really are. The test, although it differs in details, is in nearly every case the same: something occurs to make the employer unable to pay the servant's wages; the employer urges the servant to leave; the servant, to pass the test, must refuse; and in Gaskell he always does. Martha, for instance, rejects the idea that she should leave Miss Matty in *Cranford* simply because Miss Matty has now lost what little money she had. Indeed, she abuses a fellow servant who is striking for higher wages (2:155). And when she marries, she and her husband rent the house Miss Matty has lost and take her in to be their boarder. Thus they enable her to remain a resident in the home she loves but which she can no longer afford. In "The Moorland Cottage," Mrs. Browne, drained of her income by her son's extravagance, cannot afford to pay Nancy her wages. Nancy, however, does not mind. She is happy to work for nothing (2:328). In *Ruth,* we find a slight variation. Benson has no financial difficulties. In fact, he wants to give Sally a raise. But Sally, having his interests at heart so completely above her own, refuses to have her wages increased. She only agrees, when he insists, because she intends to save the money and leave it to him in her will (3:191 ff.). Even better, in *Sylvia's Lovers,* Kester, worried that Sylvia's father is growing lonely without company, living out on the moors as he does, actually hires, with his own money, people in town to pay him a visit (6:51).

These situations are replete with political implications. A Marxist could and would make much of the economic assumptions on which these relationships rest. But Gaskell's interest is not in political or in economic questions. The question for her is the nature of service. A servant who only works for wages is a bad servant. He works for himself. The servant who does not ask to be paid is a good servant. He works for others. The good of his master is his good. His joys and sorrows are his master's. He has no individual life. He has no individual identity. And these, the characteristics that make, to Greg and to Gaskell, the ideal servant, make the ideal woman too. Those who knew Gaskell in Manchester said she had a "special gift" for the "training" of "maids" and had trained many in her house.[4] Perhaps she had that special gift because, as a perfect woman, she was an ideal servant herself.

Gaskell's ideal of femininity is expressed in a short story entitled "Bessy's Troubles at Home," which she wrote for the *Sunday School Penny Magazine,* where it appeared in 1852. Gaskell did not think much of this story (*L* 260), and from an artistic point of view, although it has its moments of charm, there is not much to recommend it. It is written chiefly for children and intended as a lesson. The lesson, however, spells out clearly what a woman's duty must be.

The story is simple. It concerns a family in which the mother, going away to recover from an illness, leaves the role of "the woman of the house" to be filled by her daughter Bessy. Bessy has yet, however, to learn what it means to be a woman. She has, from the first, the best intentions, but nothing she does seems to succeed. Although she is eager to please, which is good, Bessy always assumes she knows what it is that everyone needs. Of course she is wrong, and hard as she tries, she still makes everyone unhappy. Her sister Mary, who is slow-witted—intellect being in this story not only unnecessary in a woman but a hindrance to her success—turns out to have a far better instinct for the womanly work she must do. She understands that it is her place not to make plans for other people but to be ready when she is needed to help them in plans they make for themselves. When Bessy finally learns this lesson, Gaskell turns to the reader to say that her experiences have "taught" Bessy "several lessons, which it is good for every woman to learn, whether she is called upon, as daughter, sister, wife, or mother, to contribute to the happiness of a home" (3:535). It is no accident that Gaskell gives the heroine of this story a name that is a diminutive of her own. There are a great many Bessys in Gaskell, more than coincidence could account for, and like the Bessy in this story, they all embody the feminine ideal.

Bessy is being trained in this story to become a wife and mother, and Gaskell believed a wife and mother was what a woman ought to be. Women, she felt, were made to marry. This, of course, was the general view. Greg once more suggests the norm when he remarks, in "Why Are Women Redundant?" that in such matters we must consult nature. And nature, he argues, says that for women marriage is and must be "*the* rule." Greg concedes that nature allows for a percentage of exceptions by creating more women than men. These are "redundant," superfluous, women. But single life is not, he insists, a happy or natural state for a woman.[5] Gaskell's views are very similar. In *Cranford,* for instance, Miss Matty observes that gentlemen always say " '*If* I marry' " (2:128) while "ladies" always " '*When* I marry' " (2:128). For men, marriage is an option. For women, it is a sheer necessity. Whenever a woman becomes engaged, the narrator observes in *Cranford,* "the unmarried ladies in" the neighborhood "flutter out in an unusual gaiety and newness of dress, as much as to say, in tacit and unconscious manner, 'We also are spinsters' " (2:140). Gaskell believed women were made not only to marry but to have children. Underlining the word as in *Cranford* to distinguish between the sexes, Gaskell in a letter writes that "*women . . .* naturally yearn after children" (*L* 453). This is the point of one short story entitled "Christmas Storms and Sunshine." The story, published in *Howitt's Journal of Literature and Popular Progress* in 1848, concerns two couples, one of which has been recently blessed by a baby and the other of which has not. The husband of the childless couple adjusts pretty well to his condition, but for the wife it has become the "great unspoken disappointment of her life." Being childless has "soured her temper," "turned her thoughts inward, and made her morbid and selfish" (2:200). Miss Matty in *Cranford* does not turn sour, but, we are told, she always feels " 'a strange yearning at my heart whenever I see a mother with a baby in her arms' " (2:129). In her own "Diary," Gaskell wrote on the birth of Marianne: "How all a woman's life, at least so it seems to me now, ought to have a reference to the period when she will be fulfilling one of her greatest and highest duties, those of a mother" (p. 10). Just as fully as Coventry Patmore, Gaskell believes that women were made to be angels in the house. She often uses this very image to describe her ideal women. In *Mary Barton,* one young woman who embodies the feminine ideal is described as "an angel from heaven" (1:223). In "The Moorland Cottage," Mr. Buxton finds that, on the death of his wife, he cannot "speak of" his "lost angel without a sudden burst of tears" (2:303). And in *North and South,* Margaret's father looks to her, when her mother dies, to become his "angel of comfort" (4:297).

Gaskell not only believed in this image, she needed to fulfill it herself. Her need was the basis of her belief. Deprived as a child of the home and family to which she felt she had been entitled, Gaskell needed more than anything to have a home and a family of her own. One could not replace the other but to an extent at least it could make up for the loss. Gaskell was well aware of her need, although as usual she projected it into someone else's mind, not this time a fictional character but a young girl she wanted to help. To one of her friends she wrote that this girl, being an orphan, needed a home far more than an education, and that she wanted therefore to find for her not a school but work in a family that would treat her as a daughter. "It seems," she writes, "to me so very desirable to surround an *orphan* with something of the love & duties of a home, to place her as nearly as possible in the relation of a daughter, and to secure for her the nearest approach to the domestic relationships of which she has been deprived, that I think I should consider this education of the affections, and the domestic duties that arise out of them, as more than an equivalent for the accomplishments & languages which she would learn by the other plan" (L 181).

Gaskell thought, as we have seen, of the parental love she had lost as of a birthright taken from her. In her fiction it is significant that birthrights are often embodied in houses. Houses were a Victorian obsession, but even in Victorian fiction there are seldom as many houses as there are in Gaskell's works. Some are simple, ordinary houses, as in "The Moorland Cottage," for instance, "The Schah's English Garden," "Bessy's Troubles at Home," and "A Dark Night's Work." But often the houses are ancestral, homes, that is, which have become not only associated with the families that have lived in them for centuries but which, through association, have become the very embodiments of the families themselves. This is the case in "The Old Nurse's Story," "Morton Hall," "My French Master," "The Poor Clare," "The Doom of the Griffiths," "My Lady Ludlow," "The Grey Woman," "Crowley Castle," and "Curious if True."

The house is thus for Gaskell an image, a metaphor for family life, and what that metaphor means to her is nowhere defined more fully and clearly than in the resolution provided in her story "My French Master." The central character of this story is M. de Chalabre, a Frenchman whom the French Revolution has driven out of his native land. M. de Chalabre has thus lost his homeland. He has also lost his home, having forfeited in his flight his family's ancestral castle. Although he is not unhappy in England, where he takes refuge in his exile, he yearns to return to his home in France. During his many long years in England, he marries and fathers two beautiful daughters, one of whom, when she grows up, meets the grandson of the man to whom the revolutionary government has meanwhile given his castle in France. They fall in love, of course, and marry, and when they move into the castle, they invite M. de Chalabre to come to France and live with them, making it possible, thus, for him to reclaim his ancestral home. A letter he writes at the end is revealing for the particulars it dwells on. " 'I have,' " he writes, " 'the very apartment in Chateau Chalabre that was mine when I was a boy, and my mother came in to bless me every night' " (2:530). M. de Chalabre has repossessed for Gaskell the very bed from which, as a child, she had been removed when her father had sent her to Knutsford. He has reclaimed the very blessing that she had been, like Esau, denied.

Gaskell was not, for a Victorian, especially young when she married William at the age of twenty-one. But neither was she especially old. She wanted to be a wife and mother, and she became one as soon as she could.

There is no question she loved William, but giving and receiving love was not unrelated to her need. She needed a home. She needed a family. And she very quickly settled into the domestic life. The wedding took place on August 30 in 1832. Her first child was the stillborn daughter, born in July of 1833. Marianne was born on September 12, 1834, Margaret Emily on February 5, 1837, and Florence Elizabeth on October 7, 1842. William, Gaskell's only son was born on October 23 of 1844. Julia Bradford, the last daughter, was born in 1846, on September 3. These children, even more than her husband, made up to Gaskell for what she had missed. She often suggests as much in her fiction. A typical scene is to be found, for example, in *Sylvia's Lovers*. Sylvia's story is not identical to the last detail to Gaskell's, but, like all of Gaskell's plots, it is archetypally autobiographical. One by one Sylvia has lost the members of her immediate family until she suddenly finds herself, in her late teens, "Alone! Alone!" All she has now is her husband Philip and their newly born child. Her husband she does not particularly care for, but she is fiercely attached to her baby. It takes the place of those she has lost. "Sometimes," the narrator writes, "in the nights" Sylvia "would waken, crying, with a terrible sense of desolation; every one who had loved her, or whom she had loved, had vanished out of her life; every one but her child who lay in her arms, warm and soft" (6:442). For Gaskell the future redeemed the past.

If we wished to find a myth in which to embody this aspect of Gaskell it would be the myth of Undine. And this is the myth Gaskell chooses herself to describe the transformation that a woman undergoes when she becomes a wife and mother. "How often," she writes in "The Doom of the Griffiths" about the flighty young girl Nest, "do we see giddy, coquetting, restless girls become sobered by marriage? A great object in life is decided, one on which their thoughts have been running in all their vagaries; and they seem to verify the beautiful fable of Undine. A new soul beams out in the gentleness and repose of their future lives. An indescribable softness and tenderness takes the place of the wearying vanity of their former endeavours to attract admiration" (5:257). Like the water sprite Undine, who could only gain a soul by marrying a mortal and bearing his child, Gaskell could only regain her identity by becoming a wife and mother.

It was, thus, her own private needs that made Elizabeth Cleghorn Stevenson become that model of femininity that we have come to call "Mrs. Gaskell." She needed what that image entailed. The fact, however, that the image fulfilled a public ideal as well was not without importance to Gaskell. Gaskell needed love from everyone, she needed everyone's approval. She "clung tenaciously," like Ruth, "to every symptom of regard, and could not relinquish the love of any one." If "Mrs. Gaskell" happened to be, as Walter Allen remarks in describing her, a "wholly admirable woman in harmony with the society" she lived in, to Gaskell that was all to the good.[6] Society was a larger family. Being in harmony with its views meant that she would be a part of it. Representing its ideal meant that she would earn its love. Who would reject or abandon an icon?

The image of "Mrs. Gaskell" worked. Like Maggie in "The Moorland Cottage," "Mrs. Gaskell" lived and died "rich in the love of many." When she died the congregation of the Cross Street Chapel in Manchester, of which her husband was the minister, erected a tablet in her memory. It reads:

Mrs. Gaskell
In Memory of
+
Elizabeth Cleghorn Gaskell, wife of the Rev. William Gaskell, M.A.,
one of the Ministers of this chapel. Wisely honoured for her genius and the
spirit in which it was exercised, endeared by her rare graces of mind and
heart to all by whom she was known, she fulfilled the duties of a wife and
mother with a tenderness and fidelity which secured for her undying love,
and so lived in Christian faith and hope, that death, which came without
a moment's warning, had for her no sting.
Born Sep. 29, 1810   Died Nov. 12, 1865
Erected by the Congregation in token of their respect and regard.

Elizabeth Stevenson may not have married William Gaskell until 1832. But the ideal Victorian woman who was known as "Mrs. Gaskell" was born on that day in 1811 when Elizabeth's mother died and her father sent her away.

IV

Lucy and Her Daemonic Double

ALTHOUGH "MRS. GASKELL" was as much one of Elizabeth Gaskell's inventions as any of her fictional heroines, Gaskell was not being hypocritical in assuming her identity. Her truthful nature would not allow her to lie about herself to others. And her intuition told her mere dissembling would not work. She had to believe in "Mrs. Gaskell" for the image to serve its purpose. She had to lie therefore to herself. Thus, before she returned to London for her last visit with her father, Elizabeth Stevenson had become, as far as she knew, an ideal girl. But where was the bitterness? the resentment? Where was the anger she had felt as an abandoned and rejected child? What had become, in "Mrs. Gaskell," of the passionate little girl who had hurt and vexed her father?

With the wisdom of the serpent and the innocence of the dove, Gaskell knew, without knowing she knew it, that "Mrs. Gaskell" was a forgery. This she confided to her fiction in the image of the forger and the crime that he commits. Both are prominent in her fiction. The circumstances of the crime are, in every case, the same, the same if not exactly in detail—although often in detail too—always in the larger pattern. And in every case the forgery is, it is obvious, no mere theft but a symbolic representation of what the forger is himself. We find a typical case in *Ruth* in the character of Richard Bradshaw. Richard's father, Mr. Bradshaw, is a prominent man of business who, although not really bad, is—as Gaskell writes in words she might have used for her own father—"severe and arbitrary" in his conduct (3:402). His family has suffered greatly as a result of his behavior. His wife, whom he has long ago reduced to absolute submission, has become a permanent invalid. She reminds us of Mrs. Gradgrind and she may have been her source, for Dickens had certainly read the novel and he began to publish *Hard Times* immediately after *Ruth* appeared. Neither is exactly mad, but there is in both a derangement that is a comment on their husbands. The Bradshaws have a number of children. One of their daughters, who has inherited the weakness of her constitution, seems to be following in her mother's footsteps. Another, although she is strong and resilient, finds that her life is a constant struggle against the tyranny of her father. On no one, however, has Mr. Bradshaw had so devastating an effect as he has had on his son, Richard. Richard is, like his mother, weak and, having been pretty much neglected—his mother being too debilitated to fulfill her responsibilities and his father much too busy— he has grown up to be a prey to temptations and dissipations. But these he has tried, of course, to conceal. His father expects him to behave like the ideal of the young gentleman, and Richard, who is easily "cowed," pretends to be what his father expects (3:407). Bradshaw accepts the pretense as truth. But the "set sentences of goodness" Richard utters in his father's presence are, the narrator explains, "like the flowers that children stick in the ground, and that have not sprung upwards from roots—deep down in the hidden life and experience of the heart" (3:210). Richard borrows a great deal of money to pay for his vices and his pleasures, which one day he finds himself unable to repay. Afraid to tell his father the truth, he does the only thing he can think of. He cashes a note by forging a signature. It happens—in Gaskell it always does—that this occurs just at the time Richard can no longer stand the strain of acting the part he is playing in order to satisfy his father, and it does not take much insight to see that, for Gaskell, Richard's forgery has a psychological meaning. Not only is Richard stealing back, like Benjamin in "The Crooked Branch," the love his father has denied him by stealing the money that stands in its place, he is confessing metaphorically that the ideal his father sees is not his real self but a forgery.

In her own unconscious way, Gaskell wondered all her life about the ideal she had become and what she had denied to do so, and in 1856 she published a story, "The Poor Clare," in which she came to understand how she had become "Mrs. Gaskell." Like many nineteenth-century novelists, Gaskell felt freer to express herself in her stories than in her novels. Novels had for her the character more of official public statements. Stories were more like private confidences. In her stories she is, therefore, willing or able to take risks and to do away with layers of defensive self-deception. Sometimes she pays in artistic ways for gaining psychological freedom. As she pushes towards an insight that she wants also to avoid, Gaskell often moves forward and back many times before her conclusion. The story thus grows overly long or loses momentum and direction. Absorbed, moreover, in her thoughts, Gaskell is so much more concerned with her psychological conflicts than the action that projects them that the narrative progresses not from a cause to an effect but from one scene to another in the drama of her mind. Often her stories appear in consequence loosely connected or disjointed. In one or two, it even seems as though she has pieced her tale together out of several different narratives. Very few of her stories, therefore, are entirely good artistically, although there are many parts of stories that are utterly magnificent. But bad or good, they are revealing records of her inner life.

"The Poor Clare" is a typical case. The story is long, and parts of it seem only loosely related to others. The thoughts on which the segments are based form, however, in Gaskell's mind a logical and coherent argument. One of the portions of this story concerns a young woman named Lucy Gisborne, and her purpose in the narrative is to embody the ideal. If we collect the various adjectives Gaskell uses to describe her or the instances she creates to imply her characteristics, we find that Lucy is tender, good, sweet, kind, timid, gentle, shy, generous, modest, pure. She is in every way a paradigm, thus another "Mrs. Gaskell." Lucy's behavior is ideal too. She walks lightly, she speaks softly, and she keeps her eyes lowered except when she is spoken to. And she is happy. She lives with her father, Mr. Gisborne, who is completely devoted to her.

One thing, however, troubles Lucy, and that is the fact that she is haunted by a curse that takes the form—and these are Gaskell's very words—of a "demon" which is her " 'Double' " (5:361–62). Gaskell's stories are full of ghosts, demons, and other Gothic beings, and many readers in the past have insisted, as Chadwick did, that although "most practical and endowed with much common sense, Mrs. Gaskell was always superstitious." It is true that Gaskell once said that, since she was "half-Scotch," she had "a right to be superstitious" (L 442), but she was obviously speaking in jest. It is also true, as Gérin notes, that she once claimed she had seen a ghost, but it is very much to be doubted, from her account of the event (L 48), that she meant to be taken literally. It is significant that Gaskell does not, in her longer works, meddle with supernatural beings. Seeing her novels as public statements, she speaks in realistic terms, finding other ways to express her hidden and subversive meanings. But in her stories she allows herself to use what Ellen Moers has called the language of the "female Gothic,"[1] a language in which she is able to formulate thoughts about herself in code.

The story must therefore be read metaphorically, and metaphorically "The Poor Clare" is a most remarkable narrative, an insight well ahead of its time, for it foreshadows by thirty years Robert Louis Stevenson's tale of the divided self, "Dr. Jekyll and Mr. Hyde."[2] Stevenson tells his story, of course, in an entirely natural way, in fact as though he were reporting it as a scientific experiment, and this Gaskell could not do, not only because in

1856, no one had yet the conceptual terms available thirty years later, but because, aware that she was betraying something of crucial importance, Gaskell, to prevent "Mrs. Gaskell" from knowing what she had in mind, was compelled to write the narrative in her secret symbolic language.

Gaskell describes the confrontation between Lucy and her double in a classic mirror scene (5:361). Gaskell might, although it has both mythic and medieval precedent, have appropriated the device from Charlotte Brontë's *Jane Eyre*. She had read *Jane Eyre* when it first appeared (L 25a), and she might well have remembered the novel as she wrote "The Poor Clare" not just because *Jane Eyre* is memorable but because she was, at that time, also writing Brontë's biography. Jane is awakened, we recall, on the night before her wedding, by hearing something in her room, and looking around she soon sees Bertha, or her reflection, in the mirror. As Gilbert and Gubar have noted, of course, Bertha is Jane Eyre's alter ego. Seeing her image in the mirror, Jane is really seeing herself.[3] Lucy also sees herself in the demon in the mirror.[4] The demon looks exactly like her. In "form and feature," Gaskell writes, "and the minutest touch of dress" the demon was her "complete likeness." Lucy herself describes the demon as " 'another wicked, fearful self' " (5:361). It is " 'another,' " but it is a " 'self.' " It differs from Lucy in one way only. Since it has a "demon soul," it is not an ideal woman (5:362). While Lucy, thus, sits quietly at home, the demon freely roams abroad doing its " 'detestable work' " (5:361). And, since the two are completely identical, it is Lucy who is blamed for the things her demon does.

Consciously, Gaskell deals with this contrast primarily in moral terms. At this level, one of the characters praises Lucy for resisting the " 'wicked thoughts' " the demon, he says, must have tried to " 'suggest' " to her and the " 'wicked actions' " to which the demon must have tried to " 'tempt' " her. In " 'her saintly maidenhood,' " Lucy, he concludes, has managed to escape " 'undefiled by evil thought or deed' " (5:368). But psychologically Gaskell knows it is Lucy who wants to do the deeds she attributes to the demon. Several times the narrator tells us that the demon is "mocking" Lucy (5:360–62). The demon is always laughing, in fact, and it is clear it is laughing at Lucy. Bertha was always laughing too. If it had really failed to tempt her, the demon would have had no reason to mock. The demon laughs because it knows that to emerge " 'undefiled' " from temptation, Lucy has had to emerge divided, split between the " 'holy nature' " (5:366) she accepts as her identity and those wicked thoughts and deeds that, since they have been disowned, have become her daemonic double.

It is important here to say that men need not, in Gaskell's fiction, be divided from their demons. Jekyll and Hyde must be two women but they are allowed to be one man. A good example of the relationship between a man and his daemonic self is to be found in "The Squire's Story," a tale Gaskell published in *Household Words* in December of 1853. The story concerns a man named Higgins, who arrives in the neighborhood of Barford and makes himself so generally welcome by his affability and charm that soon he marries an eligible young woman and settles down to lead the life of a respectable country squire. At the very end of the story, we learn, however, that Higgins has been leading a double life as a highwayman, riding under cover of night to do dark and bloody deeds. Eventually, he is caught and hanged.

"The Squire's Story" is not very good, not in what it achieves at least, although it contains stunning flashes of nearly Dostoyevskian insight. These are so brilliant that one wonders whether Gaskell failed in this story because she could not sustain her vision or because she was afraid to face the truths she had perceived. The fact that she ends the story abruptly suggests not ineptitude but fear. Just as she comes to the heart of her subject, she suddenly says "There is no need to add much more" (2:549), hurries to tie up her loose threads, and brings the story to an end, although not to a conclusion.

By then she has told us enough, however, to make us see it is not greed that has turned Higgins into a highwayman. The money is again a metaphor. Higgins is a man possessed, very much as is Raskolnikov, by a demon that compels him, finding no other expression apparently, to lash out in rage and fury. This demon has haunted Higgins since childhood. As a child, we are told, he had dreamed that he would commit a murder, but at the time his mother had soothed him and all had been well. Now, however, his mother is dead—Higgins is one of those motherless children for whom nothing is ever right—and there is no one left in the world who can restore him to inner peace. Higgins struggles with his demon, for he is really a good man. He is also deeply religious and looks on his crimes as terrible sins. But, in a Dostoyevskian twist, it is his morality and religion that drive him to his bloodiest deed. This bloody deed is the brutal murder of a wealthy old woman. He takes her money once he kills her, but this is not his motive at all, any more than it was Raskolnikov's. Higgins could rob her without harming her. His own explanation, which he gives later, is that he killed her because she had never given alms to the poor and because, breaking into her house, he had found that she had fallen asleep while she was reading her Bible. But as we listen, it becomes clear that he is merely skirting the truth. What had angered him was the sight not of the neglected Bible but, on the contrary, of a woman piously sitting with the Good Book. As Lucy's demon mocks and laughs at her, knowing that the ideal is a fraud, so the nocturnal, daemonic Higgins kills the old woman because for him at that moment she embodies the fraudulent piety he himself has been pretending to by day.

There is a split here of a sort between the nocturnal and the diurnal Higgins. But both are contained in the same body. In Lucy, the demon must be expelled and displaced in another form. Gaskell's definition of the male allows for both the man and the demon. Her definition of the female allows only for the ideal. Yet, for reasons to which I shall turn later, there are exceptions to this rule, and one is provided in "The Poor Clare" in Lucy's grandmother, Bridget Fitzgerald. Bridget, who lives alone in the woods, is a fierce and brooding woman who, the narrator remarks, looks as though she had been "scorched in the flames of hell" (5:338). Bridget is obviously not divided. She is daemonic. The demon in her has been allowed to remain within. Her neighbors think she is a witch, and Gaskell, while she hedges a little, allows the narrator to say that his uncle, who "had lived many years, and learnt many things," believed that people could be "bewitched" (5:368). That image, as Gilbert and Gubar have shown, often appears in Victorian fiction.[5] It often recurs in Gaskell's work, and it always means one thing: a witch is a woman who has kept her demon. Thus, although Bridget and Lucy seem, as one of Gaskell's readers has noted, but loosely connected at the level of the realistic narrative,[6] there is no question, metaphorically, they are two parts of the same tale. Bridget is the whole of the woman of which, a split having taken place, Lucy and her daemonic double are the separated halves.

There is a third woman in the story, Bridget Fitzgerald's daughter, Mary, who left home as a young woman, met a man who seduced and betrayed her, and bore an illegitimate child. Mary is thus a fallen woman, of which there are many in Gaskell's fiction, and which, like the demon and the witch, is an image in Gaskell's mind.[7] The image is explained in part when Bridget, repenting of her witchcraft, decides to join—providing the title—the order of the Poor Clares. On joining, Bridget must choose a new name, and she chooses Sister Magdalen (5:381). If we consider the facts alone, her choice is entirely inexplicable. Bridget herself has never done anything that even remotely makes her a Magdalen. She seems, on the contrary, fiercely virginal. Although once married, we are told, she has been a widow long and is a totally continent woman. There is no literal connection between Bridget and the Magdalen sin. But there is an imagistic connection. In Gaskell's language, it is clear, the demon Bridget has kept in her heart is the same that her daughter Mary has acted out in her fall.

A woman who acts out her demon sexually also seems to spend it in Gaskell. It is not altogether clear how Gaskell comes to this conclusion. She seems to believe, and understandably given her particular history, that every relationship makes a woman dependent on someone else for love and therefore vulnerable to rejection. And a relationship with a man not only makes rejection more likely—men having in Gaskell's mind a tendency to resemble her father—it forces a woman, because she needs love, to act in a way that will make him love her. It forces her, thus, to become an ideal and therefore to deny her demon. And this is especially the case in an illicit sexual union in which a man, as Gaskell sees him, is bound to the woman by no real ties. A woman expressing her demon sexually also surrenders it, thus, in Gaskell.

And this has happened to Mary Fitzgerald, who is, in consequence, no longer whole. But since she has expressed her demon, she is not yet the full submission to the demands of the ideal that is next created in Lucy. Lucy is the final step in the demon's repudiation. Gaskell makes sure we understand that the demon Lucy repudiates is the demon she inherited ancestrally through the female line. First she connects the demon to Bridget. It happens Lucy Gisborne's father had been a neighbor of Bridget's once. And hunting one day, never concerned with whom his pleasures happened to hurt, he had by accident killed her dog. Bridget had loved this dog so passionately that in anger she had cursed him, saying she hoped he would live to see the creature he loved best in the world " 'become a terror and a loathing to all' " (5:341). Gisborne, of course, turns out to be the man who seduces Bridget's daughter so that the demon that haunts Lucy proves to be her grandmother's curse. As Gaskell explains it, Lucy's " 'demon' " is the " 'hate' " in Bridget's " 'heart' " (5:382). Gaskell also connects the demon to its sexual expression in Lucy's mother, Mary Fitzgerald, Lucy's double being "voluptuous" (5:362) and spending much of its time at the stables where it becomes " 'unduly familiar' " with the " 'wild grooms' " Mr. Gisborne keeps (5:361).

Gaskell considers Lucy's predicament another instance in which the child is made to pay, as one of the characters actually says in the course of the story, for the " 'sins of the fathers' " (5:363). And it is certainly for her father that Lucy gives up her daemonic self. Until her double appears in the mirror, Lucy is, without a rival, the object of her father's love. But the behavior of her demon causes Mr. Gisborne to speak " 'fierce and angry words' " to his daughter (5:360). Even on learning that Lucy is innocent, that the behavior he finds abhorrent is not Lucy's but her demon's, the very thought that she has a double hovering somewhere in the house preys on Mr. Gisborne's mind to such an extent that its very presence is " 'past his patience to bear.' " At length, Lucy concludes a narrative she gives in the story of her past, " 'my father drove me forth' " (5:361). Perhaps Mr. Stevenson, vexed by his daughter, also spoke fierce and angry words. Certain it is he drove her forth. And driven out of her home in this way, Lucy takes up her life in exile, hoping, as Gaskell did in Knutsford, that somehow through " 'piety and prayer' " she will be freed of her dreadful demon so that her father will love her again.

It is not only her father's love Gaskell imagines Lucy losing. Before her double made its appearance, Lucy was loved by one and all. After her double has done its mischief, there is no one left who loves her. Eventually, Lucy, still in exile, meets a young man who falls in love with her before he knows she has a double. When he proposes Lucy replies she cannot marry him because his " 'love,' " she knows, " 'could' " never " 'stand' " to encounter her "fearful companion" (5:382). Lucy has learned her lesson well. Driven away by a father who could not tolerate even the thought of her demon, she has generalized to conclude that no one will love her unless she is good. And good she becomes, the ideal woman, although at the price of being haunted by the demon she has denied.

The three women of this story, Bridget the witch, Mary, and Lucy, are metaphorically one woman who, because of external circumstances, has had to split herself in three. "Mrs. Gaskell" knew as little of how she had come to be what she was as Lucy Gisborne understood how she had engendered her double. But Gaskell could not have written this story had she not realized she had begun as a whole woman, like Bridget Fitzgerald, but had been forced, like her daughter Mary, to give up her daemonic self because, like Lucy, she needed love. The story of her inner life, which is the story of her fiction, is the record of Gaskell's struggle to become a witch again.

V

The Autobiography
of a Suicide

WIVES AND DAUGHTERS was the last novel Gaskell wrote, or almost wrote, for she did not live to finish it. Many consider it Gaskell's best book, and indeed it does not appear to be as troubled at first glance by the uncertainties that mar some of her other novels and stories. But that is because it is "Mrs. Gaskell" who is in control of the narrative here. Whenever "Mrs. Gaskell" takes charge and the demon is subdued there are few contradictions visible. "Mrs. Gaskell" is in control as well of *Cranford* and "Cousin Phillis," and those who have loved the benign ideal have always preferred these works to the rest.

But Gaskell's demon, though subdued, has not been silenced in this novel. It has only taken up residence at a deeper level of the text. The novel is not, as it seems to be, a sweet reminiscence in middle age of childhood and its joys and sorrows. The title itself tells us as much. Gaskell, as she worked on the novel, had trouble thinking of a title. This was not at all unusual. Titles generally reflect themes, and Gaskell always had great difficulty, struggling as she always did to avoid the very insight that her demon was pursuing, recognizing her real concerns. Sometimes only near the end does she see what she is writing. In *North and South,* she does not discover what the theme of her novel is until she has almost finished the story. Sometimes Gaskell never perceives what it is she is trying to say. Others have to do it for her. When she published "Right at Last" it was Dickens who, discerning the underlying point of the tale, called the story "The Sin of a Father." For a time it seemed as though someone else would have to find a title for *Wives and Daughters* too. In May of 1864, she sent her publisher a projection of the outline of her tale, adding at the end of her letter "you will find a title for yourself for I can not. I have tried all this time in vain" (*L* 550).

At last, however, she chose a title, one that clearly has to do not with recollections of childhood but with the nature of female life. If the book is a retrospective, it is another work in which Gaskell sought to understand the genesis of "Mrs. Gaskell." In "The Poor Clare," Gaskell had realized that to become the ideal woman she had had to deny her demon. In *Wives and Daughters* she goes further. Here she comes to understand that the act of denying her demon had, in effect, cost her her life. Far from being a nostalgic recollection of her childhood, *Wives and Daughters* is, in reality, the autobiography of a suicide. But it is something else as well. It is the novel in which Gaskell saw where her daemonic self, rejected and condemned by the world, had found a refuge for itself.

Although it is not a mere reminiscence, nowhere does Gaskell in her fiction deal as extensively as here with her own early life. She is less concerned with facts—although she uses them when she wants to—than with archetypal images. And these are conceived in a complex way. Quiet as the text may be, the subtext is full of conflicting intentions, and while they do not collide in the novel but indeed enrich and deepen the characterizations and the plot, they spring, nonetheless, out of different impulses and cast Gaskell's past in different lights..

The novel's heroine, Molly Gibson, is without question Gaskell herself, not only because she relives her history, but because she mirrors Gaskell in personality and character. Playful, cheerful, forthright, sweet, simple, serious, the soul of integrity, shrewd but innocent as a dove, no other character in her fiction seems as much the very image of how Gaskell must have appeared to those who knew her as a girl. Equally clear is that Molly's father is a portrait of Mr. Stevenson. Part of Gaskell sees the truth but finds it so painful to admit that she displaces what she believes had been her father's feelings towards her. Mr. Stevenson had seemed, by his behavior, to be saying that he did not love his daughter. In the novel Mr. Gibson is made to hate all womankind. He is a terrible mysogynist. Conduct that had seemed to Gaskell to be a personal rejection has been reinterpreted here simply as a character trait. All through the novel Mr. Gibson makes snide remarks on the subject of women. "I 'wish I'd a five-pound house,' " he says, annoyed one day by a woman servant, " 'and not a woman within ten miles of me' " (8:108). " 'I think the world would get on tolerably well,' " he snarls on yet another occasion, " 'if there were no women in it' " (8:605). When Mrs. Hamley, one of his neighbors, offers advice, he rejects it rudely, adding that her suggestion " 'is just like a woman's idea: all kindness and no common sense.' " (8:110). Mrs. Hamley is not a feminist, but she is an intelligent woman, and she understands the contempt implied in Mr. Gibson's words. " 'Well, well,' " she says, addressing Molly who happens to be standing with her, " 'I submit I am a woman. Molly, thou art a woman! Go and order some strawberries and cream for this father of yours. Such humble offices fall within the province of women' " (8:111).

Many of Mr. Gibson's comments are made not only in Molly's presence but, in fact, directly to her. When she announces she intends to buy herself some new clothes, Mr. Gibson says he wishes, and not to spare himself the cost, " 'girls could dress like boys' " (8:64). He does not, however, want his daughter to have a boy's education. Molly is bright, curious, alert, potentially an ideal student. On her own she has indeed read "every book that came in her way." But Mr. Gibson is determined to "daunt" her "in every intellectual attempt" (8:65). To her governess, Miss Eyre—Gaskell has obviously borrowed the name from Charlotte Brontë's novel—he gives the following instructions: " 'Don't teach Molly too much; she must sew, and read, and write, and do her sums; but I want to keep her a child, and if I find more learning desirable for her, I'll see about giving it to her myself. After all, I'm not sure that reading and writing are necessary. Many a good woman gets married with only a cross instead of a name; it's rather a diluting of mother-wit, to my fancy.' " Eventually, he relents a little: " 'but, however,' " he continues, " 'we must yield to the prejudices of society, Miss Eyre, and so you may teach the child to read' " (8:65).

But for the most part Gaskell indulges, in the creation of Mr. Gibson, in transparent wish fulfillment. Reenacting some of the facts of her own early years, she changes the details just enough to make them happy rather than painful. This she had often done before. In many of her stories, for instance, fathers turn, when mothers die, to seek comfort from their daughters. In "A Dark Night's Work," the "tie between" Ellinor and her father becomes, when Mrs. Wilkins dies, "very strong and tender indeed" (5:413). The same occurs in *Wives and Daughters* between Molly and her father. The tie becomes so close, in fact, that it verges on the incestuous. This is not just another case of different kinds of love being fused. We do not have to be Freudian readers to see an Electra complex at work in the feelings Gaskell imagines Molly having for her father. Similar hints of incestuous feelings are to be found in many relationships Gaskell conceives between fathers and daughters. Daughters, for instance, often compete with their mothers in Gaskell's fiction for a place in their father's hearts. Many want to replace their mothers. And in surrogate ways they do. In "Cousin Phillis," for example, Gaskell sees the mother and daughter as rivals for the father's regard. Mrs. Holman, Gaskell tells us, is so inferior to her husband both in intellect and character that Mr. Holman has nowhere to turn but to his daughter for companionship (7:34–35). In

Ellinor's case in "A Dark Night's Work," the daughter replaces the mother literally. Ellinor, on her mother's death, is actually moved from her seat at the dinner table into the one her mother had occupied. Molly, who occupies the room that had once belonged to her mother, also in this way replaces her. Gaskell even imagines Molly taking the place once of her stepmother. When the second Mrs. Gibson leaves to spend a few days in London, Molly feels as though a "restraint" has been lifted from her heart, which now "danced at the idea of three whole days . . . of perfect freedom of intercourse with her father" (8:507). And the implicit sexual overtone suggested in the lifted restraint and the dancing of the heart is made explicit a few pages later when the narrator remarks that "there was only one little drawback to this week of holiday and happy intercourse with her father. Everybody would ask them to tea. They were quite like bride and bridegroom" (8:511).

Fathers, generally in Gaskell, experience a reciprocal interest, although it manifests itself in a more sublimated form, not as sexual desire but as a wish to keep their daughters in a prepubescent stage. Thus, Mr. Holman not only discourages all the suitors Phillis attracts, he actually keeps her dressed in pinafores, although, by the time the story opens, she is well into her teens. Ellinor's father, who "never seemed to understand how she was passing out of childhood" (7:418), finds it difficult to believe someone has fallen in love with his daughter. Even when he accepts her suitor, he cannot see why they must marry rather than "continue just as they" are (7:447). In *Wives and Daughters*, Mr. Gibson is the most possessive of all. When one apprentice, to whom Gaskell gives the suggestive name of Coxe, seems to have fallen in love with Molly, Mr. Gibson not only ejects him, almost bodily, from the house, he attacks him with his wit and determines on the spot that he will have no more apprentices. All "young men," he is now convinced, are merely "wolves in chase of his one ewe-lamb" (8:61). But Molly does not really object. Gaskell's daughters are always willing to become as little girls if the reward of their regression is a place in their fathers' hearts. Indeed, in one fantasy in which she confuses parental sexes, Gaskell imagines Molly tied by an umbilical cord to her father. " 'I should like,' " Molly says to him one day, " 'to get a chain . . . just as long as your longest round, and then I could fasten us two to each end of it, and when I wanted you I could pull, and if you didn't want to come, you could pull back again; but I should know you knew I wanted you, and we could never lose each other' " (8:27). How often in Knutsford must Elizabeth have said "I want you" to her father. Had he been tied to her by a chain, as she was tied to him by her need, they could not have "lost each other." She, at least, could not have lost him.

One of the wish-fulfilling devices Gaskell uses in this novel is for her a new invention and a triumph of ingenuity. Instead of altering the facts and changing the historical record, she recalls events as they happened but interprets them in a different way. This is especially the case in her handling of Mr. Gibson. Gaskell imagines that Mr. Gibson is a warm and affectionate man, deeply devoted to his daughter. But, because he feels so deeply, he must protect himself from excess, and this he can only do if he says and does the opposite of what he means. To Molly his manner is gruff and distant. Some might think he does not love her. Molly would certainly think so herself, were it not that she is endowed with the feminine intuition that allows her to understand what her father's feelings are (8:33). If Mr. Stevenson, "hurt or vexed," had spoken the "fierce and angry words" that Mr. Gisborne speaks to Lucy, Gaskell in *Wives and Daughters* convinces herself that the words were meant to convey a meaning that was loving and sweet. Likewise, it is for Molly's good and because he loves her so much, that Mr. Gibson sends her away. He wants to avoid another suitor coming to steal away his ewe lamb. He sends her to stay for a time with the Hamleys, and since Mrs. Hamley is one of the dowagers in whom Gaskell recalls Aunt Lumb, it is obvious that Gaskell here is reenacting her exile in Knutsford. The words Mr. Gibson speaks in parting are undoubt- edly the words Gaskell believed her father meant. " 'You're a plague,' " Mr. Gibson says, " 'and I mean to leave off loving you as fast as I can' " (8:65). Through Molly, however, Gaskell persuades herself that, as a child, she had misunderstood, that, had she known his temperament better, she would have known that what he meant was not at all that he did not love her but, on the contrary, that he did and that he would miss her terribly.

Reinterpreting her past, Gaskell is able to look differently at her father's remarriage now. Just as it was because he loved her that Mr. Gibson sent Molly away, so it is because he believes that she needs a mother to guide her, and not because he wants a wife, that he feels he must remarry.

The woman Mr. Gibson marries is one of Gaskell's most brilliant creations. Gaskell always does stepmothers well. All are wicked, but it is perhaps a clue to how long and hard she thought about the second Mrs. Stevenson that not a one is a cliché. Thelka alone, in "Six Weeks at Heppenheim," is an exception, if there is one, to the image of the wicked stepmother. Thelka decides to marry Herr Müller when the man she loves betrays her. Herr Müller, married twice already, has children by his first wife, children whom Thelka knows and loves. We are sure that when she marries him, she will become a loving stepmother. It is significant, however, that Thelka's marriage to Herr Müller is projected beyond the end, not contained in the story proper. Gaskell often places in the peripheries of her narratives events that she needs to create in her fictions but in which she cannot believe. They happen before the story begins, after it ends, or at least off-stage. The fact that Thelka's marriage, therefore, is predicted at the end makes it a nonevent for Gaskell. In the story itself, in fact, what we find is a wicked stepmother in the second Mrs. Müller who, although she will shortly die, is still alive when the story opens. It is because Herr Müller's children are so unhappy with this stepmother that they turn for love to Thelka. Thus, although she will be a stepmother, in the narrative itself Thelka is really more an Aunt Lumb.

The most extraordinary stepmother Gaskell created before Mrs. Gibson is Robert Griffiths's second wife in "The Doom of the Griffiths." The stepmother here is a minor character, but she plays no minor role. Although she only appears briefly and is not developed very far, Gaskell has imagined her so well and has understood her so deeply that, in just a few quick strokes, she has conveyed a complex character. The plot that concerns her is simple and typical. As soon as she marries Robert Griffiths, she begins to do what she can to turn him against his son, Owen, who, in very short order, becomes one of Gaskell's rejected children. Other wives in Gaskell's fiction whine and cajole and beg their husbands to get them to do what they want. Mrs. Griffiths is far deadlier. By sheer ingenuity and an iron will she makes her husband, who is weak, see as she sees, feel as she feels, and want only what she wants. Soon, although he still believes he is making his own decisions, Robert Griffiths is no more than an echo of his wife. In the end he does her bidding not because he has given in but because her will and purpose have, in his mind, supplanted his.

But Mrs. Gibson in *Wives and Daughters* is cast in a very different mold. Playing several parts at once, as a character she is deeper, for the interconnections among them make for a greater degree of complexity. As a stepmother, however, she has been diminished in size. Mrs. Griffiths, evil and cruel, has stature and a tragic dimension. She is a kind of Lady Macbeth. We may despise her, and we do, but we are forced to take her seriously. Mrs. Gibson is only comic. And by reducing her to comedy, Gaskell has removed her sting.

She has not, however, ceased to blame her. On the contrary, unwilling to believe her father guilty of her sufferings in her childhood, Gaskell transfers responsibility totally to her stepmother here. A typical scene, which illustrates too how Gaskell fuses blame and comedy, is to be found when Mrs. Gibson first moves into the Gibson house. Gaskell had written this scene before in a variety of versions. One had appeared in "The Doom of the Griffiths." As soon as his father had remarried, Owen had given vent to tears not only because he had "hitherto considered himself (and with justice) the first object of his father's life," but because a second wife had seemed to him to "slight" the first (5:245). In *Wives and Daughters* Gaskell again looks on the second wife as a slight both to the child and to the former wife. As soon as she moves into the house, Mrs. Gibson lets Molly know that she intends to begin redecorating and will start with Molly's room. Since this is the room that had been her mother's, Molly protests. She begs Mrs. Gibson to start instead with her own daughter's room. Mrs. Gibson has every intention of redecorating that room too, but she must do Molly's first, she says. Otherwise people might say—and it is only what people say that matters to her, hardly ever what she does—that she was taking better care of her daughter than of her stepdaughter. " 'Really, Molly,' " she concludes in a state of exasperation, " 'you are either very stupid or very obstinate, or else you don't care what hard things may be said about me: and all for a selfish fancy of your own!' " (8:210).

As this scene so amply illustrates, Mrs. Gibson is a vain, self-involved, and foolish woman, and it is clear Gaskell designs her not only to prove that Molly was right to fear, as she did, her father's remarriage and to resent the woman he chose, but as a punishment to her father. It does not take Mr. Gibson long to realize he has made a mistake. He rues his decision before, in fact, he has finished his proposal. The "question as to its wisdom came into his mind the instant that the words were said past recall" (8:120). Long before the wedding takes place, he has had so many times to sell the idea to himself of his marriage to Hyacinth Clare that when he tells Molly about it he rattles his reasons off by rote, "recapitulating all the advantages of the remarriage; he knew them off by heart now" (8:126). Too late does he come to understand that his new wife has been responsible for separating him from his daughter. His greatest regret, once he is married, is that Mrs. Gibson has cast so deep a pall over his house that "his little Molly," with whom he had once enjoyed such a free and happy exchange, has become "quiet and undemonstrative . . . in her general behavior to him" (8:373). His marriage, Gaskell thus concludes, may have cost her the loss of her father, but it also cost Mr. Stevenson the loss of his beloved child.

None of this make-believe, however, keeps Gaskell from seeing the truth at last. And in the truth about her history she finds the truth about herself. The revelation is so terrible Gaskell divides it into two parts, parts that are separated in the narrative by some intervening action. But in her mind this is one scene, the central scene of the book, in fact. The first part of the scene begins when Mr. Gibson informs Molly that he is planning to marry again. "She did not answer. She could not tell what words to use. She was afraid of saying anything, lest the passion of anger, dislike, indignation—whatever it was that was boiling up in her breast—should find vent in cries and screams, or worse, in raging words that could never be forgotten. It was as if the piece of solid ground on which she stood had broken from the shore, and she was drifting out to the infinite sea alone" (8:125–26).

Whenever Gaskell uses the phrase, as she does here, "whatever it was," it is always because she is thinking of something so painful she cannot name it. But as soon as Molly runs into the garden, having spoken angry words, and breaks out into a "passion of grief"—Owen Griffiths had broken out into a passion too on hearing that his father had remarried—Gaskell does tell us what she felt. "She did not care," the narrator writes, "to analyse the sources of her tears and sobs." Her "father was going to be married again—her father was angry with her; she had done very wrong—he had gone away displeased; she had lost his love; he was going to be married—away from her—away from his child—his little daughter" (8:128). Tucked away among the clauses, hidden almost in the string of devastating facts and feelings, are those words that must to Gaskell have been the most dreaded in the world: "she had lost his love." And what is worse, she had, by her anger and the angry words she had spoken, proved that she was unworthy indeed of the love that she had lost.

Molly, in this state of despair, has hurled herself, sobbing, on the ground, and it is in this prostrate state that Roger Hamley happens to find her. Roger is neglected himself, both his parents preferring his brother. Osborne, his brother, is a poet—his mother at least wants him to be one and has filled him with idle dreams. Roger, in contrast, is a scientist. He may have been, as some believe, intended as a portrait of Darwin, whom Gaskell had met on several occasions.[1] He is certainly meant to be taken as a young man of merit and promise. In the outline Gaskell made before she started writing the book, the name she used for him is Newton (*L* 550). Roger is extremely likeable, a male version of Molly Gibson. He is intelligent, like her, honest, serious, forthright, generous. Pained to find her in this condition, Roger picks her up from the ground and offers her what he considers to be the best advice he can give. If, he assures her, she does as he tells her, she will regain her father's love and earn the love of all besides. And the advice is very simple. " 'One has always,' " he says, " 'to try to think more of others than of oneself' " (8:133).

Molly is grateful for his kindness, but, on thinking over his words, she realizes their implications. "Thinking more of others' happiness than of her own was very fine; but did it not mean," she asks herself, "giving up her very individuality, quenching all the warm love, the true desires, that made her herself?" On reflection, she thinks it does. In offering "comfort," Molly now sees, Roger has actually recommended she assume a state of "deadness" (8:152). "Deadness" is a startling word, but death is precisely what Gaskell means. The metaphor reappears in the novel over and over again. When Roger repeats his advice to Molly in a subsequent conversation, which constitutes part two of this scene, adding " 'by-and-by you will be so much happier for it,' " Molly, returning to the metaphor, answers " 'No I shan't. It will be very dull when I shall have killed myself, as it were, and live only in trying to do, and to be, as other people like. I don't see any end to it. I might as well never have lived' " (8:154).

It is not by accident Gaskell chooses Roger to speak these words. He is the man Molly will marry. The moment, therefore, in which he finds her fulfills the title of the book. Molly has thrown herself to the ground in her grief as a daughter. She is raised again from the ground by the man who will make her a wife. But she can be neither wife nor daughter unless she takes Roger's advice.

For Molly this is the hour of decision. She has lost her father's love and she has not yet earned Roger's. There is a way she can possess herself of the love of both these men and she now knows what that is. But, by her own evaluation, what it requires her to do is nothing less than kill herself. At first she rebels. Why should she submit, she asks in her reply to Roger. Why should she only do and be what other people like? But Gaskell and her surrogate selves cannot turn love down on any terms. Even if it costs them their lives, they are willing to pay the price. Despite her protests, Molly decides that she must do as Roger says. From this moment on she strives to become what others wish. "Mrs. Gaskell" continues the story as though nothing has occurred. She does not even seem to remember the insight she has had through Molly. Molly continues to be delightful, charming, appealing, even lively. But something in Gaskell knows what has happened, and, at another level of the book, Gaskell makes sure we understand that the remainder of the narrative is the story of a suicide.

It is just at this moment that Mrs. Gibson's daughter, Cynthia, arrives. At the level of the plot, Cynthia enters the narrative now because

Mrs. Gibson, who had been afraid to let her come to her wedding lest her beauty make her own look faded and pale, feels she can, now safely married, allow her daughter to return. One of her functions, by far the simplest, is, as the daughter of Molly's stepmother, to embody the children of the second Mrs. Stevenson. The parallels are not precise. Mrs. Stevenson had, for instance, both a son and a daughter, while Mrs. Gibson has only Cynthia, although, in one of those gratuitous comments Gaskell always adds not because the stories need them but because they recall her life, Mrs. Gibson happens to mention that she had always wanted a son (8:141–42). If only in the realm of desire, both of Gaskell's half siblings exist. As a stepsister, moreover, rather than a half sister, Cynthia's relationship to Molly is not as close as Gaskell's was to her stepmother's children. But Gaskell again betrays the fact that she is thinking autobiographically when she entitles a chapter that deals with the two girls not "The Stepsisters" but "The Half-sisters" (ch. 21). It is true that the Victorians used these terms more interchangeably, but it is not by accident surely that Gaskell, having both available, chose the one nearest herself.

We cannot doubt that as a child Gaskell looked on her stepmother's children with a fiercely competitive eye. Sitting in Knutsford, always waiting, Gaskell must have imagined these children usurping her place in her father's house. She must have envied and resented them. In her fiction she extended the rivalry she must have felt to every kind of sibling relationship, although half siblings and stepsiblings are especially competitive. In "The Doom of the Griffiths," for instance, even before the stepmother arrives, Angharad,[2] the older of the children of the first Mrs. Griffiths, feels displaced, "almost neglected," as soon as her brother, Owen, is born. Owen becomes "the king of the house" (5:242), although, when Robert Griffiths remarries, Owen is himself displaced by the new Mrs. Griffiths's son (5:246). And Gaskell makes very little distinction between one displacement and the other.

Gaskell is generally open enough, as she is here, in her shorter fiction to tell us how siblings compete for love, but in her novels she often denies it. In *Wives and Daughters,* she insists that Molly and Cynthia are really good friends. Up to a point they actually are, and their friendship is, in fact, one of the very best accounts of friendship between adolescent girls. And yet, in her very protestations that Molly loves Cynthia as a sister, Gaskell embeds the truth we know. "Molly's love," she writes for example, "for Cynthia was fast and unwavering, but if anything tried it, it was the habit Roger had fallen into of always calling Cynthia Molly's sister" (8:362). Similarly, when she describes Cynthia's power to make herself

loved, she adds that had it not been that Molly had "the sweetest disposition in the world she might have become jealous of all the allegiance laid at
Cynthia's feet" (8:264). The hidden resentment she cannot acknowledge in
the attitudes of the characters, Gaskell embeds in the plot of the novel, in
which Cynthia and Molly are rivals. "Rivalry" is, in fact, the title of the
chapter in which their relationship is explained and explored (ch. 28). And
it is revealing, finally, that the various ways in which Molly and Cynthia
are shown to be rivals all end up in the same competition: they are always
rivals for love. This is especially the case in their most important rivalry,
which is for Roger Hamley's affections. Roger is not the first young man
who comes to the house to visit Molly and leaves enamored instead of
Cynthia. Even Mr. Coxe, who returns in the hope of wooing Molly, finds
himself, before he leaves, hopelessly in love with Cynthia. Roger is simply
another instance in which Cynthia steals the love that would rightfully
have been Molly's.

Important as it must have been for Gaskell to enact these feelings,
there were things even more important she wanted Cynthia to do for her.
One was to show what had happened to Molly after she had agreed to kill
herself. Cynthia, in one of her roles, is a mirror. It had been, we recall, in a
mirror that Lucy had encountered her double. Cynthia, whom Gaskell
calls a mirror (8:389), is the double Molly sees. At this level, their relationship is virtually symbiotic. As incidents are transformed into images,
Cynthia becomes not a fictional version merely of a historical fact but a
projection through which Gaskell, unable to press her inquiry further
through the heroine of the book, creates another in whom the consequences of Molly's suicide can be seen.

Molly has two mirrors in fact. Socially and economically, Gaskell
mirrors Molly's suicide in the second Mrs. Gibson. Gaskell calls her a
mirror too. Suggesting that in her self-involvement she is impervious to
experience, Gaskell observes that things had a tendency to slip "off the
smooth surface" of her "mirror-like mind without leaving any impressions" (8:152). Gaskell is halfway through the book before she is aware of
the fact that Mrs. Gibson is one of her surrogates, and we can point to the
very scene in which the realization takes place. It occurs when, having
discovered her failings, Mr. Gibson has begun so thoroughly to despise his
wife that he cannot even speak to her without becoming "dry and sarcas-
tic." Mrs. Gibson does not imagine how greatly she is held in contempt,
but she knows she is in "disfavour" and it renders her "uneasy." And this,
it now occurs to Gaskell, places her in the very predicament in relation to
Mr. Gibson in which she was placed herself in relation to her father. Both

are the victims of rejection. Suddenly, she imagines Molly as sympathetic to Mrs. Gibson. "Molly sometimes took her stepmother's part in secret; she felt as if she herself could never have borne her father's hard speeches so patiently; they would have cut her to the heart, and she must either have demanded an explanation, and probed the sore to the bottom, or sat down despairing and miserable" (8:477).

Such replication is common in Gaskell and especially in this book. Nothing goes in singles here. Everything in the story is duplicated, triplicated, sometimes more, like an Andy Warhol portrait, and, in a sense, for the same reason. Gaskell wants to make us see that the stories of individuals are also stories of their types. There are many victims thus in the novel of father figures—Roger Hamley, his brother Osborne, even Osborne's wife, Aimée. But it is not the fathers only who make victims out of women. Mrs. Gibson as a type is the victim of all men. So, as Gaskell knows, is Molly. The juxtaposition of father and lover, encompassing all the woman's roles that are suggested in the title, implies that Roger asks Molly to kill herself not just on his own behalf, not just on behalf of her father, but in the name of all the men with whom she could possibly have a relationship.

This is the truth that, denied in Molly, is projected in Mrs. Gibson. Every reprehensible trait that makes Mrs. Gibson wicked as a stepmother to Molly becomes another visible bruise of her victimization by men. When we first meet her at the Cumnors, the local gentry for whom she works, Mrs. Gibson is trying to think how to make do on her limited income and hoping that she can find a husband who will relieve her of her troubles (8:110). Gaskell understands her need. Equating money and love in her mind, she feels compassion for Mrs. Gibson. When Molly later judges her harshly, the narrator intervenes to remark that Molly is judging with "a girl's want of toleration, and want of experience to teach her the force of circumstances, and of temptation" (8:420–21). Mrs. Gibson may be deceitful, hypocritical, and manipulative, but for a woman, dependent and powerless, these are merely the skills of the trade. Mrs. Gibson does not need Roger to tell her women must kill themselves. She has discovered on her own that women are required to adapt and become what men desire.

What they desire Gaskell makes clear when Mr. Gibson decides to propose. The proposal occurs at the home of the Cumnors, and when he arrives, although Mr. Gibson has almost decided to remarry so that Molly will have a mother and considered Hyacinth Clare as one of many possibilities, he has not yet made up his mind. Her "voice," however, "was so soft, her accent so pleasant, that it struck him as particularly agreeable. . . . Then the harmonious colours of her dress, and her slow and graceful movements, had something of the same soothing effect upon his nerves that a cat's purring has upon other people. He began to think that he should be fortunate if he could win her" (8:118). This is not, it would appear, the first time that Mr. Gibson has succumbed to such allurements. When he is praised for being constant to his dead wife by one of the characters who remarks it is not every man who is " 'faithful to' " his " 'first love,' " Mr. Gibson winces uncomfortably. "Jeanie," in fact, had been "his first love; but her name had never been breathed in Hollingford. His wife—good, pretty, sensible, and beloved as she had been—was not his second; no, nor his third love" (8:162). As Robert Griffiths was weak psychologically, Mr. Gibson is sexually weak, unable to resist the seduction of a woman's powerful charms. The weakness is not unique to him. Roger Hamley has it too. As Mr. Gibson is taken in by the allurements of the mother, Roger is taken in by the daughter. This is to Gaskell the way of the world, the way of the male world, that is.

Cynthia mirrors Molly's suicide in a psychological sense. Except for sexes, which are reversed so that their parents can marry each other, Cynthia's history duplicates Molly's. But many details Gaskell denies, through make-believe, in Molly's tale are openly admitted in Cynthia's. Cynthia, thus, has lost her father at a very early age, as Molly and Gaskell lost their mothers, but while Molly is only sent for a short visit to the Hamleys and only because her father loves her and wants to protect her from Mr. Coxe, Cynthia is banished by a mother who very clearly does not want her. Like Gaskell, she is sent to boarding school. But unlike Gaskell, who maintained that she was happy at the Miss Byerleys', Cynthia considers herself an exile during the years she is at school. Molly is angry with her father, but she very soon forgives him. Cynthia never forgives her mother. " 'Somehow,' " she says, and the details duplicate Gaskell's own history again, " 'I cannot forgive her for her neglect of me as a child, when I would have clung to her. Besides, I hardly ever heard from her when I was at school. And I know she put a stop to my coming over to her wedding" (8:257).

Through Cynthia Gaskell is able to make several important revelations that she could never consciously make in the role of "Mrs. Gaskell." One of the most important of these is that she finds herself incapable of feeling very much for anyone. Having had, Gaskell explains, "too little true love in her life" (8:384), Cynthia finds it impossible now to feel any real love herself. " 'I wish,' " she remarks to Molly one day, " 'I could love people as you do. I never seem to care much for anyone' " (8:252). "Mrs. Gaskell" loved and was loved, and this was real up to a point. But somewhere beyond "Mrs. Gaskell's" connections to her family and friends, there was a part of Elizabeth Stevenson that no one was ever able to penetrate. Another important revelation concerns Cynthia's relationships with men. Unable to feel any genuine love, Cynthia has no real relationships. But men are very important to her. Her mother, although "she liked to be liked" (8:457), does not really care very much about them. They are mere instruments to be used, in themselves of no significance. But Cynthia cares a great deal about them. She needs, as Gaskell did, their approval. She needs, as Gaskell did, their love. When, for example, she meets Mr. Gibson, she makes a good impression on him. "Indeed," the narrator remarks, "she made something of the same kind of impression on all men. They were first struck with her personal apperance; and then with her pretty deprecating manner, which appealed to them much as if she had said 'You are wise, and I am foolish—have mercy on my folly.' It was a way she had; it meant nothing really; and she was hardly conscious of it herself; but it was very captivating all the same. Even old William, the gardener, felt it" (8:263–64). Cynthia cannot meet a man without wanting to make him love her. She was, Gaskell writes, "one of those natural coquettes who, from their cradle to their grave, instinctively bring out all their prettiest airs and graces in order to stand well with any man, young or old, who may happen to be present" (8:540). Defending herself against the charge that she set out to beguile Mr. Coxe, Cynthia says " 'I merely meant to make myself agreeable. I can't help doing that.' " " 'I knew he liked me, and I like to be liked; it's born in me to try to make everyone I come near fond of me' " (8:471–72). The reason, of course, that Cynthia needs to win the regard of every man is that she never really believes that any man can love her truly. She cannot believe she deserves to be loved. One of Gaskell's shrewdest insights into Cynthia and therefore herself is to to be found in the moment in which she tells us that Cynthia, being unloved, always inevitably feels unworthy. " 'You ought not to care so much for me,' " Cynthia remarks to Molly one day, " 'I'm not good enough for you to worry yourself about me. I've given myself up a long time ago' " (8:382). Gaskell makes it a point to show us that Cynthia is wrong to think ill of herself. She is endowed with many gifts and in possession of many virtues. Her view, however, of herself has nothing, of course, to do with her merit. It is the product of her past. Since no one, abandoned as she was, seemed to have any faith in her, she finally ceased to have faith in herself.

Cynthia is, in many ways, a kind of F. Scott Fitzgerald character. " 'Molly, you don't know how I was neglected,' " Cynthia says, in words that Gaskell might have used to describe herself, " 'just at a time when I wanted friends most. Mamma does not know it; it is not in her to know what I might have been if I had only fallen into wise, good hands. . . . I try not to care, which I daresay is really the worst of all; but I could worry myself to death if I once took to serious thinking' " (8:508–9). Cynthia's frivolity, her flirtations, her inconstancy, and her restlessness, are the distractions of a character trying desperately not to care. For if she did care that her life had been shattered irremediably, she would surely be driven mad. Many times in the novel, in fact, Cynthia seems on the edge of madness. Even Mr. Gibson realizes that her behavior at one juncture— "merry, full of pretty mockeries"—is nothing but the "constant brilliancy" of a perennial " 'mental fever' " (8:400). Carrying the mirror image forward, the narrator adds that in her brilliancy Cynthia resembles "not the sunshiny rest of a placid lake," but "the glitter of the pieces of a broken mirror" (8:389).

For lack of love, Cynthia has ceased long ago to have a self. When Molly rebels against Roger's advice, she understands that what he means is that, to earn the love of others, she must give up her individuality, she must quench her own desires. For a desire may, after all, put us in conflict with another, which may lead to angry words that may alienate affection. But without individuality one can never anger anyone. One may be what others wish. Cynthia has long ago learned this lesson. This is the secret of her success. Her "power of fascination" depends, Gaskell is only too well aware, on her gift of "adaptation." Cynthia is never this or that. She adapts to "various people" as well as to their "various moods." When Osborne Hamley comes to call, Cynthia is, like him, "gay and sparkling." When Roger calls, since he is earnest, she becomes "soft and grave" (8:384). This is not only how love is won, it is how love is won *back*. Nowhere does Gaskell betray as poignantly her own identification with Cynthia as when she writes that

> Never had any one more than Cynthia the power spoken of by Goldsmith when he wrote—

(8:493)

> "He threw off his friends like a huntsman his pack,
> For he knew when he liked he could whistle them back."

To win love is good. But to win it back is to have what Gaskell craved. She envies and covets this power in Cynthia. But she knows what Cynthia has paid for it. Cynthia is loved because she is able to be " 'all things to all men' " (8:249–50). Becoming, however, all things to all men, she has become nothing to herself.

In Cynthia Gaskell thus spells out what happens to Molly in her suicide. But Cynthia is not just Molly's mirror. She is her daemonic double as well. The demon does not in *Wives and Daughters* take a supernatural form, as it did in "The Poor Clare." Like other images in her fiction, which are given freer rein in the structures of her stories, the demon she had conceived for Lucy as a ghostly apparition is translated in the novel into realistic terms. Cynthia cannot, like Bridget Fitzgerald, be conceived as a literal witch, but she can be a witch metaphorically. Thus, in a playful way, for instance, Roger Hamley calls her a " 'witch' " (8:430) and speaks of himself as being " 'bewitched' " by her (8:748).

Another image that identifies Cynthia as a daemonic double accounts for her association with France. All through her fiction Gaskell uses nations in metaphoric ways. She is aware of these nations as places, and when she does not use them as metaphors, she is capable of dealing with them in a realistic way. Indeed, when she is not metaphoric, she has a shrewd journalistic eye for the manners of different places. In 1864, for instance, Gaskell published, in *Fraser's Magazine,* a delightful essay entitled "French Life" in which she commented on the French as she had herself observed them on her many trips to France. Proceeding in her typical manner, not in a strictly logical way but through her own associations, Gaskell in this essay discusses everything from tradition and history to the thriftiness of the French, especially with regard to butter. And not only does Gaskell seek here to give a true picture of the French, she is at pains to correct what she knows are the false assumptions of her readers. At one point, therefore, she writes, for instance, that the "prevalent English idea of French society" as "very brilliant, thoughtless," and "dissipated" is entirely mistaken (7:654). Yet this is precisely the view of France that she accepts in "Crowley Castle," a story that she had just finished when she began to write this essay. Of a French duchess there, for instance, she writes that she was "a gay Parisian, absorbed in her daily life of giddy dissipation" (8:693). France as a country and France as a metaphor are entirely different things. As a country it is complex. As a metaphor it is a stereotype. That is precisely why it is useful. Just as the Gothic and the supernatural provided Gaskell with ghosts and demons for her metaphoric vocabulary, national stereotypes offered her images through which to project her inner life.

France she associates with the demon. As its enemy in war and its rival in countless enterprises, France had always seemed to England its antithesis, its other. In *Wives and Daughters* Gaskell, in fact, alludes to this enmity to remind us how to interpret her national metaphors (8:344). The French Revolution, in addition, which was still in Gaskell's lifetime within the memory of some, and smaller revolutions after, proved to the English, who prided themselves on their Bloodless Revolution and in general on restraint, that the French were passionate, volatile, and altogether a violent people that might erupt at any time. To Gaskell they were the perfect nation to embody her passionate demon.

"Mrs. Gaskell" is not French. How much she identified with England is obvious in a remark she made in *The Life of Charlotte Brontë*. Gaskell is writing here of the year in which Emily and Charlotte were attending school in Belgium, a country Gaskell metaphorically considers a variation of France. In the class to which the Brontës were assigned in the Athénée, there were sixty pupils, Gaskell writes, "all foreigners," she adds, "excepting the two Brontës and one other."[3] By "foreigners" Gaskell here, of course, means native Belgians attending school in their native land. It does not occur to "Mrs. Gaskell" that *foreign* might be a relative term.

When she is not thinking in metaphors, Gaskell is not a flag-waving patriot. Indeed, she dislikes the trait in others. In *Sylvia's Lovers,* for example, which is set in northern England, the narrator speaks satirically of "southerners" who, perhaps because they "lived closer to the capital— center of politics, and news . . . felt more of that patriotism that consists in hating all other nations" (6:7–8). But when her mind turns metaphoric, she is blindly chauvinistic. This is the case in "The Schah's English Gardener," a piece she published in *Household Words* in June of 1852. Written in Gaskell's hybrid form, halfway between a story and essay, the piece is journalistic in style. It purports to be the report of an interview granted the writer by a Mr. Burton, an Englishman who worked for years as a gardener to the Persian schah. Even by the ethnocentric standards of the nineteenth century, "The Schah's English Gardener" is extreme in its contempt for foreign ways. Every fault and every vice that most deeply offends the English, and above all an English woman, is attributed to the Persians. To cite but a few, the Persians are seen as lazy, dirty, dishonest, obsequious, lewd, and cruel. Gaskell attacks them on every front. Their government is corrupt and incompetent, their religion is foolish and sensual, and their social customs are crude. She even takes issue with their cuisine. And worst of all, she adds, as though summing up all their deficiencies, they do not know how to tend a garden. What more need an English citizen say? There is in this piece much intentional humor, but

Gaskell does not intend by her humor to retract her accusations. She clearly sends Mr. Burton to Persia because he embodies, as an English-man, all the virtues the Persians lack.

The English are virtuous but not daemonic. A typical English type for Gaskell is to be found in "Crowley Castle" in the character of Bessy. Bessy has every conceivable virtue. She is "gentle and quiet" (7:684), "sweet-tempered" and "sensible" (7:684), "pure and good to the heart's core" (7:697). She reminds us of Bessy in "Bessy's Troubles at Home" in that she is ideally "feminine" (7:710). All of Gaskell's Bessys are. And for that reason, they are all English. In "Crowley Castle," Gaskell, in fact, adds, in describing each of her qualities, the adjective "English," as though her virtues were inherent traits in the nation. Bessy is thus an "English beauty" (7:684), "a daisy of an English maiden" (7:697). Being English and being feminine are to Gaskell one and the same. As France is to her the land of the demon, so is England the land of women. There are no Bessys in *Wives and Daughters*. There is, however, a variant, Betty, who is the cook in the Gibson house. She is an English cook, of course, and she is fired by Mrs. Gibson, who arrives determined to turn the kitchen into a French cuisine (8:203–4).

Cynthia, although she was born in England, is to Gaskell really French. Like many young women in her fiction who play for her a similar role, Cynthia was sent to school in France and was so thoroughly trans-formed there that, to all intents and purposes, she has become a French girl. Very early in *Wives and Daughters,* Molly had been daemonic too. Gaskell, describing her as a child, says that some called her "naughty and passionate" (8:363). It is her passionate, naughty demon that utters the angry words she speaks on learning her father plans to remarry. And it is revealing that Gaskell, writing about her at this period, characterizes her in images that she will later use for Cynthia. Thus, Lady Harriet, the Cum-nors's daughter and a very perceptive woman, says to Molly, whom she is meeting for the first time at the home of her parents, " 'I like you;—you are a little wild creature, and I want to tame you' " (8:182). Later, when she introduces her, Gaskell calls Cynthia a "wild animal" (8:250). Similarly, one of the guests at a gathering at the Cumnors, noticing Molly who seems to him " 'wild,' " inquires whether she is " 'French' " (8:21). In Gaskell's metaphoric vocabulary, the answer at that moment is "Yes." Molly begins, like every woman, with a daemonic self of her own, which is to Gaskell her French identity. It is only when she kills herself that she becomes an English girl.

A very similar situation is to be found in "The Moorland Cottage" which, as I suggested earlier, was a precursor of *Wives and Daughters* and in which there are two girls who anticipate Molly and Cynthia. One is the heroine, Maggie Browne, and the other is Erminia. As she does in Molly and Cynthia, Gaskell projects in these two girls different versions of her own history. Molly's precursor is certainly Maggie, although, like Cynthia, she is neglected, not by her father, but by her mother—who, we recall, dotes on her brother but does not much care for her. Maggie's father, who resembles Cynthia's father, Mr. Kirkpatrick, was a good man who died young. Maggie is willing to make any sacrifice in order to win her mother's love, and knowing that her mother loves Edward, she is willing to earn her gratitude by sacrificing herself to him. When Edward therefore commits a crime and is compelled to leave for America, Maggie, although it entails giving up everything she loves in England, offers herself as his companion. Like Molly, she is ready, thus, to commit suicide for love. As it turns out, she does not go. The ship catches fire, Edward dies, and Maggie is able to return. But she remains ideally good, dying, as we have seen already, "rich in the love of many" (2:382).

But in the process of becoming ideal, Maggie has become a forgery. Gaskell had, we recall, in *Ruth,* by making Richard commit a forgery, suggested that the respectable young man he was pretending to be was a fraud. But Richard's forgery was a metaphor intended not only for himself. Gaskell often relays her insights, passing a truth she cannot confront from one character to another, until, as each acts out a part, the whole of what she means is said. Richard had been a daemonic double acting for his sister Jemima, and she in turn had been a double for the novel's heroine, Ruth. This is what happens in "The Moorland Cottage." The crime that Edward has committed is, like Richard Bradshaw's, a forgery. And the forgery, as in Richard, tells us that Maggie is a fraud.

It is only at this point that Erminia enters the picture. The daughter of Mr. Buxton's sister, Erminia is a mirror, like Cynthia, in which the heroine sees herself. Cynthia is described, we remember, as "the glitter of the pieces of a broken mirror" (8:389). When Maggie becomes another Lucy, Erminia becomes "a shattered mirror" (2:295). Maggie and Molly, having killed themselves, are quiet, placid, tranquil, serene. As their mirrors, Erminia and Cynthia, both of whom are taut and restless, show us the consequence of their suicide. But Erminia acts as well the part of Maggie's daemonic double. Gaskell makes her French for that purpose. Maggie is English, but Erminia has been, like Cynthia, educated in France. And, like Lucy's daemonic double, she mocks Maggie for her goodness. When Maggie tells her she intends to go with Edward to

America, Erminia says, "Maggie, darling—what is this going to America? You've always and always been sacrificing yourself to your family, and now you're setting off, nobody knows where, in some vain hope of reforming Edward'" (2:365). These words are echoed in Maggie's mind as she boards the ship to sail, and in repeating them, Gaskell again uses the image of the "The Poor Clare." "The mocking daemons," she writes, "gathered round her, as they gather round all who sacrifice self, tempting" (2:372).

On the surface it would appear that a character in whom is projected the heroine's suicide is not a character who could act at the same time the part of the double. The two are, after all, antithetical. In Gaskell's mind, the contradiction is, however, only apparent, for she has yet one secret more in which the conflict is resolved. That secret too is expressed in an image, the most important image of all in the relationship Gaskell envisions between the heroine and her double. In *Wives and Daughters* Gaskell alludes to it when the narrator, remarking on Cynthia's reluctance to confess all her secret thoughts to Molly, observes that with all her "apparent frankness, there were certain limits beyond which" Cynthia's "confidence did not go; where her reserve began, and her real self was shrouded in mystery" (8:481). Molly had agreed to repudiate everything "that made her herself" (8:152). Cynthia has a "real self" but it remains "shrouded in mystery." "Shrouded" is a striking word, especially striking in a novel in which the heroine kills herself. It seems to imply that, although she has killed herself, becoming a mirror of Molly's suicide, Cynthia has, beyond the grave, survived to become a daemonic double. And this is precisely what Gaskell means. It strikes us at first as a curious notion, but the survival of the demon on the other side of the grave is one of Gaskell's central ideas and often one of her central images.

The image, found in most of her fiction, is the subtextual theme, for example, of the short story "The Half-Brothers." This is the story of two young men who are the half brothers of the title. Part of the story, its basis in fact, reenacts the old sibling rivalry, although in an interesting new form. The older, Gregory, loses his father at a very early age. Soon, his mother, Helen, remarries and gives birth to a son, a boy whose name we are never told, and who seems, in fact, not to have one. Not long after, Helen dies and her sister Fanny arrives to offer her help to the widowed father. Fanny is obviously Aunt Lumb, but, as often happens in Gaskell when archetypal identities fuse, she quickly, in her behavior to Gregory, becomes more like a wicked stepmother. Gregory is already despised. His stepfather, who is called Mr. Preston, not only favors his own son but, believing that his wife had preferred her son to him and to the child they had together, holds an additional grudge against Gregory. Gregory thus is rejected by everyone. In contrast, the nameless son is adored. Although he is spoiled by excessive indulgence, becoming selfish and even cruel, he is the "darling" of the household (5:296).

One day, however, the nameless son is caught in a terrible storm on the moors, and his death appears inevitable. Gregory has remained at home, and Mr. Preston, who is worried because his son has not returned, begins to abuse him more than usual. Gregory understands the reason. He realizes that, afraid for his son, Mr. Preston is enraged to think that his stepson is meanwhile safe. If one of the children must die, he implies, it should be Gregory, not his son. Gregory does not disagree. Like all of Gaskell's rejected children, Gregory has little sense of self-worth. He is, like all such children, ready, if necessary, to die for love. Without a word, he leaves the house and goes in search of his half brother, whom, by using his intelligence and his knowledge of the moors—for Gaskell does not miss the chance to avenge the unloved child by giving him the skills and gifts that the favored child lacks—he does not have great trouble finding. But by this time night has fallen, and the storm has grown so wild that even Gregory cannot hope to find his way home before the morning. The two must spend the night on the moors. The night is cold, and the nameless half brother, typically careless, has, apparently, left the house without his overcoat. But Gregory, ideal to the end, takes off his own and wraps it around him. The brother is saved. But by the next morning, Gregory has been frozen to death.

The metaphors here are obvious enough. As there is love for only one child, so there is only one coat for both of them. The coat is the love. The nameless brother is kept alive not by the coat but by the fact that he is loved, just as it is his stepfather's indifference that is the cause of Gregory's death. The cold is the image of that indifference. Many characters in Gaskell who are unloved die in the cold. Alice Carr in "Morton Hall," when her husband no longer loves her, wanders out into a storm and is found frozen to death. In "The Old Nurse's Story," a daughter and a granddaughter are frozen because they are unloved by the squire. Love is the warmth by which life is nourished. Without it, Gregory dies of the cold.

It is significant, however, that it is in Gregory's coat that the nameless brother returns. If he is dressed in Gregory's coat, is not the one who returns really Gregory? And is not this the reason Gaskell does not give Gregory's brother a name? We know that Gaskell had trouble with names, but even she does not leave nameless a title character anywhere else. The namelessness is a metaphor too. The brothers, in Gaskell's mind, are one, as heroines are with their mirrors and doubles. The nameless brother in this story is a mirror and a double. Like Molly, Gregory is good. The nameless brother is not, like Cynthia. The fact that he has no name suggests that he has, again like Cynthia, no identity. He is an image, the favored child, as Cynthia, being all things to all men, is the one whom everyone loves. And yet, since he is not ideal, he has not denied his demon. He has, like Cynthia, a "real self" which is the self that returns at the end. That self, however, has survived only because it has been buried, buried with Gregory in the grave, literally "shrouded," as Cynthia's self has been "shrouded" metaphorically.

The same occurs in *Wives and Daughters*. No daughter, so the title suggests, can escape a woman's fate. Cynthia herself does not escape it. As soon as Molly kills herself, Cynthia becomes her formless reflection. She also, however, becomes the grave in which Molly's real self is buried. This is what Gaskell, then, learned in this book. She learned that to gain the love she needed she had had to kill herself. She also learned that she had been able, somehow, to survive her suicide. Within her disguise as "Mrs. Gaskell," there was, though "shrouded," a "real self," one that survived and continued to live on the other side of the grave.

VI

Persephone on the
Flowery Pleasure-Path

IT WAS NOT OFTEN "Mrs. Gaskell" entered the inner world of her demon, giving up the external trappings of the benign Victorian ideal. But this is just what she did in *Ruth*. For reasons that will be evident later, *Ruth* is divided into two parts. With the second I shall deal shortly. Here I will be concerned with the first.

Ruth is one of the many stories Gaskell wrote about fallen women. A fallen woman need not be a prostitute, but Gaskell often blends the two and writes about them in similar ways. There is some external reason for this. Basch may be right to suggest that prostitutes fared far better in life than in fiction, some of them marrying and becoming typical angels in the house,[1] but often it was hard for a woman who had fallen to reclaim her place in "respectable" society, and, unable to find work, she did sometimes become a prostitute.

In Esther, the aunt of the title character, Gaskell had told just such a story in her novel *Mary Barton*. Esther, not a bad woman really, only a little vain of her beauty, is seduced by an army officer. He is not a bad sort himself, taking full responsibility both for her and for their child. Soon, however, he is transferred, and, although it is not clear why he cannot take her with him or send money to support her, Esther finds herself abandoned. Esther is able to work for a time, but when her little boy falls ill, the cost of caring for him is so high that she is forced to walk the streets. This is the beginning of the end. Her child dies, she turns to drink, ends up in prison, and finally dies shortly after she is released (ch. 14). There were many women like Esther in Manchester in the nineteenth century, as Friedrich Engels had reported only four years earlier, in fact, in *The Condition of the Working Class in England,* and Gaskell, in her parish work with the ailing and the poor, must have met a great many of them.

Gaskell blames Esther to an extent, but she is also sympathetic. Always and by inclination on the side of those in need, Gaskell takes up Esther's cause. "Who will give her help," she asks, "in her day of need?" (1:182). Gaskell is calling on society to look on the prostitute with compassion. But she is also implying that Esther could have been saved from prostitution had someone helped her after her fall. This is precisely the kind of help Gaskell is offering in her novel. Making Esther sympathetic, Gaskell wants to stir her readers to extend a helping hand to women in Esther's situation.

On its surface, *Ruth* appears a novel written for the same purpose.[2] Having shown in *Mary Barton* how a woman becomes a prostitute if there is no one there to help her, Gaskell now goes on to show how a woman can be saved. In the original edition, Gaskell used, on the title page, a poem by Phineas Fletcher whose point is that we must show to sinners the mercy Jesus showed mankind.[3] The name she chooses for her heroine is itself a plea for mercy. Gaskell makes certain in the novel that we remember the biblical Ruth, who was given the help she needed (3:276–77), and undoubtedly she intends us to recall that *ruth* means "pity."

Gaskell's protest is not limited to the fallen woman, however. She wants to make some related points. She wants to protest the double standard that brands the woman but not the man. " 'Where was her lover?' " asks Mr. Benson, the man who eventually saves Ruth. " 'Could he be easy and happy? Could he grow into perfect health, with these great sins pressing on his conscience with a strong and hard pain? Or had he a conscience?' Into whole labyrinths of social ethics Mr. Benson's thoughts wandered" (3:116). And, with the compassion she felt always for children who are made to pay for the sins of their parents, she pleads for the illegitimate child, who was, in Victorian society, very much an outcast still.

Like many other social protests, *Ruth* was very well received by those who were believers already. But the general reader was scandalized. Never before had any novel so outraged the reading public, in fact.[4] One of William Gaskell's parishioners, advanced Unitarian though he was, was so completely incensed by the book that he forbade his wife to read it (*L* 150). Even in London, where the audience was considerably more sophisticated, one of the libraries was forced to withdraw it from circulation because its subscribers found it " 'unfit for family reading' " (*L* 151). Gaskell had anticipated difficulties. She had known, she writes to a friend responding to the ongoing furor, that the writing of such a book would require "all one's bravery." But she had refused to hide her head "like an ostrich" in the sand and, because some thought the subject unsuitable for fiction, "forget"—and here she refers not to the fallen woman herself but to how fallen women are treated—that such "evil exists" (*L* 154).

But why did Gaskell, believing this, ban the book from her own house and forbid her daughters to read it (*L* 148)? She writes to Anne Robson that she intends to sit down with Marianne "some quiet time or other" and read the book with her (*L* 148). She writes these words as though she were speaking of a very small child still. But, at the time, Marianne was nineteen, and while it is true that young women were protected in the nineteenth century from overtly sexual material, Gaskell had already said that the subject needed discussion. Shortly after the book was published, Gaskell wrote to Eliza Fox "I think I must be an improper woman without knowing it, I do so manage to shock people" (*L* 150). The truth is Gaskell had shocked herself. She had, at least, shocked "Mrs. Gaskell," and not because "Mrs. Gaskell" was prudish, which in fact she was not. Gaskell was worried about Marianne because, with the wisdom of the serpent and the innocence of the dove, she knew that she had written in *Ruth* a novel that was dangerous reading for daughters who were destined to become wives.

Pleading for the fallen woman, Gaskell was pleading for her demon. The ostensible point of the novel is moral, but moral arguments in Gaskell often mask psychological truths. Indeed, it is often in Gaskell necessary to make a distinction between a position that is her natural point of view and one that is her official stance. The former is what she thinks and feels. The latter is how "Mrs. Gaskell" deals with realities she will not recognize. There is a world of difference, for instance, between Gaskell's goodness and her "goodness," between her moral and "moral" selves. Gaskell was by nature good. And she was by nature moral. She only becomes a model of "goodness" when she behaves as the ideal Lucy, and she only becomes "moral" when a psychological insight has to be contained in a form "Mrs. Gaskell" can approve of. Gaskell is well aware that art must pay a price for having a "moral." When Molly Gibson in *Wives and Daughters* tells a tale with what the narrator describes as a "mental squint," Gaskell adds that having a bias is "the surest way to spoil a narration" (8:726). Gaskell herself is often discomforted when she feels compelled to sermonize. Publishing "Libbie Marsh's Three Eras," in June of 1847, in *Howitt's Journal,* which was dedicated to what it called improving literature, Gaskell felt she was, for instance, required to end with a "moral" point. Instead, however, she wrote the following: "Do you ever read the moral, concluding sentence of a story? I never do, but I once (in the year 1811, I think) heard of a deaf old lady, living by herself, who did; and, as she may have left some descendants with the same amiable peculiarity, I will put in, for their benefit, what I believe to be the secret of Libbie's peace of mind, the real reason why she no longer feels oppressed at her own loneliness in the world—She has a purpose in life; and that purpose is a holy one" (1:489). Gaskell thus gets her "moral" in, but not without defusing it first.

It is not difficult in Gaskell to distinguish moral from "moral." There are many telltale signs, not the least of which is the prose. When Gaskell is moral, she is eloquent. When she is "moral," she is dead. She herself remarked in one story, "Mr. Harrison's Confessions," published in *The Ladies' Companion* in 1851, that she had found the " 'secret of eloquence' " to be " 'believing what you've got to say' " (5:443). Gaskell believes in her moral vision. She does not believe in her "moral" points. Another sign that helps us distinguish between the moral and "moral" Gaskell is the fact that a "moral" tale often contains a conflicting subtext written in Gaskell's daemonic images. In *Ruth* both the prose, which is often dead, and the imagistic language tell us that a hidden meaning lies beneath the "moral" text.

Like Mary Fitzgerald in "The Poor Clare," Ruth is acting out the demon. There are a number of reasons the demon is acted out in a sexual fall. One anticipates John Fowles in *The French Lieutenant's Woman*. The heroine here pretends to be, although she is not, a fallen woman because she wants to escape becoming the stereotype of the Victorian ideal. She realizes she will be tempted to yield to the pressure of society, which holds out many happy rewards to those who are willing to comply, marriage with a respectable man and the establishment of a household being, of course, the chief among them. That is why she tells the lie. The lie, in the minds of those around her, creates a barrier to respectability that, once erected, even she cannot ever break down. Who would believe her if she confessed that her story was not true? Her lie protects her from herself. Only by telling it can the heroine be and remain what she really is rather than the public image of the feminine ideal. Fowles, of course, is far more modern than any Victorian writer could be, but several nineteenth-century novelists dealt with this question in similar ways. Hawthorne, for instance, in 1850 had written, in *The Scarlet Letter*, a novel in which an adulterous woman, although reintegrated at last into the Puritan community, gains from her period as an outcast a degree of independence from the mores of her time. Gaskell had probably read this novel (*L* 89) and may, as we shall shortly see, have appropriated parts of it in the writing of her own.

Gaskell is not only fascinated by fallen women in her fiction, she is fascinated as well by women who fall only in part, women who are believed to have fallen, women who do not but almost fall, and, perhaps the most interesting of all, women who fall in a surrogate manner, many of whom are shown to fall literally, in a physical way, that is. The heroine of *Mary Barton,* who bears a great resemblance to Esther especially in that she is vain and susceptible to flattery, is—since she is saved in time—not like her aunt a fallen woman but, for a time, a falling one, flirting with the millowner's son who is trying to seduce her. Mary, who works in a milliner's shop, has a friend who is falling too, or has fallen already perhaps—a girl named Sally, who appears to have a questionable reputation. For "Mrs. Gaskell," Sally and Esther are a warning to Mary Barton. For Gaskell, they are Mary's proxies, acting out what she cannot. Mary is not allowed to fall, or even to progress very far, but Sally, as in a relay race, carries it further and Esther completes it.

Relays in Gaskell are common not only within the boundaries of a work but from one work to another. What Gaskell leaves undone in one she feels compelled to do in the next. The fall that Mary does not complete is thus passed on to other characters, not only in the novel itself but to the heroine of "Lizzie Leigh," the story to which Gaskell turned after she had finished the novel. The story, which had been solicited for the first issue of *Household Words* in the spring of 1850, is almost a miniature of the novel. It deals with all the same public issues and all the same private woes. And the circumstances of the heroines are essentially the same. But all the facts that in *Mary Barton* had been potential, as it were, are actualized in "Lizzie Leigh." In *Mary Barton* it is the son of the millowner who courts Mary. Although one day he will own the mill, he is, for the moment, only the heir. The heroine of "Lizzie Leigh" is courted by the millowner himself. Mary had wanted to work in a mill, but her father, who had feared girls were vulnerable to seduction in a place of such loose morals, had forbidden her to do so. Lizzie does work in a mill, where, in fact, she is seduced. It is as though Gaskell could not rest until Mary Barton had fallen, and since she could not let her fall in the novel as she conceived it, she had to write another story in order to complete the tale.

Another falling character is Cynthia, who, in falling a part of the way, drags Molly Gibson a little down with her. Cynthia's falling is implied not only in her outrageous flirtation but in the secret relationship she has had, as it turns out, with a man named Preston. Nothing, as far as we know, has happened, but the very fact that Cynthia has a relationship of this kind, as well as the fact that it is secret, makes her, if not a fallen woman, certainly a falling one. And Molly becomes involved in her fall when she learns that Preston has a hold on Cynthia. Deciding that she must confront the man, she arranges to meet him secretly, risking her reputation, thus, and becoming, in a sense, a bit of a fallen woman herself.

It was her preoccupation similarly with the doings of her demon and not her social conscience alone that prompted Gaskell to take an interest, late in 1849, in the case of a young woman whose story was the germ of *Ruth*. Miss Pasley, as the young woman was called, had been seduced, become a prostitute, and finally been imprisoned for theft. Gaskell had determined to help her, and, in the hope that he would help too, she wrote to Dickens to relate the essentials of her story. The letter is sufficiently important to warrant being quoted at length:

> *I am just now very much interested in a young girl, who is in our New Bayley prison. She is the daughter of an Irish clergyman who died when she was two years old; but even before that her mother had shown most complete indifference to her; and soon after her husband's death, she married again, keeping her child out at nurse. The girl's uncle had her placed at 6 years old in the Dublin school for orphan daughters of the clergy; and when she was about 14, she was apprenticed to an Irish dress-maker here, of very great reputation for fashion. Last September but one this dress-maker failed, and had to dismiss all her apprentices; she placed this girl with a woman who occasionally worked for her, and who has since succeeded to her business; this woman was very profligate and connived at the girl's seduction by a surgeon in the neighbourhood who was called in when the poor creature was ill. Then she was in despair, & wrote to her mother,* (who had never corresponded with her all the time she was at school and an apprentice:) *and while awaiting the answer went into the penitentiary; she wrote 3 times but no answer came, and in desperation she listened to a woman, who had obtained admittance* \to the penitentiary / *solely as it turned out to decoy girls into her mode of life, and left with her; & for four months she has led the most miserable life! in the hopes, as she tells me, of killing herself, for "no one had ever cared for her in this world,"—she drank, "wishing it might be poison," pawned every article of clothing—and at last stole. I have been to see her in prison at Mr Wright's request, and she looks quite a young child (she is but 16,) with a wild wistful look in her eyes, as if searching for the kindness she has never known.*

Gaskell concludes by saying she wants Miss Pasley to have a fresh start in life. She wants to arrange for her emigration and to make sure that she goes out "with as free and unbranded a character as she can; if possible, the very fact of having been in prison &c to be unknown on her landing" (*L* 61). Dickens was, as always, helpful, and within a very short time, Gaskell had arranged for Miss Pasley to emigrate under the protection of a kind and respectable family.

Many of Gaskell's readers have noticed that there are significant parallels between Miss Pasley's life and Ruth's. But no one has, to my knowledge, remarked on the extraordinary similarities between Miss Pasley's life and Gaskell's. Gaskell herself must have been aware of them, although not consciously perhaps, for, in telling Miss Pasley's tale, she not only focuses attention on events they both experienced, she interprets them as having had the effect on Miss Pasley that they had actually had on her. The roles are reversed in Miss Pasley's life of the father and the mother, just as Gaskell herself reverses them sometimes in her fictional characters, but they are otherwise very similar. As Gaskell lost her mother in infancy, so Miss Pasley lost her father. As Gaskell's father then remarried, so in Miss Pasley's case did the mother. Gaskell's father banished Elizabeth. Miss Pasley's mother banished her, sending her to an orphan school. For Gaskell this orphan school may recall the boarding school to which she was sent and to which she then sent Cynthia when she was exiled by Mrs. Gibson. Miss Pasley's mother did not write or visit her while she was in school just as Gaskell's father did not. Gaskell underlines this clause surely because she remembers the pain she felt under similar neglect. And it is her own experience that she is recalling again when she quotes Miss Pasley as saying that in consequence she had felt " 'no one had ever cared for her in this world.' " Gaskell sees in her "wild wistful look" the mark of someone who was "searching," as indeed she was herself, "for the kindness she has never known."

When Gaskell heard Miss Pasley's story, she must have felt as Lucy does when, on looking into her mirror, she is confronted by her double. Here in Miss Pasley, who shared her history, was the very incarnation of an image that had become, in her own imagination, one of the major representations of her own daemonic double. If "Mrs. Gaskell" thought Miss Pasley gave her a chance to lodge a protest against what she felt was a social wrong, Gaskell's demon must have recognized that this fallen woman's tale was a literalization of its own metaphoric life.

In the novel itself the history Gaskell provides for her heroine is a combination of elements from her own and Miss Pasley's past. Mrs. Hilton, Ruth's mother, is, as Mrs. Stevenson had been, a woman of very delicate health. She does not, like Gaskell's mother, die when her daughter is an infant, but she dies when Ruth is twelve, still a child who needs to be protected by a mother's love from the cruelties of the world. Mr. Hilton

for the most part is an image of Mr. Stevenson. One of the many significant parallels by which Gaskell must have been struck as she heard Miss
Pasley's story is the fact that, like her father in the first of his vocations, Mr.
Pasley had been a clergyman. In the novel Gaskell, however, recalls
another of her father's vocations, making Mr. Hilton a farmer, and a very
poor one, at that. He seems to differ in the fact that he does not abandon
Ruth. But, since the death of his wife so affects him that he withdraws into
himself and dies very shortly afterwards, in a sense he does abandon her.
Ruth soon acquires a surrogate father in an old family friend who is
appointed as her guardian, a figure who is certainly modeled on the uncle
by whom Miss Pasley was first sent to the orphan school, then apprenticed
to a dressmaker. The guardian in *Ruth* is not as kind. He does not bother to
send her to school. He sends her directly to the dressmaker, where she is
apprenticed immediately. He says he is acting in her best interests, but we
suspect he does not care (3:37). The role played by Mrs. Mason, the
woman to whom Ruth is apprenticed, is that of the second Mrs. Stevenson. She may not be exactly evil, but she is so absorbed in herself—with
her comfort and her profit and (which is always a telltale sign) with the
care of her own children—that, without actually wishing them ill, she fails
so completely to extend the "tender vigilance" and "maternal care" (3:53)
that her apprentices require that, in the effect she has on them, she is a
thoroughly wicked stepmother. Gaskell on her visits to London, so unhappy her heart was breaking, had alleviated her sorrow by sitting,
presumably at a window, looking for hours at the river. This scene,
recalled again and again as an archetype in her fiction, is reenacted at Mrs.
Mason's when Ruth, who is also so unhappy that she feels her "heart" will
"break," sits on Sundays in her room, "at the window, looking out" (3:9).
And, to complete the factual parallels, at Mrs. Mason's Ruth attaches
herself to another apprentice named Jenny, who is only a little older but a
great deal more mature. Jenny becomes a second mother, but, like Mary
Anne Lumb, she is ill and dies soon after.

But Ruth resembles Gaskell most not externally but internally. Characters like Molly Gibson let us see the young Elizabeth as she must have
seemed to others. Ruth allows us to experience her as she must have felt to
herself.

Like most of Gaskell's surrogate selves, Ruth is robbed of her identity
by the experiences of a childhood that has made her desperate for love. In a
passage I quoted earlier but that must be repeated here, Gaskell, recalling a
number of details of the history she shares with Ruth, writes that "Love
was very precious to" her. "It was one of the faults of her nature to be ready

to make any sacrifices for those who loved her, and to value affection almost above its price; . . . lonely as the impressionable years of her youth had been—without parents, without brother or sister—it was, perhaps, no wonder that she clung tenaciously to every symptom of regard, and could not relinquish the love of any one without a pang" (3:246).

Her need for love has rendered Ruth "child-like in her dependence on others" (3:79). Ready to be whatever they wish, she is prepared, like Molly Gibson, to kill her individual self. In fact her suicide occurs early, almost before the story begins. Many readers of the novel have complained that Ruth is passive, unable either to act or to react. She seems to accept without resistance everything that happens to her. But Ruth is not passive. She is dead, in Gaskell's metaphoric sense. Gaskell already describes her as "deadened" when we first meet her at Mrs. Mason's (3:9). And, except for one part of the book, she always dresses her in black. Characteristically, Ruth has died to become a "Mrs. Gaskell."

Molly continues to live a corpse, projecting her demon into Cynthia. In *Ruth,* however, Gaskell achieves, at least in this part of the story, an extraordinary victory. Not only does she preserve the demon within the character herself, she lets us enter her inner world. Gaskell herself, in one of her letters, suggests a distinction that helps us to see how she conceives in *Ruth* the relationship between the inner and outer identity. Written to Eliza Fox, the letter is bolder than most of Gaskell's, and in it she is able to recognize that there are in her different selves. She calls them here her different "mes." "I have a great number," she goes on to say, "and that's the plague. One of my mes is, I do believe, a true Christian . . . and another of my mes is a wife and mother. . . . Now that's my 'social' self I suppose. Then again I've another self with a full taste for beauty and convenience. . . . How am I to reconcile all these warring members?" (*L* 69). The Christian and the social selves I shall take up in later chapters. Here I shall focus on the self that loves beauty and convenience.

The immediate occasion of this letter is a new house the Gaskells have found. In 1850, the date of this letter, the Gaskells needed a new home, not only because their lease on the old one was on the verge of running out but also because there were now four children, many more visitors, and much more to do for the household and the parish. The house they found at Plymouth Grove delighted Gaskell no doubt in part because it was larger, but mostly it delighted her because it was so very beautiful. The fact that it was expensive as well made her feel a conflict about it. The cost might be too great for their income. And it seemed selfish to spend so much on such a luxury for themselves when so many were going hungry. "But," she writes, defending herself, "here we have no great external beauty either of nature or art." "Well!" she writes again, "I must try and make the house give as much pleasure to others as I can and make it as little a selfish thing as I can." But there would be, she adds, no conflict if she "had neither conscience nor prudence." Then she would simply "be delighted, for it certainly is a beauty."

Gaskell was always ravished by beauty. Although it disturbs her to believe it, beauty is one of the things she loves best. She has an eye for physical beauty, for colors, for textures, and for forms. Gaskell's senses were all acute. Very few writers—very few people—have relished sensation as much as she did. Gaskell is alive in her fiction to every kind of sensory experience. In *North and South,* we virtually smell the roses that grow on the Hale's cottage and we veritably taste the pears that grow along its south wall (4:28). The opening paragraph of *Mary Barton* is a sensory cornucopia. Writing, in alliteration, of the characteristic sounds to be heard in the countryside just outside the city of Manchester, Gaskell speaks of "the lowing cattle, the milkmaids' call, and the clatter and cackle of poultry"; she describes, again alliteratively, a "deep, clear pond, reflecting in its dark green depths the shadowy trees that bend over it"; and she points out "the little garden" in which "a medley of old-fashioned herbs and flowers" have been allowed to grow in "scrambling and wild luxuriance—roses, lavender, sage, balm (for tea), rosemary, pinks and wallflowers, onions and jessamine" (1:1–2). Sometimes sensory inclinations are a means of characterization. Lady Ludlow's idiosyncrasies are, for instance, all spelled out through her preferences in scents (5:46–48). More perhaps than she knew herself, Gaskell experienced the world through her senses. She writes in her "Diary" about Marianne: "when I see her looking very intently at anything, I take her to it, and let her exercise all her senses upon it, even to tasting, if I am sure it can do her no harm." Gaskell needs to add that her "object" in this practice is "to give" Marianne the "habit of fixing her attention" (p. 6), but the real reason is that she believes children are creatures of the senses. "When young," she writes in her "Diary" once more, "their feelings, especially those under the direct control of their senses, are so acute, while the powers which will eventually, it is hoped, control their feelings are in a dormant state" (p. 14). No one was more energetic than Gaskell, more dedicated, or more sincerely committed to the cause of social good. But under that "social" and "Christian" "me," there was a sybarite in Gaskell. When she wrote to George Smith that she hoped "Heaven" would be a place in which "amusement" would consist of "driving in an open carriage . . . and eating strawberries & cream" (*L* 561), she was, it is true, particularly tired from trying to do too many things. But only someone as susceptible as she was to the sensory world could have conceived of the hereafter in such a gustatory way.

Gaskell was not just extremely sensual, she was also extremely sexual. She had a healthy interest in sex, as her fiction clearly shows us, and a healthy appreciation of the power of sexual passion. When Ruth begins to meet with Bellingham, Gaskell comments on her ignorance in the following way: "She was too young when her mother died to have received any cautions or words of advice respecting *the* subject of a woman's life—if, indeed, wise parents ever directly speak of what, in its depth and power, cannot be put into words—which is a brooding spirit with no definite form or shape that men should know it, but which is there, and present before we have recognised and realised its existence" (3:43). Sexual passion in her fiction is often expressed in fiery metaphors. Thornton, for instance, in *North and South,* when he falls in love with Margaret, seems to be in a fiery "furnace," "struggling" "in the midst" of "flames" (4:401). Always it is intense and furious. Morin, thus, in "My Lady Ludlow" is in love with Virginie who, however, loves another. Since he is French, and thus belongs to the nation of the demon, his love for Virginie is fierce. It is "terrible." He is "convulsed" at the very thought of her. He would "kill" her, he confesses, rather than "see her" with another. (5:101–2). He cannot even look at her without " 'devouring her with his eyes' " (5:101).

One of the reasons Gaskell embodies the demon in a fallen woman is that her sense of sexuality is so encompassing it becomes a metaphor for all the passions. This is what she implies when Bradshaw, condemning sexual sin in *Ruth,* remarks that " 'wantonness,' " as he calls it, for him " 'includes all other sins' " (3:334). This is also why fallen women are not for Gaskell just sexual creatures. The body for Gaskell is much more than sensuality or sexuality. Gaskell attributes to the body capabilities and effects that are generally attributed to entirely different causes. Writing, for instance, in her "Diary," Gaskell remarks that she believes the root of Marianne's moral character is nothing else than her good health (p. 14). "I sometimes fear," she writes, in fact, "there is too much pride in my heart in attributing" Marianne's "goodness to the success of my plans, when in reality it is owing to her having hitherto had such good health, and freedom from pain" (p. 9). When "*children,* at any rate," she concludes, after seeing that Marianne had behaved badly during an illnesses, "are irritable something is physically the matter with them" (p. 17).

In her fiction Gaskell did not limit this observation to children. Nowhere, not even in the naturalists, are mind and body as connected as

they are in Gaskell's books. Thus, for example, she explains the dis-
similarities in *Ruth* between Faith and Thurstan Benson wholly in terms of
physical differences. His childhood injury, she writes, so "affected" his
"constitution," that it determined the condition of his "mind as well as of
his body," making him tenative and uncertain (3:374). Similarly, the fact
that Faith had a "superior" "constitution" gave her a "greater decision of
character" (3:112). Bodies in Gaskell have lives of their own. Ellinor in "A
Dark Night's Work" realizes she is recovering after a long and debilitating
illness brought on by great emotional distress "when day after day she felt
involuntary strength and appetite return. Her body seemed stronger than
her will; for that would have induced her to creep into her grave, and shut
her eyes for ever on this world, so full of troubles" (7:477). Physical
instincts have to Gaskell almost a kind of reasoning power. They provide
knowledge of inner things. In *Mary Barton,* Gaskell speaks of the "instinct"
of one character as something "by which almost his body thought" (1:92).
Gaskell may not be ready to say that the body is the soul, but she has, like
D. H. Lawrence, a sense that there is a mysterious world of truth and
wisdom in it.

This is the world we enter in *Ruth*. And this is what the narrator
means when he says that Ruth is beautiful. Her beauty is not just how she
looks. It is the essence of her being. It is significant that Gaskell, although
she dwells on her beauty often, never provides a picture of Ruth. We have
only a few bare hints of her actual appearance. But her appearance is not
important. Although we are obviously meant to believe in its physical
manifestation, the beauty Gaskell is thinking of here characterizes her
inner life. When she remarks that Ruth knew "she was beautiful" but that
her beauty "seemed abstract, and removed from herself" because she felt
that her "existence was in feeling and thinking, and loving" (3:73), it is as
though, changing her setting, Gaskell takes us from the external, in which
we only observe Ruth, to the subjective world of experience in which we
cannot see how she looks, any more than Ruth herself can, but in which,
feeling what Ruth feels, we can know how she seems to herself. Her
beauty now is the projection of the life Ruth lives within.

Like most of Gaskell's characters, Ruth functions in her outer life in a
religious and social context. But from this her inner life is entirely detached. Just as in her letter Gaskell distinguishes the "me" that loves beauty
and convenience from the Christian and social "mes," so in the novel she
divides Ruth into her inner and outer existence. The outer life is represented in the second half of the book. There we are moved to another place
that is to Gaskell the embodiment of the Christian and social world. In the

first half of the narrative, when we enter Ruth's inner being, we find ourselves in a pagan world.

This is precisely how Thomas Hardy was to remove Tess in *Tess of the D'Urbervilles* from the censure of society. Hardy knew that culpability depended on conceptual frames. In the light of Christian society, Tess is a sinner, a fallen woman. But if we see her in pagan terms, we see her, not as a fallen Magdalen, but as the fertility goddess Persephone. Gaskell had certainly not articulated the argument consciously to herself, but she anticipates Thomas Hardy both in purpose and in method. Gaskell does not write mythically often, and when she does it is not by using actual myths in her own narrative but, as in *Cranford* and "Curious if True," more by imagining her story in a mythopoetic way. In *Ruth,* however, she uses the myth of the vegetation goddess, although she expands it, mythopoetically, into a larger myth of her own. And in this pagan, mythic context, Ruth is as guiltless in Gaskell's view as Tess was later to be in Hardy's. All through the novel she is called "innocent"—not only before (e.g., 3:43), but during her fall (3:56), and, even more significantly, after it (3:95). At Mrs. Mason's, which she envisions as a house of death, a Hades, Gaskell dresses Ruth in black. But when she sends her out with Bellingham, although it is he who is her seducer, she always dresses her in white. Nor does she trust to our understanding to guess what the color imagery means. She tells us herself on several occasions, bringing "white" and "sinless" together (e.g., 3:150).

Even more important here than the narrative perspective is the perspective in which Gaskell allows Ruth to see herself. Hardy—it is part of his irony—shows us that Tess, completely trapped in the perspective of her society, never exonerates herself. But, in the first part of the novel, Ruth does not, as Gaskell writes, feel any "consciousness of error" (3:93). By convention, the fallen woman always blames herself for her deed so as to let the reader know that sin is followed by regret. Esther does so in *Mary Barton* (ch. 14). But Esther is someone we see from without. She herself sees her sin externally. Even when she speaks for herself, it is to express the views held about her, which she shares, by her society. But this is not the case in *Ruth*. Ruth is the first daemonic character who sees herself in Gaskell's fiction not as her society sees her, but as she feels to herself within. With Ruth we have entered the self of the demon, and we have seen that to itself the demon does not appear to have sinned.

Gaskell reveals more about Ruth than about anyone else in her fiction. Yet there are levels of realization beyond which she simply cannot go. But what she cannot convey about Ruth, she manages still in the novel to tell us by attributing it to nature. Nowhere is nature in Gaskell's fiction as present and as powerful a force. Gaskell is always fond of nature, but it figures in her fiction generally in conventional ways. Thus, for instance, it offers characters a Wordsworthian restoration. In *Wives and Daughters,* for example, Molly, sitting by the window in the archetypal scene while Roger is proposing to Cynthia, feels as though her heart will break. "Gradually," however, "the consciousness of the soft peaceful landscape stole into her mind, and stilled the buzzing confusion. There, bathed in the almost level rays of the autumn sunlight, lay the landscape she had known and loved from childhood; as quiet, as full of low humming life as it had been at this hour for many generations" (8:433). Often Gaskell uses nature—weather especially and clouds—to describe the states of minds and the moods of her characters. Thornton, for instance, in *North and South,* passes through a year of seasons and a meteorological display as he tries to ascertain whether or not Margaret loves a man with whom he happens to have seen her. When it seems to him she does, he becomes "frost-bound" and "wintry." When it seems to him she does not, it is "as if some soft summer gale had blown all anxiety away from his mind." But when he fears again that she does, his face becomes "cloudy once more" (4:503).

Sometimes, Gaskell's sense of nature is conventional in *Ruth.* But more often Gaskell uses nature for a different purpose. Let me quote two typical passages. In the first, we find Ruth sitting by a window once again just after Bellingham has abandoned her. The narrator describes what she sees: "Across the moon, and over the deep blue heavens, large, torn, irregular-shaped clouds went hurrying, as if summoned by some storm-spirit. The work they were commanded to do was not here; the mighty gathering-place lay eastward, immeasurable leagues; and on they went, chasing each other over the silent earth, now black, now silver-white at one transparent edge, now with the moon shining like Hope through their darkest centre, now again with a silver lining; and now, utterly black, they sailed lower in the list, and disappeared behind the immovable mountain; they were rushing in the very direction in which Ruth had striven and struggled to go that afternoon; they, in their wild career, would soon pass over the spot where he (her world's he) was lying sleeping, or perhaps not sleeping, perhaps thinking of her" (3:98–99). A similar scene occurs much later. This time it is Ruth's friend Jemima who, abandoned as Ruth had been, sits, unhappy, by the window. "The clouds were hurrying over the moon's face in a tempestuous and unstable manner, making all things seem unreal; now clear out in its bright light, now trembling and quivering in shadow. The pain at her heart seemed to make Jemima's brain grow dull; she laid her head on her arms, which rested on the window-sill, and grew dizzy with the sick weary notion that the earth was wandering lawless and aimless through the heavens, where all seemed one tossed and whirling wrack of clouds. It was a waking nightmare" (3:329). Gaskell above, in *North and South,* uses meteorological language to describe the mood of the character. In *Ruth* she does not describe the character. Here it is the mood itself that is externalized in nature. Nature itself does not exist. The storm is not outside the window. It is raging in Ruth's heart just as the "whirling wrack of clouds" is Jemima's very spirit. As Persephone in the myth is the divinity of nature, in the novel Ruth is nature and the natural world is Ruth. Nature thus becomes the demon in which Gaskell can explore what beyond a certain point she can no longer explore in Ruth. Gaskell herself was perhaps aware of the substitution she made here. When she remarks that Ruth is using the flowers of the bouquet she is holding as a "veil to hide her emotion" (3:424), Gaskell is describing precisely how she uses nature herself.

It is this inner, natural, life that Gaskell projects in the relationship she describes between Ruth and Bellingham. Bellingham is no vegetation god, as by rights he ought to be to play his part in this rite of fertility. But Gaskell cannot see him that way. At the beginning it almost seems as though he might be an interesting character. Like Alec D'Urberville in *Tess,* he seems a restless, searching soul, bereft, in the world he has inherited, both of purpose and of meaning. Later, Gaskell also allows him a moment in which he is gentle and brave, risking his life to save a child. She even provides him with a mother who, behaving like a stepmother, is responsible for destroying him, as she subsequently destroys Ruth when she persuades her son to leave her. But this complexity does not last. Bellingham soon becomes a cliché, which he remains for the rest of the novel. The difference, indeed, between him and Ruth shows us the difference in the novel between a character who remains part of Gaskell's social protest and a character who escapes to the daemonic level of the book.

Bellingham, thus, for most of the novel, is nothing more than Ruth's "seducer." Ruth, however, like Persephone, is the flower that blooms in spring after the long death of winter. Gaskell actually tells Ruth's story primarily in floral terms. Although she is not trying for parallels in any precise and schematized way, the general outline of the myth informs the outline of the novel. Not only does she, therefore, use images of vegetation, she follows the seasonal calendar too that structures the progress of the myth. When Ruth is living with Mrs. Mason, it is winter, for example. But, as the seeds are found in Hades of the flowers that bloom in spring, so we find at Mrs. Mason's the seeds of Gaskell's floral metaphors. It happens that Mrs. Mason is using, as the site of her dressmaker's shop, a building that once had been a mansion, and one of the walls of the sewing room is covered with a "magnificent" mural. The mural depicts what Gaskell describes as "the most lovely wreaths of flowers," and while she says they are "profuse and luxuriant beyond description," she does proceed to describe them in fact in a passage so important it must be quoted here at length:

> *It was divided into panels of pale sea-green, picked out with white and gold; and on these panels were painted—were thrown with the careless, triumphant hand of a master—the most lovely wreaths of flowers, profuse and luxuriant beyond description, and so real-looking that you could almost fancy you smelt their fragrance, and heard the south wind go softly rustling in and out among the crimson roses—the branches of purple and white lilac—the floating golden-tressed laburnum boughs. Besides these, there were stately white lilies, sacred to the Virgin—hollyhocks, frax-*
> (3:6–7) *inella, monk's-hood, pansies, primroses; every flower which blooms profuseful in charming old-fashioned country gardens was there, depicted among its graceful foliage but not in the wild disorder in which I have enumerated them. At the bottom of the panel lay a holly branch, whose stiff straightness was ornamented by a twining drapery of English ivy, and mistletoe, and winter aconite; while down either side hung pendent garlands of spring and autumn flowers; and crowning all, came gorgeous summer with the sweet musk-roses, and the rich-coloured flowers of June and July.*

Although it has meant she has had to take the darkest and the coldest corner, Ruth has chosen to sit in the spot from which she can best survey this mural. She is enchanted by the scene. She wants to enter its flowery world.

When she meets Bellingham, she does. It happens like this. Having been sent by Mrs. Mason to a ball to wait in readiness in case a young woman tears her gown and needs to have it mended immediately, Ruth one evening finds herself watching a group of young people at a dance precisely as she had watched the mural. To her it seems an animation of that painted floral world, and she describes it in floral terms. How happy these people must be, she thinks, living amid "such profusion of flowers" (3:14). Later that night at Mrs. Mason's, cold and hungry and alone, Ruth remembers those happy people whom, again in floral terms, she imagines to herself walking through life on "flowery pleasure-paths" (3:17). It is on this very path that Gaskell arranges for her to walk with Bellingham. They meet at the very ball that Ruth had attended as a seamstress. Bellingham has come as the escort of a young woman who tears her gown. When Ruth is summoned to repair it, he is enchanted by her beauty. He hands her a flower, a camellia, that he happens to have in his hand. That gesture engenders a sexual dream. Recalling the scene that very night Ruth imagines Bellingham courting her, giving her "flower after flower" (3:18).

Later, the dream becomes literal fact when Ruth and Bellingham go walking through the fields on flowered pathways. These walks are synchronized with the seasons. Since Ruth works every day but Sunday, the two can meet but once a week. But every Sunday they go walking into the neighboring countryside. Weekly, their relationship grows, and, as spring turns into summer, weekly the flowers bloom more abundantly. First there are only "pale-coloured" blooms (3:44–45). Then the shrubs become "luxuriant" (3:49). Then the entire hill they climb is covered with luxurious flowers whose "delicious scent" has "perfumed" the air around them on every side (3:51).

The seduction scene recalls the abduction of Persephone. In the myth, Hades discovers Persephone dancing in a field in which she has been picking flowers. He sweeps her into his horse-drawn carriage and takes her to the land of the dead. Hardy's seduction scene in *Tess* also reenacts this moment. Tess is walking home from a dance when Alec suddenly overtakes her and sweeps her up onto his horse. In *Ruth,* Bellingham comes upon Ruth as she is walking through a field after Mrs. Mason has dismissed her. She is miserable and alone. Promising that he will take her to a family friend, old Thomas, Bellingham sweeps her into his carriage and so drives her away.

Needless to say, he has no intention of taking Ruth to see old Thomas. Once in the carriage, he takes her to Wales. Wales is another of the places Gaskell uses metaphorically. Samuel Holland, Gaskell's uncle, had a country house in Wales, and Gaskell had often visited there. And she had honeymooned in Wales. Perhaps she chooses Wales as the scene of Ruth's first sexual experience because it was there that she had had hers. But something else is here at work. Whether it was because she remembered it as the site of her own honeymoon or whether it just impressed her so, metaphorically for Gaskell, Wales is where nature is wild and free. When Gaskell writes to one of her sisters-in-law—whose name was Elizabeth Gaskell too—to say that she longs to be in Wales, she speaks of returning to "those wild places." "Welsh" and "wild" become synonymous. The place, in fact, becomes an adjective. William's sister lives in Warrington, and Gaskell laments that she is not located "in a wilder more Welshy place" (*L* 9). It was the metaphoric significance that Gaskell attached to it in her mind that made her set stories like "The Doom of the Griffiths" and "The Well of Pen Morfa" in Wales. Many a woman falls, in Gaskell, in a story set in Wales. Nest is on the verge of falling in "The Well of Pen Morfa," for instance, and Owen's wife, also called Nest, nearly falls in "The Doom of the Griffiths" (5:253).

And it is there that Ruth falls too. In the central scene of this section, Gaskell fully identifies Ruth with the free and natural world that she associates with Wales. Ruth and Bellingham, walking again, have chosen this time a path that leads them through the woods into a grove. Groves are frequently the site in ancient myths of sacred rituals, and something ritualistic in fact does take place in the novel here. In the grove there is a clearing, and in the clearing "a circular pool" that is completely surrounded by "flowers." The hour is "noon" and all is "still." Lilies are floating on the water, and Bellingham, braiding a "coronet," places it on Ruth's dark hair. And there she "stood," Gaskell writes, "in her white dress against the trees which grew around; her face was flushed into a brilliancy of colour which resembled that of a rose in June; the great, heavy white flowers drooped on either side of her beautiful head, and if her brown hair was a little disordered, the very disorder only seemed to add a grace" (3:74). Ruth is no longer a character here. She is the goddess of the grove, nature personified, like Persephone. Earlier, Gaskell had written that Ruth, running through the fields one day, "knew not if she moved or stood still, for the grandeur of this beautiful earth absorbed all idea of separate and individual existence" (3:64). Like Persephone she has become the embodiment of the earth.

Many readers have felt that Gaskell was inspired to write this scene by the scene in *The Scarlet Letter* in which Hester and Arthur Dimmesdale have their meeting in the woods. Some have believed that Hardy in turn was influenced by reading Gaskell.[5] Whether either or both are true, it is important to stress that Gaskell is closer to Hardy here than to Hawthorne. Hawthorne, although he may be ambivalent, sees the meeting in the woods as a release of the natural passions that are a threat to civilization. Gaskell sees something entirely different. When she stands at the edge of the pool looking at her reflection in the water, Ruth, the narrator remarks, cannot help "seeing her own loveliness" (3:74). Ruth, like Lucy in "The Poor Clare," looks in a mirror and sees her double. But unlike Lucy, who does not recognize that the demon is herself, Ruth is aware whose reflection she sees. And rather than turning away in horror, like Lucy, from the sight of her demon, Ruth sees loveliness in the pool. She has accepted her natural self. She has here embraced her demon. Perhaps as Gaskell wrote this sentence, she accepted her demon too.

VII

Religion Kills
Lois the Witch

GASKELL IN *RUTH* HAD COME to see that her daemonic self was lovely. She had come to love it, in fact. But she still could not believe that other people could love it too. It is this fear that finally changes the direction of the book. The critical scene that marks the turning point occurs one day when Ruth and Bellingham, walking down a village street, happen to come upon a baby. Ruth bends down to "smile" and "coo" at it, but as she does so, the infant's brother, who is only a child himself, lifts his arm and slaps Ruth's cheek. His nurse reprimands him for behaving so rudely to the " 'kind lady,' " but, with righteous indignation, the child replies " 'She's not a lady. . . . She's a bad, naughty girl—mamma said so, she did; and she shan't kiss our baby' " (3:70–71). Ruth is devastated. From that day, she "habitually avoided encountering these happy—innocents, may I call them?—these happy fellow-mortals!" (3:94). The lesson of this scene is enforced in a second confrontation that takes place a little later. Reluctant to meet people now lest she be reviled again, Ruth begins to take her walks, not in the village, but in the fields where she will not encounter anyone. One day, however, a group of children, "gathered from all four corners of the hamlet," sees her and begins to follow her. Afraid to come out into the open, the children hide themselves in hedges so that the only thing Ruth sees are their "curious" "peering" "eyes" (3:94). There is, in these disembodied eyes, something a little Kafkaesque. One never feels paranoia in Gaskell, but there are characters in her fiction who, as in Kafka's, although they are innocent, begin to feel guilty when accused. And this is just what happens to Ruth. The demon, lovely to itself, becomes, when others accuse it, guilty.

Gaskell could never resist the world. She could not stand against its judgment. Brave as she was in taking on difficult and unpopular subjects, she could not face accusing eyes. She wrote to Charles Eliot Norton once that she admired Barbara Leigh Smith, a woman of very advanced opinions, but that she did not really like her. The reason, she explains, was that Smith was "a strong fighter against the established opinions of the

world,—which always goes against my—what shall I call it?—taste—
(that is not the word)" (*L* 461). We know that Gaskell becomes aphasic
only when she does not wish to know what it is she wants to say. She did,
however, find the word in an unrelated letter that she wrote to Richard
Monckton Milnes, the poet, critic, and politician. Commenting on *Ruth*,
in fact, Gaskell explains that she had tried to "quiet" the story so that
" 'people' (my great bugbear) might not say that they could not see what
the writer felt to be a very plain and earnest truth" (*L* 152). *Bugbear* is a
revealing word for Gaskell to use in such a context. It is a word a child
would use to name the object of its fear. Literally it means a hobgoblin used
to frighten naughty children, and *naughty* is precisely the word the boy had
used who had slapped Ruth. The boy, of course, had only spoken in his
own childish idiom, but in the act of being called "naughty" Ruth is
reduced to a child again. To Gaskell she seems a child in any case. Often she
is described as "child-like" (e.g., 3:79). Ruth herself, in relation to others,
invariably sees herself as a child. She speaks as a child would speak to
adults. She even calls Bellingham "Mr." and "Sir." If Gaskell projected
herself in Ruth and seeing her demon found it lovely, she also discovered
she could not stand up to the accusing eyes of the world.

It is in her effort to "quiet" the demon—the word she had used above
to Milnes—so as to appease those accusing eyes that, in the second part of
her story, Gaskell transforms the daemonic Ruth into an image of "Mrs.
Gaskell." We are familiar with this pattern. It is the archetypal pattern
through which Bridget the witch is transformed into the ideally feminine
Lucy. It is significant, however, that Gaskell sees this transformation in
social and religious terms. Thus, while the earlier Ruth embodies the self
that Gaskell had described in her letter to Fox as the "me" that loved
beauty and convenience, the later Ruth allows us to see the genesis of the
selves she had called the social and the Christian "mes."

Very few readers have ever questioned the nature of Gaskell's religious views. The facts seem altogether too simple and too obvious for
debate. Both by circumstance and by choice, she lived, from birth to
death, a part of the Unitarian world. Her parents had been Dissenters both
and so indeed had most of her ancestors. Her father, in fact, as we have
seen, had been a Unitarian minister before he conceived the scruples that
forced him to resign from his post. In Knutsford too Gaskell had been
wholly surrounded by Unitarians. And her religious instruction there had
been at the Unitarian chapel. The only non-Unitarian moment in her
Unitarian childhood had occurred at the Miss Byerleys', who were in the
habit of taking their pupils on Sundays to the established church. But they

themselves were Dissenters too. After boarding school, Gaskell had spent, to complete her education, two successive winters at the home of the Reverend William Turner, a Unitarian minister and schoolmaster. And finally, she had, at twenty-one, married a Unitarian minister, assuming, thus, a central role not only in the immediate parish of his Cross Street Chapel in Manchester but an active part in the affairs of the large Unitarian community that existed then in the city.

Up to a point these facts do not lie. Had anyone asked Elizabeth Gaskell what her religious opinions were, she would undoubtedly, in reply, have outlined the Unitarian position. But this is not the whole of the story. It is the story of "Mrs. Gaskell." The demon, however, had other views and wholly different inclinations. And it is these we must examine to understand Gaskell's inner life.

This is no easy task, however. In neither her letters nor her fiction does Gaskell ever say enough to tell us what we want to know. About religion she says, in fact, altogether very little. The subject turns up now and again, but Gaskell is not preoccupied by it. Unitarians seldom were. Unlike their Anglican contemporaries, they had not suffered a crisis of faith. On the contrary, Unitarians, long convinced that Providence worked only through natural law, prided themselves on keeping pace with the progress of rational thought and of scientific discovery. Unlike their neighbors, they walked unscathed through the Higher Criticism that was subjecting scriptural claims to historical scrutiny, remained untroubled by geological findings that challenged the biblical age of the earth, and even listened with interest to Darwin, a man, we recall, whom Gaskell knew and on whose early life she may have based her portrait of Roger Hamley. While other Victorians wrestled with doubts, Unitarians could take their faith for granted and turn calmly to other things.

Their emphasis had, in any case, always been on social concerns rather than theological issues. They tended to focus on earthly things rather than on heavenly matters. A good Unitarian was more to be measured by his good works than by his beliefs. The Unitarian creed was simple, and there was little that counted as orthodoxy. The only important point of faith was the Unitarian conviction that Jesus was human, not divine, a model to be admired and followed but not a divinity to be worshipped.[1]

The Unitarian "Mrs. Gaskell" never liked mystery or abstraction. Enough of a child of the Enlightenment to see the world as a rational place, she felt that God spoke intelligibly to her through her reason and through nature. Sometimes Gaskell writes in this spirit. In "Cousin Phillis," for example, she makes fun of metaphysics in a typically Unitarian way when one of the characters, an engineer—who is himself inclined to see the world in a practical way—defines *metaphysics* to the narrator. When " 'a man talks to you,' " he says, " 'in a way that you don't understand about a thing which he does not understand, them's metaphysics' " (8:43). She did not like to discuss theology. "Mind!" she writes to one correspondent with whom she suspected she might disagree, "I won't talk theology—Unitarian or otherwise" (*L* 593). Nor did she like discussing doctrine. One of the characters in *Ruth* rises from a doctrinal discussion to comment, in an impatient way of which Gaskell clearly approves, " 'if we've talked doctrine long enough, I'll make the beds' " (3:147). She did not care for dogma at all. She liked it less than most Unitarians, and she disliked even the little she found in the Unitarian creed. In "Lois the Witch," the title character speaks for Gaskell when she claims that " 'no one has a right to limit true godliness for mere opinions's sake' " (7:126).

But the Unitarian creed, right as it was for "Mrs. Gaskell," failed to provide the depth and passion that "Mrs. Gaskell's" demon needed. As H. P. Collins rightly says, there was a "religious hunger" in Gaskell that Unitarianism could not satisfy.[2]

"Mrs. Gaskell" may have thought there was nothing unintelligible, but the demon often felt a "deep mystery" in the universe that encompassed all "existence" (1:441). "Mrs. Gaskell's" God was benign, but the demon's was not always. This is especially the case in the "Diary." As Winifred Gérin has remarked, the "Diary" is "intensely religious,"[3] but nothing is less Unitarian than the divinity conceived there. The God of the "Diary" can be angry, fierce, possessive, raging, and menacing. And the fear that Gaskell expresses there for the health and life of her children obviously rests on the suspicion that He may also be unjust.

"Mrs. Gaskell" may have found a natural God to her satisfaction, but the demon wanted a deity radiant with supernatural glory. Gaskell once wrote to Charles Eliot Norton that, in her religious views, she was "more I suppose what would be called Arian than Humanitarian" (*L* 648). In most Christian sects, the Arians' claim that Christ is not God's equal is heretical because it lowers Christ in the heavenly scheme. Among Unitarians it is heretical because it endows a human Jesus with a degree at least of divinity. In proclaiming herself an Arian, Gaskell was not, like most Arian heretics, moving towards a secular view. As an Arian Unitarian, she was reaching towards transcendence.

Gaskell, as she longed for transcendence, longed for church observances too that were filled with passion and song. She always liked the

Anglican church, which she frequently attended when she traveled on the Continent. And in a letter to Marianne written in 1854 she herself understood why. This letter is extremely important, since it is one of the very few in which Gaskell expresses herself on the subject of religion in a specific, substantial way. "I agree with you," she writes to Marianne, "in feeling more devotional in Church than in Chapel; and I wish our Puritan ancestors had not left out so much that they might have kept in of the beautiful and impressive Church service" (*L* 198a). She writes something similar to Norton. While discussing her husband's affairs, Gaskell suddenly interupts herself to utter one of her exclamations. "Oh!" she writes, "for some really spiritual devotional preaching" (*L* 418). But in her letter to Marianne she urges her daughter not to indulge her preference for the church service too much. Before she indulges herself at all, she hopes that Marianne will try to define her beliefs carefully. For, she explains, "with our feelings and preference for the Church-service I think it is a temptation not to have a fixed belief." She herself, she concludes, considers it her "duty to deny myself the gratification of constantly attending a service . . . in a part of which I thoroughly disagree." The morning service, she believes, is especially to be avoided, since it calls for a commitment to the Anglican creed. This is the service she avoids. The evening service, which contains less to "offend one's sense of truth," she allows herself to attend (*L* l98a). Recognizing in herself a subversive inclination, "Mrs. Gaskell" warns her daughter so as to admonish herself.

The Anglican church was not, however, the only one that attracted Gaskell. In her fiction Gaskell creates characters of many faiths, and she does so, not because they reflect Victorian society, but because they let her experiment imaginatively with different creeds. The established church is, for instance, important in *The Life of Charlotte Brontë*. In *Sylvia's Lovers* it is the Quakers who are given a prominent place. Often in her shorter works Gaskell likes to include religions lesser known or of other days. She deals with the Puritans, for example, in "Morton Hall" and "Lois the Witch" and with Calvinism in "Curious if True." In "Traits and Stories of the Huguenots," which she published in *Household Words* in 1853, Gaskell turns to the Protestants of France of the sixteenth and seventeenth centuries. Nowhere are there as many religions as there are in *North and South*. Margaret, the heroine, is an Anglican. Her father begins as an Anglican minister but, conceiving religious doubts, resigns his post and becomes a Dissenter. Frederick, her brother, living in Spain, has married a Roman Catholic woman and become a convert himself. Bessy Higgins, a factory girl, is also a convert, but to Methodism. And her father, Nicholas Higgins, is, to complete the list, an atheist.

But no religion attracted Gaskell, as Yvonne ffrench has rightly said, as much perhaps as Roman Catholicism.[4] It was her fascination certainly that inspired her to create so many Roman Catholic characters. Most appear in the shorter fiction, although there is in *North and South* Frederick and his Spanish wife and in *Wives and Daughters*, similarly, Osborne and his French wife, Aimée. In the short stories, Roman Catholics appear, for example, in "My French Master," "Morton Hall," "The Grey Woman," "Crowley Castle," and "The Poor Clare," the most important instance of all, since the Roman Catholic here is none other than Bridget the witch.

Too little has been made, I think, in this connection of the fact that Gaskell's daughter Marianne came very near once to converting. The details of the event are not clear. We know, however, that Marianne, twenty-seven at the time, while visiting family friends in Rome, had surrendered to the spell of Dr. (later Cardinal) Manning, the charismatic English priest who had already converted many. "Mrs. Gaskell" was distressed to think of Marianne embarking on this "wrong & terrible way" (*L* 500a). Reporting on her very slow progress back to the fold on her return, "Mrs. Gaskell" hopes her father, who is trying to win her back, will dispel this "evil influence" (*L* 504). But she is not overly sanguine (*L* 507).

Gérin suggests that Gaskell was troubled, on receiving the news from Rome, because she felt she had failed as a mother, failed to instruct Marianne correctly on the subject of religion and failed to earn the trust that would have made Marianne confide in her before she determined to take such a step.[5] And this was probably true in part. But Gaskell was troubled more, I think, because she could imagine herself standing where Marianne now stood. Of all her children, Marianne was the one that resembled her most. The two shared many strengths and weaknesses, many tastes and inclinations, many preferences and needs. And, as Gaskell proved she knew in the letter she wrote to her on their fondness for Anglican services, they were virtually identical in their religious sensiblity. Gaskell, on her visit to Rome, had found Dr. Manning exciting herself.[6] Both had been drawn to the passion and poetry and mystery of the Anglican church. Roman Catholicism had these attributes to an even greater degree. Learning what Marianne intended, Gaskell, "Mrs. Gaskell," felt threatened. However great her attraction to Rome, "Mrs. Gaskell" could not choose to leave the Unitarian fold. But here was her daughter doing it for her.

Another part of Gaskell was drawn, as we have seen especially in *Ruth,* to the gods of pagan creeds. Not only does Gaskell suggest in *Ruth* the pagan mysteries of Persephone and, in such scenes as the one by the pool, invent new versions of pagan rituals, in her narrative voice she implies that the passions of the heart and the nature that embodies them constitute their own religion. Whenever she writes of passion or nature, not only in *Ruth* but in all her fiction, she always uses religious terms. The linnets in the woods in *Ruth* are described as singing "vespers" (3:51). In *Sylvia's Lovers,* Charley Kinraid, whom Sylvia loves, becomes for her the "blessed" subject of her "thoughts" (6:221). Passion and nature embody the demon, and it is clear that in her fiction Gaskell envisions the demon's religion as the antithesis of "Mrs. Gaskell's." It is significant that it is on successive Sundays in *Ruth* that the heroine is seduced. The practical explanation, of course, is that this is Ruth's day off, but Gaskell makes a point of the fact that Ruth should be in church on Sunday, so that every day she chooses to go out with Bellingham instead is a day she has made a choice between her official faith and her demon. Ruth still has this choice to make in the second half of the novel. When Bellingham turns up by chance in the town that she has moved to, Ruth suggests they meet on Sunday, and the place that she selects lies in the shadow of a church. "Mrs. Gaskell" wants to say that Ruth could have avoided sinning had she gone to church instead, but the official position here is not the position we intuit. What we feel is, not that Ruth has made an error in choosing Bellingham, but, in a Hardyesque sense again, that she has, in following passion rather than the Christian faith, chosen to live a different creed.

But "Mrs. Gaskell" could not accept the pagan religion of her demon. It meant accepting her demon too, and she did not have the courage. Nor could she become an atheist. Atheism was another of the demon's predilections. Even "Mrs. Gaskell" has moments when she is not secure in her faith. To Norton, for example, she writes that "about doctrines" she could feel "certain" only that she could "never be certain" (*L* 418). And her demon, it seems clear, felt a powerful attraction to the philosophic materialism that was later in the century to turn Hardy into an atheist. This is evident in her portrait of Nicholas Higgins in *North and South.* Higgins is a remarkable creature, a representative of the new intellectual industrial worker. Novelists like Frances Trollope and Disraeli had conceived him, but Gaskell went on to develop him further, first in Job Legh in *Mary Barton,* then in Higgins in *North and South.* The university and the professions are still not available to such men. But education in the form of popular lectures and evening classes was becoming increasingly possible. Gaskell's own husband was one of those who gave such lectures and classes in Manchester. Legh is a scientist, an entomologist—a bit of a working man's Darwin, in fact. Higgins too is a man of learning. He has opinions on many subjects and, what is more, a point of view that speaks for a philosophic perspective. Gaskell does not give it a name, but when he says that he believes only in what he can actually see (4:105), she makes it clear that he is one of the new philosophic materialists. It is on this philosophic perspective that he rests his religious views. This is important. Higgins is not an atheist simply by default. He is an atheist by conviction. He sees the world in material terms and finds no room in it for God. The fact that Gaskell conveys his views accurately and sympathetically does not mean she shares them, of course. But if it is true, as I believe, that she experimented with religions in her fiction because she found other religions more attractive than her official Unitarianism, it is equally true that in Higgins, she is experimenting with atheism because she finds it attractive too. She does, as she makes her way through the novel, try to soften his position. She explains he is an "infidel" only because "he had never yet found any form of faith to which he could attach himself" (4:267). After his daughter, the Methodist, dies, he takes to teaching the hymns she had sung to the children in the neighborhood (4:414). And there is one ecumenical moment in which "Margaret the Churchwoman, her father the Dissenter," and "Higgins the Infidel, knelt down together" and discovered it "did them no harm" (4:277). But Gaskell never makes Higgins believe. He is an atheist to the end.

Living in Manchester, Gaskell must have met a great many men like Higgins, but we have no record of them. We do, however, know there were atheists and almost atheists among her friends. One of the latter was Catherine Winkworth. The Winkworths were Unitarians officially, but Catherine was of a different mind. Reading Harriet Martineau's *Letters on the Laws of Man's Nature and Development* published in 1851, Catherine had, for instance, remarked that she had found in its materialism and its atheistic point of view a "sense of relief and freedom at escaping from belief in God and a future life."[7] Harriet Martineau herself was one of Gaskell's friends in Manchester, and in one of her letters Gaskell defended her against detractors who objected to the views she had expressed in this very book (*L* 138). We need not assume that Gaskell always shared the opinions of her friends, any more than those of her characters, or that she defended their views only when she agreed with them. We do, however, know that Gaskell was enormously intrigued by the figure of James Anthony Froude, who had begun as one of the group that made up the Oxford Movement but who had later lost his faith. Gaskell alludes in one of her letters to *The Nemesis of Faith* (*L* 49), the book in which Froude describes his apostasy. Gaskell had fallen under his spell as soon, appar-

ently, as she had met him. "If any one under the sun," she writes in a letter
to Catherine Winkworth, "has a magical, magnetic, glamour-like influence, that man has. He's '*aut Metphistophiles* [*sic*] *aut nihil,*' that's what he
is." Froude was visiting in Manchester and was staying with the Darbishires, whom the Gaskells knew as well. The Darbishires, Gaskell
continues, "bend and bow to his will, like reeds before the wind, blow
whichever way it listeth. . . . He disbelieves, they disbelieve; he wears
shabby garments, they wear shabby garments; in short, it's the most
complete taking away their own wills and informing them with his own
that ever was." Gaskell herself nearly bends and bows. "I stand," she
writes, "just without the circle of his influence; resisting with all my
might, but feeling and seeing the attraction. It's queer!" (*L* 49).

Resisting thus with all her might, Gaskell held on to her faith. At
least, she held on intellectually. But in her letters and in her fiction, during
moments of trial and pain, it is often the case that Gaskell, or in her stories
her surrogate self, finds it impossible to believe either in a benevolent deity
or in a deity at all. The thought, we recall, that she might die and leave her
children without a mother had prompted her to write to her sister-in-law
that, in thinking of her daughters, she found it difficult to "have the right
trust in God almost" (*L* 16). Likewise, when she thinks of her son, whom
she lost to scarlet fever, Gaskell finds it hard to believe that God's purpose
has a logic. "I wish I were with him," she writes, "in that 'light, where we
shall all see light' for I am often sorely puzzled here" (*L* 70).

Gaskell often makes it a point to show in her fiction that those who are
troubled or who have suffered in some way find no solace in religion. We
do not wonder in *North and South* that Higgins cries "wildly" " 'Get thee
gone!' " when Margaret tells him his daughter's death is part of God's
benevolent plan (4:260). He is an infidel, after all. John Barton, however, is
a believer, and yet he turns "a deafened ear" when one of his neighbors
quotes the Bible to comfort him on the death of his wife (1:20). Emotional
crises often, in Gaskell, turn believers into atheists. Mr. Hale is as much a
skeptic as John Barton and Nicholas Higgins when he learns that his wife is
ill. A friend—there is always a friend in Gaskell whose task it is to speak
for religion, usually in the stilted way that the friend is speaking here—
urges Hale to " 'Be a man, sir—a Christian. Have faith in the immortality
of the soul, which no pain, no mortal disease, can assail or touch.' " But all
that Hale can answer is " 'You have never been married; . . . you do not
know what it is" (4:318).

This is not to say that Gaskell found no consolation herself in religion
or Holy Scripture. We know she did and so occasionally do a number of

her characters. Margaret Hale in *North and South,* for instance, although she fails to comfort her father when she reads to him from the Bible, finds a solace in it herself in the ninth chapter of John. And Gaskell, in a tone that tells us she had read those very words in her own moments of sorrow, speaks of that chapter as having the power to offer "unspeakable consolation" (4:297).

But generally in Gaskell's fiction there is nothing in religion to stand against the fact of pain. Facts, in Gaskell, have, in any case, enormous power on the mind. Experience is for her irrefutable. When Roger, thus, in *Wives and Daughters,* finds Molly weeping on the ground because her father plans to remarry, he tries to give her a perspective through which she can try to see her pain. In ten years' time, he says, this incident will hardly seem important to her. But Molly rejects this point of view. " 'I daresay it seems foolish,' " she says. But " 'perhaps,' " she continues, " 'all our earthly trials will appear foolish to us after a while; perhaps they seem so now to angels. But we are ourselves, you know, and this is now, not some time to come, a long, long way off. And we are not angels, to be comforted by seeing the ends for which everything is sent' " (8:154). For Gaskell the only tense is the present, the only eternity is now. Gaskell writes a similar speech for one of the characters in "Lois the Witch." " 'But do you never,' " the character asks, " 'feel as if you would give up all that future life, of which the parsons talk, and which seems so vague and so distant, for a few years of real, vivid blessedness, to begin to-morrow— this hour—this minute? Oh! I could think of happiness for which I would willingly give up all those misty chances of heaven' " (7:165). It is no accident that the character who is given this speech is called Faith. Faith itself cannot in Gaskell resist the power of the here and now.

For sorrow, then, there can be no comfort, not in heaven, not on earth. Pain annihilates the world. Sitting with her dying mother, Margaret Hale, for instance, thinks "What a vain show Life seemed! How unsubstantial, and flickering, and flitting! It was as if from some aërial belfry, high up above the stir and jar of the earth, there was a bell continually tolling, 'All are shadows!—all are passing!—all is past!' " (4:201). Whatever "Mrs. Gaskell" thought, this is the desperate cry of one who lives in a world that has no God. A similar passage in *Sylvia's Lovers* makes that desperation explicit. Writing about a poor old man who has come to bury his son, Gaskell, as he enters the church, says that he "felt, in his sore perplexed heart, full of indignation and dumb anger, as if he must go and hear something which should exorcise the unwonted longings for revenge that disturbed his grief and made him conscious of that great blank of consolation which faithlessness produces. And for the time he was faithless. How came God to permit such cruel injustice of man? Permitting it, He could not be good. Then what was life and what was death, but woe and despair?" (6:73). Similar thoughts occur to Ruth. While she had wandered the flowering landscape still with Bellingham at her side, she had had no trouble believing implicitly in a benign plan. She had "thought the land enchanted into everlasting brightness and happiness; she fancied, then, that into a region so lovely no bale or woe could enter, but would be charmed away and disappear before the sight of the glorious guardian mountains." But when Bellingham abandons her, instantly she loses her faith. "Now," the narrator concludes, "she knew the truth, that earth has no barrier which avails against agony" (3:83). There is an existential absurdity in the universe described here. And Jemima, another character, makes that absurdity clearer yet. She too has been, like Ruth, abandoned, or at least she believes she has. In her agony she feels that she is growing "dizzy with the sick weary notion that the earth" was "wandering lawless and aimless through the heavens" (3:329).

As paganism is thus the creed of the demon's passionate nature, atheism is the creed of its anger and despair. Bessy Higgins in *North and South* provides a striking illustration of these connections in Gaskell's mind. Speaking to Margaret, Bessy remarks she wishes her father were not an atheist. She herself, she insists, disagrees with his position on religion. " 'But yo' see,' " she soon continues, " 'though I don't believe him a bit by day, yet by night—when I'm in a fever, half-asleep and half-awake—it comes back upon me—oh! so bad! And I think, if this should be th' end of all, and if all I've been born for is just to work my heart and my life away, and to sicken i' this dree place, wi' them mill-noises in my ears for ever, until I could scream out for them to stop, and let me have a little piece o' quiet—and wi' the fluff filling my lungs, until I thirst to death for one long deep breath o' the clear air yo' speak on . . . I think if this life is th' end and there's no God to wipe away all tears from all eyes' "—and here, the narrator intervenes, Bessy sits up, "clutching" Margaret "violently, almost fiercely," before she continues—" 'I could go mad and kill yo', I could' " (4:117–18). The pain of life, without a God, is unbearable, she is saying. And being unbearable, the pain makes her so angry she could kill.

If paganism asked too much, atheism asked even more. It asked Gaskell to accept herself as an unloved and abandoned child, it asked her to accept her anger, it asked her to accept despair. And this she simply could not do. She had to believe there was a God so as to believe she was loved. Gaskell implicitly makes this clear in a very revealing moment in the story

"A Dark Night's Work." Ellinor, having now established a happy relationship with her father, happens, looking out the window, to notice that the
day looks grey. But, the narrator writes, she was "too happy to feel this
much, knowing that absent love existed for her alone, and from this
knowledge unconsciously trusting in the sun behind the clouds" (7:455).
There is an implied equation here. Secure in the knowledge that she is
loved, Ellinor trusts that the sun is there even though she cannot see it. But
the reverse is true as well. If she were not secure in love, her faith in the sun
would vanish too. The terms, moreover, in this equation seem to function
also reciprocally. The very fact that she believes in the existence of the sun
is evidence that she is loved. The consequence is the proof of the cause.
Faith—in the sun, in God, in anything—is for Gaskell the guarantee that,
although she cannot see it, somewhere there is "absent love." Gaskell said
something to this effect once to Charles Bonsanquet, a lawyer she met on a
trip to Germany. In a letter, she remarked "we must just put our lives into
God's hands, and feel that He knows best, for otherwise certain additions
to sorrow would be inexplicable" (*L* 424a). The key phrase here is "for
otherwise." Gaskell could just as well have written—most religious people would have—that we must put our trust in God because He really does
know best. Gaskell as a Unitarian did in fact believe He did. But this is not
what she says here. Here we must trust in God because sorrow is otherwise inexplicable. It is the inexplicability that she is seeking to avoid.
Again the consequence is the cause. She has to believe that God is there
because the alternative is unbearable. And whatever is unbearable is for her
inconceivable too.

Gaskell needed her religion not only so she could convince herself
love was real and pain was not, she needed those things she imagined in
God that made up for what she had lost as a child. Again and again she
alludes, for example, to the kindness of the deity, pointing out how great a
contrast it is to the cruelty of men. In *North and South* one of the workers
who has lost his job, for instance, and can no longer feed his family
commits suicide in despair. A neighbor who tries to comfort his wife
speaks the familiar words in Gaskell: " 'He thought God could na be harder
than men; m'appen not so hard; m'appen as tender as a mother; m'appen
tenderer' " (4:355).

This image of God as a tender mother is unusual in Christianity, but it
is very common in Gaskell. Having in her mind transformed her mother
into an image of love, Gaskell conceives of God, the embodiment and the
ultimate source of love, as a tender, loving mother. Whenever she does not
speak in this way, and the times are rare indeed, Gaskell almost always

corrects herself. Philip thus, in *Sylvia's Lovers,* remarks that " 'God pities us as a father pities his poor wandering children' " (6:524). But when the subject comes up again only a couple of pages later, Philip observes that while God's love is " 'wiser, tenderer,' " and " 'deeper,' " it is of the same kind as the love of a mother (6:527). Even when Gaskell deals with a text in which God is called the Father, He is very soon transformed in her work into a mother. Thus, in "Libbie Marsh's Three Eras," the title character, while attempting to comfort a friend on the loss of her son, takes up the Bible, which falls open to the fourteenth chapter of John. "How often," the narrator remarks, "these large family Bibles do open at that chapter! as if, unused in more joyous and prosperous times, the soul went home to its words of loving sympathy when weary and sorrowful, just as the little child seeks the tender comfort of its mother in all its griefs and cares" (1:482). This is a chapter in which Jesus, urging his disciples not to be troubled, speaks of God in nearly every one of the thirty-nine verses as a kind and caring Father. Nevertheless, in Gaskell's text, God is turned into a mother. It is as a mother too that He appears in Gaskell's letters. Writing, for instance, to Catherine Winkworth, Gaskell remarks on one occasion that she believes God loves her "with an individual love tenderer than any mother's" (*L* 223).

Often in relation to God Gaskell imagines herself a child, not in the usual sense in which all human beings are called God's children, but in the personal sense in which she was in fact her mother's child. Thus, in the passage I quoted above from "Libbie Marsh's Three Eras," Libbie opens the family Bible seeking the comfort of God's word "just," the narrator explains, as "the little child seeks the tender comfort of its mother" (1:482). Sometimes the object of God's love is metaphorically an infant. This is how, in *North and South,* Bessy Higgins thinks of herself when she says she is ready to die. " 'I could die away into silence,' " she tells Margaret at one point, " 'and rest o' God, just as a baby is hushed to sleep by its mother's lullaby' " (4:236). Nearly the identical image is to be found in "The Crooked Branch." Here the narrator remarks that hearing the Bible read is as "soothing" to him "as a lullaby to a tired child" (7:240).

Religion, as Gaskell interpreted God, not only offered her a mother, it offered her the home she needed, both in heaven and on earth. Whether or not she believed there was literally a home in heaven to which she would be summoned one day, the image of a heavenly home could not but appeal to Gaskell. She uses the image herself in her fiction. Again in the passage I quoted above from "Libbie Marsh's Three Eras," she speaks, for example, of the Bible and its comfort as a "home" (1:482). Likewise in "The

Crooked Branch" when the protagonist's mother dies the narrator writes: "Before night the mother was stricken with paralysis, and lay on her death-bed. But the broken-hearted go Home, to be comforted of God" (7:258).

Gaskell's imagination dwelt not only on her heavenly home but on the members of her family whom she expected to see there. Perhaps the most poignant and telling words Gaskell wrote on the comfort of religion are to be found in a hymn she quotes in "Libbie Marsh's Three Eras":

(1:479)

> Here we suffer grief and pain,
> Here we meet to part again;
> In Heaven we part no more.
> Oh! that will be joyful, &c.

In childhood she had been parted from everyone. Religion promised that one day she would meet them all again.

Just as important was the fact that religion provided an earthly home in the Unitarian community. Had there been no other reason to prevent her from becoming either a Catholic or an atheist, this in itself would have been enough. More than most, as we have seen, Gaskell needed to belong, and the world she did belong to happened to be the Unitarian. This is the point on which, significantly, she focuses in *North and South* when the Reverend Mr. Hale announces that he has resigned his ministry. " 'You cannot mean,' " his daughter cries, " 'that you are really going to leave the Church—to give up Helstone—to be for ever separate from me, from mamma—led away by some delusion—some temptation! You do not really mean it!' " (4:43). His scruples, whatever their nature might be, are dismissed as insignificant. All that matters is that he is cutting himself off from his family and from the village he had once served. And Margaret, it is important to note, makes no distinction between the parish and the family he is leaving. For Gaskell, the religious community was her family in a sense.

Thus, in religion Gaskell found just what she found in "Mrs. Gaskell." As she had tied the two together in her letter to Eliza Fox, the Christian and the social "mes" are fused for her in her religion. And, as she had in that letter suggested that her social "me" included her life as a wife and mother, so it is clear that the needs that turned her into the ideal Victorian woman were the needs that turned her too into the perfect Unitarian. The two were, indeed—religion and woman—so indistinguishable metaphorically that they became a binary image. Describing the character of some letters Charlotte Brontë exchanged with a friend, Gaskell, for instance, in the biography, writes that "the *womanly* consciences of these two . . . were anxiously alive to many questions discussed among the stricter religionists" (*LCB,* p. 110; italics mine). She does not pause to consider the adjective. Religion is necessarily female. Not only is it female, in fact, it has a feminizing power. When she creates a religious man, Gaskell, as we shall later see, almost invariably calls him "feminine."

The conflict between "Mrs. Gaskell's" religion and the attitudes of her demon is a question that is often the subject of Gaskell's subtextual themes, and nowhere is it explored as fully as in the story "Lois the Witch." The story, set in the days of the Puritans, concerns a young woman who, being orphaned, travels from England to New England to live with her uncle, Ralph Hickson, his wife, Grace, and their three children. Her cousin Manasseh, a strange young man, falls in love with her and proposes. When she rejects him, he denounces her as a witch. Lois is tried, found guilty, and hanged.

On the face of it, the story seems a warning against the religious fanaticism represented by the Puritans. Gaskell had never been fond of Calvinism. She was, like most Unitarians, friendly to virtually every other creed, but there were some important exceptions. Officially, Roman Catholicism was one. Calvinism was another. Writing to Charles Bonsanquet, for instance, Gaskell observes that in religion she has "only one antipathy—and that was to the Calvinistic" creed (*L* 485).[8] And of all the Calvinist sects Gaskell liked the Puritans least. Her reasons are given throughout the story: the Puritans are too abstract, too theological, too absorbed in studying their "mysterious doctrines" (7:159), too obsessed with the supernatural. Gaskell, who is elsewhere ready to play with the supernatural herself, makes certain here we understand that every instance in her tale that was attributed by the Puritans to a supernatural cause could be explained by "common sense" (7:135). And the Puritans would have known it had they not been, by their religion, so intellectually deluded and so emotionally warped that they could not see the truth either of the physical world or of their own inner motives.

And yet, although she clearly despised them, Gaskell was fascinated by the Puritans. Not only did she write about them in a number of her stories, when she published a collection of the first three stories she wrote—"Libbie Marsh's Three Eras," "The Sexton's Hero," and "Christmas Storms and Sunshine," all of which appeared originally in *Howitt's Journal* in June, August, and January of 1847–48—she chose as her pseudonym for the volume, which was entitled *Life in Manchester,* the name Cotton Mather Mills. Gaskell was obviously making a joke. Cotton was

Manchester's major industry and it was woven in the mills. Still, the choice is very curious, since none of the stories has any connection with anything in the Puritan world. Would Gaskell have taken the name of a man whom officially she detested had she not been fascinated too? In "Lois the Witch" it is clear she has read him, for she quotes at length from his works (7:182 ff.).

It was this fascination with Puritanism, rather than her objections to it, that prompted Gaskell to write "Lois the Witch," that actually compelled her to write it. For Gaskell, as she wrote to Norton, thought—she was mistaken on this, for it is one of her very best—her story was "not very good." But she could not put it away. "I have grown," she ends her letter, "interested in it, and cannot put it aside" (*L* 418).[9]

Gaskell was fascinated by the Puritans as one would be by the guillotine that was about to fall on one's neck. In Gaskell's case the blade had fallen. She was, as she came to see herself, living on the other side of the grave. In "Lois the Witch," she saw what share religion had had in her execution. It is important to remember that Unitarians, having begun as a sect of Presbyterianism, had an historical connection with the Puritans, and Gaskell—who had, we recall, spoken of "our Puritan ancestors" in one letter to Marianne—was fully aware of it herself (*L* 198a). By Gaskell's day the Unitarians had, it is true, evolved a religion very different from the Calvinists. But it was religion of any kind that was deadly to the demon. Gaskell would have found it difficult to tell the truth her demon saw had she tried to set her story in the Unitarian world. "Mrs. Gaskell" would not have allowed it. But writing about the Salem Puritans—so long ago, so far away—she felt she could say whatever she liked. The difference between the sects was so great that it protected "Mrs. Gaskell" while it let her demon speak, speak not only of religion but of the ancestral creed, and in images, moreover, Gaskell had conceived already for her metaphoric vocabulary. She had established in "The Poor Clare," which she had published three years earlier, that the witch was one of the images she had created for her demon. And it so happened that it was witches that the Salem Puritans killed.

Gaskell attributes various pieces of her own history to Lois. Like her, Lois is orphaned early. As Gaskell went to live with her aunt, Lois goes to live with her uncle. Her father, like Gaskell's, is a minister, and his church turns out to be the very church that Gaskell attended in Barford while she was at the Miss Beyerleys'.[10] Gaskell projects herself in Lois psychologically as well, most particularly in the fact that, as Gaskell saw herself, Lois is paying, in her suffering, for a sin her father committed. This is made clear in a striking scene near the beginning of the story. Lois, while she is yet a child and is still living in England, happens to witness a dunking one day of a woman thought to be a witch. For reasons that are never revealed, the woman, Hannah, blames Lois's father for her unfortunate predicament and, to be avenged on him, utters a curse against his child. " 'Parson's wench,' " she cries out, drowning, " 'thy dad hath never tried for to save me; and none shall save thee, when thou art brought up for a witch.' " Like Lucy, thus, in "The Poor Clare," Lois is victimized by a curse for which her father is responsible.

There are, incidentally, in this scene several details that allow us to observe how Gaskell works when her mind is on the subtextual rather than the textual tale. One accounts for an imbalance in the choices Gaskell makes of the particulars she tells us. While she does not bother to mention why it is that Hannah holds Lois's father to blame for her plight, although it is something we should know, she takes the trouble to inform us, with unnecessary specificity, that Lois was almost four at the time. Nothing in the story itself makes this information necessary. But something outside the story does. Gaskell herself was almost four when the event, her father's remarriage, occurred on which she blamed so much of the misery she experienced. A second detail is responsible for a serious inconsistency that in turn is brought about by the fact that "Mrs. Gaskell" and her demon are engaged in entirely different narratives and express themselves in idioms of entirely different sorts. Although it is Gaskell's official argument that the events that seem to the Puritans to be the work of supernatural forces have completely natural causes, although she insists that there are no witches except in the twisted Puritan mind, the fact that Lois is hanged as a witch seems to fulfill the curse that Hannah had spoken against her years earlier, and this would seem to prove that Hannah, having such powers, was truly a witch. But Gaskell is really writing two stories. Taking a realistic view of the events she is creating, "Mrs. Gaskell" sees the witch trials from the rational perspective of a sensible Unitarian. The demon, however, who is concerned only with telling its own tale, needs to assume the existence of witches in order to speak to us in code.

Lois in the story is offered the usual choice of Gaskell's heroines. She can become an ideal woman or remain, like Bridget, a witch. The ideal woman is represented in the story by Lois's mother. Mrs. Barclay functions, like Lois, as one of Gaskell's surrogate selves, sharing the details of Gaskell's history. She is, for example, the youngest of eight of whom only two survived, herself and the brother who lives in Salem. And she is perfect in the same way Lucy is perfect in "The Poor Clare." Should Lois follow in her footsteps, she will become like her a Lucy. Just before she leaves for Salem, Lois is on the verge, in fact, of becoming a literal Lucy, for she is planning to be married to a man whose name happens—not by accident surely—to be Hugh Lucy. The alternative for Lois is to become, like Hannah, a witch. Hannah is Mrs. Barclay's antithesis, a woman who has kept her demon. And, in a classic recognition scene that occurs when she is dunked, Hannah recognizes Lois as a fellow daemonic type. A crowd has gathered to witness the dunking, and looking around at the circle of faces, Hannah spots Lois and stares at her. Her " 'eyes . . . met mine,' " Lois remembers as she retells the story in Salem. They held her in their powerful gaze. This is really a mirror scene and it recalls the scene in which Lucy sees her daemonic double. Here, however, the terms are reversed. It is the demon that looks in the mirror and sees its reflection in Lois's eyes. Lois is aware of the bond between herself and Hannah the witch. Later she is haunted by nightmares reenacting Hannah's dunking, but in her nightmares it is herself she sees standing in Hannah's place (7:122).

Faced with this choice, Gaskell's heroines generally split themselves in two, as Molly Gibson does when she kills herself, engendering the daemonic Cynthia. But "Lois" is a bolder tale. It is one of the few in which the heroine chooses to keep her demon. Not only does she keep it, in fact, Gaskell defends her against her accusers and, against the voice of the world, refuses to grant that she is wrong. Hannah's prophecy does come true, but this time the heroine does not surrender to her executioners willingly.

Gaskell signals this bolder attitude by moving the action to America, another of the places she uses in a metaphoric way. She is still thinking in simple stereotypes. America is the land of the free. A very large number of her characters end up going to America: Mary Barton, for example, sails to Canada at the end, as does Holdsworth in "Cousin Phillis," Canada being a country Gaskell fuses with the United States just as she fuses Belgium with France; the heroine's daughter in *Sylvia's Lovers* also sails at the end to America. Gaskell lets us know the meaning of this metaphoric place as it is used in "Lois the Witch" when she tells us, at the beginning, that it was to escape persecution and to find freedom that Lois's uncle had fled to America years earlier (2:112). England is the land of women. Lois, had she stayed in England, would have been turned into Mrs. Lucy. Gaskell sends her to America so she can live in the land of the free.

But Lois cannot escape the curse, any more than Gaskell could. The fact that even in America Lois has come to the one community in which witches are put to death tells us that Gaskell has come to see freedom for her as an impossibility. It is not the external world that has inhibited her demon. It is the internal restraints that have enchained it in her mind. This is the insight Gaskell projects in the discussion of free will that she suddenly introduces in the denouement of the story. Predestination is, of course, part of Calvinistic doctrine, but the discussion of free will has little to do with the textual theme. For Gaskell it is a subtextual issue. The question is raised at Lois's trial. No sooner has Manasseh denounced her than he volunteers to defend her. But he defends her not by saying that she is really not a witch. His argument, rather, is that her witchcraft had been made known to him in a prophecy. And, he continues, " 'if there is prophecy, there must be foreknowledge; if foreknowledge, no freedom; if no freedom, no exercise of free-will' " (7:189). Lois is innocent not because she is not what she is said to be. She is innocent because she had no choice in what she became.

"Lois the Witch" is not the only story that raises the question of free will. Less explicitly, the subject is also at issue in "Curious if True." Gaskell published "Curious if True" shortly after "Lois The Witch," and, as "Lizzie Leigh" takes up the story of the fallen woman left unfinished in *Mary Barton,* so does "Curious if True" take up what Gaskell had left unsaid in "Lois." "Curious if True" is different in mood. It is a funny, delightful fantasy. The hero, an Englishman whose name, Richard Wittingham, intentionally recalls Dick Whittington, turns out to be a descendant of Calvin who has come to Tours to examine archives that may help him find "other descendants of the great reformer" who might still be living in France (7:259). Taking a walk through a dark wood, Wittingham, as we only learn at the very end of the story, falls asleep and has a dream, much as in a medieval dream allegory. The recollection of the dream is the substance of the tale. In his dream, he comes upon another of Gaskell's many mansions, this one being an old chateau that is hidden in the forest. He enters and meets there a good many people. None is identified by name, but all seem both familiar and strange. It takes a while for us to realize that all these people are really characters we have met in nursery rhymes and fairy tales. But they are not as we remember them. Sleeping Beauty, for example, whom we discover still asleep, lies disheveled on a sofa, not because she is enchanted, but because she is lazy and fat. The Prince, although he does his duty by awakening her with a kiss, finds her thoroughly unappealing. When she looks tenderly into his eyes, he answers in words that Gaskell says she cannot allow herself to repeat (7:269). Similarly, Cinderella is an aging beauty now, a little plump, a little dowdy, complaining constantly about her feet, to which she did irreparable damage when, out of vanity as a girl, she tried to wear shoes that were too small for her. Her stepsisters, sorry they were wicked, are pathetic and middle-aged. And so the entire story goes. We meet Puss-in-Boots, Jack-the-Giant-Killer, Bluebeard, and a great many others, all presented in this way.

The story is extremely amusing, but humor is not the whole of its point. Its deeper purpose is to free the characters from the roles that imprison them. Within the stories in which they exist, these characters live forever fixed in the roles that are assigned to them. Gaskell, in her narrative, frees them from their fictional incarceration. Here, they are allowed to develop. Here they grow old, grow fat, grow weary. Gaskell is not quite Pirandello in *Six Characters in Search of an Author* or Tom Stoppard in *Rosencrantz and Guildenstern Are Dead,* but she does want to let these characters live, not, as in the stories they come from, trapped in someone else's mind, but independently, for themselves. As "Mrs. Gaskell," Gaskell too had been shackled in a role that had been written for her by others. She too wanted to break free. But—and this is the reason Gaskell uses the frame of the dream allegory—the freedom these characters have achieved exists for them only in a dream. In the real and waking world they remain forever imprisoned. That is why the story's narrator is made to be a descendant of Calvin. They are predestined. So is he. So is the writer of the story.

Lois is predestined too, not by supernatural forces, but because Gaskell, having created her as a projection of herself, can only provide her with the choices that she envisioned for herself. And, as it was with "Mrs. Gaskell," it is society and religion that condemn her to her fate. The two are inextricably fused, as were the Christian and social "mes" in Gaskell's letter to Eliza Fox. Fused as well, as they were for Gaskell, are the community and the family. In the story all are embodied in the Hicksons, with whom Lois has come to live in Puritan Salem.

When she first arrives in Salem, Lois finds a family there that to an extent reminds us of the Stevensons in London. Her uncle is a surrogate father, but it turns out that he is weak, both emotionally and physically. And having failed to make her feel welcome against his wife's resentment at the presence of his niece, he abandons her by dying. Lois continues to live with her aunt, the Hickson daughters, Faith and Prudence, and the Hickson son, Manasseh. Mrs. Hickson, although an aunt, behaves like one of Gaskell's stepmothers, and like all of Gaskell's stepfamilies, she and her children are brilliant creations, chilling studies of the derangement to which Puritan thought can lead. Each is different, but the four are a kind of group psychosis. Grace is hard, cold, indifferent, except in the love she bears her son, about whom she is fiercely possessive in an almost incestuous way. About her religion she is smug, claiming that Cotton Mather himself told her she could instruct him in godliness (7:129). And she is wholly without principles. If she is not exactly evil, she is very little short of it in the effect she has on Lois. Faith and Prudence, in different ways, are egocentric, jealous, angry, and as unprincipled as their mother. Most of all they seem to like the thought of exercising power, which they discover they can do by accusing people of witchcraft. Manasseh is the worst of the lot. Having "pondered," Gaskell writes, "too long" on the "doctrines" of his faith "for the health either of his mind or his body" (7:159), Manasseh has been completely perverted by the Puritan religion. Even his mother admits he has bouts of depression and delusion. Once he even tried to kill himself. And at some earlier point he appears to have been attached incestuously to his sister Faith (7:174).

By placing Lois in the position of having to find a home and family, Gaskell has placed her in the circumstances in which she herself became "Mrs. Gaskell." In England, Lois escaped the fate of becoming Mrs. Lucy. But, predestined, in America, when Manasseh proposes to her, she seems about to become "Mrs. Hickson," which is much the same thing. The manner in which Manasseh proposes lets Gaskell define the alternatives here. He tells her he has had a vision in which it has been revealed to him that God has offered Lois the chance to choose for herself one of two lots. Either she must marry him or she must be hanged as a witch. Most of Gaskell's heroines yield. But Lois is different. She does not. Refusing Manasseh, she chooses rather to be executed as a witch. Death waits for Lois either way. Just as she would have had to kill herself to become the ideal Lucy, she would have to kill herself now to become Manasseh's wife. And she dies if she dies as a witch. But Gaskell sees an important difference in the fact that, as a witch, Lois has only to die in the flesh. By coming to America, therefore, although she has not been wholly liberated, for that is beyond conception for Gaskell, Lois has gained the important freedom of being able to choose her fate. Although it has been at the cost of her life, she has been able to keep her demon, she has been able to save her self.

Religion had been responsible too for killing the witch in "The Poor Clare," but there the witch had been killed in spirit just as much as in the flesh. At the end she had been transformed into an image of "Mrs. Gaskell." Lucy had been told, we remember, that she could exorcise her demon only if her grandmother Bridget cast out the hatred from her heart.

And Bridget, seeking to cast it out, had entered a convent to become a sister of mercy, a Poor Clare, whose task it was to care for the needy. The moment of Bridget's transformation occurs when a mendicant one day comes to the convent to ask for food. Bridget has only just enough food— as there had only been one coat for the two brothers in "The Half-Brothers"—to keep one of them alive. She chooses to give the food to the mendicant, and he turns out, needless to say, to be Mr. Gisborne, Lucy's father, the very man she had hated before. Bridget has expiated her sin and thus done away with Lucy's demon. But she has, at that same moment, done away with her own as well. In the doing of her good deed she has become "a good woman." She is no longer Bridget the witch. She is the Poor Clare of the title.

Thus, although she could not imagine herself giving up her ancestral faith or living outside a religious community, Gaskell understood very well what the relationship had been between religion and her demon.

VIII

The Sweet Insanity Within

JUST AS RELIGION kills the witch in "Lois the Witch" and "The Poor Clare," so, in the second half of the novel does it kill the demon in *Ruth*. "Mrs. Gaskell" wants to show here that the sinner can be saved, and it is itself revealing that to save Ruth from her sin, which is to save her from her demon, Gaskell feels the need to shift to a Christian point of view. The Ruth who had been a pagan Persephone while she still possessed her demon now becomes a fallen "Magdalen" (3:118, 347). Bridget too had become a Magdalen, choosing Magdalen, we recall, as her religious name in the convent. Shifting perspective in Gaskell often entails shifting venue as well, and it is equally revealing that to save her Gaskell feels she must physically move Ruth out of Wales, which is the home of nature, passion, and pagan rituals, into Eccleston, the home in the novel of Christian society.

The social and religious worlds are not as closely connected in Eccleston as they are in Puritan Salem. Religious and secular power here are, although related, divided between the Reverend Thurstan Benson and his parishioner Mr. Bradshaw, a businessman whose active involvement in the community and the town makes him function in the novel as the official voice of "the world." "The world" is here a palpable presence, almost a character in the book, and Gaskell often uses the term as though, in fact, it were a name. Ruth in Wales had been allowed to live in herself, in her own consciousness, unaware and unconcerned with how she seemed to other people. But having seen herself reflected in the accusing eyes of the children, she has come to live in Eccleston in the shadow of religion and under the scrutiny of "the world."

"The world" in *Ruth* has inflexible opinions. Gaskell frequently makes this clear, but nowhere as pointedly as in connection with Ruth's son. As an illegitimate child, Leonard is one of the novel's causes, and Gaskell, intent on pleading his case, is determined to make him appealing. She therefore makes him essentially good, loving, devoted, intelligent, promising. Still, she cannot quite forget that he is a child of passion. She lets him have one rebellious gene, and this is the gene that prompts him to argue constantly with Mr. Benson. Gaskell describes this trait in Leonard virtually in the very words that she was later to use in writing to Charles Eliot Norton about Barbara Leigh Smith. Smith was illegitimate too, and Gaskell believed that it was "in consequence," as she wrote in her letter to Norton, "of her birth" that she was such "a strong fighter against the established opinions of *the world*" (*L* 461; italics mine). "There was," Gaskell writes about Leonard in *Ruth,* "an inclination in him to reason, especially and principally with Mr. Benson, on the great questions of ethics which the majority of *the world* have settled long ago" (3:380; italics mine). And Gaskell, "Mrs. Gaskell" at least, does not here mean simply "settled." What she means is "settled rightly."

In this second part of *Ruth* Gaskell does not allow herself or her heroine to question the opinions of "the world." Lois had resisted "the world." Ruth considers herself a sinner as soon as she faces accusing eyes. Lois had faced accusing eyes too. When she has the recurring nightmares in which she remembers Hannah's dunking but imagines herself in her place, she feels that "'all men hated me with their eyes because I was a witch'" (7:122). Yet she is able to stand her ground, even when she is put in prison. She does for a moment, on being imprisoned, wonder whether she might be guilty even as her judges claim. Reminding us of Bridget the witch, she thinks of "every angry thought" she has harbored in her heart, wondering whether these might not "have had devilish power given to them by the father of evil, and, all unconsciously to herself, have gone forth as active curses into the world" (7:192). But soon she regains her faith in herself. Insisting once again on her "'innocence'" (7:203), she tells her accusers she will "'choose death . . . rather than life to be gained by a lie'" (7:199). Lois refuses to blame herself. But Ruth cannot maintain her innocence once she has been accused by "the world."

Ruth is saved by Mr. Benson. They meet while he is on holiday in Wales. When she is abandoned by Bellingham, Benson offers to take her in. This, of course, is the story's moral. Thus must good Christians, Gaskell implies, offer a helping hand to the sinner. Benson has a sister, Faith, a name that Gaskell uses ironically, we recall, in "Lois the Witch," this being the Hickson girl who would trade the promise of heaven for a moment of earthly delight. Benson's sister is very different, but there are ironies here as well. When Benson writes to her from Wales telling her that he intends to bring a pregnant young woman back to Eccleston, Faith is shocked by his rash decision and replies in a letter that shows she has very little faith in the possibility of redemption. Eventually, she comes to love Ruth, and her help proves indispensable in effecting Ruth's salvation.

Saving Ruth for Gaskell means turning her into a mirror image of the "social" and "Christian" "mes" she had described to Eliza Fox, and doing so for the very reasons she had assumed those identities herself. Benson, meeting her in Wales after Bellingham has abandoned her, finds Ruth homeless and alone. She is in desperate need of love, and love, in the form of Christian compassion, is precisely what he offers. Gaskell, projecting herself in Ruth, imagines Benson as the embodiment of the very image of love. She sees him as a tender mother. This is an instance in which religion, being a female characteristic, feminizes the man who has it. At their first meeting, Gaskell remarks, Benson reminds Ruth of her mother (3:96). His home, when she arrives in Eccleston, also reminds her of the home that she had, as a child, lived in with her "gentle, blessed mother" (3:140). Although not in the literal sense in which M. de Chalabre had repossessed his childhood bed at the end of "My French Master," Ruth, on moving in with Benson, finds the home she had once lost.

Writing to Eliza Fox, Gaskell had called her "social" "me" the self that was a wife and mother, and it is a wife and mother she feels the need to make of Ruth. Although she never marries in Eccleston, in a spiritual way, she plays the role of Benson's "wife." Gaskell is very explicitly thinking of their relationship as a marriage. She even invents a kind of ceremony that places on Ruth's hand the ring that, in fact, she would have worn had she indeed married Mr. Benson. Appropriately, the ceremony takes place soon after Ruth arrives in Eccleston. To make it possible for Ruth to be accepted by the community, which is essential, they believe, if the sinner is to be saved, Benson and Faith have invented a story—as Gaskell believed one should be invented for Miss Pasley, we recall—designed to conceal the truth of her past. Since she is pregnant, it must be claimed that she is actually a young widow, and, since a widow must have a ring, Benson gives her the family wedding ring that he happens to have in the house (3:142). This is the ring that had been worn as her wedding ring by his mother, and it is obviously the ring he would have wanted to give his bride. By putting it on, Ruth has therefore metaphorically married Benson. His relationship to Ruth parallels Bellingham's in every way. One is the husband in the flesh, the other the husband in the spirit. As Bellingham had courted Ruth with the flowers of pagan passion, Benson courts her with the flowers that have spiritual associations. When they meet, for instance, Benson, leading Ruth out of the woods into which Bellingham had led her—and there is obvious allegory here—stops as they walk to admire a foxglove. Gaskell herself admired the foxglove because she had heard a story about it that seemed to her especially "poetical," namely that it always "knows when a spirit passes by and always bows the head" (*L* 12). Benson tells this story to Ruth as they pause to admire the flower, and they thus become the spirits in a sense to which it bows (3:68).

In Eccleston too Ruth becomes a mother. The child had been conceived in Wales, in the natural pagan world, and is Bellingham's in the flesh. But it is born in Benson's house, and it belongs to him in spirit. The natural child had been Ruth's sin. The spiritual child is her salvation. Gaskell is using an image here, popular in Victorian fiction, that derives from the Christ child. She makes the religious connection herself when she has the Reverend Mr. Benson, who is trying to reassure Faith, say that he is praying God, in the name of His " 'Holy Son,' " will make the birth of Ruth's child her " 'redemption' " (3:120). Gaskell had already used the child in this way in "Lizzie Leigh" (2:239–40). In *Ruth* it becomes Ruth's " 'purification' " (3:117–18). It is, however, important to note that the redemption is achieved, not by a change taking place in Ruth, but by the substitution of selves. In a typical and revealing scene, Ruth, recalling her earlier life, happens to remember Bellingham. But just as she does so, Leonard appears, and his appearance, Gaskell writes, "*changed* her from the woman into the mother" (3:270; italics mine). The woman remembers the man she loved. The mother drives out all thought of passion. Gaskell once observed in her "Diary" "If *we* could but consider a child properly, what a beautiful safeguard from evil would its presence be" (pp. 10–11). She does not name the evil here, but we can guess what evil she means. A child is protection from the demon. The moment Ruth learns she is pregnant, she promises Benson she will be " 'good' " (3:162). When he is born, both she and her son become "angels" to one another (3:365).

But here the narrative splits in two. In the first part of the novel, in which Ruth is one with her demon, Gaskell has only one story to tell. The moment, however, she moves her to Eccleston, Gaskell is forced to double the narrative. The Ruth who is saved is one of the stories, the inner life of the demon the other. The fact that the book is about to be split is signaled at the point of transition. There are in fact two transition scenes. One, which is written by "Mrs. Gaskell," continues the official text. It is set in the Benson's garden on the first Sunday Ruth spends in Eccleston. This garden is made a contrast to Wales. In Wales, nature was wild and free. Here, it is contained and controlled. Later, after Leonard is born, Ruth will sit many times in this garden holding her child on her lap, creating thus a picture of Mary as she holds the infant Jesus. And this is the picture Gaskell anticipates on the Sunday she arrives. Although Leonard is not yet born, Ruth picks up a neighbor's child who has wandered into the garden. As she places him on her lap, Ruth is not only shown as pure, she is transformed into the image of the most ideal of women. The other scene is a transition to the novel's daemonic subtext. On her arrival, the Bensons decide to tell their invented tale about Ruth even to their servant Sally. But Sally is too shrewd to believe it. And, as though to make her act the part that she is pretending to play, Sally marshalls Ruth upstairs, sits her down, and cuts her hair off, tucking the jagged ends that remain tightly under a widow's cap (3:143–44). This is the same dark beautiful hair on which Bellingham had placed the coronet of water lilies in the scene beside the pool. There, Ruth's passion had transformed her into a fertility goddess. Here, it brands her as a sinner who must therefore be desexed. Sally, of course, in desexing Ruth, has metaphorically killed her demon. The scene is a parallel imagistically to the scene of Molly's suicide. It tells us that the ideal Ruth is not a happy wife and mother, an image of the Virgin Mary holding the Christ child on her lap, but the mutilated remains of a once daemonic woman. When Bellingham had first abandoned her, Ruth had become like one who was "dead" (3:101). Sally now completes the process. In a sense Ruth is a widow, the widow of her former self. Bellingham does not even recognize her when he meets her again in Eccleston. " 'Where are the water-lilies?' " he asks, " 'Where are the lilies in her hair?' " (3:442).

"Mrs. Gaskell" keeps insisting that Ruth in Eccleston is happy, but she is surrounded everywhere here by images of death. As Mrs. Mason's had been the Hades that preceded the resurrection of Persephone in the spring, Eccleston is the Hades to which she eventually returns. Gaskell, in this part of the novel, largely abandons the myth of Persephone—itself a significant indication of what has happened here to Ruth—but certain features of it persist, and one of these is the image of Hades. Thus, it is always dark in Eccleston. Describing Ruth in Wales with Bellingham, Gaskell had written that the "future lay" for her "wrapped in a golden mist, which she did not care to penetrate; but if he, her sun, was out of sight and gone, the golden mist became dark heavy gloom, through which no hope could come" (3:56). The dark is always hopeless to Gaskell. She is an Apollonian woman. Her spirits rise and fall with the sun. Thus she writes in "The Moorland Cottage" of a "mizzling rain," for instance, which, since it has "obscured the light," threatens to "obscure hope" as well (2:351). And weather that is dark and hopeless Gaskell always associates with death. In "The Moorland Cottage" again, describing yet another day, Gaskell writes that there "was incessant rain, and closing-in mists, without a gleam of sunshine. . . . Every Colour seemed dimmed and darkened . . . and it looked as if the heavy monotonous sky had drawn closer and closer, and shut in the little moorland cottage as with a shroud" (2:339). This is also the darkness of Eccleston. Being an industrial city, Eccleston seldom sees the sun. There seems to be on its horizon always "a low grey cloud" (3:132). And it is always winter in Eccleston. The seasons come and go, of course, but, in the progress of the years, the narrative almost always pauses on the action in the winter. Winter too belongs to death, especially since it is a season that Persephone spends in Hades. There is almost always snow. In the novel's cyclical seasons there had been snow and winter before, first when Ruth was still a child (3:5), then again at Mrs. Mason's (3:5). In Eccleston the snow returns, not only in a literal sense but in connection with other images. The flowers that had carried, for instance, in the first part of the book, much of the novel's daemonic passion, become, in the second, flowers of snow. The room in which she lives at the Bensons reminds Ruth of a "snowdrop," thus, and it is a "snowdrop" too that Benson gives Ruth on the birth of her son (3:160).

It is not difficult to guess what Gaskell's conscious intention is here, but she herself interprets her image when she comments on Leonard's birth. "The earth," she writes, "was still 'hiding her guilty front with innocent snow,' when a little baby was laid by the side of the pale, white mother" (3:159). The guilt of the earth had been implied in an earlier passage too. Here Ruth's mother, "blessed" and pure, had been described as being "removed from any of earth's stains and temptations" (3:140). The earth is guilty. The snow is pure. It hides, as it falls, the guilt of the earth, just as the guilty Ruth of Wales is hidden now in snowy Eccleston.

In the subtext, Gaskell, however, uses the snow in a different way. Subtextually, *Ruth* is a winter's tale, a tale of the death of beauty and passion, a story of flowers that bloom in spring but come at last to lie in winter under the cold snow-covered earth. Ruth herself, at the end of the novel, comes to lie under the earth. And the earth, since like Persephone Ruth is laid to rest in winter, is indeed covered with snow.

The death of the demon, however, engenders a daemonic double in Jemima, a daughter of Bradshaw's who, like Cynthia, enters the narrative precisely at the moment the heroine dies. As Cynthia is born of Molly's suicide, Jemima is born of Ruth's redemption. In the moral scheme of the book, Jemima is intended to show that sin dwells potentially in everyone. Every one of us can fall. " 'With a father and mother, and home, and careful friends,'" Jemima explains, making the point, "'I am not likely to be tempted like Ruth.'" But "'if you knew all I have been thinking and feeling this last year, you would see how I have yielded to every temptation that was able to come to me; and, seeing how I have no goodness or strength in me, and how I must just have been like Ruth, or rather worse than she ever was, because I am more headstrong and passionate by nature'" (3:361). Gaskell had made this point before, in *Mary Barton* when she had chosen, as a motto for the chapter in which Esther's story is told, the cautionary words to the reader "Know temptation ere you judge the crime" (ch. 14). And Lizzie's mother in "Lizzie Leigh" had said to Susan, the "good woman," "'Everyone says you're very good, and that the Lord has keeped you from falling from His ways; but maybe you've never ben tried and tempted as some is'" (2:222). Jemima is there as the world's daughter who, but for the grace of God, would have ended up like Ruth.

But Gaskell misrepresents the facts here. "Mrs. Gaskell" is misreading what her demon has conceived. Jemima is really not loved and cared for. On the contrary, like Ruth, she is a rejected child. Jemima's parents are still alive, but that is the whole extent of the difference. Mr. Bradshaw, severe and arbitrary with her brother, we recall, has been as abitrary and severe with Jemima and her sisters. And like her brother too she has been neglected by her abstracted mother. To all intents and purposes, therefore, Jemima is an abandoned child. Jemima is not a contrast, thus, but a very double of Ruth. She is a daemonic double, in fact. Although "Mrs. Gaskell" insists she is good because she has not fallen like Ruth, her demon is aware there are subterranean depths in Jemima. When, for example, Jemima answers her father one day in angry words, the narrator speaks of "the sullen passion which seethed below" her "stagnant surface" (3:333). Gaskell's demon sees Jemima's and at one point calls it by name. Wrestling with her temper one day, Jemima is made to ask herself: "'What was this terrible demon in her heart? Was she, indeed, given up to possession?'" (3:242).

Jemima is Gaskell's boldest double. Cynthia, acting as a mirror of Molly Gibson's empty self as well as the part of her daemonic double, buries the anger and resentment Molly denies when she becomes "good." Jemima, however, expresses herself openly. And, although she cannot admit the anger expressed by Jemima is Ruth's, Gaskell does construct the narrative in a way intended to show that, in her daemonic behavior, Jemima is acting out Ruth's demon. Seldom, for one thing, does Gaskell provide a reason for Jemima's behavior. Often, in fact, as in the passage in which she asks herself, above, whether she is possessed by demons,

Jemima herself is left to wonder why she does the things she does. Gaskell wants us to believe that it is her seething passion that accounts for her strange outbursts and to ask for nothing more. But if we correlate events, it is almost always, we realize, the case that when Jemima erupts, Ruth has experienced an event which, if she could vent her feelings, would occasion an eruption. What is thus suppressed in Ruth is given utterance through Jemima. Whenever Ruth is most serene, Jemima is moodiest and most troubled. When Ruth accepts the will of God, as Mr. Benson interprets it for her, Jemima explodes with furious rage at the rules her father lays down. And when Ruth is resigned and submissive, Jemima is obstinate and perverse. Gaskell achieves some wonderful moments transferring the demon from one to the other. While Ruth is out on a picnic, for instance, sitting in the cool of the shade, Jemima, left at home alone, paces back and forth in her garden in the "intense heat" of the sun (3:243).

There had been sun at the picnic too. Ruth had sat in the cool of the shade, but she had let Jemima's sister Elizabeth wander off in the sun. Elizabeth, as it turns out, is delicate, and by the time Ruth gets her home, the sun has already, it seems, debilitated her. Jemima, however, is not aware of this. Eager to hear about the picnic, since Ruth's companion was Mr. Farquhar, with whom Jemima is in love, she detains Elizabeth in the garden, once again in the heat of the sun. This is altogether too much for Elizabeth, who falls in a faint. The sun is here a sexual metaphor. Gaskell may actually be thinking of the tradition Shakespeare recalls when, in the mad scene, Hamlet observes that if he wishes her not to conceive, Polonius must not allow Ophelia to walk in the sun. Elizabeth's fall is no mere faint, thus. In a metaphoric way, Elizabeth falls as Ruth had fallen. Jemima is not allowed to fall, but Elizabeth, by falling in consequence of the heat of the sun, has, in Gaskell's relay fashion, become the double of Ruth's double. Gaskell in her shorter fiction had already used literal falls in this meta-phoric way. As soon as Lizzie Leigh is redeemed, her daughter, for instance, assuming her state, instantly tumbles down the stairs. Another kind of substitute fall occurs in the story "The Well of Pen Morfa." Nest, the heroine, being Welsh, is a daemonic, passionate woman and her consuming love for a man who has little concern for her seems to be heading her for a fall. Thus, she is a falling woman. But, instead of letting her fall, Gaskell provides a "treacherous rock" that trips her one day when she goes to the well (2:248) and makes her fall literally instead. Dickens, in fact, found Gaskell's heroines so inclined to stumble and fall that he remarked to W. H. Wills he wished "to Heaven her people would keep a little firmer on their legs!"[1] The fallen is the daemonic state, and being rejected in one guise, it must somehow be achieved in another. This is what happens in *Ruth* to Elizabeth.

Not only does Gaskell express in this novel more openly what the double feels, she grapples with the very question that had first engendered the demon. Ruth is transformed behind the scenes. We see her one minute a daemonic girl and the next an ideal woman. We do not witness her transition nor the struggle she must have endured. We do see the struggle in Jemima. Jemima, as it happens, finds herself in the very situation in which girls in Gaskell's fiction usually turn into perfect Lucies. She is in love with Farquhar, and she wants him to love her. Farquhar is one of the characters in whom Gaskell fuses roles. As Mr. Gibson in *Wives and Daughters* was in a literal sense a father and metaphorically a lover, Farquhar is a literal lover and a metaphoric father. A man much older than Jemima as well as her father's business partner—thus in a sense her father's double—Farquhar had always acted, when Jemima was a child, as a kind of paternal surrogate. Even now, although she is grown and he has become her lover, he continues to behave toward her in a fatherly way. Jemima, like Ruth, is eager for love, and from Farquhar she seeks the love her father has denied her. But, like other fathers in Gaskell, Farquhar is willing to love her only if she will be "good." This is suggested in an exchange Gaskell conceives in the same floral language she had used in Ruth's relationships. Once, as a child, Jemima had given Farquhar a bouquet of "wild" blossoms. He had given her in exchange a "nosegay of greenhouse flowers" (3:239–40). A question here has been asked and answered. Jemima has asked him to accept her in her wild, natural state. Farquhar has replied he wants her only in a greenhouse version. To earn his love, she must be tamed. Gaskell seems prepared, initially, to quiet Jemima as she had quieted Ruth. Indeed, she makes it Ruth's occupation to calm the demon in Jemima. This is an instance, incidentally, in which, dramatizing a metaphor, Gaskell turns a figure of speech into an element in her plot. The Bensons have decided that Ruth ought to have employment in Eccleston, and Bradshaw, not knowing what to do with his uncontrollable daughters, and seeing that Ruth is completely controlled, decides to hire her as a governess. Gaskell is playing word games here. Since Ruth has now become " 'self-governed,' " as Gaskell describes her at one point (3:239), she can be assigned the task of being the "governess" of her demon. One result of the relationship that develops between the girls stresses Jemima's role as a double. The Bensons have told Ruth's secret to no one, but Jemima finds it out. Sharing her secret, Jemima becomes, in a sense, Ruth's secret sharer, thus, by literary tradition, in effect her other self.

Ruth does manage to tame Jemima, but not until the very end and only to a limited degree. Although she begins to sound like Ruth when she thinks she might be willing "to become and to be all" Farquhar wishes her to be, and even, if only he will love her, "to change her very nature for him" (3:217), Jemima in the end concludes that he must "love her as she was or not at all. Unless he could take her with all her faults, she would not care for his regard; 'love' was too noble a word to call such cold, calculating feeling as his must be, who went about with a pattern idea in his mind, trying to find a wife to match. Besides, there was something degrading in trying to alter herself to gain the love of any human creature" (3:217). "She felt as if she would rather be bought openly, like an Oriental daughter, where no one is degraded in their own eyes by being parties to such a contract" (3:238). Gaskell had earlier told us that Ruth "valued affection almost above its price." In the same metaphoric language, Jemima refuses to be bought.

Ruth is bolder than *Wives and Daughters* in another respect as well. In *Wives and Daughters,* once the demon has been projected into Cynthia, Molly has no inner life. She walks, she talks, she falls in love, or so the narrator reports. But her inner life has vanished. This is not the case with Ruth. In *Ruth* Gaskell follows the demon not only into the heart of the double but into its secret life in the grave. Ruth may be dead, like Molly Gibson or like Gregory in "The Half-Brothers," but within she still conceals what Gaskell calls a "vital secret" (3:388). Gaskell is trying to explain here why it is Ruth seems detached, alienated from herself and from everyone around her. "Anyone," she writes, "who has been oppressed with the weight of a vital secret for years is naturally reserved" (3:388). The secret officially is Ruth's sin, which no one in Eccleston is aware of except for the Bensons and Jemima. And it is true that such a secret might make someone seem reserved. But Gaskell, playing with words again, really means *vital* etymologically. Ruth has been killed to become the ideal. She herself has become a corpse, and Eccleston, the land of Hades, is the grave of her former self. But, as Cynthia has maintained within her "shrouded" state a "self," Ruth has kept a "living" self secreted in her deadened state.

That secret lives in every sense. First, it lives because, as Gaskell every so often is forced to admit, Ruth is still in love with Bellingham. "'They think I have forgotten all,'" Ruth remarks on one occasion, "'because I do not speak.'" But "'O my God!'" she soon continues, "'I do believe Leonard's father is a bad man, and yet, oh! pitiful God, I love him; I cannot forget—I cannot!'" (3:270–71). Often, as she does elsewhere, Gaskell describes Ruth sexual passion in the imagery of fire. Her "heart," for instance, "burned," she writes, with the desire "to see" Bellingham (3:274). At the end, this fiery passion is the fever that kills Ruth. Passion frustrated in Gaskell often turns into a physical fever. Thus in "Half a Lifetime Ago," Susan Dixon succumbs to "a fever" as soon as she sends her lover away (5:313). In "Cousin Phillis," Phillis falls ill with a fever when she discovers the man she loves has married another (7:103). So does Sylvia in *Sylvia's Lovers* when she loses the man she loves, and Gaskell here, when Sylvia speaks during her illness of the "fire" that is "burning" in her heart (5:425), makes the metaphoric connection explicit. Ruth had already suffered a fever when she had been abandoned by Bellingham (chs. 10 and 11). When he turns up again to stir the fire still burning in her heart, the fact that she must reject him now engenders in her a fatal fever. Her passion is so intense, in fact, that it brings on an epidemic in the entire town of Eccleston. Just as Ruth refuses Bellingham, who is now proposing marriage, Eccleston breaks out in a plague. The plague makes a moral point as well in the novel's social theme. As Carlyle shows in *Past and Present* by using a plague in a similar way, Gaskell wants to show the community is an interconnected whole, that we all live or die together. But when she describes the plague in the narrative as "the blaze of a fire which had long smouldered" (3:420), it is clear that Gaskell is thinking, not of the moral point she is making, but of the fire in Ruth's heart. And the events seem to confirm this. For it is Bellingham who falls ill of the fever that is raging, and it is in taking care of him—she has become, like Bridget the witch, a Sister of Mercy now in Eccleston—that Ruth is fatally infected. If the fever is Ruth's passion and she catches it from Bellingham, being infected by the fever is like being seduced again.

Of those who read the novel first, many objected to Ruth's dying. They felt that Gaskell was punishing Ruth. Sexual sinners did, of course, often die in English fiction. Richardson had killed Clarissa, although she had in fact been raped. Hetty dies in *Adam Bede* and Tess as well in *Tess of the D'Urbervilles*, although, as a determinist, Eliot insists that Hetty is not responsible, and, as a sexual rebel, Hardy insists that Tess has not really sinned. The English were, of course, conservative. But Tolstoy in Russia killed Anna Karenina, and even Flaubert could not in France allow Emma Bovary to live. But there were exceptions to this rule. Hawthorne had not killed Hester Prynne, and Gaskell herself, who had killed Esther, had allowed Lizzie Leigh to live.[2] Many hoped Ruth would be spared as well. Charlotte Brontë, for example, having received an outline from Gaskell of the novel and its ending, wrote in reply, "but hear my protest! Why should she die? Why are we to shut up the book weeping? My heart fails me already at the thought of the pain it will have to undergo. And yet you must follow the impulse of your own inspiration. If *that* commands the slaying of the victim, no bystander has a right to put out his hand to stay the sacrificial knife; but I hold you a stern priestess in these matters" (*LCB,* pp. 421–22). Gaskell received a similar letter, as soon as the novel appeared in print, from Elizabeth Barrett Browning. "Was it quite impossible," she asked, "but that Ruth should *die?*" W. R. Greg, reviewing the novel, used its ending as an example of the excessive punishment novelists meted out to their sexual sinners.[3] Had she wished to, it is obvious, Gaskell could have let Ruth live. But Gaskell needed to kill Ruth, not to punish her but to free her.

Gaskell's logic is complex here, but she provides the links herself between the explicating metaphors. One thing of which we are aware in the second half of the novel is that for Gaskell the real Ruth was forever arrested in Wales. That is why, at least in one sense, she never really changes in Eccleston. Ruth is aware of this herself. She knows that changes are taking place in all the people she sees around her. "Mr. and Miss Benson grew old, and Sally grew deaf, and Leonard was shooting up, and Jemima was a mother," Ruth, as we near the end, reflects. She alone has remained unaltered. "She and the distant hills . . . seemed the only things which were the same" (3:388). Ruth does not change because she lives, not in the real world of time, but in the timeless world of memory. She lives in her memories of Wales. As soon as she learns that she must leave, Ruth walks around the inn in Wales looking through windows from room to room, "learning off each rock and tree by heart. Each had its tale" in her life in Wales "which it was agony to remember; but which it would have been worse agony to forget" (3:130). The sights are branded on her mind, and it is to them in Eccleston that she returns in memory and dream. Many readers have observed that the narrative of *Ruth* passes in and out of dreams. Many have found this practice puzzling. But when she calls the day on which Ruth runs away to Wales with Bellingham the beginning of her "dream" (3:58) and remarks, when Bellingham leaves her, that Ruth had now "dreamed out her dream" (3:130), Gaskell makes it clear she means Ruth's dreams to stand for her daemonic life. A dream is where, as in "Curious if True," freedom can be found in Gaskell. Eccleston is for Ruth a "nightmare" (3:92). Her only escape is to reenter in her mind the "haunts of memory" (3:148) and to live thus in her dreams where her demon can be free. That is why Ruth is so detached. She is not where her body is. Whatever her body may be doing,

she is within forever "absorbed" in her "thoughts" of Wales and Bellingham (3:148). On one occasion, in which we see Ruth abstracted from
her surroundings, Jemima and her mother are visiting and are received by
Ruth and Faith. Ruth lets Faith do all the talking, while she takes this
"opportunity" of "retreating" to her thoughts, to her memory of a night
she had spent in Wales with Bellingham. "Which was the dream," the
narrator asks, "and which the reality? That distant life or this? His moans
rang more clearly in her ears than the buzzing of the conversation between
Mrs. Bradshaw and Miss Benson" (3:148).

The answer is obvious. For Ruth and Gaskell, reality lies in the
passionate life. And this is the life Ruth dies to enter. Officially, the death
is conventional. The sinner redeemed, having acted nobly as a Sister of
Mercy at the hospital, dies in a state of peace and happiness as all around
lament her loss (2:447), showing that even fallen women can be saved by
love and kindness. But several elements in the narrative suggest that in the
novel's subtext Gaskell has something else in mind. One is the very
curious fact that Ruth on her deathbed recognizes no one with whom she
has had a connection in Eccleston. "She never looked," the narrator
writes, "at any one with the slightest glimpse of memory or intelligence in
her face; no, not even Leonard" (3:444). By wiping completely from her
memory everyone she knew in Eccleston, Gaskell has done away entirely
with this segment of Ruth's life. She has negated her salvation. Ruth has
become again the Ruth of the first part of the novel. She is no longer the
perfect woman she had come to be in Eccleston, but the daemonic girl of
Wales. This is implied in the fact that Gaskell mentions specifically that
Ruth did not even remember Leonard. The perfect woman—"Mrs. Gaskell"—is an angel in the house, the ideal wife and mother. But at the
moment of her death, Ruth has forgotten her Eccleston "husband." She
has forgotten her "savior" child. They have ceased to exist for her. For she
no longer exists as they knew her. Her mind has now returned to Wales.
Gaskell had already predicted, in the earlier scene in which Ruth had run
from room to room memorizing the inn in Wales, that the sound of the
running waters she had heard outside the inn would be "in her ears . . . on
her death-bed" (3:130). There it had seemed as though the sound would be
a simple recollection. But it is not. It is a sound that she really hears in her
"ears" because in her mind she has returned to her daemonic self in Wales.

And it is again to Wales that Gaskell sends her when she dies. As Ruth
stares vacantly before her the very last second of her life, Gaskell describes
her as withdrawing to "a sweet . . . insanity within" (3:444). The word
insanity seems odd here, but madness is one of Gaskell's images, and while

it is not explained in *Ruth,* it is explained in "Lois the Witch." Here it is Hannah who goes insane in this metaphoric way and the nature of her insanity is made clear when, to describe it, Gaskell uses not a contemporary but an old English expression. Hannah, Gaskell writes, "went double" (7:122). *Double* has in Gaskell's mind yet another meaning, of course, and it is plain in "Lois the Witch" that the two meanings are connected. Hannah, by remaining a witch, has been able to keep her demon. Thus, she has not engendered a double. But to escape one kind of doubling, she has had to "go double" instead. Thus, in a metaphoric sense, madness is not a derangement. It is that state in which the demon, having detached itself from "the world" that has rejected and condemned it, finds a retreat in the inner self where it can live secure and free.

The very year she published *Ruth* Gaskell used the image of madness in a very similar way in the history of Alice Carr in her short story "Morton Hall." The hall is itself the story's focus, this being yet another tale about a home that is restored eventually to its rightful owners, or their descendants in this case, for Gaskell is tracing the generations of the Mortons through the centuries. But the narrative is long, and it contains a number of tales. One, which is set in the time of Cromwell—her fascination with the Puritans has a hold of Gaskell again—tells the story of Alice Carr, the daughter of a Puritan family, and John Morton, a loyal Royalist. Alice and John, the moment they meet, take "a fancy to each other." But each falls in love in a different way, Alice "in the deep, wild way in which she took the impressions of her whole life, deep down, as if they were burnt in" (2:452), and John only in "a man's way," Alice being "a beautiful woman" to him who requires "to be tamed" (2:452). Their marriage from the start is doomed, but it deteriorates even more on the day of the Restoration. Being a Royalist, John insists that his wife support the Stuarts. Alice meanwhile is as adamant that she will continue a Puritan. They are, thus, engaged in a contest of wills, John attempting to get Alice, as Gaskell understands his actions, to "come to his beck and call" (2:452), Alice resisting and "defying him" (2:453). Morton decides to forget her at first by going to London to live at court, but soon he returns determined to "punish" her (2:453). So far the story proceeds as usual, but here the narrator, quite inexplicably, claims not to know what happened next. All he can do is to offer the rumors he has heard of Alice's fate. The rumors, however, are important. Each lets Gaskell write an ending in another of her images. One of the rumors tells the story of Alice being frozen to death as Gregory is in "The Half-Brothers." Another, which reports that John sent her to be confined in a convent, shows us a woman who has, like

Ruth, been imprisoned by religion. Similarly, in another ending, John, returning to the hall, spreads the word around the countryside that his wife has gone insane. He, of course, is only doing so so that he can "shut" her "up" in an insane asylum in London (2:457–59)—thus containing her again—but, to those who see her, Alice does in fact appear insane. Yet it is clear she is insane, not in an ordinary sense, but in the sense of Hannah the witch. Fierce and passionate, Alice Carr is obviously a daemonic woman. Morton has attempted to tame her, but she has refused to be bullied into becoming his ideal. She cannot, however, withstand the power—which Gaskell in this story transforms into sheer physical force—exerted on her by a man who, like Mr. Bradshaw, embodies—being a member, under the Stuarts, both of the established religion and the established secular government—the opinion of "the world." Thus she withdraws as Ruth has done to the "insanity within."

Ruth, redeemed, had been doubled in Eccleston, projecting her demon into another. Returning in death to her inner life, she had "gone double" in a way that had undoubled her split self. Thus, it was not to punish Ruth that Gaskell killed her at the end. Her death is a metaphor through which, the demon saved from its salvation, she can enter her world of memories and live forever in her dreams.

Here we have the answer, then, to where the demon goes in Gaskell. The "Christian" and the "social" "mes," are, as we have seen in Ruth, only the corpse that remains of the witch Christian society has killed. Buried in that corpse, however, lies a "secret" that is "vital." The secret is that the demon lives. "Shrouded" so as to keep itself safe from the censure of the world, it survives and even flourishes in the realm of memories and dreams.

IX

Social and Political
Fiction: Expiation
in Good Works

IT IS SIGNIFICANT THAT Gaskell requires Ruth to be redeemed in the community through good works. Good works have always been a part of the Judeo-Christian tradition, and it is true that the Unitarians, holding that God could only achieve his plan for the world through human agents, gave them a special place in their scheme. Works of charity were, moreover, just the practical turn Unitarians liked to give to their religion. Gaskell herself remarks in *Ruth* that, although she "did not talk" about it as she went about her work as a Sister of Mercy at the hospital, Ruth was following, nonetheless, the "unseen banner" of "religion" (3:388).

But every fallen woman in Gaskell atones for her sin in this same way. Lizzie Leigh, as we are told at the very end of the story, proves that she has been reclaimed when she assumes the task of comforting all who have suffered pain and sorrow. Esther, in a variation, to be purged of her transgression, is assigned just one good deed, that of saving Mary Barton from succumbing like herself to the compliments of a flatterer. And Bridget, of course, in "The Poor Clare" is told she can expiate her demon only if, taking the veil, she devotes herself to good deeds (5:382). Gaskell requires good works, in fact, not only of fallen but of falling women. Thus, in "The Well of Pen Morfa," for instance, Nest, although she does not fall, must still do penance for her demon by undertaking works of charity.

Margaret Ganz is right to say that it was a Victorian convention for fallen women to do good works. She cites Hester Prynne in *The Scarlet Letter* as a paradigmatic example.[1] But Gaskell uses conventions only if they meet her personal needs, and the reason she uses good works to redeem her sexual sinners is that she sees the "moral" self as the antithesis of the "daemonic." If, as she says in connection with Cynthia, it is the daemonic "self" that is "real," to be undaemonic one must be self-less. Gaskell means self-less psychologically, but here as often in her fiction—

finding it easier to speak in moral rather than psychological terms—she translates one into the other. Self-less thus becomes selfless. It was selflessness, we recall, that Roger recommended to Molly. Nest, in "The Well of Pen Morfa," is told to give up all " 'thought of self' " (2:260), Ellinor in "A Dark Night's Work" is said to be finally "weaned from self-seeking" (7:532–33), and Ruth, when Leonard is born, is instantly drawn " 'out of herself' " (3:118). But being selfless is not enough. Daemonic women, those especially who have acted out their demons, must give evidence of their selflessness by undertaking to do good works.

Gaskell did not impose on her characters what she did not impose on herself. We might imagine a minister's wife, especially in the nineteenth century, had no choice in such a matter, but Gaskell apparently felt she did. According at least to A. Cobden Smith, who had himself known Gaskell in Manchester, she had no sooner arrived and settled there "than she steadily and consistently objected to her time being considered as belonging in any way to her husband's congregation for the purpose of congregational visiting, and to being looked to for that leadership in congregational work which is too often expected of the 'minister's wife.' " And yet, as we shall later see, she did work tirelessly in her community. Smith believes she elected to do so "of her own choice and desire."[2] And he is very probably right. Many of the things she did she certainly did because she was a generous and compassionate woman. But to the extent that she conceived of her actions as "good works," Gaskell was, in her philanthropies, seeking to expiate her demon.

Such expiation always, in Gaskell, wins the affection of "the world." The ending of "The Moorland Cottage" in which the long-rejected child dies, by having served the community, "rich in the love of many," is a typical example. But Gaskell is always, as we know, thinking of earning the love of one even more than of the many, and in *Ruth* she makes it clear that the many are the one. Although it is the town of Eccleston that she serves during the plague, Ruth, as Gaskell lets us know, has offended—not her father, who has long been dead, of course—but his surrogates in the novel, of which there are no fewer than three. The first is Bellingham. As Jemima does with Farquhar, Ruth, in her childlike way, regards Bellingham as a surrogate father. The critical word that had appeared in the letter Mrs. Stevenson had sent Aunt Lumb about Elizabeth appears in Ruth's relationship with Bellingham. On learning that he has come to Eccleston, Ruth insists that she must see him, not—at least this is her claim—to rekindle their relationship but to ask why he abandoned her. " 'If I might see him!' " she cries in a passion, " 'If I might see him! If I might just ask him why he left me; if I had *vexed* him in any way' " (3:270; italics mine). Jemima too, having angered Farquhar, also wonders how she had "vexed" him (3:371). It happens that Ruth did not "vex" Bellingham, it having been his mother in fact, acting to Ruth like a wicked stepmother, who had whisked him away from Wales. But when she tends him in his fever as a Sister of Mercy at the hospital, Bellingham comes to love her again. A second father Ruth offends is Mr. Bradshaw when she allows his daughter Elizabeth to walk in the sun, causing her thus to collapse and "fall." But Bradshaw comes to admire Ruth when he learns of her good works. And, as Mr. Benson implies on many occasions in the novel, Ruth has by her sin offended above all her Heavenly Father. He too, however, comes to forgive her through her good works.

Gaskell, as the tablet attests erected by William's congregation, won the "undying love" herself of the community through her good works. The help she offered and gave Miss Pasley, whose story was a model for *Ruth,* was one of her many good works in Manchester. So, however, was *Ruth* itself. We cannot understand what Gaskell both achieves and fails to achieve in her socioeconomic and in her political fiction unless we realize that this fiction was in her mind a form of the work through which, by expiating her demon, she could reclaim her father's love. This is, again, not to imply that Gaskell did not care for the people whose social and economic miseries she depicted in her works. She had, it cannot be stressed enough, a warm and affectionate and generous heart. Human suffering troubled her deeply. She wanted to help, especially since, as a Unitarian believing in the ultimate perfectibility of all human institutions, she was convinced there was no problem for which a solution could not be found.

But Gaskell had no genuine interest in social, economic, and political questions. These are hardly ever mentioned, for example, in her letters. If her letters tell us anything, it is that she found these subjects, important though she knew they were, boring, difficult, and alien to her natural inclinations. In one, for instance, she alludes to the dullness of a lecture on political economy (*L* 624). In another, she confesses, half in jest and half in earnest, that she will have nothing to say to a woman she has invited because, instead of novels and poetry, the woman reads only Adam Smith (*L* 443a). The proof perhaps of how little interest Gaskell actually had in these issues is that she knew very little about them, opening, as we recall, *Mary Barton* by stating in the very Preface that she knows "nothing of Political Economy, or the theories of trade" (1:lxxx). Nine years after *Mary Barton,* when she rejects an idea from her publisher, Gaskell not only confesses her ignorance, she adds she is ignorant by choice. The story her publisher wants her to write would "require," she writes, "a greater knowledge of politics than I either have *or care to have*" (*L* 370; italics mine). Some have believed she disclaimed too much.[3] Gaskell was certainly aware—living in Manchester she could not fail to be—of some contemporary events and of some of their implications. The Chartist movement, for example, weaves in and out of *Mary Barton*. And it would seem that she herself had at some point read Adam Smith (*L* 93). But her knowledge is very minimal and extremely imprecise. Sometimes she actually gets things wrong. Louis Cazamian has, for example, pointed out that her "frequent use of the form 'trades' union' shows that she still confused unions of men in one craft or occupation with a general league of all workers."[4]

One of the reasons Gaskell would not have, had there been no other compulsion, written on subjects of this kind is that she did not like abstractions, preferring to deal with the concrete. She makes this very clear in her fiction. In one situation in *Mary Barton,* in which the story calls for comments on unions, strikes, wages, and scabs, she hurries through a brief discussion that she ends with the following words: "So much for generalities. Let us now return to individuals" (1:200). Nor does she have—like George Bernard Shaw, a genuine sociopolitical thinker—a particular point of view that she is eager to promote. The conclusion she usually comes to is that everything is a muddle. " 'Of course,' " says Job Legh in *Mary Barton,* articulating the uncertainty Gaskell feels on how to solve the conflict between the masters and workers, " 'it would take a deal more thought and wisdom than me, or any other man has, to settle out of hand how this should be done" (1:448). Sometimes Gaskell is aware that she ought to have an opinion, and she feels she must explain why it is that she does not. Commenting thus on the "terrible years"—1839–40, which were very bad in Manchester—the narrator writes that "Even philanthropists who had studied the subject, were forced to own themselves perplexed in the endeavour to ascertain the real causes of the misery; the whole matter was of so complicated a nature, that it became next to impossible to understand it thoroughly." (1:94).

It is not difficult to see that Gaskell would have been much happier had she been able to avoid questions of this sort entirely. But she felt that she could not. Political and economic matters are central concerns in two of her novels, and in the rest, as in her stories, they turn up in peripheral ways. She herself provides, however, the clue to the reason she undertook subjects so uncogenial to her when, on finishing *Mary Barton,* she asks her publisher whether she may use as her pseudonym Stephen Berwick (*L* 28).

"Stephen" is derived from Stevenson, but Gaskell is not thinking of her own maiden name. She is thinking of her father who had been born in Berwick-on-Tweed. The book, she admits without knowing she does so, has in fact been written for him. As an appeal on behalf of the workers, as an attempt to redress their plight, it is a "good work," an expiation for the demon that had "vexed" him.

The needs that compelled her, thus, to write economic and political fiction were the needs that had transformed her into an angel in the house. The good works she did in the community simply enlarged in the public sphere the role of the domestic ideal. To the extent that they are political, social, and economic narratives, works like *Mary Barton,* therefore, are the fictions of "Mrs. Gaskell." Officially, it is her views that these narratives express. And "Mrs. Gaskell," as we know, needed to be in complete agreement with the opinions of "the world." She does not even want to risk inadvertent confrontations. "If my accounts agree or clash," she writes in the Preface of *Mary Barton,* "with any system, the agreement or disagreement is," she assures us, "unintentional" (1:lxxx).

For Gaskell, "the world" was her community, and the views of that community on the questions of these novels were the views of Adam Smith.[5] Theorists like Jeremy Bentham and James and John Stuart Mill had adapted *The Wealth of Nations* to contemporary conditions, and the economic philosophy thus created had become the favored view in all of England. But it was held with special zeal by what was called the Manchester School, the social, economic, and political party led by Manchester factory owners like John Bright and Richard Cobden, both of whom were friends of the Gaskells. The economics of Adam Smith were Unitarian orthodoxy too, partly because the laissez-faire principles of Adam Smith suited the Unitarian doctrine of individual freedom and effort and partly because the Manchester School counted among its prominent members a very large number of Unitarians. Harriet and James Martineau were two, both acquaintances of the Gaskells.

In *Mary Barton,* "Mrs. Gaskell" holds the orthodox positions. The story consists of the usual elements found in a "condition-of-England" novel. Its action, for instance, concerns a conflict between rich and poor, masters and workers. It touches such important issues as working conditions in the factories, working hours, wages, unions, strikes, and government regulations.

Like the Manchester economists, Gaskell always favors capitalism. Officially, she takes her stand almost always with the masters. Gaskell is still defending the masters six years later in *North and South.* This later novel is not by any means a rewriting of *Mary Barton* but the issues that it deals with are the same to an extent and the positions Gaskell takes tend to be the same as well. Holding still with Adam Smith, Gaskell thus defends the masters once again in *North and South*. It is they, she argues there, who, since they must take the risks, are entitled to the profits (4:378).

Gaskell's official view of the poor resembles that of W. R. Greg, another Manchester School supporter who, in his review of the novel, suggests that the reason masters suffer less in bad times than the factory workers is that "*they,* in the days of prosperity, had laid by a portion of their earnings," while "the operatives had not."[6] In *North and South* Gaskell expresses a similar view when Thornton calls the workers "'ignorant and improvident'" (4:96). And, although she otherwise sees him as a sane and sensible man, Gaskell officially insists that Barton brings on his own sufferings partly by "his improvident habits" (1:3).

Clearly, there is class bias here. "Mrs. Gaskell" undoubtedly thought that she was describing herself when Mrs. Gibson in *Wives and Daughters* calls Molly "'a democrat in rank'" (8:724). But Gaskell is only a democrat upwards. She is always aware of class when she deals with the aristocracy. Its faults are always evident to her and she rarely misses a chance to satirize its manners and attitudes. On rare occasions she also sees class from the perspective of the workers. In *Mary Barton* and *North and South,* in a very important example, Gaskell, for instance, takes to task the masters for calling the workers "hands," as though they were only tools for profit rather than full-fledged human beings. But Gaskell is very rarely aware that she belongs to a class herself and that many of her opinions are rooted in its point of view. She takes the middle class as her norm. The middle class was, of course, her audience, but that is not the only reason Gaskell writes, for example, a passage such as this from *Mary Barton:* "The people rise up to life; they irritate us; they terrify us, and we become their enemies" (1:196). She and her readers are "we" and "us"; "the people," the workers, to her, are "they."

The most extraordinary instance, however, of Gaskell's middle-class bias is to be found in *Wives and Daughters* in her attitude to Preston. Although a man of lower rank, Preston, who works on the Cumnor estate, has managed not only to rise in the world by virtue of his affable manner, his very good looks, his great intelligence, and his great athletic ability but to gain, as Gaskell writes, "admission into much higher society than he was otherwise entitled to enter" (8:174). Everyone seems to be impressed with him. But he irritates Lady Harriet. She "'cannot bear,'" she says, a man who gives "'himself airs of gallantry towards one to whom his simple respect is all his duty' " (8:183). She means, of course, that instead of behaving as he should to a social superior, Preston treats her as an equal. Lady Harriet is a snob, but Gaskell obviously agrees when she later writes that Preston had been "presuming on his handsomeness" when he had assumed "a tone of gallant familiarity with Lady Harriet, and paid her personal compliments as he would have done to an equal" (8:618). Preston can, it is true, be unpleasant, but one might take a different view of him and see him not as an arrogant upstart but as a new kind of man, determined to make it on his merits and not altogether sure that these are not intrinsically above the merits of inherited rank. His very unpleasant-ness may be seen as part of his self-conscious struggle against the bias of society. Gaskell understands all this. It is she who created him, after all. But she cannot admit it consciously. Consciously, betraying her bias, she can only find him insolent (8:618).

There is great suffering in *Mary Barton,* and much of it could be alle-viated by regulations on employment and on conditions in the factories. But—adamant with Adam Smith on the subject of laissez-faire—"Mrs. Gaskell" opposes these. When the workers in the novel set out to bring their charter to Parliament, Gaskell, through Job Legh, suggests that the best thing they can do is ask for trade to be set free. The workers then can earn the money that, when they spend it, will stir the economy so that the masters can pay their wages, and thus begin the cycle again (1:99). One of the problems is that wages are so far below subsistence that the workers cannot survive on them, let alone make the kind of purchases that will in-vigorate the economy. Gaskell is aware of this problem, but she does not want to let the government determine the workers' pay. "Mrs. Gaskell" backs laissez-faire even when it comes to regulating how many hours children may work. A number of bills had been enacted in the thirties that had placed limits on working hours for children, but Gaskell wants these laws rescinded (1:98–99). Gaskell continues to oppose child labor laws in *North and South,* in which she shows one family starving because its chil-dren cannot work (4:158). But here, although still for laissez-faire (4:95, 393–94), Gaskell does allow exceptions. At least, for instance, she makes no comment when Bessy Higgins says that government should make laws requiring millowners to air the fluff out of their factories so that others will not contract the brown lung disease of which she is dying (4:117).

Economists of the Manchester School did not uniformly oppose unions. Harriet Martineau did not. "Mrs. Gaskell," however, does. She offers a large number of reasons, all important to the plot. Misled by passion, unions can turn to violence in their cause (1:200). The workers, united, do in fact become violent in *Mary Barton,* violent against the masters—Barton himself being assigned the task of killing the mill-owner's son—and violent too against those workers who refuse to join their ranks. One of these, Boucher, in *North and South* kills himself because he cannot resolve his difficulties with the union. And unions— "Mrs. Gaskell" protests, proving she has misunderstood the entire point of unions—do not let individuals settle with the masters for themselves. During the strike, Job Legh, for instance, says, half a loaf being better than none, he would work for lower wages. But the union will not allow him to negotiate for himself (1:228). The saintly character in the novel, Alice Wilson, hearing that John has been attending union meetings, shakes her head in great dismay (1:179). And "Mrs. Gaskell" clearly agrees with her. She still, although her position is softened, dislikes unions in *North and South.* Strikes, however, although she doubts that they can have an effect on wages, which will always find their level simply by demand and supply (4:272), she is prepared there to accept, as long as they are not divisive and bitter (4:516).

The fact that these are the views of "the world" is enough to make them Gaskell's, but there is another reason Gaskell dislikes unions and strikes, and that is that she is afraid to let the workers claim their rights. The claiming of rights always makes her nervous. When there begins to be agitation for the rights of the lower orders in "My Lady Ludlow," for instance, the title character remarks, " 'When I was a girl, one never heard of the rights of men, one only heard of the duties' " (5:59). This question of rights as opposed to duties is at the heart of one short story Gaskell published in 1849 in the *Sunday School Penny Magazine.* The story, titled "Hand and Heart," is one of Gaskell's children's stories intended chiefly to teach a lesson. But, like "Bessy's Troubles at Home," with which Gaskell herself grouped it as one of her "moral & sensible" tales (*L* 260), the lesson it teaches is revealing. The story concerns a boy named Tom, whose widowed mother, although poor, manages, by working hard, spending little, and wanting less, to be a happy, satisfied woman. When Tom one day expresses a wish for money to purchase some childish object, his mother explains to him that real good consists, not in the acquisition of things, but in the doing of good deeds. A few years pass. Tom's mother dies and he is taken in by an uncle. His uncle's house is not, however, the peaceful home his mother ran. Everyone in this house is cross, everyone is always complaining. And the reason, Gaskell explains, is that everyone is selfish, always wanting things for themselves. Tom is the only one who is not. Having learned his mother's lesson, Tom now teaches it to his aunt, who, by precept and example, turns her once frenetic household into a happy home. The moral of the tale is given when the narrator remarks that "Whenever, in a family, every one is selfish, and (as it is called) 'stands up for his own rights,' there are no feelings of gratitude; the gracefulness of 'thanks' is never called for; nor can there be any occasion for thoughtfulness for others when those others are sure to get the start in thinking for themselves, and taking care of number one" (3:554). Morally, Gaskell is calling for altruism, but altruism, as we know, is the means through which the demon must be expiated in Gaskell. The claiming of rights is to Gaskell "selfish." It is an expression of the "self," so an expression of the demon. Gaskell speaks in *North and South* precisely in these terms of unions. When Nicholas Higgins says, for example, he would rather starve than work for the lower wages that the union is requesting, he asks the heroine, Margaret Hale, why this attitude, which is acknowledged to be honorable in a soldier, should not be honorable in a weaver. Margaret replies that a soldier is selfless, dying in the cause of the nation, while a weaver, if he died, would only be standing up for himself (4:157–58). What bothers Gaskell about the union, what bothers her about the strike, is that, created to claim rights, they are assertions of the self. The strike has the added disadvantage of being a challenge to authority, which "Mrs. Gaskell" also dislikes. The workers who ask for help and kindness are handled with sympathy in her fiction. They are not to her a threat. But those who insist on claiming their rights become a daemonic force in the novel, and this very greatly disturbs "Mrs. Gaskell."

"Mrs. Gaskell's" attitude, thus, to the struggle of the workers is determined by the fact that it is for her associated with the struggle of her demon. And the answer she gives the workers is the answer she gave herself.

In *Mary Barton* and later again in *North and South* she rejects any economic solution. Money is not the problem to Gaskell, partly because she does not know enough about economic realities, partly because she is not interested in the economic ends of things, but mostly because she thinks of money not as an entity in itself, but primarily as a metaphor. Only at the end of her life, in *Wives and Daughters,* does she begin to understand it as a reality. Coral Lansbury exaggerates in saying that through the entire novel money "runs like a tarnished thread,"[7] but it is true that in *Wives and Daughters* Gaskell sees, as never before, that money can be, as in the case of Mrs. Gibson who only marries Mr. Gibson because she is in need of money, the cause of what characters say and do.

In *Mary Barton,* however, money is seen as a corrupting influence.

Most "condition-of-England" novels included an attack on mammonism. Gaskell includes such an attack not only in her industrial novels but in "The Moorland Cottage" as well, in which a secondary theme concerns, as one of the characters puts it, the " 'evils' " that have beset " 'a nation whose god is money' " (2:336). But Gaskell is more zealous than most in showing that money is corrupting. Wealth, for instance, in *Mary Barton* has completely corrupted the Carsons, Mr. Carson having turned callous, Mrs. Carson idle and bored and a hypochondriac too, and the children spoiled and selfish. Although there are a few exceptions, Gaskell generally concludes that, as long as it is not penury, poverty is better than wealth.

One of the reasons Gaskell insists money corrupts is that, if it does, she does not have to acknowledge the conflict she sees between the rich and the poor. If money were something really worth having, she would have to admit there was a reason for the classes to struggle. But Gaskell cannot deal with conflict. Every time a conflict arises, Gaskell finds a way to deny it. This is not only because she believes, as the Unitarians did, in the harmony of the universe. It is because she cannot face the conflicts of her own past. As she attempts in *Wives and Daughters* to reinterpret, through Mr. Gibson, what her father did and said, so she refuses to acknowledge that there are conflicts and collisions for which there can be no solution. Everywhere in *Mary Barton* there are irremediable clashes, but Gaskell manages to avoid them or insists they can be resolved. Thus she insists that, while it seems profits and wages are at odds, in reality they are not. Leaping right over the question of how profits are to be divided between the masters and the workers, which is really the point at issue, Gaskell says that both must realize that they rise and fall together. If there is work, they both can prosper. If there is not, they both will fall.

The real problem, Gaskell argues, far from being economic, is the personal relationship between the masters and the men. The "most deplorable . . . evil," she writes, arising out of the present conflict between the masters and the workers is the "feeling of alienation" that exists "between the . . . classes" (1:95). Money, thus, not only corrupts, it does not even address the question. What the workers want, she says, is to know that the masters care. What " 'we all,' " Job Legh remarks in a conversation with Carson, " 'feel sharpest is the want of inclination to try and help.' " All the workers want to hear, Job continues, is the masters saying " 'Poor fellows, our hearts are sore for ye' " (1:449–50). The answer, thus, for Gaskell is love. But it is clear that she is projecting into the workers her own need. She knows very well that love will not solve the real problems of the workers. In one of the scenes she writes, for instance, to illustrate her official position, the facts contradict the generalization. Some workers in this scene have gathered to help the Davenports, their neediest friends. They themselves have little to give, and one among them has nothing at all. But, the narrator intervenes with the novel's official message: offering "love-works" and "heart-service," he gave them what was "of far more value" (1:66–67). The events that follow, however, tell us this is not the case. The Davenports need food and medicine and a warm, dry place to live. Without these necessities Davenport dies and two of his children very soon after him.

The fact that Gaskell here projects into the workers her need for love makes intelligible the solution on which she comes to rest in the book. The solution is paternalism, and she is thinking of the term in its etymological sense. The master and worker are father and child. This is especially clear in one scene in which the telltale word appears that Mrs. Stevenson had used in her letter to Aunt Lumb. Job, as he explains to Carson that all the workers want is love, feels the need to excuse himself for speaking in so bold a manner. He would be loth, he says, to "vex" him (1:449). The union had vexed him, the strike had vexed him. Job does not want to vex him more. He wants to establish a relationship in which, instead of claiming their rights, the workers will earn the love of their masters. It is significant that for Gaskell the ideal worker in the novel is not a worker in the factory but the servant Alice Wilson. We know what Gaskell thinks of servants. They are the paradigmatic woman, creatures that have shed their demons. In *North and South* Gaskell almost escapes the paternalism of *Mary Barton*. Thornton is prepared to let the workers have an independent existence, claiming the right to dictate their actions only while they are at work. But Margaret protests. She calls his views "unchristian isolation" (4:141 ff.). Eventually, there is a compromise. In some distant future perhaps the workers may become independent. For now, however, they need, like children, a father who will love and direct them.

Thus did Gaskell in her first novel seek to expiate her demon. The demon, however, would not be expiated. Angry, defiant, by nature rebellious, it finds its way into the narrative despite the resistance of "Mrs. Gaskell." Its interest in economics and politics is no greater than "Mrs. Gaskell's," but its instincts are very different, and its attitudes and views are of a very different kind. It therefore becomes a subversive force, a radical voice, contradicting, challenging "Mrs. Gaskell's" official position. Much of the novel suffers, in consequence, from an ambivalence in which it seems to be arguing with itself, which, of course, is what it is doing. But while this ambivalence sometimes diminishes the quality of

Gaskell's art, it also allows us a further glimpse into the nature of Gaskell's demon.

"Mrs. Gaskell" and her demon often wrestle for the text, intruding into each other's thoughts and breaking into each other's sentences. Sometimes, just as the demon appears about to arrive at a conclusion, "Mrs. Gaskell" interrupts to prevent the subversive thought. Thus, in the Preface, just when the demon has finished describing the workers' feelings and entered so fully into their "anguish" that we are likely to take their side, "Mrs. Gaskell" leaps in to say "Whether the bitter complaints made by them . . . were well-founded or no, it is not for me to judge." Sometimes it is "Mrs. Gaskell's" narrative that is interrupted by the demon. Thus, unable to prevent "Mrs. Gaskell" from concluding that the workers are mistaken to think the masters do not care, the demon slips in a conditional. "If it be an error," it says, "that the woes, which come with ever-returning tide-like flood to overwhelm the workmen in our manufacturing towns, pass unregarded by all but the sufferers, . . . it is an error . . . so bitter in its consequence" that whatever can should be done "to disabuse the work-people of so miserable a misapprehension" (1:lxxx). The demon is never afraid to speak, however hard or bleak its conclusions, and "Mrs. Gaskell" often finds the only thing she can do to soften what her demon has to say is to interject a "seem" word. In the Preface alone, for example, which is shorter than two pages, there are the following typical instances: the "care-worn men," the narrator writes, "looked *as if*" they were "doomed to struggle"; they felt they were "tossed to and fro . . . *apparently* in even a greater degree than other men"; the poor "were sore and irritable against the rich, the even tenor of whose *seemingly* happy lives *appeared* to increase the anguish caused by the lottery-*like* nature of their own." The demon knows these things are so. But "Mrs. Gaskell" cannot admit it.

Not infrequently, however, the demon, more agile of the two, manages to usurp a paragraph—sometimes even a page or more—and "Mrs. Gaskell," unable to stop it, is thrown into a virtual panic. This, for example, occurs when the demon, having appropriated the narrative, points to the contrast in hard times between the lot of the rich and the poor. The "houses" of the rich "are still occupied," however difficult the time, "while spinners' and weavers' cottages stand empty, because the families that once occupied them are obliged to live in rooms or cellars. Carriages still roll along the streets, concerts are still crowded by subscribers, the shops for expensive luxuries still find daily customers, while the workman loiters away his unemployed time in watching these things, and thinking of the pale, uncomplaining wife at home, and the wailing children asking in vain for enough of food, of the sinking health, of the dying life of those near and dear to him. The contrast is too great. Why should he alone suffer from bad times?" (1:23). These are very dangerous thoughts, and "Mrs. Gaskell" instantly panics. "I know," she assures us, wresting the helm, "this is not really the case; and I know what is the truth in such matters; but what I wish to impress is what the workman feels and thinks. True, that with child-like improvidence, good times will often dissipate his grumbling, and make him forget all prudence and foresight." (1:24).

Gaskell herself was faintly aware that she was, on political matters, not fully at one with herself.[8] To Catherine Winkworth she once wrote "I never can ascertain what I am in politics; I veer about from extreme Right,—no, I don't think I ever go as far as the extreme Left" (*L* 29). "Mrs. Gaskell" tends to the Right. Her demon, however, is antiestablishment. "Government," she writes to George Smith in a clearly daemonic moment, "is always my '*they*'" (*L* 443).

The demon is a political radical. There is an implicitly radical purpose in how the novel presents the workers. The very fact that the novel focuses, not on the masters, but on the workers, the fact that it is with the workers we live—in their homes and in their thoughts—means that the novel makes us see the world as they see it, through their eyes. The novel, in fact, is extremely visual. Nowhere in all of Gaskell's fiction are we made to "see" so much, and greatly as this enhances the narrative, vivifies the story and characters, the ultimate reason for the visual is essentially political. Gaskell herself tells us as much. When Carson claims that in bad times the rich suffer as much as the poor, Job replies "'Not so much, I'm sure, sir; though I'm not given to Political Economy, I know that much. I'm wanting in learning, I'm aware; but I can use my eyes'" (1:447). Job is clearly Gaskell's voice here. His admission that he is ignorant of political economy echoes Gaskell's in the Preface. But his eyes show him the truth that disproves what Carson says. Gaskell had been a witness herself to most of what she depicts in her novel, and by showing us what she saw, she lets us also see the truth that refutes the official position on which "Mrs. Gaskell" stands.

For what we see is pain and suffering. There is almost nothing else. The grimmest scene perhaps in the book occurs when John Barton and George Wilson go to visit the Davenports. The demon walks us through the streets to the cellar the Davenports live in. The streets are "unpaved; and down the middle a gutter forced its way. . . . As they passed, women from their doors tossed household slops of *every* description into the gutter." The "putrid" conditions have brought about a dreadful typhoid epidemic, and all the Davenports are ill. The cellar to which they had to move when Davenport, laid off at the mill, could not pay their rent on their cottage, is cold and "dark." "The window-panes were many of them broken and stuffed with rags, . . . and the smell so foetid as almost to knock the two men down." We see "three or four little children . . . rolling on the damp, nay wet, brick floor, through which the stagnant, filthy moisture of the street oozed up." The wife is crying. When Barton gives her the piece of bread that he has brought to alleviate their hunger, she is so weak the effort to take it causes her to collapse on the floor. Davenport himself is lying on "straw, so damp and mouldy no dog would have chosen it in preference to flags" (1:65–70). The misery is unalleviated. And even "Mrs. Gaskell" here does not try to make us think it is inevitable or deserved.

Not every home is as bad as the Davenports' but there is none that is very good. Hunger is everywhere. There is not much food in the best of times, and in the worst there is literally none. Workers get drunk so as not to feel hungry and give opium to their children to alleviate their pangs. Barton remembers seeing a father kill his own child so it would not suffer the agony of death by starvation. And he, Barton adds, " 'were a tender-hearted man' " (1:217). Death is no easier than life. The undertaker, for example, takes advantage of Mrs. Ogden, the widow of one of the workers who dies, forcing her to go into debt (1:49). And Davenport, although he had paid for years a monthly fee to a burial club, having missed the last few payments after he has lost his job, is not even given a funeral. For him there is only a pauper's grave. Gaskell not only describes this grave, she gives a footnote for the description, assuring the reader that this was the case, "to my certain knowledge" at least in one churchyard in Manchester. The "pauper bodies" are "piled up within a foot or two of the surface." Then "the soil" is "shovelled over, and stamped down, and the wooden cover" goes "to do temporary duty over another hole" (1:80–81).

Conditions at work are not much better. Sometimes they seem much worse, in fact. Employment is never very certain. Those who are working, work long hours. When they grow tired, they have accidents, especially since the repair of machinery is, being costly and not profitable, something the masters try to avoid. Many workers hobble about, having been maimed by their equipment or lost limbs to the machinery that the masters did not repair. And, of course, there is always the lint, the fine cotton lint that fills the air with particles that the workers swallow, causing the brown lung disease from which many are suffering. There is some health care, but it is primitive, and entirely in the hands of the masters, who dispense it in a careless and arbitrary manner. Carson, for instance, likes to save infirmary orders for serious accidents. When Wilson, one Friday, comes to ask for an order to bring Davenport to the infirmary immediately, Carson suggests he wait for Monday (1:77–78). By Monday, Davenport is dead.

We cannot be made to "see" these things without feeling a moral outrage that calls for radical solutions. And that is what the demon wants. "Mrs. Gaskell" is laissez-faire, but her demon, in these conditions, wants to lend a helping hand. Carson and Job are made at one point to debate this very issue. Carson asks Job whether it is not better for everyone to be independent, to rely on himself. Job replies, we must help one another (1:448). Cazamian may see too unequivocal a position in the novel when he remarks that Gaskell wants the "law to step in,"[9] but there are moments in the novel in which the narrative calls implicitly for some form of legislation. We learn, for instance, that Mrs. Wilson, when she had worked as a girl in the factory before the government had stepped in to enact some safety regulations, had been crippled by a wheel (1:100). Barton has already reported that the surgeon at the infirmary had mentioned to him that most accidents occur in the last two hours of work, when the workers are too tired to be careful with the machinery (1:93). One of the things he intends to do when he takes the charter to London is to ask Parliament to pass a " 'short-hours' bill" so that the workers can go home before they maim themselves out of weariness (1:97).

It would be an exaggeration to say that Gaskell's demon was a communist. Yet many of those who felt that Gaskell had been too partial to the workers called her a socialist and a communist, and while the words in the 1840s carried different connotations, their meaning was similar for the most part to the meaning they have today. Gaskell said that she was neither, that she was only a good "Christian" (*L* 69). Movements like "Christian Socialism" saw the ideas, it is true, of Christianity as leading to something essentially socialistic, and Gaskell was tremendously attracted both to the movement and to its members—Francis Newman, J. A. Froude, and "my *hero*," Charles Kingsley (*L* 55). But the idea of taking Christianity to so literal a conclusion in economic and political ways is a radical one itself. Little moments of "Christian Socialism" are to be found throughout *Mary Barton*. Barton, at the beginning of the novel, asks, for instance, " 'does the rich man share his plenty with me, as he ought to do, if his religion is not a humbug?' " (1:8). And Job remarks at the end that Barton had found it difficult to reconcile great wealth with Christ's gospel

(1:446). But this is only a very small part of the communistic tendencies that we find in Gaskell's demon. Much more often, and this is not entailed in "Christian Socialism" at all, the demon writes something of this sort: "At all times it is a bewildering thing to the poor weaver to see his employer removing from house to house, each one grander than the last, till he ends in building one more magnificent than all, or withdraws his money from the concern, or sells his mill to buy an estate in the country, while all the time the weaver, *who thinks he and his fellows are the real makers of this wealth,* is struggling on for bread for their children, through the vicissitudes of lowered wages, short hours, fewer hands employed, &xc." (1:59; italics mine). The view that the workers make the wealth and should share equally in the profits is repeated in *North and South* (4:159). And some of the workers who speak for the demon add that, just as the masters have a capital in the money they invest, so do the workers have a capital in the labor they contribute. And they should be able to draw interest on it like the masters (1:72). Greg does not, in his review, doubt that Gaskell meant that wealth should be considered the joint production of capital and labor.[10] The Manchester School was opposed to the notion that profits should be distributed equally to the masters and the men, and "Mrs. Gaskell" fully agreed. The demon, however, saw it differently.

The demon, in fact, seems to be ready for revolution in *Mary Barton*. Leaving the Davenports' cellar, for instance, Barton finds himself on the street walking by expensive shops whose windows are filled with expensive provisions. Looking in, John Barton "felt the contrast between the well-filled, well-lighted shops and the dim gloomy cellar, and it made him moody that such contrasts should exist. . . . He wondered if any in all the hurrying crowd, had come from such a house of mourning. He thought they all looked joyous, and he was angry with them" (1:69–70). Hearing Barton speak these words, "Mrs. Gaskell" panics again, jumping into the text to say: "you cannot . . . read the lot of those who daily pass you by in the street. How do you know the wild romances of their lives; the trials, the temptations they are even now enduring, resisting, sinking under?" (1:69–70). But it is clear the demon is angry. Anger is always a sign of the demon. It is never hard to tell, in Gaskell's political positions, even when they are very similar, which is the demon's and which "Mrs. Gaskell's." It is "Mrs. Gaskell," for instance, who writes to Charles Eliot Norton to tell him that she stands with him in the American Civil War. Generous, kind, compassionate, caring, "Mrs. Gaskell" like her demon takes the side of the downtrodden, but the gentle words in which sympathy is expressed for the slave tell us the letter to Norton is hers (*L* 384). "Mrs. Gaskell" certainly sympathizes with the American "Indian" no less than with the American slave, but it is the demon's voice that we hear in "Lois the Witch" when the narrator conveys the thoughts of the "Indian" woman, Nattee, hired to care for the Hickson girls. Gathering the girls to tell them a story, Nattee, the narrator writes, takes "a strange, unconscious pleasure in her power over her hearers—young girls of the oppressing race, which had brought her down into a state little differing from slavery, and reduced her people to outcasts on the hunting-grounds which had belonged to her fathers" (7:134). In "Traits and Stories of the Huguenots," it is "Mrs. Gaskell" again we hear in the kindly, liberal tone of her defense of the persecuted. But in "An Accursed Race," which Gaskell published in *Household Words* in August of 1855 and in which she deals with the Cagots, another persecuted race, we hear the angry voice of the demon. In "Traits and Stories," Gaskell calls for "Mrs. Gaskell's" usual remedies, tolerance and understanding. But in "An Accursed Race," the demon agitates for revenge (5:222). Gaskell even gives gory details, reporting that the Cagots, for instance, having fought and won one battle, withdrew to relax by playing ninepins with their enemies' bloody heads (5:222).

The demon seems here prepared for violence. "Mrs. Gaskell" was pacific, but the demon in her fiction accepts violence as a natural expression of political frustration. Alluding to the French Revolution, which "Mrs. Gaskell" always condemns, the demon, for instance, in "My French Master" accepts the revolution as being the product of "the silent horrors endured for centuries by the people, who at length rose in madness against the rulers" (2:513). The demon speaks in a similar manner in *The Life of Charlotte Brontë*. There we are told that Charlotte's teacher Miss Wooler remembered "when the people of England, represented by the workers of Yorkshire, Lancashire, and Nottinghamshire, were being trained for the day when they should make their voice heard in a terrible slogan, since their true and pitiful complaints could find no hearing in parliament" (*LCB*, p. 92). The demon is completely fascinated by the Camorra, the secret society formed in Naples during the Bourbon occupation to resist the French oppressor, on which Gaskell wrote the essay "An Italian Institution," which she published in *All the Year Round* in March of 1863. Ostensibly formed for self-protection, the Camorra soon became as bloody as the oppressing French. But the demon admires its courage, and its dedication to freedom,[11] just as, in "Modern Greek

Songs," it admires the people called Klephts, Greeks who resisted, often violently, the occupation of the Turks.

The demon not only accepts revolution, it rather imagines itself as leading one. Gaskell always took to rebels. The coming of Louis Kossuth to Manchester sent her into a virtual tizzy. I intend, she writes to Eliza Fox, to see him "by hook or by crook" (*L* 51). Her heroes are men like Garibaldi, for a book about whom Gaskell wrote a dedicatory preface.[12] In the summer of 1854, Gaskell, using one of the phrases that she was to use in the *Life of Charlotte Brontë* in the passage I quoted above, wrote to Eliza Fox she had heard someone say that Manchester seemed "on the verge of a precipice." Gaskell continues: "I don't know what they meant; but don't be surprised if you hear of a rising of the weavers, headed by a modern Boadicea" (*L* 206). It is not hard to picture the demon leading an angry people to war.

But this is too much for "Mrs. Gaskell." She cannot sanction revolution, and while we are often on the verge of that precipice in *Mary Barton,* the revolution never takes place. But something equivalent to it does. In the metaphoric language that the demon always uses, there are insurrections everywhere. The plot itself is insurrectionary in the sense that it erupts into wild, outrageous incidents. Gaskell herself is well aware that such incidents have no place in her realistic tales. Commenting on the art of fiction in *The Life of Charlotte Brontë,* Gaskell observes it is "but a poor kind of" plot that depends "upon startling incidents rather than upon dramatic development of character" (*LCB*, p. 255). But she really has no choice. As soon as "Mrs. Gaskell" refuses to let events take their natural course, the demon explodes into the text. Many of these explosive moments have no connection with the narrative. They are simply dramatizations of one of Gaskell's daemonic metaphors. One daemonic metaphor dramatized is the fire of chapter 5. Fire, as we recall, for Gaskell is a metaphor for passion, and passion is often in her fiction embodied in a sexual way. Gaskell here describes the fire in an openly sexual manner. The fire, she writes, for instance, at one point, "sent forth its infernal tongues from every window hole, licking the black walls with amorous fierceness." She might be describing a fallen woman to whom, it is clear that in her mind, the fire here is very close kin. It is also close kin to Boadicea. At other moments in the description, Gaskell sees the fire as rising, as though it were a conquering king, as a crown from the mill, "triumphant" (1:55). In *North and South* the demon identifies itself in the fire even more explicitly. Here the narrator explains that the fire has been ignited, set as it has been by the men who are angry with their master, by the "passion" of the workers (4:210). There is a riot here as well, and, describing the savage crowd as it attacks the mill "mad for prey" (4:210), Gaskell calls its howl the voice of "demoniac desire" (4:209).

The closest we come to a real revolution in *Mary Barton* is the murder of young Henry Carson. The workers and the masters have met and not only has the meeting produced no resolution of their conflicts, young Henry Carson has sat through the meeting sketching caricatures of the men. Later the workers find these caricatures, and they are understandably outraged. So is Gaskell, as she suggests when she describes these drawings as mockeries (1:213). When the workers afterwards gather to discuss their futile meeting, Barton begins to speak to the group, saying the masters are responsible for the suffering they endure and, since they cannot be made to listen, they surely ought to be made to pay. The workers are desperate. They agree. They settle that the act of revenge will be to kill the man who ridiculed them. To see who will do it, they draw lots, and the assignment falls to Barton. Gaskell picks Barton because for her—I disagree here with Kathleen Tillotson, who holds that Barton is not meant as a type[13]—he is the embodiment of the workers. The narrator, introducing Barton, calls him "a thorough specimen of a Manchester man" (1:4). Every deprivation and insult Barton undergoes in the novel represents one of the sufferings that the workers must endure. And the growth of Barton's rage parallels the desperation and frustration of the workers. In committing the murder, therefore, Barton is acting for the class. And he is acting for Gaskell's demon. Gaskell from the very beginning describes him as a daemonic man. There is a "vehemence" in his manner, there is a "fire" in his eye (1:8). And, as sorrow follows sorrow and one calamity upon another, these develop into an obsession against the indifference of the rich, a "monomania," Gaskell calls it (1:194). In the violence, in the murder, Barton thus becomes for Gaskell the Boadicea she dare not be.

There are a good many men in Gaskell who express their demon violently. The Squire in "The Squire's Story" is a typical example. The one that most resembles Barton is, however, the protagonist of the story "The Heart of John Middleton." Having lost his mother early and been mistreated by his father, Middleton is clearly intended to be Gaskell's surrogate self. And, as Gaskell felt she had, he must pay for the sins of his father. His father had been not only vicious but a drunkard and a criminal, and it is because of his crimes that, when Middleton grows up and goes to work in the local factory, he finds himself the object of hatred, especially by one fellow worker. Middleton is a daemonic man. He has, we are told, a terrible "temper" (2:392). And he is furious when this worker, named Dick Jackson, calls him names. His hatred of Jackson, Gaskell writes using one of her daemonic images, "raged like a fire" (2:390). He wants revenge, and when he sees that for the moment he cannot have it, he, like his father, begins to drink and to commit crimes (2:390). Eventually he discovers religion and a good woman who reforms him. They have a daughter, whom they call Grace, as angelic as her mother. Many years later, when Dick Jackson, purely by chance, arrives at his door, his wife, in the spirit of Christian forgiveness, persuades him not to take the revenge for which all these years he has been waiting.

Except for the ending, which transforms him, Middleton is full of the anger that is seething in John Barton. And, as Gaskell makes it obvious by giving Middleton her own history, it is the anger she felt herself. But Barton and Middleton not only act as daemonic surrogates for Gaskell, they are daemonic projections as well of their daughters and their wives. This is a common pattern in Gaskell. A woman often projects her demon into one of the men in her family. His violent deeds act her own demon out. To understand this pattern, however, we must consider another distinction Gaskell makes between the roles that she assigns to women and men.

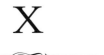

X

Men Do, Women Are

THE CHARACTERISTICS GASKELL DESIGNATES as especially male or female are for her not necessarily embodied in a man or a woman. There is a prima facie connection between a person's sex and gender—and I use this latter term, although it is strictly a term in grammar, simply because it serves to distinguish between psychological and physical sex and has recently gained some currency—but the connection is not invariable or insoluble in Gaskell. It can be loosened. It often is. In many of her characters, therefore, sex and gender are dissociated, and we have to examine the circumstances in the individual instance before we can be sure who is which. The point, however, is not androgyny. Male and female are, for Gaskell, entirely different from one another. In her stereotypical way, Gaskell always assigns her characters, of whatever sex they are, characteristics that belong to one or to the other gender. And her distinctions are not limited by any means to people alone. Places, feelings, ideas, conditions, and a good many other things also have genders in her fiction. To an extent this is not unusual. Most societies, making divisions between what men and women do, distinguish their activities also, and many of Gaskell's associations are those common in her day. Courage, for example, is male. Charity, however, is female. Men have the right to express their feelings; women, by implication, do not (4:253).

Most of the metaphors Gaskell uses have genders in a similar manner. The demon is unequivocally male. Made of the passions she denied in creating "Mrs. Gaskell," the demon is "Mrs. Gaskell's" antithesis. As she is the ideal woman, the demon is the unideal man. It is significant that Gaskell—clustering metaphors, as she does—thinks of France, the land of passion and in consequence of the demon, always as a male domain just as she thinks of England as female. It is common in her fiction for male characters to be French and for female to be English. The narrator's parents in "My French Master" are divided in this way. In "the Grey Woman," there is again a man who, being daemonic, is French and a woman who is German, Germany being another country that is for Gaskell female like England.

The most important distinction for Gaskell between the female and the male is to be found in her description, in *The Life of Charlotte Brontë,* of the different lots awaiting Branwell and the Brontë girls. "There are always," Gaskell writes, "peculiar trials in the life of an only boy in a family of girls. He is expected to act a part in life; to do, while they are only to *be*" (*LCB,* p. 153). Gaskell had used these very words, also italicized, years earlier, in her conclusion to "The Moorland Cottage," in which she had eulogized Mrs. Buxton, a woman who would be, she wrote, remembered as one "who could *do* but little during her lifetime; who was doomed only to 'stand and wait'; who was meekly content to *be* gentle, holy, patient, and undefiled" (2:383). Men do, women are.

"The Moorland Cottage" develops this notion further when Mrs. Buxton attempts, being herself ideally feminine, to teach Maggie to become heroic in a female way. Maggie, like most of Gaskell's girls, begins with daemonic characteristics. She wants to play a heroic part, but she envisions herself in the role of someone who acts like a Joan of Arc. Joan of Arc was, of course, a woman, but not to Gaskell a female type. Mrs. Buxton tries, instead, to teach Maggie what she calls "noiseless" heroism by reminding her of women who have gone "through life quietly, with holy purposes in their hearts, to which they gave up pleasure and ease, in a soft, still succession of resolute days" (2:296). "Mrs. Gaskell" suggests that Maggie, nagged and mistreated by her mother, "showed no little heroism" herself "in bearing meekly what she did every day" (2:296). A woman, thus, it is implied here, should not seek to act heroically. She must teach herself to endure, to invest her heroism in being.

Even a man, if he is female, must learn to realize his heroism, not in *doing,* but in *being.* This is the lesson Gaskell seeks to teach in her story "The Sexton's Hero," a tale she published in *Howitt's Journal* in September of 1847. The story concerns a man named Dawson who, being extremely religious, refuses to fight for the woman he loves when he is challenged by the sexton. The woman marries the sexton instead, and Dawson is branded a coward by everyone. He proves, however, he is not when, at the cost of his own life, he saves the sexton and his wife, who are about to drown in a flood. Leaping into the water, of course, Dawson is engaged in *doing,* but this is not his heroic moment. It is the moment only in which the sexton suddenly comes to realize that what was really heroic in Dawson was his initial refusal to fight and, even more, his quiet endurance of the contempt in which he was held all those years he was thought a coward. Having been feminized by religion, Dawson must for Gaskell become heroic in a female way. The sexton who, on Dawson's death, acquires his copy of the Bible and is converted to its ways, is feminized himself in turn. It is to preach this female heroism that he writes the story, in fact.

Nowhere in all of Gaskell's fiction is the idea that women *are* embodied as fully as in *Cranford,* a work that began as a single short story entitled "The Last Generation in England" and appearing in *Sartain's Union Magazine* in July of 1849, but that, growing by installments published irregularly in *Household Words* between December of 1851 and May of 1853, reached the length of a short novel. The work is unusual in many ways, not in the patterns it reveals, but in the forms the patterns take. Generally, Gaskell does not, for instance, physically isolate what she sees as the male and female worlds. Most of her settings mix the two. But in *Cranford* she creates a place that is entirely female. There is, as well, a male place in the neighboring town of Drumble, but neither she nor we go there. We only hear of it now and then. To the extent that events in Drumble have an effect on events in Cranford, Drumble is important in the narrative. It is important too as a guide to the genders Gaskell assigns to a variety of *doings,* since she considers exclusively male all the activities of Drumble. Drumble is a large manufacturing town, concerned with business and with money, both of which are here defined as exclusively male domains. We know that money in Gaskell's mind is associated with love. Here we learn that men and women have different relationships to the image. Women need love. Men have it to give. And since the possession of love is male, so is the possession of money. The Cranford ladies know nothing of money. They never mention it, in fact (2:3). They know nothing of business either. The "most earnest and serious business" for the ladies of Cranford are card games, of which they are, in fact, very fond (2:80). Whenever a woman attempts to deal with money or business in Cranford, she fails. Thus, the heroine, Miss Matty, loses her money because her sister, rejecting advice from a Drumble businessman, invested their inheritance herself. Inevitably, the bank she chose for their investment goes bankrupt.

The man whose advice Miss Matty's sister would not take is the narrator's father. Gaskell must have begun the story not intending to make the narrator more than a formal figure through whom she would be able to tell her tale. At the beginning she is peripheral, mostly a witness to the events and only minimally a participant. She does not even acquire a name until we are halfway through the book, at which time she is called Mary Smith (2:164). But, as she kept on adding installments, Gaskell must have come to see her as an individual character. Little by little she gains a voice, then an actual personality, and eventually even a history. And it is obvious, as she develops, that Gaskell projects in Mary Smith her recollection of herself when she was about eighteen. The focus is on the usual details. Her mother is dead, her father is living, as Gaskell's was when she was eighteen. And her manner, which is kindly, gentle, funny, charming, sweet, yet incisive, shrewd, and impish, is exactly Gaskell's own.

Mary is a Drumble resident. Every so often, however, she feels the need to get away to Cranford. And this is the very need that drives Gaskell herself to write the tale. Since Drumble is male, it is the place in which, for Gaskell, the demon lives. There, she must always face confrontation, an endless struggle against her self. Therefore, like Mary Smith, she needs every so often to escape. She needs to get away from her demon to a completely female world, a world that does not threaten, that is, the composure of "Mrs. Gaskell." Gaskell created such a world for herself in her actual life. As Haldane has rightly pointed out, within her large circle of friends there was a very special group—Eliza Fox, the Winkworth sisters, Parthenope Nightingale, Mary Mohl, and a number of others as well—that consisted wholly of women. A similar circle exists in *Cranford,* some of the characters being modeled perhaps on people she knew in Manchester, others undoubtedly recreated out of the elderly ladies of Knutsford.

The town itself, whatever the source of the individual characters, is, as a fictional setting, a metaphor for the female place in the mind. That is why it is literally female.[1] As Mary observes in her opening sentence, "In the first place, Cranford is in possession of the Amazons; all the holders of houses above a certain rent are women. If a married couple come to settle in the town, somehow the gentleman disappears; he is either fairly frightened to death by being the only man in the Cranford evening parties, or he is accounted for by being with his regiment, his ship, or closely engaged in business all the week in the great neighbouring commercial town of Drumble" (2:1). Nothing seems less Amazonian than the little old ladies of Cranford, but Gaskell knows what she wants to say. The ladies of Cranford are Amazonian, not because they are large or powerful, but because they have banished men, because they have exiled the male principle.

The making of this female place is the central point of the story. If the incremental installments have a unifying theme, it is the freeing of Miss Matty, who embodies the female spirit, from the domination of men. Miss Matty is Gaskell's ideal woman. She has a fairly limited intellect. " 'I never,' " she says, " 'feel as if my mind was what people call very strong' " (2:151). But she has "patience," "humility," "sweetness" (2:158). She is the stuff of which, in Gaskell, is made the angel in the house. Her sister,

Deborah, a different type, to whom I shall return in a moment, had dreamed as a girl of marrying an archdeacon so that she could write his charges, but Matty had had a different wish. " 'I was never ambitious,' " she says, " 'nor could I have written charges, but I thought I could manage a house (my mother used to call me her right hand), and I was always so fond of little children' " (2:128–29). In time she does in fact become—although she does not ever marry—an angel to those who live in her house: her servant, her servant's husband, and their child. And, like Ruth, she even extends her role as an angel to the community. When she discovers the bank has failed in which her money was invested, she insists on using her savings to help the bank pay the creditors back, even though she is, by doing so, left virtually without an income (2:151). Miss Matty is not at all competitive. On deciding to open a shop, since she has nothing now to live on, she asks the shopkeeper in the neighborhood whether her shop would threaten his trade (2:173–74). Gaskell, who does not like to imagine the conflict of a competitive market, insists that cooperation is possible even when, as it would be here, the supply is doubled and the demand on each shop is therefore halved. The two establish a happy relationship. He sends customers to her shop, helping her to earn a living, and suffers no injury to himself. Competition, of course, is male, and cooperation, female. The very last paragraph of the story is a eulogy on Miss Matty not unlike the one erected for "Mrs. Gaskell" by the congregation. Miss Matty has now brought together the factions that had of late developed in Cranford. "Ever since," Mary Smith writes, "that day there has been the old friendly sociability in Cranford society; which I am thankful for, because of my dear Miss Matty's love of peace and kindliness. We all love Miss Matty, and I somehow think we are all of us better when she is near us" (2:192). Miss Matty, living in "quiet contentment," as we are told, "with all that she could not *do,*" is obviously satisfied to *be* (2:158; italics mine).

Miss Matty, however, has all her life been under the domination of males. First, she had been oppressed by her father, who had ruled with an iron hand. Then she had been oppressed by her sister, who, when he died, had assumed his place, insisting, in fact, that things be done just as they had been " 'in my father, the rector's house' " (2:31). To Gaskell, Deborah is a male character. Her clothing is always described in male terms. The first time we see her, for example, she is wearing "a cravat" and a "bonnet like a jockey-cap" (2:14). Another covering for her head is a hat that looks like a "helmet" (2:21). She has, moreover, a manner so military, it makes her look "like a dragoon" (2:24,143). And, to confirm her masculinity, she prefers Dr. Johnson to Dickens, *Rasselas* to *The Pickwick Papers* (2:10–11). For Gaskell, writers are metaphors too. As Margaret Ganz has rightly said, Johnson embodies order, reason. Dickens embodies imagination, spontaneity, and feeling.[2] They are the male and female worlds. Captain Brown, a female character as Deborah Jenkyns is male, is an ardent admirer of Dickens. When he expresses his admiration for *The Pickwick Papers* to her, Deborah replies " 'I must say, I don't think they are by any means equal to Dr. Johnson. Still, perhaps, the author is young. Let him persevere, and who knows what he may become if he will take the great Doctor for his model' " (2:10). Being "the more decided character" (2:145), Deborah tyrannizes over Matty. It is "astonishing," says the narrator, "how such people carry the world before them by the mere force of will" (2:145). Even her memory, after she dies, continues to intimidate Matty. But slowly she begins to free herself. Slowly she begins to act, not as her father and Deborah had wished, but as she considers best. Her acts of independence are small but significant to Gaskell. Deborah held smoking in abhorrence. Miss Matty, however, when she is asked, agrees to fill Mr. Holbrook's pipe, taking his request, in fact, as a compliment to herself (2:40). She summons the courage to pick out the silk for a new gown she is to have made, and this is the first time in her life she has ever chosen "anything of consequence for herself" (2:145). And she begins to read Charles Dickens (2:27). In many ways, Miss Matty proves, subservient though she had always been, more independent than her sister. She is not tied to convention as much. When Lady Glenmire is betrothed to the surgeon, Mr. Hoggins, whom everyone considers "vulgar" (2:138–39), Miss Matty, who had always liked him, is the first to congratulate the pair (2:152).

There is in all this something truly wonderful, but there is also something unreal. Gaskell makes clear in many ways that Cranford is a land of fantasy. The magic show that comes to town, and which the ladies of Cranford attend, is a symbolic representation of the way things work in Cranford. Miss Pole, the soul of reason and logic, tries to expose the magic as trickery. The fact that she fails suggests that Gaskell intends us to accept the magic as the ruling law of the town. Many events are indeed inexplicable, not the least of which is the fact that men keep disappearing in Cranford. But even those that can be explained are so unlikely in many cases that they seem to be just as magical. Thus, when Jessie Brown, for instance, another of the Cranford ladies, is left helpless and alone after her father and sister die, the lover she had once rejected reappears to propose again. His explanation, that he read, while he was traveling through Rome, a notice of her father's death (2:25–26), is preposterous, unbelievable, but everyone does believe it in Cranford because that is how things in Cranford work.

Gaskell clearly enjoys creating this world that violates probability. But she is also fully aware that she is hiding from the truth. Her portrait of Miss Matty, for instance, warm and loving as it is, is not of a representative woman who is whole in her female self. The fact that Miss Matty had wished to marry and had been, by her father and sister, prevented from accepting Holbrook suggests that Gaskell has conceived her as a female who has been forcibly wrested from the male. Gaskell seems to realize too that there is a certain cowardice in Miss Matty's isolation. Miss Matty not only repudiates men, she is positively afraid of them (2:29–30). She even fears to open her shop because she thinks that men might come into it (2:171). The thought of a sexual encounter terrifies her even more, even when it is not hers. Before she hires her as a maid, Miss Matty insists that Martha promise she will not acquire a follower (2:43). Martha does, but breaks her word, and Miss Matty is utterly shocked when she hears kissing at the front door one evening when Martha returns home (2:72). Even sexually suggestive activities can intimidate Miss Matty. She likes, for instance, to suck her oranges, but she is reluctant to do so except in the privacy of her room (2:31). Like Mr. Bradshaw, who is outraged when Ruth lets Elizabeth walk in the sun, Miss Matty is afraid of sunshine. She covers her carpets with pieces of newspaper, which she moves around all day in order to keep the sun off her carpet (2:16–17). And when she goes to visit Holbrook, Miss Matty cannot use a knife to help pick up the peas from her plate (2:40).

The knife is, of course, a phallic symbol, and Martin Dodsworth is right in part to read such incidents in the narrative in a loosely Freudian way.[3] But Matty's fear of sexuality is, in Gaskell's metaphoric vocabulary, a fear of her daemonic self. This is emphasized in Holbrook, another character whose gender has no relation to his sex. A man whose house is filled with books, most of which are novels and poetry, and who lives an instinctual life (2:41), Holbrook to Gaskell is a female. The action shows he is, in fact, a surrogate for Miss Matty herself, carrying the metaphoric progression, as in a relay, the next step forward. Miss Matty's visit to Holbrook brings her, as though on the first lap of a journey, for the first time in many decades, into a relationship with a man, the very man she might have married had her family not objected. Unable to wield the knife, however, Miss Matty cannot go any further. Holbrook, therefore, continues for her. Immediately after this visit from Matty, Holbrook, to everyone's surprise, suddenly decides to go to Paris. France, of course, is the land of passion, and his trip makes the connection that Miss Matty could not make. His trip, however, also kills him. He dies as soon as he returns. In Gaskell's usual way in this narrative, no explanation is ever given. But no explanation is really necessary. The connection is metaphoric between Paris and Holbrook's death. Miss Pole is metaphorically right when she apostrophizes the city as she alludes to Holbrook's death as " 'that wicked Paris, where they are always having revolutions' " (2:47). A surrogate for Miss Matty, Holbrook had attempted to claim his demon. But demons in Gaskell can be dangerous, and his attempt had killed him instead. The demon kills another female that is embodied in a man when another phallic symbol, the railroad that is being built (over the vehement objections of the Cranford ladies, of course) kills Captain Brown, a female spirit. Brown, as it happens, works on the railroad, which would suggest he is a male, but the fact that he loves Dickens is the real clue to his gender. Dickens is in fact what kills him. Pausing to read *The Pickwick Papers* while he is working on the railroad, Brown is so startled when a child runs out on the track that, in trying to save it, he is struck by an oncoming train (2:19–20).

This is one of the many incidents in which the demon suddenly surfaces, proving it is not only cowardly but impossible to escape. The demon will not go away. Even in this female place, the demon can, at most, be hidden. Many daemonic males in fact do turn out to be hidden in Cranford. Some of them are hidden literally. Martha, for instance, hides her lover, since she has been forbidden followers, in the scullery of her kitchen whenever anyone enters the room (2:30). Similarly, males are hidden in the substratum of Cranford society. If "gentlemen were scarce, and almost unheard of in the 'genteel society' of Cranford, they or their counterparts—handsome young men—abounded in the lower classes" (2:30). The demon manages to hide even in the female mind. Miss Matty, for instance, is convinced there is "a man under her bed" who is waiting to grab her leg as she attempts at night to climb into it. Therefore, before she goes to sleep, she rolls a ball under the bed, and even if it meets no obstruction and comes out on the other side, she gets into bed with a running leap (2:118). All the ladies of Cranford at one point believe that there are burglars in town, and it is metaphorically significant that they believe the burglars are French (2:107–8).

The magic of Cranford lets Gaskell imagine that dreams and wishes can come true. Thus, Peter Jenkyns, Miss Matty's brother who had run away to sea never to be heard of again, returns at the end of the story miraculously, just as Gaskell undoubtedly hoped her brother, John, would one day return. The Stevensons had never learned what had actually happened to John, and they had always continued to hope that he was still alive and well. Gaskell's grandson, Bryan Holland, the son of Gaskell's daughter Marianne, claimed the family always thought John had been captured by pirates,[4] and Chadwick reports it was thought he might have gone ashore at Calcutta.[5] In what may well have been the last letter he was to write to his sister, John did mention that he was thinking of settling permanently in India.[6] Gaskell obviously hoped he had. This is where Mary finds Peter Jenkyns. When she happens to hear of an Englishman who has gained wealth and fame in India, she decides this must be Peter and writes to urge him to come home. Against all odds, she proves to be right, and, like many other sailors who disappear in Gaskell's fiction but are finally found again, Peter, as if by magic, returns.

The magic is enormously satisfying, but by making all things possible, it makes all possibilities meaningless. Make-believe answers in a make-believe world cannot help Gaskell find a place for her real self in the realm of reality. Cranford in the end proves sterile. Placing no limits on invention, it seems extremely creative at first, but as Gaskell herself suggests in the title of the story with which the narrative began, Cranford is a town in which "generation" is not possible. The story, in a comic way, reminds us a little of Joyce's "The Dead." Women may bear and nourish children, as Martha does indeed at the end, but only if they are nourished themselves by the demon, which is male.

That is why Cranford must finally change, why males must finally be admitted. Lady Glenmire marries Hoggins, and Martha, Miss Matty's servant, Jem. When Miss Matty loses her money, they in fact take over the house, not only providing a place where Miss Matty can live although she has lost her income but metaphorically repossessing for "generation" her sterile house. And the circle of Cranford ladies takes Peter Jenkyns into its midst (2:185). Peter Jenkyns is the character in whom Gaskell most clearly suggests the fact that fertility in Cranford requires the agency of a male. Peter, although not androgynous either, is both a male and a female character. This is made evident in an incident that is at the heart of his story, for it is in consequence of it he quarrels with his father and sister and decides to go to sea. As a young boy, Peter had once, dressed in an old gown of Deborah's, paraded up and down the street cradling a pillow in his arms as though it were a newborn baby (2:62–63). The act had been metaphoric, of course. The other two children, Deborah and Matty, are exclusively male or female. Peter, the third, has brought together the male and the female in himself. And this, the fusion of the two, is what he restores to Cranford. The Cranford circle, by taking him in, accepts in its midst—and indeed at its center, for Peter becomes the general favorite— the notion of an integrated whole.

XI

It Must Be a Fine
Thing to Be a Man

"MRS. GASKELL" MAY HAVE FOUND a refuge in her female place. The demon, however, found in it a prison. This is the point of "The Cage at Cranford," the sequel that Gaskell wrote to *Cranford* and published in *All the Year Round* in November of 1863. The cage of the title refers to a crinoline that arrives one day in Cranford. The ladies of Cranford, having never seen anything of its kind before, have no idea what to make of it. It looks like a birdcage, and they decide they will use it for that purpose. Their error makes the story amusing. What makes it serious is that they are right. As a symbol of femininity, the crinoline is indeed a cage, and the woman placed inside it is in reality a caged bird. Gaskell often uses birds to speak of freedom and imprisonment. Ruth, for example, at Mrs. Mason's is "a bird" that is described as pressing "against the bars of its cage" (3:4). When she is liberated by Bellingham in the scene beside the pool, Gaskell remarks on the birds in the grove—on the linnets, the water wagtails—all of which are singing and free (3:51). When, however, she moves to Eccleston, once again she is a caged bird. This is suggested in a scene that takes place in the Benson's garden. Sitting in the garden, Ruth is surrounded by a wall (3:139), just as though she were in prison. Outside "winged songsters" sing, and she can hear them "rejoice" in their freedom. One of these birds even casts its shadow on the wall as it rises in flight. But she remains enclosed, imprisoned (3:151). Gaskell spoke of herself as a bird. In one of her letters, she writes, for instance, that Margaret, her servant, has come to ask "what time I would like, & what I will have for,[*sic*] dinner; but that fixes me too much, so I despise dinners, and eat when & where I like, like Sancho Panza and the birds" (*L* 206). In another, she laments that, as she happens "to be a woman instead of a bird," she is imprisoned by "ties at home and duties to perform" from which she has "no wings like a dove to fly away" (*L* 8).[1] Many of her readers too have thought of Gaskell as a bird. Writing, thus, of *Wives and Daughters,* David Cecil observes, for instance, that the "Victorian standards in which" Gaskell "had been educated told her that Molly was indisputably better than Cynthia. And she was no more capable of questioning these standards than she was of flying." And Elizabeth Haldane once describes her as being like "a caged bird who did not struggle against his [*sic*] bars."[2]

Lucy had been imprisoned too, first in the house and then the garden, while her double had wandered about doing the things forbidden to Lucy. There are an inordinate number of "wives" who are imprisoned in Gaskell's fiction.[3] In her novels their imprisonment is generally just a figure of speech. When Sylvia marries Philip, for instance, in *Sylvia's Lovers,* Gaskell describes her as tied down by the "chains of matrimony" (6:396). When her daughter is born, she feels as though she were a "prisoner" in her house (6:370). The whole of her married life, in fact, becomes for her one long "imprisonment" (6:370). But in the short stories, in which Gaskell often turns her metaphors into plots, wives are often imprisoned literally. For instance, in "The Grey Woman," a story Gaskell published in January of 1861 in *All the Year Round,* Anna, as soon as she marries M. de la Tourelle, finds herself imprisoned in his castle. The very condition of being a woman seems to Gaskell an imprisonment. The prison is the female self.

"Mrs. Gaskell" was happy in it. Her demon, however, longed to escape the prison of the female consciousness. This is the theme of "Crowley Castle." The two central characters of this story are Theresa and Bessy. Bessy we have met already. Like other Bessys in Gaskell's fiction, she is a typically English girl, which is to say she is typically female. Theresa, who is "as different as possible," the narrator says, from the English Bessy (7:684), has the role of the daemonic double. She reminds us of Cynthia in *Wives and Daughters* and of Erminia in "The Moorland Cottage," and she shares her history with both. As Bessy is English, Theresa is French. Although she was actually born in England and is the daughter of an English father, she takes rather after her mother, a woman about whom Gaskell thinks that she has told us enough when she says that she had in her "foreign blood" and had been "brought up in France" (7:682). It is from her that Theresa inherits the "wilful" temper and "passionate" nature (7:683) that make her a daemonic type. Theresa herself has been, moreover, brought up, although on English soil, by a French bonne named Victorine, with whom, eventually in her teens, she is actually sent to France in order to "finish" her education.

Like most such pairs, Theresa and Bessy fall in love with the same man. The man is Duke, and he, at first, won over by her English virtues, marries the angelic Bessy. At the beginning, he is happy, but when he starts to develop an interest in political affairs and considers running for office, he finds he cannot talk to Bessy. Being a female, she is not bright. Besides, she is so entirely absorbed in caring for her home and child, she takes no interest in anything else (7:709). Theresa has meanwhile been living in France, where she has married a French nobleman. He, however, dies quite suddeny, and she decides to go back home. She tries to be a friend to Bessy by telling her what she considers wrong in Bessy's relationship with Duke. Whenever, she says, " 'he wants to talk to you of politics, of foreign news, of great public interests, you drag him down to your level of woman's cares.' " But Bessy is unable to change. " 'I wish,' " she says, " 'I was cleverer; but you know, Theresa, I was never clever in any thing but housewifery' " (7:706–7). Theresa herself begins to grow weary of hearing Bessy's domestic talk, which centers always on her servants, on her mother, on the parish (7:707). Theresa, daemonic, has nothing to do with these typically female activities. Her interests are entirely male. She much prefers to talk to Duke about the things that he is doing. Very soon, Theresa becomes, as Bessy is not, his "true companion" (7:714). She takes an active part in seeking to further his political career, partly, as the narrator says, because, perceiving the "powers" of his "mind," she is "impatient of their remaining dormant in country seclusion." But it is not for his sake alone that, when a seat in Parliament falls vacant, Theresa urges Duke to run for it. She herself longs "to find herself in the thick of the struggle for place and power" (7:708). If she could run for office herself, we have no doubt that she would do it. Since she cannot, Duke is her surrogate. This is why she becomes so angry when Bessy, in her "passive" manner, seems to be "opposed to the scheme" (7:708). By standing in her husband's way, Bessy is standing in Theresa's.

But in Gaskell's imagination Theresa and Bessy are not two women. They are, like Lucy and her double, the male and female halves of one. This may be another reason Gaskell chose Bessy as the name of so many typical females. Beside thinking of herself in her role as "Mrs. Gaskell," she was recalling perhaps a character popular in the Middle Ages, in the Mummers' Play for instance, always called Bessy by convention. Versions of such entertainments survived all through the nineteenth-century, especially in rural towns like Knutsford, and it is very possible Gaskell saw such performances as a child. In these, Bessy is a man who is dressed in woman's clothing. The female Bessy is a disguise. Within her, there is a latent male. Theresa is thus not Bessy's rival but the male demon she contains.

It is through Theresa that Gaskell seeks to escape her female prison. But Bessy blocks her at every turn. At last, in anger, Gaskell realizes that she cannot ever be free until she has done away with Bessy, until she has killed her female self, precisely as, in "Professions for Women," Virginia Woolf was later to write that, so as to become a writer, she had had to "kill" that part of herself that still embodied the image of "The Angel in the House."[4] "Mrs. Gaskell" cannot allow Theresa to kill Bessy with her own hand, but she can allow Victorine, Theresa's surrogate, to do it. Here the relationships of the women recalls the relay relationships in *Ruth.* As Jemima was Ruth's double, and her sister Elizabeth hers, so is Theresa Bessy's double, while Victorine in turn is hers. Being French, Victorine is daemonic. And her existence is bound up in every particular with Theresa's. She lives not only for Theresa; in reality she lives through her. In Paris, for instance, Victorine would ask Theresa a thousand questions when she returned at night from her balls. Theresa would report her "triumphs." She would give details of every "conquest." And Victorine would feel as though in them she were "triumphing" herself (8:692–93). It is not by chance that Gaskell here uses words like *conquest* and *triumph* to describe Theresa's evenings. They are merely variations of the meaning of Victorine's name. In the same vicarious way, Victorine shares Theresa's frustration in seeing that Bessy is holding Duke back. One night, after Theresa unleashes another angry attack on Bessy, Victorine sees what she must do. An expert in deadly potions, apparently, she decides to poison Bessy. It is important, however, to note that she considers herself an instrument, acting out what seems to her the "secret" desire in "Theresa's heart" (7:709). She thinks of this secret as a " 'joint secret,' " the secret she and Theresa share (7:712), and the fact that they share a secret makes Victorine, like Jemima in Ruth, the secret sharer, the other self. And, when Theresa later accepts responsibility for the murder, it is a virtual confirmation that Victorine had read her right. The act of accepting responsibility is part, of course, of the "moral" ending. Theresa, who on Bessy's death had married Duke and helped to make a brilliant career for him in politics, has by the end been discovered guilty and abandoned by her husband. To punish herself, she chooses to live at Crowley Castle all alone and in "retirement" from the world (7:714). She is, in fact, replacing Bessy. Having killed her, she is now becoming the imprisoned wife. But before she reaches her "moral," Gaskell has told us something important. She has told us that the male wants to kill the female self.

Gaskell needed to kill the female so that she could become male. Female characters in Gaskell often wish that they were male, and it is not for Freudian reasons. There is no penis envy here. Gaskell only wants the means to realize her daemonic identity. Sometimes, when they wish they were men, her women wish merely to escape from the confinement of being female. Maggie in "The Moorland Cottage," seeing how narrow is the sphere in which, according to Mrs. Buxton, a woman is allowed to function, says " 'I wish I was not a woman. It must be a fine thing to be a man' " (2:271). Bessy Higgins in *North and South,* poor and sick and bored with her life, says " 'I've longed for to be a man to go spreeding, even if it were only a tramp to some new place' " (4:161). Similarly, in *Mary Barton,* Mary says " 'I wish I were a boy; I'd go to sea' " (1:223). But sometimes Gaskell's women want more. Margaret Hale in *North and South* wants the right to speak and act just as a man would, freely and openly. When she believes that she has earned the disapproval of Thornton by lying, Margaret says " 'I wish I were a man, that I could go and force him to express his disapprobation, and tell him honestly that I knew I deserved it' " (4:367). Jemima in *Ruth* wants the ultimate right, the right to be angry, the right "Mrs. Gaskell" was never able to grant herself. When Mr. Farquhar makes her angry, Jemima longs "to be a man" so that she can "speak out her wrath" (3:253).

Gaskell's females were all once males, just as once they were all witches. Molly in *Wives and Daughters,* for instance, before she killed herself, was a "tom-boy" (8:273). Becoming male is not, in Gaskell, for a woman a change of sex. It is only a return to her true, original gender. Being male, like being a witch, is simply being whole again. The journey to *Cranford* had been easy. Becoming female was letting go. The journey back, however, was difficult. But Gaskell achieved it in *North and South.*

XII

Men Do *What* Women Are

ALTHOUGH IT IS SET in an industrial city whose economic and social conflicts provide not only a frame for its plot but a quarry for its incidents, *North and South* is not primarily, or even to a great extent, concerned, as *Mary Barton* had been, with the plight of the suffering workers. There might be several reasons for this. For one thing, as Margaret Ganz has observed, Gaskell's "emotional involvement with the miseries of the poor had," by the time she wrote *North and South,* "lost some of its immediacy."[1] For another, conditions had changed in the years between the novels. Things were to get worse again during the American Civil War when the supply of cotton grew short and many mills had to be closed, causing bankruptcy among the owners and unemployment among the workers, but for a time in the mid–fifties it looked as though the worst had passed. Gaskell may have felt the workers no longer needed her passionate pleading. England, besides, had been made nervous by revolutions on the Continent, and Gaskell may have been reluctant, as so many others were, to encourage workers to contemplate or to voice the wrongs they felt, lest in doing so she helped to foment revolution at home.

The most important reason, however, was undoubtedly the fact that she had been severely criticized, by those who had read the subtextual narrative on the pages of *Mary Barton,* for identifying too completely with the workers of the book. Even while she had written the novel, she had wavered, as we have seen, in her attitude to the workers. But when she saw her radical views reflected in the eyes of her critics, as Ruth saw in the eyes of the children the reflection of her sin, Gaskell found it increasingly difficult not to believe she had been mistaken. Her letters show her growing progressively more uncertain, more intimidated. "I'm sure," she writes to Catherine Winkworth, trying at first to defend herself, "I *believe* I wrote the truth" (*L* 35). Thinking of the accusations that had been leveled at the book, Gaskell, however, is not so sure that the truth was as she saw it. "I wanted," she writes in another letter, "to represent the subject in the light in which some of the workmen certainly consider to be *true,* not that I dare to say it is the abstract absolute truth" (*L* 36). To Mrs. Greg, whose husband had been, on the subject of the workers, one of her very harshest critics, Gaskell sends a letter in which she hides, as she had hidden in the novel, behind the protection of "seeming" words. "I can remember now," she explains, "that the prevailing thought in my mind at the time when the tale was silently forming itself and impressing me with the force of a reality, was the *seeming* injustice of the inequalities of fortune" (*L* 42; italics mine). Finally, she is convinced that she has committed a sin. "I do think," she writes in another letter, "that we must all acknowledge that there are duties connected with the manufacturing system not fully understood as yet, and evils existing in relation to it which may be remedied in some degree, although we as yet do not see how; but surely there is no harm in directing the attention to the existence of such evils. No one can feel more deeply than I how *wicked* it is to do anything to excite class against class; and [and here is the telltale word] the sin has been most unconscious if I have done so" (*L* 36).

The critics had to be appeased. Gaskell felt she had to write a novel in which she redressed the balance. It is not that she is not compassionate to the workers in *North and South*. It is just that she does not dwell on the raw misery of their lives. The workers are not her subject at all. Some of the critics had suggested that, since she had been so entirely absorbed by the workers in *Mary Barton* and had therefore shown the masters in such an unfavorable light, Gaskell write another novel in which the masters, now portrayed with good will and understanding, were the center of her story. Gaskell had at first demurred. To Lady Kay-Shuttleworth she had insisted that she did not feel as strongly about the masters as the workers and that an attempt to write about them would undoubtedly end in "failure." But even here she had equivocated, saying that she could imagine someone taking as a model a man like Samuel Greg, an idealistic industrialist whom she had come to know in Manchester, and writing a story that depicted "the trials of a conscientious rich man, in his dealings with the poor" (*L* 72a). Whether it was Greg or not that she did use as her model, it was on a master she focused, and sympathetically, in *North and South*. Thornton, the hero of the novel, is nothing at all like Henry Carson. He is likeable. He is good. In some respects, he is an idealist. His interest is not in making money (4:397). What he is working for is progress, which, in his view, business and industry will eventually achieve. And he is generally a good master. He makes mistakes, but he wants to learn, and he does learn, partly from Margaret, who teaches him the human values that she brings with her from the south, and partly from workers, whom he respects, to whom he listens, and whom he invites in the end to share with him the actual running of his factory. Gaskell's critics were appeased. As A. W.

Ward has pointed out, W. R. Greg liked *North and South* a good deal better than *Mary Barton* (4:xviii).

Even the masters are not, however, the true subject of *North and South*. Much as it may, in some respects, seem a "condition-of-England" novel, *North and South* is more a sequel to *Cranford* than to *Mary Barton*. In *Cranford*, Mary Smith had traveled, as a surrogate for Gaskell, from the male city of Drumble to the female town of Cranford. In *North and South*, the heroine Margaret travels that road back again.

Like many another of her heroines, Margaret is one of Gaskell's surrogates, sharing, with variations, her history. Although her mother is still alive, she has been brought up by an aunt, and her exile has, like Gaskell's, made her desperate for love. When she comes home—just at the age Gaskell herself had gone to London to care for her father in his last illness—she feels threatened by a servant whom her mother seems to prefer. Her mother, like Gaskell's father, falls ill, and Margaret longs for the right to take care of her. " 'Let me be in the first place, mother,' " Margaret pleads with Mrs. Hale. " 'I am greedy of that. I used to fancy you would forget me while I was away at Aunt Shaw's and cry myself to sleep at nights with that notion in my head' " (4:151). Very soon her mother dies. Her father is the Reverend Mr. Hale, who resembles Mr. Stevenson in that he resigns his ministry on conceiving religious scruples. And he dies too after a time, leaving Margaret Alone! Alone!

Again like many another heroine, Margaret had been a daemonic child, a creature, as the narrator calls her, of the "forest," "untamed" (4:5). On becoming a woman, however, she had had to conceal her demon. Gaskell describes the demon's concealment in one of her most dramatic metaphors when she remarks that within Margaret was contained a "latent Vashti" (4:446). Vashti and her successor, Esther, were popular Victorian images, the latter for the ideal woman (one of her better-known incarnations being the Esther of Dickens's *Bleak House*), the former for the unideal self (one of her most remarkable appearances being in Charlotte Brontë's *Villette*, where, as the name of the fiery actress who is Lucy's alter ego, she gives so fiery a performance that it seems to cause a fire literally to break out in the theater).

The fact that Margaret harbors a Vashti, a demon still vital though concealed, makes her for Gaskell more male than female, and all through the novel, interspersed with such remarks as when the narrator says she assumed a "womanly softness" (4:233), are hints of the male identity within. Gaskell, for instance, imagines that Margaret seeks, above all, to live heroically, and the heroic ideal she gives her is very clearly not female but male. Margaret does not seek the self-sacrifice Gaskell had praised in "The Moorland Cottage" as the feminine form of the virtue. She seeks, as males do in Gaskell, to live a "brave and noble . . . life."[2] Even her fear that "her courage" will "fail her in an emergency" (4:206) is, in Gaskell, a male rather than a female anxiety.

But Gaskell sees this male in Margaret constrained to lead a female life. The feminine destiny is projected in the very opening scene in which we come on preparations being made for Edith's wedding. Daughters, as in *Wives and Daughters,* are expected to become wives. Edith, although she is Margaret's cousin, is a thoroughly female character, having no "very strong will of her own" (4:2). Marriage is her natural end. But this is not the end that Gaskell has in mind for Margaret Hale. When Henry Lennox proposes to her shortly after Edith's wedding, Gaskell has her turn him down. Henry, the brother of Edith's bridegroom, offers Margaret a life like Edith's, and that is precisely the kind of life Gaskell does not intend her to have.

What Gaskell wants is to find a way for Margaret to live her life as a male. It is not until the end of the story, this being one of the works in which Gaskell discovers her subject only as she nears her conclusion, that she articulates the question. Margaret, now alone in the world, has to decide what to do with herself. She has "to settle," the narrator writes, "that most difficult problem for women, how much was to be utterly merged in obedience to authority and how much might be set apart for freedom in working" (4:497). As it happens, there is no authority to impose its will on Margaret, and she has no work to do. Gaskell is thinking less of Margaret, it would seem, than of herself. And the alternatives she envisions are extreme and absolute. A woman may claim the "freedom" to "work," or she must be "utterly merged in obedience to authority." Margaret, early deprived of love, is a candidate for the latter. But, instead of letting her yield, Gaskell, observing that Margaret herself is surprised by the unexpected "firmness" with which she "asserted" herself (4:491), decides to "take her life into her own hands" (4:497), to claim the "right to independence of action" (4:491). And these—assertion, rights, independence, and, above all, action, of course—are to Gaskell male ideas, ways of *doing* not of *being.*

Margaret *does* a number of things in the progress of the novel, but the most important of these is the lie she tells the police to protect her brother, Frederick. Many characters lie in Gaskell. Lying is one of her central images.[3] In *North and South* it occurs in this way. Frederick, who has been living in Spain to avoid being prosecuted for the part he took in a mutiny—this is one of those wild eruptions that occur in Gaskell's plots—returns in secret to see his mother, who is ill and dying in England. On her death, he leaves again. But as he waits for his train at the station, he is recognized by someone who attempts to apprehend him. Frederick pushes the man away as he leaps onto his train, and the man, hitting his head, dies of the injury he sustains. Margaret has accompanied Frederick, and being recognized herself, she is named to the police as a witness to the fatality. When the police arrive, however, unaware that Frederick is safe, Margaret, to protect her brother, denies the incident took place.

Margaret's lie distresses Gaskell to an extraordinary degree. " 'Oh, Frederick! Frederick!' " Margaret cries, " 'what have I not sacrificed for you!' " (4:336). "Oh! what slight cobwebs of chances," Gaskell echoes Margaret's cry, "stand between us and Temptation!" (4:339). "Where now," Margaret laments again, "was her proud motto, 'Fais ce que dois, advienne que purra?' If she had but dared to bravely tell the truth as regarded herself, defying them to find out what she refused to tell concerning another, how light of heart she would now have felt!" (4:339). Time does not soothe the agitation Gaskell feels about the lie. Whenever she recalls the incident, it troubles her all over again. Her "plans for Frederick," Margaret thinks over seventy pages later, "had failed, and the temptation lay there a dead mockery,—a mockery which had never had life in it; the lie had been so despicably foolish, seen by the light of the ensuing events, and faith in the power of truth so infinitely the greater wisdom!" (4:411). Truth telling is, of course, important. It was especially so to Gaskell, not only because she was herself an exceptionally truthful woman but because she held very seriously the Unitarian view of truth. Margaret alludes to this view in the novel when she remarks that in telling a lie she has not only betrayed her convictions but "failed in trust" toward God (4:339). God, the Unitarians argue, is guiding the world to an ultimate good through a causal chain of events. We must not, with our limited vision, attempt to interrupt that chain. What we may see as a dreadful evil to be averted at all costs may be a necessary link in the completion of God's plan.

But Gaskell's reaction to Margaret's lie is neither religious nor moral really. If it were, she would react always to lies in the same way, and the fact is she does not. In *Mary Barton,* for example, Gaskell disapproves of lying, but she is not overwrought when Job Legh tells Mrs. Wilson that her nephew has been found to be a witness for her son who is being tried for murder. The fact is he has not been found, but Mrs. Wilson is very tired and Job is aware she will not sleep unless she feels her son is safe. Later

Gaskell does point out that the falsehood was shortsighted, (1:358–60). But that is the limit of her protest. In *Cranford,* Gaskell is ambivalent about the moral status of lies. When Miss Matty loses her income with the failure of the bank, her friends take up a collection for her. They know she will not accept their charity, but having been put in charge of the sale of her furniture and books, they add their money to the proceeds and persuade Miss Matty to take the whole amount as her rightful profit. Gaskell records her official view when Mary Smith remarks that in principle she does not approve of lying (2:175), but even Mary does not attempt to intervene in the events. In "The Well of Pen Morfa," Gaskell seems even more casual about lies, undermining, in a way, even their religious status. Here the lie is told to Nest by her mother, who does not want her to know her lover has abandoned her. She knows she should not tell a lie, but she is sure that God will forgive her. And Gaskell does not say He will not (2:249). In *Wives and Daughters* Gaskell actually seems to take pleasure in Cynthia's lies. There was, the narrator writes, "no ill-nature, and, in a general way, no attempt at procuring any advantage for herself in all her deviations; and there was often such a latent sense of fun in them that Molly could not help being amused with them in fact, though she condemned them in theory" (8:254). Sometimes she is even defiant when she imagines that the reader might offer an objection to lying. Thus, in "Christmas Storms and Sunshine," describing a journalistic compositor who fills empty spaces in his newspaper with "interesting phenomena" he has "invented for the occasion," Gaskell flippantly inquires of the reader "but what of that?" (2:193–94).

If Gaskell were troubled by Margaret's lie for religious or moral reasons, she would have to be troubled as well, one assumes, by the fact that Frederick has been responsible for the death of the man, whose name is Leonards, who had recognized him at the station. There are, it is true, a number of factors that have contributed to Leonards's death. Leonards is drunk when Frederick meets him. Presumably, he would not have been as easy to push had he been sober. Also, he suffers from a complaint that, for reasons we are not given, makes him more vulnerable to the blow. But none of this can alter the fact that Leonards is dead and Frederick has killed him. If he is not guilty of murder, Frederick at the very least is guilty of involuntary manslaughter. And if Margaret has interfered with the divine chain of events, Frederick must have done so too, and in a much more serious manner. Whatever perspective we care to take—legal, moral, or religious—if Margaret's lie merits such wailing, surely a dead man merits a word. But Leonards does not bother Gaskell. Only the lie disturbs her so.

To be precise, it disturbs "Mrs. Gaskell." And it disturbs her because the lie is an expression of the male demon. In telling the lie, Margaret has taken affairs indeed "into her own hands." Had she merely told the truth, she would have been a passive witness to events she had not caused, just a reporter, as it were, of the *doings* of others. In telling a lie, she is, however, herself the author of events, herself the cause of subsequent consequences. It may be true she errs religiously, morally, and even legally. But she is acting out her demon. She is not satisfied to *be*. Lying, she has chosen to *do*.

Not only is the lie daemonic, Frederick, whom the lie protects, is himself a daemonic character. Gaskell identifies him as such by having him take part in the mutiny. The mutiny plays a part as well in the novel's conscious purpose. As a rebellion against the oppression of a captain who acts tyrannically, which is how Gaskell describes the event, the mutiny is meant to be a parallel to the strike of the workers. Most economists would, of course, argue that workers have to their masters a very different kind of relationship from that of sailors to their captains, but all these issues are to Gaskell variations on the theme of the relationship between obedience to authority and freedom. Margaret is trying to settle this question. Women, Edith being the paradigm since she has no will of her own, are expected to obey the authority placed over them. Men, however, are, like Frederick, permitted, indeed required, to rebel. Rebellion itself is male to Gaskell. This is especially made clear with regard to the French Revolution in the story of Virginie, one of the characters whose history is reported in "My Lady Ludlow." Virginie, who is French and daemonic, is to Gaskell a male type. Her father has given her, in fact, the education of a man, and she has, as an adult, every male characteristic. She is, for example, "daring and wilful," "independent and original," and an atheist as well. And she is for the French Revolution, which she identifies as male when, by contrast, she describes the side of the monarchy as "effeminate" (5:75–76).

But Frederick is not just a male demon, he is Margaret's daemonic self. Gaskell makes it a point to tell us that Frederick not only looks like Margaret, he shares in all of Margaret's feelings and he even communicates with her without needing to say a word. "The brother and sister," she writes for example, "arranged the table together, saying little but their hands touching, and their eyes speaking the natural language of expression, so intelligible to those of the same blood" (4:291). They do not need to talk to communicate, as they would if they were two people. All they need to do is think, as they would if they were one. When Gaskell writes that Margaret is happy Frederick has come to see their mother because he stood "in precisely the same relation" to her "as that in which" she "stood" herself (4:289), she is describing the brother and sister standing in the very same place. They share a space because to Gaskell what they share is an identity. This sharing of space often identifies brothers and sisters in Gaskell's fiction as variations of one self. In "The Doom of the Griffiths," for example, Angharad and Owen, rivals at first for the love of their parents, begin to identify with one another when they suffer the same neglect on the birth of their stepbrother.

Sometimes brothers and sisters in Gaskell are so close in emotional space that their relationship seems incestuous. Often they behave like lovers. In "Six Weeks at Heppenheim," for instance, Herr Müller's sister is so jealous of her brother's love for Thelka that she fiercely opposes his marriage. Michael, in "Half a Lifetime Ago," says that if Susan wants to marry him, she must get rid of her mad brother. He " 'might,' " Michael says, " 'be a cast-off lover and jealous of me, he looks so dark and downcast at me' " (5:292). Faith and Thurstan Benson too behave in *Ruth* like a husband and wife. Ruth, as I have suggested already, is one kind of "wife" to Benson. But his sister is another. Faith, in fact, refuses to marry, Gaskell says, because she cannot bring herself to leave her brother (3:163). Gaskell throws out incestuous hints about Margaret and Frederick too. Thornton, not knowing who Frederick is and seeing him at the station with Margaret, takes him in fact to be her lover (4:319–20). Gaskell may be confusing here different kinds of love again, but brother and sister seem incestuous far more importantly, I think, because they are fused in Gaskell's mind, much like Lucy and her demon. Lucy's demon had been male, since every demon is in Gaskell, but it had taken a woman's form. In *North and South* the demon assumes finally its rightful sex. One of the ways that Gaskell implies that she intends a man to be the male demon of a woman is by making him look feminine. He looks, in short, like what he is, a woman whose male demon is showing. Frederick, male in every way, has, nonetheless, such "delicate" features that he is "redeemed from effeminacy" only "by the swarthiness of his complexion" (4:293). Frederick, however, must be distinguished from Mr. Hale, who is "feminine" too (4:92). He is not a male woman. He is rather a female man. Although she uses the same vocabulary sometimes to describe these types, they are different in Gaskell's mind, and we can always tell them apart. A female, whether a man or a woman, has no daemonic characteristics. A male, however, always does. In "The Doom of the Griffiths," Robert Griffiths is "almost feminine" in his manner (5:241), but every so often he explodes in "tremendous bursts of passion" (5:244). And these, the product of a demon, tell us that his effeminate manner does not identify him as a female

but as a woman's male demon. The same is true in "The Grey Woman" of
M. de la Tourelle, who has a "handsome effeminate face" that looks
"ferocious as any demon's" (7:346). Mr. Hale is not daemonic. He is
therefore a female man. Frederick is feminine but not female. He is rather a
female's demon.

Frederick for Margaret is thus the demon that every woman in
Gaskell conceals. Concealment is the heart of his story. Arriving in England by stealth, as he does, Frederick requires that he be hidden. As in a
woman the demon is hidden, so in the land of women is Frederick.
Concealment is what the lie achieves. Because he must be hidden in
England, Margaret denies that Frederick is there. In doing so, as in
England she must, Margaret also denies her own demon. Frederick, as a
male, is a doer. Gaskell calls him a "Man of action" (4:328)—the terms
being redundant for her—and even provides him with a theory, a kind of
philosophy, of doing. Whenever he feels distressed, he says, he looks for
something he can do. He advises Margaret to do the same. " '*Do* something, my sister, do good if you can; but, at any rate, *do* something'"
(4:295–96; italics mine). Being a doer, a daemonic double, Frederick is
Margaret's doing self. As Lucy's demon had acted out the thoughts and
feelings Lucy herself had been too feminine to express, so Frederick acts
out Margaret's demon, the "latent Vashti" in herself. The fact that Margaret's Vashti is *latent*—a word, of course, whose etymology makes it a
synonym of *hidden*—indeed associates it with Frederick. Vashti had been a
rebel too, refusing to obey authority. Frederick's mutinous rebellion is
Margaret's demon acted out.

Between "Men Do" and "Women Are" there seems, in Gaskell's
imagination, thus to be a hidden connection. Men in her fiction seem to do
not only while but *what* women are. Certain things in Victorian society,
men were expected to do *for* women. Gaskell already shows this in
Cranford. Whenever they need certain things to be done, the women of
Cranford call on men. Miss Matty at one point says, in fact, " 'I don't deny
that men are troublesome in a house. . . . but still a man has a sort of
knowledge of what should be *done* in difficulties, that it is very pleasant to
have one at hand ready to lean upon" (2:153; italics mine). In *North and
South* Gaskell extends this nineteenth-century convention into a psychological metaphor. Gaskell imagines Margaret a male, a Vashti, a rebel, a
doer, someone who wants to take charge of her life. She wants to let
Margaret act out her demon. But this she can do only up to a point.
In Frederick she creates a character who, as Margaret's male self, can,
through his daemonic actions, *do* what his sister *is*. Most of Gaskell's

brothers and sisters have a relationship of this kind. Jemima, as the heroine's double, had been able to express Ruth's daemonic nature in *Ruth,* but she had not been able to act. Her acting self had been her brother. Committing the forgery, Richard had *done* what his sister Jemima *was.* Edward in "The Moorland Cottage" and Benjamin in "The Crooked Branch" are also brothers who are required to act for their sisters in this manner.

It may be that brothers and sisters in Gaskell have this particular kind of relationship because it was how Gaskell herself conceived her relationship to her brother, John. She felt very close to John, we recall. He was a father and brother both. She must, as a child, sitting in Knutsford waiting for her father to claim her, have pictured John precisely as Margaret pictures Frederick in *North and South,* sailing the seas, his life an adventure, happy in his "wild career" (4:293). Later, when she made the distinction between the male and female self, the contrast perhaps came back to her mind. As John had done and she had been, so she divided her brothers and sisters. And John in a sense had done for her, at least he had done what she desired. It was not just literally to go to sea, although that was part of it for Gaskell, for John was not the only Stevenson who had conceived a love for the sea. The sea was a family tradition, many Stevensons having served in the Merchant and Royal Navies. Gaskell also loved the sea. Whenever she writes of it in her fiction, it is in a romantic way and with a romantic love both for the life she imagines on it and for the exotic lands to which she pictures it carrying its sailors. Even the letter Mary Smith writes that brings Peter home in *Cranford* is pictured as being "tossed about on the sea, . . . stained with sea-waves . . . and . . . carried among palm-trees, and scented with all tropical fragrance." The "little piece of paper, but an hour ago so familiar and common-place, had set out on its race to the strange wild countries beyond the Ganges!" (2:154). John, in going to sea, had thus done, in a sense, what she had been. He had become her doing self. Had Gaskell had a chance to know him, had she seen him every day, John, although he would undoubtedly have found his way into her fiction like every other person she knew, might not have been so romantic a figure. But he was never a person to her. His visits and letters were too infrequent, and at the time she was too young, for her to know him as a person. She only knew the dashing young man who loved her and took an interest in her. The rest was all imagination. And in her imagination John was turned into an image. Peter and Matty enact in *Cranford* the classic pattern in her fiction of the relationship that Gaskell imagined between herself and John. While Matty remains at home to bear all the oppression that her father and her sister can impose, Peter rebels and goes to sea, precisely, in fact, as Frederick rebels against the authority of the captain. John for Gaskell had become the myth of the rebellious male demon.

One development of this relationship between brothers and sisters in Gaskell is to be found in the recurring pattern of the idolized son. Gaskell is altogether fascinated by the subject of idolatry. Sometimes she takes a religious view of it. Unitarians, who believed that God alone should be revered, made a particular point of stressing the impiety of idolatry, and Gaskell sometimes writes in this vein. When one of the characters, for example, in "Mr. Harrison's Confessions" remarks that her sister, being a spinster, cannot imagine what it is to be concerned about the " 'illness of a worshipped husband,' " the sister replies " 'I hope I know my duty better. I've not learned my Commandments for nothing. I know Whom I ought to worship' " (5:458). Sometimes we sense a psychological rather than a religious reason. Gaskell's own history must have convinced her, so many of those she had loved having died, that she would lose whomever she cared for, and in her fiction to idolize someone is to ensure he will be lost. The loss may come in many forms. In *Sylvia's Lovers,* which Gaskell considered calling at one point *Philip's Idol* (L 493), Sylvia is only lost to Philip because she does not return his love. But idolized people frequently die, or, as it happens in "Cousin Phillis," nearly die, the heroine here, an only child her parents idolize, almost dying of a fever (7:105). All through her "Diary," Gaskell prays she may not idolize Marianne.

But the most common configuration suggests a somewhat different pattern. Unlike Phillis, for example, the idolized child is usually male. Generally he has a sister who is neglected for his sake. The sister is almost always good. She has to be so she can try to win the love she has been denied. The idolized son, however, is wicked. Sometimes he only behaves very badly, but usually he has committed a crime. Part of this is sibling rivalry, but that is not the whole of the point. The central point is that a son can be daemonic and still be idolized. A boy does not cease, that is, to be loved simply because he acts out his demon. The bad behavior, even the crime, is partly a test of how far the boy can go without his being rejected. It turns out he can go very far. Whatever he says, whatever he does, he cannot lose his parents' affection. The paradigm case is that of Edward in "The Moorland Cottage." Idolized as he is by his mother, Edward grows up to be selfish and spoilt, eventually committing the forgery that compels him to leave for America. His sister is his complete antithesis, good and selfless in every way. And yet she finds she cannot elicit a single affection-ate word from her mother. Even at the end of the story when Edward has died and Maggie has grown, so greatly admired is she for her goodness, "rich in the love of many," her mother continues to dote on her son, idolizing even his memory, and pays no attention to her daughter (2:382). In "The Doom of the Griffiths," Angharad receives the same treatment from her parents once her brother Owen is born. She is angelic and Owen is spoilt, but it is him their parents idolize (5:242). In *North and South* there are two such cases that Gaskell clearly intends as parallels. As Mrs. Hale is cool towards Margaret but idolizes her son Frederick, so Mrs. Thornton worships John but has complete contempt for her daughter.

In all these examples, the brothers *do*. They *do* what their sisters *are*. This is made clear in "The Crooked Branch." Benjamin, also an idolized son, grows up to be spoilt and selfish, which he proves when he returns to rob his parents, as we have seen. Benjamin does not have a sister. He has a surrogate sister, however, in the cousin whom his parents are bringing up as their own child. Bessy, which is the cousin's name, she being typically ideal, is not by any means unappreciated. Her aunt and uncle know her virtue. But it is Benjamin they idolize. When he therefore robs his parents, money standing again for love, it cannot be on his own behalf. He has his parents' love already. There is no need for him to steal it. The one who needs to steal it is Bessy, and through Benjamin she does.

XIII

A Latent Vashti
in a Male Camp

BROTHERS ARE NOT THE ONLY male characters Gaskell uses as male selves. Not every man is a male surrogate, but any man, if Gaskell needs him, is a candidate for that role. Many are brothers, but some are not. In two of the novels, the male self of the heroine is projected, not entirely but in part, into and acted out by a father. One of these novels is *Mary Barton*. Here, as I began to suggest at the end of chapter 9, John is an agent for his daughter. "Mrs. Gaskell" has agents too, one in the character of Alice Wilson and another in Margaret Legh. Alice is the ideal woman. This is clear in her behavior, which is entirely self-sacrificing, and is metaphorically stressed in the fact that she is a servant, thus a perfect female self. Margaret, although a little less saintly, is essentially of the same type. Gentle, thoughtful, deeply spiritual, Margaret is often the means through which "Mrs. Gaskell" quiets Mary, speaking through her words intended to subdue her daemonic self. It is no accident that Gaskell introduces Alice and Margaret in the same chapter of the novel and that the motto of that chapter, which is a verse from Ebenezer Elliott's poem "Withered Wild Flowers," suggests the feminine ideal:

> "To envy nought beneath the ample sky;
> To mourn no evil deed, no hour mis-spent;
(ch. 4) > And, like a living violet, silently
> Return in sweets to Heaven what goodness lent,
> Then bend beneath the chastening shower content."

"Mrs. Gaskell" wants Alice and Margaret to have political implications. Both are poor and Margaret is blind, but as they bear their suffering silently, so, "Mrs. Gaskell" wants to suggest, should the factory workers bear theirs. They are the voice of resignation, submission to the will of Providence. When he returns from London, for instance, where Parliament has refused to hear the sorrows and complaints of the workers, John is understandably angry. Just at that moment he happens to hear Margaret singing the hymn "Comfort ye, comfort ye, my people, saith your God"

(1:111). Alice too is resigned to God's will. To Mary, Alice remarks one day that God, in her view, "is against planning. Whene'er I plan over-much, He is sure to send and mar all my plans, as if He would ha' me put the future into His hands" (1:86).

John, daemonic, brooding, violent, is Alice Wilson's complete antithesis, and Mary stands between the two. Mary, at heart, is really good. All through the novel, despite her vanity, her thoughtlessness, her self-absorption—much of which Gaskell blames on the fact that she is a motherless girl—Mary shows in countless acts a warm and genuinely good nature. When Mr. Davenport dies, for instance, she comes to comfort the rest of his family, and is so moved by the grief she sees that she forgets an assignation she had arranged with young Henry Carson. When she goes home, she decides to remake her own black dress so that Mrs. Davenport will have a mourning gown for the funeral (1:80–81). Mary, however, vibrant, passionate, a little wild, is also daemonic. Even in this early work, Gaskell uses her usual metaphors to substantiate her nature. Mary wishes that she were a boy, she wishes she could go to sea (1:223), and she is "bewitchingly" charming (1:90). But "Mrs. Gaskell" cannot allow her to act out her demon for herself. Her demon must be projected in others. One of those in whom her demon is projected is her aunt Esther, whom she resembles not only physically (1:144) but, since both are driven by vanity, in her character as well. Thus she is in a surrogate way a daemonic fallen woman. But Mary's demon is projected in her father even more. This explains a curious fact in the story, incidentally, namely that Esther and John Barton are later buried in the same grave (1:456). Had Gaskell's mind been on her characters, she would have buried John with his wife. Barton deeply loved his wife. Esther he did not even like. But Gaskell is thinking not of the characters but of the role they play in her mind. Esther and John are both Mary's surrogates, acting out the crimes in her heart. They are one person and must therefore be buried in a common grave. The demon passes from Esther to John partly because Esther is saved and ceases thus to be daemonic. But it would have passed from her even if she had not been saved. The demon, being male itself, gravitates to male characters. John was the character, in fact, in whom Gaskell was chiefly interested when she first conceived the book—"the central figure to my mind," as she wrote to one correspondent (*L* 39). She wanted to call the book *John Barton,* and it was only because her publisher persuaded her to change her title— probably because he wished to attract the female readers who made up a very large portion of the reading public—that she called it *Mary Barton* (*L* 39).

Unlike "Mrs. Gaskell" and her surrogates, the demon in Barton is not resigned. The demon rebels, just as Frederick mutinies. And as she explains the reasons that drive him to kill Carson finally, Gaskell reveals that she is thinking in John Barton of herself. The final link in the chain of causes that make Barton commit the murder is the indifference of Parliament when the workers petition for help. The workers, Gaskell writes in words she could have used to describe herself waiting in Knutsford for her father, "could not believe that the government knew of their misery; they rather chose to think it possible that men could voluntarily assume the office of legislators for a nation, ignorant of its real state; as who should make domestic rules for the pretty behavior of children, without caring to know that those children had been kept for days without food" (1:95–96). Only when they go to London to tell Parliament the truth do they find, as Gaskell did when she went herself to London to discover that her father was indifferent to her pain, that the government does not care. The anger Gaskell had felt then, the anger that had made her act in a way to "vex" her father, grows to such a rage in Barton that he is ready to commit murder. "Mrs. Gaskell's" official attitude to the murder is to condemn it, but the demon, in the subtext, takes a different view of the crime. For one thing, the demon makes the murder pivotal in the novel's resolution. If wisdom can only be learned through suffering, as Gaskell insists at the end of the book, the murder is absolutely necessary to teach the elder Carson the lesson. While "Mrs. Gaskell" thus insists on resignation to God's will, the demon has so constructed the plot that even "Mrs. Gaskell's" solution must be effected through itself.

Gaskell's sympathy, moreover, for John Barton as a criminal struggles constantly to invalidate "Mrs. Gaskell's" condemnation. Even writing to Mrs. Greg, Gaskell is at odds with herself on the question of the murder. Although she quickly goes on to say that in violating God's law Barton doomed himself to suffer the "punishment of an avenging conscience," she begins by admitting that she had "fancied," as she wrote, she could see how so much suffering had led "to a course of action which might appear right for a time to the bewildered mind of such a one" (*L* 42). In the novel itself, "Mrs. Gaskell" quiets, qualifies, and subdues, but, in a similar way, the demon concedes that it shares Barton's feelings. Thus, for example, seizing the narrative, the demon tells us it is aware that the workers are bitter and angry, and it knows why they are so. "There were," the daemonic narrator writes, "desperate fathers; there were bitter-tongued mothers (O God! what wonder!)" (1:63). The demon knows they want revenge, and it understands their reasons. Describing the years of Barton's poverty and recalling the death of his son, the demon thinks that even the reader will be able to "fancy, now, the hoards of vengeance in his heart" (1:25). And the demon knows oppression must inevitably lead to violence. As she remarks in a similar case in "An Accursed Race," whenever people are treated badly, "it is not surprising" that we hear "of occasional outbursts of ferocious violence" (5:222).

Yet Barton, although he succeeds in expressing the anger and violence of Mary's demon, fails in an ultimate way as her agent. For one thing, he dies. Daemonic fathers invariably do in Gaskell's fiction. Daniel Robson, as we shall see, also dies in *Sylvia's Lovers* and Edward Wilkins in "A Dark Night's Work." Gaskell's own rage against her father may be in part responsible for this. She tends to divide her fictional fathers into two groups, those she idealizes, like Mr. Gibson in *Wives and Daughters,* and those on whom she allows herself, although these too are sometimes idealized, to vent to the full the wrath she feels. The latter she very often kills. One is actually killed by his child, Owen, in "The Doom of the Griffiths." Brothers fail as agents too, although they do not generally die. Edward in "The Moorland Cottage" is an exception, but he dies not as a brother, one suspects, but in his second role as a father. But brothers fail in another way. Like brother John, they disappear. Frederick, for instance, goes back to Spain in order to avoid being captured. Richard Bradshaw is sent away to begin his life anew. Brothers do return occasionally, but, like Frederick who returns only to see his dying mother, they often disappear again. Peter alone returns in *Cranford* not to disappear again, but he returns too late to make a genuine difference to his sister.

Fathers and brothers having failed her, Gaskell turns to husbands next in her attempt to find a surrogate. And this is the role in *North and South* that she assigns her hero, Thornton. Thornton to Gaskell is more than a character. He is the very incarnation of the town of Milton-Northern, the town in which the novel is set. Gaskell's readers have usually taken Milton-Northern to be Manchester and Margaret's journey from south to north a fictional record of Gaskell's journey on her marriage from Knutsford to Manchester. This to me seems both true and false. It is true that when she married William, Gaskell did make such a journey. Although it was not a southern town, Knutsford, like Helstone in the novel, was a peaceful, quiet village in an agricultural area. And it is true that Milton-Northern is a reproduction of Manchester. Certainly, writing Margaret's story, Gaskell used portions of her own. But it is not just historical fact that Gaskell wants to record in this novel. She is concerned in *North and South* not so much with the move she made as with the metaphoric significance that it came to have in her mind.

It is generally held that Gaskell always hated life in Manchester, hated the large industrial city, hated not only the dirt and grime but the hurry and scurry of Manchester, and would have gladly returned to Knutsford or another place of its kind. Gérin, for instance, who grants that Manchester may have "stimulated" Gaskell, insists that the city "repelled her" as well. Pollard is of the same opinion: Knutsford, he says, "remained to the end of her life the home of her spirit." Hopkins too alludes to "Gaskell's passion for the country, a longing to be settled in rural surroundings, that came out again and again during a life that had to be spent for the most part in the grime of one of England's most depressing of industrial cities." And even Ganz, who believes her "allegiance was divided between . . . the appeal of a simple rural existence and the challenge of urban complexity," concludes that in *Wives and Daughters* "the universe of Knutsford with its archaic charm wins out at last in the final celebration of country life."[1] Sometimes in her letters Gaskell writes nostalgically about the country. In May of 1838, writing to William and Mary Howitt, she says "I was brought up in a country town, and my lot is now to live in or rather on the borders of a great manufacturing town, but when spring days first come and the bursting leaves and sweet earthy smells tell me that 'Somer is ycomen in,' I feel a stirring instinct and long to be off into the deep grassy solitude of the country" (*L* 8). Sometimes she writes this way in her fiction. The opening of *Mary Barton,* returning to the month and year of her letter to the Howitts, brings the inhabitants of Manchester out of the city streets to celebrate the coming of spring in the outlying fields (1:2–3). Gaskell often returned to Knutsford, as Mary Smith returns to Cranford. She returned not only in fact—to see Aunt Lumb, to visit old friends, and to be in familiar places—but in her mind when she created settings that she modeled on Knutsford, settings like Duncombe in "Mr. Harrison's Confessions," Barford in "The Squire's Story," Hamley in "A Dark Night's Work," Eltham in "Cousin Phillis," and Hollingford in *Wives and Daughters.*[2]

This is the point in *North and South* at which we first find Margaret Hale. Margaret, when the novel begins, is nostalgic for the home she has left in southern England. The Leighs in the story "Lizzie Leigh" have also moved from a town like Knutsford, and Gaskell, describing them as they try to settle into their "Manchester home," adds immediately "if they could ever grow to consider that place as a home, where there was no garden or outbuilding, no fresh breeze outlet, no far-stretching view, over moor and hollow,—no dumb animals to be tended and, what more than all they missed, no old haunting memories" (2:213). The past is hard to leave behind, and it is no surprise that Margaret, having been brought up in the south, begins the novel as a southerner yearning to return to her home.

Dividing the world, however, in genders, as it is her habit to do, Gaskell sees to it we realize that Margaret's southern home is female and that, living in the south, Margaret must be female too. Much of the gender is suggested in the imagery of flowers, flowers used, not as in *Ruth*, to project the hidden demon but, in the more conventional way Gaskell associates women with flowers, to embody femininity. Margaret, who is the rose herself, as we are constantly reminded, of which Thornton will be the thorn, is the very incarnation of the feminine ideal. Roses surround the cottage too in which the Hales are living in Helstone, and the landscape is floral as well. Whenever we find ourselves in the south, as in the novel we do occasionally, we are never far from flowers—roses, honeysuckle, ferns.

Knutsford settings are always female. Cranford, twenty miles from Drumble, is the quintessential Knutsford, which was sixteen miles from Manchester, and it is in Gaskell's mind the definition of female place. Being female, the south is defined as a place of *being*, not *doing*. Mr. Bell in *North and South* remarks, for instance, that while Milton-Northern changes so rapidly that he himself, although a native, can never recognize the streets after he has been away, in Helstone every " 'stick and stone' " stands as it has for " 'the last century' " (4:455). Margaret, on a journey back, realizes, as she sees "the golden stillness of the land," that there is nothing in the south like "the bustle and stir" of "London" and of the cities of the north (4:459–60). In *The Life of Charlotte Brontë*, Gaskell was to write again, in a very similar manner: "nothing can be more opposed than the state of society, the modes of thinking, the standards of reference on all points of morality, manners, and even politics and religion, in such a new manufacturing place as Keighley in the north, and any stately, sleepy, picturesque cathedral town in the south" (*LCB*, p. 15).

It is no accident that the southerner in the novel is a woman and the northerner a man. In the conscious theme of the book Gaskell wants to suggest a fusion. The south and the north, both good and bad, can each correct the other's faults. But Margaret and Thornton, at the beginning, are both so blinded by pride and prejudice that they are unable to see what each can learn from the other's culture. The theme of pride and prejudice here is a conscious appropriation. *North and South,* as Arnold Kettle and A. B. Hopkins have remarked, is meant to be an industrial version of Jane Austen's *Pride and Prejudice.*[3] Austen in her novel deals with an earlier social adjustment, the landed gentry in Elizabeth marrying the aristocracy in Darcy. Gaskell's novel, taking up the subject at a later point, shows the northern manufacturer seeking acceptance from the established "aristocracy" of the south.

It is her prejudice that determines Margaret's initial response to the north. Having conceived before she arrives a "repugnance" to the "idea of a manufacturing town" (4:66), Margaret, when she reaches the north, finds Milton-Northern very ugly. Gaskell had already complained of the ugliness of Manchester on the pages of *Mary Barton,* and she complains of it again here. Remarking on an October morning, the narrator, speaking for Margaret here, contrasts the "silvery mists" of the south with the "fogs" of Milton-Northern (4:298). Maragert arrives with great contempt for the manufacturers too, and when she meets them she feels vindicated, concluding that, though they are wealthy, they are endowed with no style, no taste. Thornton's house appears to her ostentatious, overdone, and the dinner that is served there ostentatiously luxurious (4:189). Margaret even feels contempt for Thornton's effort to improve himself. She wonders why he has hired her father as a tutor in the classics. She is fond of the classics herself, but she thinks that a manufacturer can have no use for that kind of learning (4:42). " 'You are quite prejudiced,' " says Mr. Hale, hinting thus at Austen's novel, " 'against Mr. Thornton, Margaret' " (4: 197). Thornton, however, is prejudiced too. Preparing for the Hales to come, he rents a house for them in town that he is aware is vulgar but that seems, before he meets them, good enough for a tutor's family (4:71–73). As Margaret feels a pride in the south, Thornton feels it in the north. " 'I would rather be a man toiling, suffering,' " he says, " '—nay, failing and successless—here, than lead a dull prosperous life in the old worn grooves of what you call more aristocratic society down in the South, with their slow days of careless ease. One may be clogged with honey and unable to rise and fly' " (4:93).

Gaskell's official view in the novel, calling for north and south to fuse, is suggested in a discussion between Margaret and Mr. Hale. They are talking about Mrs. Boucher, the wife of the man who kills himself because of the economic conflicts between the masters and the workers. Mrs. Boucher is high-strung, and Margaret attributes her frayed nerves to the fact that she lives in a city. The " 'nerves,' " she says, of city people " 'are quickened by the haste and bustle and speed . . . to say nothing of these pent-up houses, which of itself is enough to induce depression and worry of spirits. Now in the country, people live so much more out of doors.' " But Hale replies that people sometimes are so stagnant in the country that they become fatalistic. Margaret then draws the official conclusion: " 'each mode of life produces its own trials and its own temptations. The dweller in towns must find it as difficult to be patient and calm, as the country-bred man must find it to be active, and equal to unwonted emergencies. Both must find it hard to realise a future of any kind; the one because the present is so living and hurrying and close around him; the other because his life tempts to revel in the mere sense of animal existence, not knowing of, and . . . not caring for any pungency of pleasure, for the attainment of which he can plan, and deny himself and look forward" (4:358–59). Officially, it is this fusion that is intended at the end in the marriage of Margaret and Thornton.

Officially Gaskell wants to fuse not only north and south, in fact, the agrarian and the industrial, but England's urban culture too, and even the heritage of the classics that she sees embodied in Oxford. At this level of the narrative, Gaskell seems to want to offer a kind of cultural anthropology in her analysis of the nation. This is an interesting idea, and Gaskell develops it very well. But this is not where her energies are. Her energies are devoted, rather, to turning Margaret into a northerner and to repudiating, in turn, each of the novel's other cultures. Each, like north and south, acquires a metaphoric signification. Each, except for the north, becomes in Gaskell's mind a female place. And sooner or later, Margaret discovers that, however much she appreciates its special character and virtue, she must take leave of it and move on.

London we come to know through the Shaws, Margaret's aunt and her daughter, Edith. It is a trivial, frivolous place—idle, bored, and superficial (4:2,64). Margaret, even when she had lived there, had never been a " 'London girl' " (4:27), and once she settles in the north and compares its "earnest" men with the men who used to talk "in the used-up style that wearied her so in the old London parties" (4:193), she comes to like London even less. When she returns for a brief visit after both her parents die, to see whether she wants to live there, she finds the city sleepy, "placid" (4:392), and herself there "sleepily deadened" (4:445). London too is *being,* obviously, and describing it Gaskell here seems as tired of it as Margaret.

She does not exactly tire of Oxford. Represented in the novel by Mr. Hale's good friend Mr. Bell, who boasts of its " 'beauty,' " " 'learning,' " " 'history' " (4:397), Oxford is England's cultural center as London is its social and political. Gaskell greatly respects the heritage carried in the traditions of Oxford. She even allows the northern men to admit the value of giving their sons, along with an education in business, a little "mental cultivation" (4:78). Thornton himself agrees that knowledge of the past forms the best basis for conjecture about the future (4:197). But when it is compared to the north, Oxford appears a stagnant place. Bell, when he visits, says that Miltonians seem incapable of sitting still. Hale replies that to Miltonians Oxonians seem unable to move. Again, the official answer is fusion. " 'It would,' " Mr. Hale says, " 'be very good if they mixed a little more' " (4:394). Stagnation, however, is once more an aspect of *being,* not of *doing.* Mr. Bell, we are not surprised, is depicted as an effeminate man.

After Margaret has seen the north, the south, to which she once returns, proves to be equally disappointing. When she leaves, she leaves for good. She takes some honeysuckle with her because it symbolizes the south (4:479–80). Knowing she will not return, she wants a token to remind her of the life she leaves behind. It is her way of saying good-bye. Gaskell is saying good-bye here too to the Knutsford of her childhood. In literal fact she did return. And she returned to it in her fiction. The farewell she is saying here is to the female place in her mind. Although she will continue to love it for the sake of her mother and father (4:480), Margaret knows she does not belong there. Having lived now in the north, she knows the south is a prison for her. Introducing her at the beginning, Gaskell had shown us Margaret sitting in a "garden" in which the "trees" had "shut" her "in" as in a "nest" (4:20). We know what these images mean to Gaskell. Enclosed in this way, Margaret, in fact, reminds us of Ruth in the Benson's garden. Outside a bird had risen in flight, but Ruth, who could only see its shadow, had been surrounded by the wall that represented her incarceration. But something very important has changed. In *Ruth,* the garden was salvation. Here it is recognized as the prison from which the heroine must be saved.

Thus, in the end, Gaskell rejects London, Oxford, and the south. What really interests her in this novel is the nation's Teutonic stock. Gaskell herself claimed Teutonic heritage. Whenever she took to traveling extensively, as she did in later years, she would explain her restless spirit by citing her Scandinavian ancestors, saying that their Viking blood ran in her own veins.[4] This is the blood she sees in the north. " 'Teutonic blood,' " Thornton remarks, " 'is little mingled in this part of England' " with the blood of other races. In the north the Teutonic " 'spirit,' " he says, is still alive (4:398). The fact that Gaskell adds a hyphenated "Northern" to the name of the town—which she might simply have called Milton, as she occasionally does for short—suggests that its Teutonic heritage is the most important aspect of the novel's setting to Gaskell.

In *Mary Barton* Gaskell had focused primarily on Manchester's problems, and some of these are explored here too. Beside the economic conflicts, beside the poverty, violence, and vice, the city is crowded, noisy, dirty. But most of what Gaskell notices now are the things she finds exciting. She finds enormously exciting the "exultation" northerners feel, living in a busy metropolis that is shaping England's future. She finds exciting the "sense of power" everyone seems to feel in Manchester (4:193). To Margaret it is an "intoxication" (4:193). Gaskell always found power exciting, and she was drawn to powerful people. We recall that about Froude she had written to Catherine Winkworth that he had such personal power that, although she was able to stand "outside the circle of his influence" by "resisting with all my might," she was still aware of "feeling and seeing the attraction" (*L* 49). She felt the same about Florence Nightingale, whose charismatic personality had so powerfully impressed her that she wrote to Catherine Winkworth "She must be a creature of another race" (*L* 211). William Shaen, a family friend who later married Emily Winkworth, understood one aspect at least of Gaskell's fascination with power. "Mr. Shaen accuses me always," Gaskell writes in a letter to Forster, "of being 'too much of a woman' in always wanting to obey somebody" (*L* 191). "Mrs. Gaskell" was not powerful. Power was not a feminine virtue. It was a male characteristic. It was an attribute of the demon. "Mrs. Gaskell" liked to obey and she liked to obey especially those whose powerful personalities let her project her demon in them. Obeying them, she was obeying, in a sense, her daemonic self. Many characters in her fiction feel precisely in this way. Preston, for instance, in *Wives and Daughters* inspires such a feeling in Cynthia. He is a daemonic type and Cynthia feels the need to obey him. " 'Have you never,' " she asks Molly, " 'heard of strong wills mesmerizing weaker ones into submission?' " (8:474). In *North and South,* the north itself becomes that powerful personality.

Part of what makes the power of the north is its industrial machinery. Gaskell trembles with excitement as she alludes to the "power" of steam (4:92), as she describes "the might of the steam-hammer" (4:92), and reproduces the "ceaseless roar and mighty beat, and dizzying whirl" of all the "machinery" in the factories (4:498). The north is energetic, dynamic. As she had done in *Mary Barton*, Gaskell walks us through the streets, not, however, to see, this time, putrification in the gutters, but to marvel at the people who are hurrying to and fro, full of purpose, full of confidence.

Gaskell is amazed by the people. They are eager, vibrant, active. Thornton explains to Mr. Hale that the Teutonic race is different from the race of ancient Greece. To the latter " 'beauty was everything.' " We, he says, " 'do not look upon life as a time for enjoyment, but as a time for action and exertion' " (4:398). Action, of course, is *doing* to Gaskell. The south, being female, merely *is*. The north, which *does,* however, is male. This is confirmed in the fact that the north, unlike the south, is not at all floral. The narrator of *Mary Barton* had already observed that Manchester was utterly deficient in "flowers" (1:110). The narrator of *Sylvia's Lovers* was at a later time to observe that the north had not yet learned, like the rest of England, to garden (6:5). Milton-Northern is the same. There are no flowers, there are no gardens. What there is, instead, is rock, rock not only in the landscape but, perhaps even more, in the people. " 'There's granite,' " Margaret says at one point, in " 'these northern people' " (4:367).

Every aspect of northern life is associated in the novel with one of Gaskell's male images, and nearly every male image appears in her characterization of the north. One that she uses most extensively is the imagery of war. "Mrs. Gaskell" opposes war, but her demon finds it stirring. Everything in the north is a war. Gaskell imagines there is a " 'war' " between the powerful machinery and the material world it shapes (4:93). The masters and men are locked in " 'battle,' " as they had been in *Mary Barton,* but while "Mrs. Gaskell" there had been terrified of conflict, as the effeminate Mr. Hale is disturbed by the conflict here, the demon that had seen itself once as a possible Boadicea finds the idea of battle exciting. Thornton even thinks it is healthy for masters and men to disagree (4:96). And Margaret's relationship to Thornton, while Gaskell does not call it a war, proceeds, very much as in *Pride and Prejudice,* through the stages of a conflict. Even when Gaskell is not aware of writing in military images, she slides into the language of war, using words like "victorious" (4:398) and "conqueror" (4:78–79) where very different words would do. The business and industry of the north are also male images to Gaskell. Gaskell had already in *Cranford* indicated that business and money, being activities of Drumble, are concerns of the male world. In her biography of Charlotte Brontë, she was to suggest as well that the power of organization was an exclusively male endowment, women lacking not only the talent but the capacity to appreciate it. In the biography, Gaskell thought Charlotte Brontë was an exception (*LCB,* p. 439). Gaskell was an exception too. Although it is generally believed that Gaskell took no interest in business, the fact is that she found it stimulating. In *Sylvia's Lovers,* she seems to find the business end of the whaling industry almost more of an adventure than the romance of going to sea. There is a touch of Theodore Dreiser in Gaskell's sense of business and commerce. In *North and South* she is enthralled by Milton-Northern's textile industry. When Mr. Bell attacks the town for the philistinism of its industry, Margaret makes an impassioned speech to defend " 'the progress of commerce' " (4:393).

If Milton-Northern is therefore Manchester, and there can be no doubt it is, it is a Manchester, not in England, but in the geography of Gaskell's mind. Even the fact that the name is changed, as it was not in *Mary Barton,* tells us that Gaskell in *North and South* has once more mythified the landscape. As Cranford was in the hands of the Amazons, females hostile to the male, so is the north in the hands, like Drumble, of the mythified male spirit. It is a place in which, that is, Gaskell can release her demon. The sexuality through which the demon often reveals itself is given open expression here. Margaret is frightened when first she meets "the outspoken men" on the streets of Milton who show their "undisguised admiration" (4:81). In *Cranford* the demon had been hidden. In Milton-Northern it is not. Similarly, while women like Margaret are imprisoned in the south, in the north they are set free. Thornton objects to " 'laws' " being made in London for the manufacturers because the Teutonic spirit, he says, must be independent and free (4:398). But it is not only men who are liberated by the free Teutonic spirit. Women have "freedom" here as well (4:81). The fact that there are not many girls here who are willing to be servants, as Margaret discovers when she arrives, suggests that the feminine ideal is, in Milton-Northern, a rarity. Northern girls work in the factories not only because they are better paid there but because as factory workers they are allowed to remain "independent" (4:80). And when she finally does find servants, Margaret is amazed to see how different they are from their southern counterparts. Even the girls who are willing to serve have a more independent spirit, they are rougher, even rude. And unlike servants in the south, they are not flattered by the fact that the minister's family wants them. There is no feudal subservience here (4:79–80).

Now and then there are moments of panic, moments in which "Mrs. Gaskell" retreats. Margaret's journey south again after the death of both her parents is a retreat to female safety. It was in just such moments of panic that Gaskell herself retreated to Knutsford, both in fiction and in fact. These moments were never to cease entirely. Gaskell surely describes herself when Mary Smith remarks in *Cranford* that she has "vibrated all my life between Drumble and Cranford" (2:185). But Gaskell did not move back to Knutsford, and it was not altogether because William happened to work in Manchester. Although she continued to use Knutsford as a setting in her stories, she used Manchester as well. Among the stories set in Manchester are "Libbie Marsh," "Lizzie Leigh," "Bessy's Troubles at Home," "The Manchester Marriage," "Hand and Heart," and "The Heart of John Middleton." Among the novels are *Mary Barton, North and South,* and the second part of *Ruth.* In her imagination, she lived as much in Manchester as in Knutsford.

North and South is thus the novel in which Gaskell came to feel that she had settled in her mind in the mythical male place. Even in *Cranford,* Mary Smith had only come for a visit to Cranford. Her home, even there, had been in Drumble. In *North and South* she goes home again. Mary, as Gaskell had managed to tell us, had been even in Cranford male. Unlike Miss Matty, she had been able, on their luncheon visit to Holbrook, to use a knife to eat her peas (2:40). But Gaskell had found it hard in *Cranford* to picture herself in the male domain. In *North and South* she not only learns to see herself in her mind on male ground; she actually turns herself into a northerner. She even begins to see the south through her new northern eyes. Margaret, when she had first arrived, had spoken nostalgically of the south, comparing all its remembered virtues with what seemed vices in the north (4:116–17). But when, much later, Nicholas Higgins says that he might move to the south to avoid the northern problems, Margaret tells him he does not see that the south has problems too and the north its virtues also (4:363–64). And when visitors come to Milton, as they do in the course of the novel, bringing with them the very prejudices she had brought when she had arrived, Margaret, listening to each as though she were hearing a former self, realizes, and we do too, how radically her views have changed. Even her social and economic positions become those of a northerner. She speaks much less like "Mrs. Gaskell" and much more like Gaskell's demon. Mr. Bell is alarmed on hearing her. She has been " 'quite corrupted ,' " he tells her, by her residence in Milton. She has become, he says, " 'a democrat, a red republican, . . . a socialist" (4:393).

Gaskell, thus, in the north accepts herself fully as a daemonic male. In *Cranford,* she had remained among women. Margaret prefers the company of men. She is bored when the gentlemen leave after dinner for their cigars and happy when they rejoin the women (4:193). Gaskell herself, unlike "Mrs. Gaskell," preferred the company of men. "I wish," she once wrote to Catherine Winkworth, partly in jest and partly not, "I could help taking to men so much more than to women (always excepting the present company, my dear!) and I wish I could help men taking to me; but I believe we've a mutual attraction of which Satan is the originator" (*L* 633). Gaskell even tells us the men whom Margaret likes are especially manly. Thornton, for instance, she likes because he is not " 'a lady's man' " (4:86).

Margaret's marriage, which ends the book, is meant to be a contrast to Edith's, with which the novel had begun. Edith's had been a female marriage. Margaret's is to be a male one. In marrying Thornton, Margaret has chosen to *do* rather than to *be*. Margaret herself, in her own proper person, is allowed to *do* two things in her relationship to Thornton. The first is to throw herself in front of him to protect him from the strikers who have come to attack the mill. There is, as always, "an explosion," the workers being so enraged they have taken off their clogs and are hurling them as missiles. Margaret, watching from his house where she happens to be visiting, sees that Thornton is in danger. Not considering her own safety, she runs out into the yard, physically placing her body between Thornton and the angry workers. Thornton is thunderstruck. So are we. We know that Margaret is preoccupied with the idea of living heroically, and that her idea of heroism is not female but male. But this is an extraordinary action. Thinking about it later, Thornton believes it can only mean she loves him. As it happens, Margaret does, but that has nothing, Gaskell insists, to do with her amazing behavior. Margaret herself is greatly distressed to think that Thornton has so misread her. Gaskell is greatly distressed too. "It was," she insists, "a natural instinct; any woman would have done just the same. We all feel the sanctity of our sex as a high privilege when we see danger" (4:230). Any "woman," she repeats, "worthy of the name of woman, would come forward to shield, with her reverenced helplessness, a man in danger from the violence of numbers" (4:232). All this protestation, of course, tells us that Gaskell does not herself believe a word of her explanation. We do not believe it either. We know that this is not how women behaved in the Victorian world. This is how men were supposed to behave. And Gaskell is aware of this too. Metaphorically, she describes Margaret in this scene as male. She conceives her as a warrior, using her "body" as a "shield" (4:210–13). At the end, although not physically, Margaret saves Thornton yet again by providing the money he needs to build a new factory. The conflicts between the masters and workers have by this time ruined Thornton. He has gone bankrupt. Margaret, however, having inherited from Mr. Bell, who suddenly dies, a sizable sum can supply the funds for Thornton to rebuild his industrial empire. Money is male, as Gaskell has shown both in *Cranford* and *North and South*. And, as she hinted in *Mary Barton*, it is also power (1:16). At the end of *North and South*, it is a way for Margaret to *do*.

To what extent the money *does* is not entirely clear in the novel.

Before the two acknowledge their love, Margaret offers the money to Thornton, knowing he will not take it otherwise, as a business proposition. It will be an investment for her, and he will have to pay her interest (4:519). Whether this arrangement continues after they marry we do not know. Metaphorically it must continue if Margaret is to maintain her identity as an independent, male, woman. Charlotte Brontë has Jane Eyre insist that she continue to work as a governess for Adèle so that she can earn her keep after she has married Rochester (ch. 34), and Gaskell, inspired by Brontë perhaps, might have been thinking of letting stand Margaret's business arrangement with Thornton. The mill itself belongs to Thornton, but by providing the money for it, Margaret, in a sense, becomes an equal partner in his career.

But this is as far as Gaskell goes in letting Margaret *do* herself. The rest she passes on to Thornton. Thornton is the very embodiment to Gaskell of the northern spirit. He is defined in the very images that define the north itself. He has "resolution and power" (4:73), independence of spirit, grit, and, that most essential ingredient, the " 'Teutonic blood' " of the Vikings (4:398). Even his name, the thorn of the rose, associates him with the northern landscape. Describing, in fact, a northern park in "The Old Nurse's Story," Gaskell had named as its primary features its " 'gnarled thorn-trees' " and its " 'rocks' " (2:425). Margaret's remark that there is granite in the people of the north identifies Thornton as a rock. His name associates him with the thorn tree. Most important to Gaskell's purpose, as a northerner he is a doer. Margaret, in fact, especially admires the fact that he seems to be "a man ready to *do* and dare everything" (4:92; italics mine). But what he does, he does for his wife. He is the agent of her demon.

XIV

———✦———

Woman Wailing for
Her Demon Lover

THE SUBJECT OF *Sylvia's Lovers* is passion, and, although the demon is carried in Gaskell's usual relay fashion by a number of different characters, the novel is chiefly concerned subtextually with how husbands act it out for their wives. As always, the demon begins in the heroine. One of the ways in which Gaskell tells us that Sylvia is a daemonic character is by identifying her with the moors that lie in the neighboring countryside. The moors are a metaphor to Gaskell, projections of the inner passion of the dark and brooding soul. This is how they appear already in the short story "Lizzie Leigh" (2:208–9), and writing Charlotte Brontë's biography, which she did in the mid-fifties, must have made the moors for Gaskell, haunting the Brontës as they did, images of the passion too that was exhibited in that family. *Sylvia's Lovers* has, in fact, been compared to *Wuthering Heights,* and rightly so to an extent. Gaskell did not, as far as she knew, like Emily Brontë's book. She thought the "opening" "wonderfully fine," but she emphatically disagreed with one correspondent who considered it better than any of the works of the other Brontë sisters (*L* 385). It was not as a novel, however, that *Wuthering Heights* lived in her mind. It was as an embodiment rather of the wild Yorkshire moors. *Wild* is Gaskell's favorite word in *The Life of Charlotte Brontë.* The "moors" are "wild" (*LCB,* p. 17), the people are "wild" (*LCB,* p. 23), as is the "strength" of their fierce "will" (*LCB,* p. 29). *Wild* is similarly the word that Gaskell uses in *Sylvia's Lovers.* Here the mountain roads are "wild" (6:412), the "fells" are "wild" (6:36), the "heights" are "wild," and "wild" as well are the trees and the heather (6:3) and the "rough-flavoured fruits" (6:483). Even the grazing "black cattle" are "wild" (6:410). And, of course, "wild" are the "moors" (6:497). But all of these are projections really of the wildness of the heroine. Sylvia is "wild" in her "look and manner" (6:195); she has "wild eyes" (6:373); she weeps "wild" tears (6:389); she goes into fits of "wild" passion (6:311); and she suffers "wild" frustrations (6:400).

Sylvia does not display her passion, like Hester Prynne, in a scarlet letter, but she does wear a scarlet cloak that she acquires near the beginning and never takes off, except indoors. Like many of Gaskell's daemonic heroines, Ruth being a prime example, Sylvia is torn between two men, in each of whom is projected a part of her own divided nature. These are the lovers of the title, Charley Kinraid and Philip Hepburn. Charley is Sylvia's male self. That is why Gaskell makes him a sailor. Having turned her brother, John, into the myth of her *doing* self, she turned the idea of the sailor into the image of her male demon. The sea and the male are one for Gaskell. In "Bessy's Troubles at Home," for instance, the female Bessy brings home for her brother a book of maritime adventures because, she says, boys love the sea (3:517). Charley, a boy in *Mary Barton,* wants to set sail on "the glorious river" because it is, as he envisions it, the "glittering highway" to the sea (1:336). Even a man as advanced in years as Mr. Holman in "Cousin Phillis," as sober a man as one could wish, devoted to his farm and parish, has "a fancy for the sea," and feels, "like other land-locked men," that "the great deep is a mystery and fascination" (7:76). To the demon the sea means freedom. Daemonic women in Gaskell's fiction always long to go to sea. Mary Barton, as we have seen, wishes she could be a sailor (1:223). Sylvia longs for the sea as well (6:370). Sometimes she also longs for the moors, feeling she can be "free" there too (6:395), but it is in the sea that Gaskell in this novel embodies "freedom" (6:379). All the descriptions of the sea associate it with daemonic metaphors. It is "wild" (6:7), tempestuous (6:388), "passionate" (6:388, 516), and, like Milton-Northern, "northern" (6:121),

Gaskell had already begun to use the sea in this way in *Ruth.* When Ruth and Bellingham meet in Eccleston, they meet, by Ruth's choice, on a sandy beach within the sound of the "moan" of the sea (3:292). Later, this encounter becomes, like the whole of her passionate life, part of Ruth's dream existence in Eccleston. She has one dream in which she is standing on the "shore, striving to carry" Leonard away "from some pursuer." "All at once, just near the shore," she is "clutched" back towards the water. But, before she is swept to sea, she throws Leonard back to shore, to the "land," she says, "which was safety" (3:307). The land is "safety," for "Mrs. Gaskell." The sea is danger. It is the demon.[1] But Bellingham had only partially been associated with the sea. Charley is its very spirit. To Sylvia he is the soul of romance. Margaret had thought of her brother, Frederick, enjoying a "wild career" at sea (4:293). Sylvia sees Charley as "dashing and brilliant" (4:7). Charley is also a spinner of yarns, and these, as Sylvia's father remarks, being an old salt himself, are how women are courted and won (4:111). That is indeed how Sylvia is won. Spinning one yarn after another, all of which are tales of the sea, Kinraid weaves a magic spell as Sylvia sits listening, like Desdemona, to the wonderful feats of men.

The role that Gaskell assigns her sailors is almost always an indication of the degree to which she is able to admit she wants her demon. In *Mary Barton,* for instance, and *Cranford,* the sailors, Will Wilson and Peter Jenkyns, are assigned the roles of brothers. Peter is literally Matty's brother and Will, the lover of Margaret Legh, is a surrogate brother to Mary. If the demon expresses its passion, as it does, in a sexual way, brothers make the demon safe. Indeed, whenever Gaskell panics, lovers themselves are turned into brothers. The heroine of *Mary Barton* for a long time considers Jem only in a brotherly way (1:205), and Molly Gibson in *Wives and Daughters* looks on Roger as a brother (8:737). Some daemonic men are kept, while Gaskell tries to summon the courage to let the demon take its shape, in a kind of halfway house by being made sons of surrogate mothers before they are allowed to be lovers. Roger Hamley and Frank Buxton are the best examples here. Another halfway house consists of cousins who begin in a brotherly way and eventually become lovers. Thus it is only when she is able to concede she wants her demon that the sailor in Gaskell's fiction turns from a brother into a lover. And this is what happens with Charley Kinraid.

Gaskell had reached a halfway point between sailor-brothers and sailor-lovers in "The Manchester Marriage," a story she published in *Household Words* in December of 1858. The story is in many respects a trial run for *Sylvia's Lovers.* The heroine, Alice, is divided between Frank Wilson and Mr. Openshaw. Frank is a sailor like Charley Kinraid but, although Alice does in fact marry him, he is not yet a lover metaphorically. He is indeed not only a cousin but the son of a surrogate mother, Gaskell obviously feeling the need to be protected from him twice. It is her own fear she projects in her heroine when she observes that Alice was quite literally "frightened" by the intensity of Frank's passion (5:493). "The seed," she writes, "of their unhappiness lay in Frank's vehement, passionate disposition, which led him to resent his wife's shyness and want of demonstrativeness as failures in conjugal duty" (5:494). It would have made Alice a good deal happier had Frank, she adds, behaved less passionately (5:493), more like a brother, that is, than a lover. Frank very soon sets sail again, and not long after disappears, leaving Alice free to marry, after waiting a suitable time, a very different kind of man. Like Philip Hepburn in *Sylvia's Lovers,* Mr. Openshaw is in trade and there is nothing daemonic in him. He "required," the narrator writes, "no demonstration, no expressions of affection from her." These indeed "would rather have disgusted him" (5:503). Alice is very happy with him. It is significant that the story, when it appeared in *Household Words,* had the title "A House to Let." If the house is the outward form of the woman, as in Gaskell it always is, the woman in "The Manchester Marriage," having evicted her daemonic tenant, is available to be let to the feminine ideal.[2]

But having worked out some of her fears, perhaps in the very process of writing, Gaskell turned from "The Manchester Marriage" to *Sylvia's Lovers* with more confidence. For one thing, the demon that had surrendered in the short story here rebels. In *North and South* Gaskell had used, as one of the images of rebellion, Frederick Hale's mutiny at sea. She uses the image again in *Sylvia's Lovers,* not as a major event in the narrative, but, reversing the usual order by which her mind turns a figure of speech into an incident in the plot, by using the plot of *North and South* as a figure of speech in this novel. When Sylvia protests against her lessons, which she not only hates in themselves but also because her teacher is Philip, a man she throughly dislikes, Gaskell remarks it is only the thought that her mother would be displeased that prevents her from rising in "mutiny" (6:113).

Another sign of Gaskell's confidence is the fact that Sylvia here is allowed to want her demon. Ruth had wanted her demon too, but there her desire had been illicit. Here the demon is embodied in a perfectly legitimate suitor. Yet Gaskell is not quite free of doubt. Although she can say she wants her demon, she does not feel certain she can trust it. All through the novel, Gaskell vacillates, wondering whether or not she can let Sylvia put her faith in Kinraid. Over and over again she provides contradictory documentation on the subject of his worth. William, who is a friend of Philip's, says that Kinraid, having made his sister believe that he would marry her, promptly abandoned her to die, presumably of a broken heart. " 'He's a bad man,' " William concludes (6:89). But Gaskell refuses to deny or to verify his story. Similarly, when he is taken by the press-gang, Charley asks Philip to let Sylvia know that, since she has promised to marry him, he considers her his wife (6:234). But when Gaskell names the ship on which Charley is put *The Alcestis,* in a rare mythological reference, she seems to imply that, like Alcestis, Sylvia will be betrayed. It is generally true in Gaskell that any man who is loved by a heroine in a daemonic, passionate, way, turns out somehow to be untrustworthy. Nest in "The Well of Pen Morfa," for instance, Alice Carr in "Morton Hall," and Thelka in "Six Weeks at Heppenheim" are three of a very long list of women who love in a wild and passionate way men who love them back very casually and who finally abandon them. Ralph Corbet in "A Dark

Night's Work"—a story Gaskell must have been working on as she was finishing *Sylvia's Lovers* since it appeared in *All the Year Round* from January to March of 1863—is another such casual lover who abandons the woman who loves him. Explaining their relationship, Gaskell writes that Ralph and Ellinor "were desperately in love with each other, or perhaps I should rather say, Ellinor was desperately in love with him—he, as passionately as he could be with any one" (7:428). The logic seems to be in part that in calling forth her passion, a man calls forth a woman's demon, making her express that self that the world cannot love. But it is also very likely that Gaskell never quite trusted men. Her father had given her reason not to. Men are inconstant, unreliable. Their love is flimsy as the wind. To love them is to court betrayal.

Charley's abduction by the press-gang makes him yet another sailor Gaskell imagines lost at sea. And, although not in the way in which we have been expecting, it also makes him another lover who abandons the woman who loves him. He does not leave by choice, it is true. But Gaskell blames him nonetheless. At the novel's literal level, it makes no sense for her to blame him. But, as always, Gaskell knows precisely what she wants to say. The abduction is a metaphor. Kinraid, captured and confined, is the containment of the demon. Kinraid, thus, has failed the test. The demon can only prove itself trustworthy if it can stand up to the world, the world that Gaskell had in *Ruth* embodied in Mr. Bradshaw and Benson. Here she embodies it in the press-gangs. It is important to remember that, although the press-gang seems utterly lawless in its behavior, it is, in reality, the lawful arm of the Royal English Navy, abduction being at the time at which the action is taking place—which is the end of the eighteenth century—one of its recruiting methods. It is not only a legitimate power but also a power Gaskell surely associated with her paternal line, since a good many Stevenson men had served in the Royal Navy. And while, we recall, the demon in Gaskell always considered the government "they," "Mrs. Gaskell," as she wrote in her letter about Barbara Leigh Smith, was always intimidated by authority. Kinraid too, by being caught, has proved he cannot resist authority. What good can he be as a demon, then?

In Sylvia's father, Daniel Robson, Gaskell provides an object lesson in how authority deals with demons. Daniel's story in *Sylvia's Lovers* is identical in outline to John Barton's in *Mary Barton,* and Gaskell uses Sylvia's relationship to him as she had used Mary's to John. Like Mary and John, Sylvia and Daniel are very much alike in temperament (6:139). Daniel is also, like Kinraid, not only a sailor but romantic, bold, adventurous, and dashing. And, as these parallels suggest, Daniel is a daemonic man, the projection, like John Barton, of the demon in his daughter. He is a father ready, therefore, to *do* what his daughter *is*. The circumstances are similar too between John Barton and Daniel Robson. Daniel is, like John, obsessed. John hates the masters, Daniel the press-gangs. Daniel is by nature a rebel. Anything that curtails his liberty he considers a " 'meddle-some' " nuisance (6:53). But the press-gangs he hates especially. Not only are they an arm of the law, they are authority in its worst form, authority that comes at night and by stealth to carry off the bravest men. This sets the scene for the crucial incident. Arriving in Monkshaven one night, Monkshaven being the name of the town in which a part of the story is set, the press-gang rings the fire bell, hoping all the young men of the town will gather to help in the town square. The young men do, and when he sees that they are carried off by the press-gang, Daniel becomes enraged. He explodes. Being one of those himself who had believed there was a fire, Daniel rightly feels betrayed. He calls on all who have not been captured to fall on the press-gang, which they do. The confrontation is fierce and bloody and characteristically ends in a fire. It is the expression of his passion. The attack on the press-gang, however, has victims, and the fire leads to a death. Rebelling, thus, against authority, Daniel, like John, has committed a crime—indirectly, in fact, a murder. Daniel's rebellion against authority is metaphorically Sylvia's rebellion, as John Barton's is really Mary's, and, as Gaskell describes it herself, his "punishment" is "prompt and severe" (6:326). Daniel is tried, found guilty, and executed. Gaskell explains that Daniel's punishment is so very swift and harsh because the authorities feel an "example must be made" of Daniel's case (6:325). Daniel is an example indeed. For Gaskell, he is an example to Sylvia. And the message to her is clear. Daemonic behavior will not be tolerated. Rebels will be captured and punished.

It is at this moment in the novel that Sylvia decides to marry Philip, the other lover of the title, who embodies her other self. As far as she knows, her daemonic self—for Philip has not conveyed to Sylvia the truth of Kinraid's disappearance; she believes he has abandoned her—has been betrayed by Charley Kinraid. It has proved dangerous in Daniel. Philip, who is Sylvia's cousin and who behaves in a brotherly way, is the safe choice. He will not rebel. He has so little heart and backbone that he actually likes authority. He does not even mind the press-gangs (6:42–43). But marrying Philip is for Sylvia a betrayal of herself. The fact that Philip is in trade not only makes him a dull comparison to the romantic sailor Kinraid, it also identifies him metaphorically as an enemy of the demon. Gaskell did find business exciting, but trade she uses as a metaphor for the selling of the self. A number of men are in trade in Gaskell: Openshaw in "The Manchester Marriage" and Farquhar and Bradshaw in *Ruth*. In *Ruth* Jemima had actually said, as Gaskell made the image explicit, that she would rather be bought openly than trade her identity for love. When Sylvia marries Philip, however, that is precisely what she does. With Philip Sylvia becomes "tamed, just as a wild animal is tamed" (6:135). Even his effort to teach her to read, as Gaskell perceives it in the novel, is not an attempt to improve her mind as much as to destroy her spirit.

Although he is safe, Philip is thus not what Sylvia's demon yearns for. Gaskell had a good deal of trouble writing the chapter in which they marry. She had begun to write the novel on April 8 in 1860 and, with the usual interruptions for household affairs, family matters, and the writing of other stories, she had worked steadily for eighteen months, until December of 1861. But then there is a break in her progress. For nearly eight months she cannot write. In August of 1862 she finds she has not advanced one sentence beyond where she had been in December. Once she resumes, her progress again is fairly steady, even rapid. By February of the following year, the novel is already in print. Only on one other occasion did Gaskell, as we shall later see, experience such difficulty with her writing, and it is important to ask what it was that stood in the way of her continuing her narrative. She was busy, it is true, at the time she was writing this novel. Manchester was just then suffering from what it called its great Distress, the period during which its shipments of cotton from the United States, since the Civil War was raging, had been stopped or severely curtailed. Many factories had closed and the unemployed were starving. Gaskell had responded, as always, by volunteering her time and energy to help in every way she could. In addition, she was concerned that her publisher did not like what she had sent him of the novel, and she was more anxious than usual about the merits of her work (*L* 499). But all these circumstances, while they certainly contributed to her long dry spell, were not the real reason, I think, Gaskell could not go on with her novel. The real impediment was the fact that the next chapter would have required her to make Sylvia marry Philip. This is not immediately evident. Explaining her problem to her publisher, Gaskell writes that she has finished the second volume of the novel but cannot get started on the third (*L* 499). This would make it seem as though she had already written the chapter in which Sylvia and Philip marry, for when these volumes were finally published, the chapter in which the wedding occurs, which is chapter 29, appeared at the end of the second volume, the volume Gaskell says she has finished. But Gaskell had, in fact, not written it. It happens that when she completed the novel, Gaskell, realizing the pages had not been evenly distributed, moved the first chapter of volume 3 to the end of volume 2 (see *L* 511a), and as Easson rightly suggests, the chapter she moved was 29.[3] Thus it was the wedding chapter that Gaskell could not proceed to write. From a fictional point of view, nothing, of course, could have been easier. Once the couple is brought together, itself a simple thing to do, the rites and the rituals alone can substitute for narrative planning. But Gaskell had actually planned the chapter. She is already in her hiatus when she offers to send her publisher a sketch of what happens in volume 3 (*L* 499). What is preventing her is not that. What is preventing her is rather the fact that she does not want to do it. She cannot bring herself to turn Sylvia into "Mrs. Hepburn." It would mean turning herself into "Mrs. Gaskell" again.

Unable to continue her novel, Gaskell left England and went to France, showing that she was not, incidentally, so busy with her charitable work that she could not interrupt herself. She went, she said, to start her research for a biography, "a sort of Memoir," of Mme. de Sévigné (*L* 501). While writing *The Life of Charlotte Brontë*, Gaskell had observed to George Smith that, if she ever finished that book, she would write no more biographies (*L* 318). But here, in the middle of a slump, she seems determined to start a project of a kind she had already found difficult once before. Gaskell had been, she said, inspired to take on the project when she had met "a supposed-to-be well-educated young lady" who knew nothing about the Frenchwoman. And since the seventeenth-century figure had been to her "a well-known friend" (*L* 499), she thought she would make her known to others. Gaskell never did write that book, and I believe she never intended to, although she may have thought she did. I think she thought of taking it on only to avoid the destiny that she had prepared for Sylvia. By leaving England, the land of women, and going to France, the demon's home, she hoped perhaps to find the courage to save Sylvia from her fate. But all she did was to delay it. She simply could not imagine Sylvia escaping the life she had lived herself. After remaining in France for a while, she realized that she had to go home, and when she returned she wrote the chapter in which Sylvia marries Philip.

But Gaskell knew, as she wrote that chapter, she was condemning Sylvia to death. Once she is married, Sylvia, in fact, constantly wishes that she were dead (e.g., 6:399, 435, 470), and once, in a scene that resembles the moment in which Ruth Hilton wants to kill herself because she must give up her demon, Sylvia actually contemplates suicide (6:399). In a sense, to marry Philip, she has had to kill herself. The wedding is, in fact, like a funeral. Gaskell makes a point of reminding us that, since she is marrying Philip shortly after her father's death, Sylvia is married in her mourning dress (6:355). And when they return to the house from their wedding, Sylvia's mother, having just thought of her husband at that moment, greets them at the door with sounds, not of joy, but of "weeping and wailing" (6:360). If you kill passion, you kill life. The moment Sylvia marries Philip is for Gaskell the moment she dies.

Through Sylvia, therefore, Gaskell has failed to take possession of her demon. And having failed, she transfers her quest, strangely enough, to Philip Hepburn. We witness perhaps the very moment Gaskell begins to identify with Philip when the narrator remarks that in trying to win Sylvia, Philip had tried "to win the love that had never been his" (6:414). These words are the story of Gaskell's life. When they become the story of Philip's, we see that he has assumed the role of being her surrogate in the novel. This is the second stage of the relay. In a new and different way, Gaskell now requires Philip to *do* what his wife *is*.

Although he does not at first appear so, Philip is a daemonic man. To use a phrase Gaskell had used to describe Jemima in *Ruth,* he is a character who is seething with a dark and sullen passion. It is, however, a passion that Philip finds it impossible to express. His demon, as in "Lois the Witch," is imprisoned by religion, Philip being one of the Quakers who let Gaskell in this novel explore the Society of Friends. The Quakers, of course, are very liberal in their theological views, and not very strict in other ways either, but Gaskell, seeing all religion as the enemy of her demon, speaks of the Quaker community here just as she does of the Salem Puritans. The "atmosphere among the Friends at this date," she writes, "partook of this character of self-repression" (6:136).

Philip is thus a demon imprisoned, his "rigid conscience" (6:217) having contained, as Gaskell puts it, his "impetuous heart" (6:141). At one point he is described as "pent up" (6:159). We feel psychologically claustrophobic whenever he is introduced on the page. He resembles Manasseh in "Lois the Witch," both in appearance and in character.[4] Like him, he is tall and thin (6:26). Like him, there is something about him—Gaskell seems to hint it has to do in some way with his thin upper lip—that, although he might have been handsome had he not had this one impediment, makes him positively repulsive. He also reminds us of Manasseh in that he is a man obsessed. This is what Gaskell meant to suggest when she considered calling the novel, not *Sylvia's Lovers,* but *Philip's Idol* (L 493). Consciously Gaskell was thinking of idols, as always, in religious terms. Philip's story, in this sense, is the story of a man who is destroyed because he loves a woman more than he loves God. We should not lightly dismiss this theme. It is important to "Mrs. Gaskell." But Philip's idolatry, in the subtext, is his obsession with the demon that is imprisoned in his soul.

Concealing an imprisoned demon, Philip represents to Gaskell the archetypal condition of woman. Gaskell clearly considers him female. All his characteristics are female, and he behaves in a female way. Thus, he is weak and undecided (6:137–39). When he and Charley visit the Robsons, Kinraid, for instance, sits with Daniel, smoking and talking by the fire, and it is clear that Gaskell sees both of these activities as male. Philip, however, sits sullen and silent, apart in a corner, not only because Sylvia seems to prefer Kinraid but also because he objects to smoke (6:116). Philip always objects to something, or he has an aversion to it, or it is something he cannot do. Thus, for example, he cannot drink, another activity that is male. Kinraid is "too well seasoned to care what amount of liquor he drank," but Philip "had what was called a weak head, and disliked mud-dling himself with drink" (6:152). It is no wonder that the press-gang that seizes Kinraid as a prize decides, upon examining Philip, that he is not worth the taking (6:232–33). Perhaps the most convincing moment on the subject of his gender occurs when Philip himself compares his appearance with Kinraid's. The only object he possesses in which he can study his reflection is a little woman's mirror (6:408). The fact itself that he owns such a mirror—we can be sure Kinraid does not—defines him as a female type. And if it is in a woman's mirror that he studies his reflection, is it not, in the novel's subtext, a woman he sees reflected there?

Gaskell not only envisions Philip as the archetypal woman, she imag-ines him as standing virtually in Sylvia's place. She is divided between two men. He is divided between two women, each a different part of himself. One of the women is Hester Rose, a Quaker who, in relation to him, plays the role he plays to Sylvia. Hester is daemonic too. She has "her own private rebellion." But like Philip's it is "hushed into submission by her gentle piety" (6:440). The other woman is Sylvia herself, who is to him a Charley Kinraid. Philip is also precisely like Sylvia in wanting to possess his demon. And this, like Margaret in *North and South,* when the oppor-tunity offers itself, he attempts to do by lying. Instead of letting Sylvia know that Kinraid has been abducted, as Kinraid begs him to do, Philip says nothing, allowing Sylvia to believe Kinraid has betrayed her. Gaskell does not become as distraught here as she had in *North and South,* but the lie does trouble her. It is always on Philip's mind, as it had always been on Margaret's. And, as in *North and South,* it becomes a part of the novel's moral drama. The moral point is made by Jeremiah, a Quaker who is

Philip's employer. " 'It was,' " Jeremiah says to Sylvia, " 'a self-seeking lie; putting thee to pain to get his own ends. And the end of it has been that he is driven forth like Cain' " (6:436). Jeremiah is doubly right. The lie is " 'self-seeking' " not only morally but psychologically as well. Through it Philip "seeks" possession of the "self" that is his demon. And the lie works. Margaret's lie in *North and South* had turned out to be unnecessary. The demon she had wanted to protect had already been safe without it. Philip's lie is not only necessary, it is entirely indispensable. Without it, Sylvia would not have married him. She only marries Philip because, thinking Kinraid has abandoned her, she sees no point in waiting for him. The lie alone enables Philip therefore to possess his demon.

And yet, in a sense, he does not possess it, even when he marries Sylvia. The only real demon for Gaskell is Charley, and once she has lost him, Sylvia herself becomes as undaemonic as Philip. Later, indeed, when she becomes a member of the Quaker community, Sylvia is actually "saved" like Ruth, although this is only in this novel a very small portion of the narrative. It is Charley Philip must seek if he wishes to claim his demon, and this is precisely what he attempts to do in the next of the novel's relays.

Superficially, Philip is meant to be a contrast to Kinraid. Philip himself, knowing he lacks them, envies Kinraid his manly virtues, most especially the virtues that make him such a gallant "sailor" (6:173–74). Gaskell is aware in this instance that the moral contrast she sees is at odds with the psychological. It is indeed a remarkable aspect of her portrayal of Philip Hepburn that we despise him for his virtues as we like Kinraid for his faults. Kinraid, for instance, flatters Sylvia, as he has flattered other girls, but neither we nor Sylvia object. Philip never flatters idly, which is certainly to his credit, but he makes us shrink and shudder as, "discontented," he stares at Sylvia at a party with "longing eyes" (6:153). Kinraid is reckless. He lives for the day. He takes no thought for the morrow. He has never saved a penny, and while he promises to begin as soon as Sylvia says she will marry him (6:207), we know that he will never be prudent. But Philip's careful frugal habits seem by comparison petty and mean. Philip worries about Sylvia. He wants to teach her how to read, and we agree that she should learn. But she would rather hear Kinraid, and we cannot but feel as she does, telling stories of dolphins and mermaids. Kinraid, if he is lax and careless, is, for that reason, flexible and free. Philip, rigorous and disciplined, is, for that reason, repressed and rigid.

The contrast is only apparent, however. In reality they are alike. Metaphorically, indeed, they are really the same person. The fact that

Philip is always watching Kinraid (6:174), always stalking him, walking behind him, walking in his very footsteps, makes Philip, in a figurative way, the very shadow of Kinraid. And this is the image Gaskell literalizes on the day of the abduction, Kinraid strolling in the sunlight on the sandy shore of the sea, Philip following him in the shade as though he were his very shadow (6:226–27). The fact that he alone, moreover, knows what has happened to Kinraid makes him, in that special sense we have seen before in Gaskell, a secret sharer, a second self. Gaskell suggested something similar in "The Manchester Marriage." Many years after he disappears, Frank comes back to look for Alice—Frank being thus another sailor who miraculously returns after he is lost at sea. Realizing she has remarried, Frank does not reveal his presence. But Openshaw discovers his "secret," becoming, like Philip, his secret sharer. Later, when Frank has committed suicide, Openshaw insists on burying him, saying he can do no less since Frank was "like a brother" to him (5:522). This, however, is very strange. There is no connection in the story between Openshaw and Frank. They did not even know each other. But Gaskell, ignoring the text completely because her mind is on her subtext, knows that she has created Frank as the hidden demon of Openshaw. It is significant that Openshaw changes radically after the funeral, becoming more impulsive, bolder, more assertive, and in general more of a daemonic type. He has internalized the demon that lies "shrouded" in the grave. Kinraid in a similar manner is in reality Philip's demon. And Philip is the captured Kinraid. The moment, in fact, that Kinraid is caught he becomes the imprisoned Philip.

To free the demon Gaskell must therefore free that part of Philip Hepburn that is in truth the daemonic Kinraid. And this is precisely what she does. The next to last lap of the novel begins when Sylvia learns the truth that Kinraid had not abandoned her. Kinraid, escaping from the navy, has returned to look for Sylvia, only to find that she is married and the mother of a child. He asks her to have her marriage annulled and to marry him instead, but Sylvia says she cannot do it. She cannot break her marriage vow, she cannot take her child from its father. Painful as it is for her, she says she must refuse Kinraid. But she is very angry with Philip and vows that she will never forgive him or live with him as his wife again (6:404). And Philip, unable to stand her anger, and blaming himself in any case, decides that he must go away. Thus begins for Philip a journey that is both literal and metaphoric. This journey is the most unlikely and unbelievable part of the novel, but it is essential to Gaskell. It is the means of liberating Philip and finally setting his demon free.

Gaskell realizes that Philip, if he is to escape his imprisonment, needs to be completely transformed. He needs to die as Philip Hepburn and to be somehow reborn in his full daemonic character. Metaphorically, this is what happens. Gaskell first releases Philip from the prison of religion. Not only does he leave the Quakers literally when he goes away, he leaves them spiritually as well when he decides to join the marines. The Quakers are pacifists, and Hester's mother can hardly believe a " 'man of peace' " would become " 'a man of war' " (6:475–76). But that is Gaskell's point precisely. Philip must break the Quaker mold. War, moreover, to Gaskell is *doing*. Restrained by his Quakerism, Philip had *been*. Now he is finally able to *do*. On the battlefield, in fact, Philip behaves in a manner quite different from the Philip of Monkshaven. He is a brave and dashing figure. He is a daring, adventurous man. In writing this section of the novel, Gaskell herself is able to *do*. Many of the events in this section—fires, riots, battle scenes— dramatize her daemonic images. It is important in itself that Philip has chosen to join the marines, not another branch of the service. The marines take Philip out to sea. Thus, once again, he trails Kinraid. Indeed, as before he had walked in his shadow, so he follows him literally now. When Sylvia had told him she could not now abandon Philip to marry him, Kinraid had left to join a war. Philip, looking now for a war, finds the one Kinraid is fighting in. And as divided selves in Gaskell always in some manner meet—Lucy her demon in a mirror—Philip, in a chapter Gaskell signifi- cantly calls "Recognition," meets Kinraid on the battlefield. Kinraid is wounded, and Philip saves him (6:455), thus preserving his demon's life. But in the act of saving Kinraid, Philip is hurt by an explosion, burned beyond recognition, in fact (6:358). Explosions too are daemonic images, and burning Philip beyond recognition, this one physically transforms him, turns him into another man. Just before he had left Monkshaven, Philip had said his life was ended (6:403). On his journey he had written to Hester to look on him as one dead (6:428). Now, at the military hospital, he says he does not want to live (6:478). The Philip we know does die indeed metaphorically at this moment. In a sense, he is even buried. On his way home, he stops for a while at a monastery to which Gaskell, clearly thinking of her imagery, gives the name of St. Sepulchre (6:486). Philip has died and been reborn in a completely different form. And, to acknowledge it, he is given an entirely new name. Gaskell had renamed Ruth and Bellingham when she had brought them from Wales to Eccleston so as to show they were different people, no longer their old daemonic selves. In *Sylvia's Lovers,* she does the reverse. Once the demon is freed in Philip, he is endowed with a new name to establish his new identity. The name in fact describes his state. Gaskell now calls him Stephen Freeman (6:414). We recall that Gaskell had wanted to use Stephen Berwick as her pseudonym for the publication of *Mary Barton,* Stephen being derived, of course, from her own family name. In *Mary Barton* she had been thinking not of herself but of her father. Here it is herself she projects. Assigning Philip her family name, she tells us, in the surname she gives him, that she has become through him—being now a *man* and *free*—both a male and a demon.

Had Gaskell ended her narrative here, *Sylvia's Lovers* would have been a most extraordinary triumph. The novel is so courageous in fact in facing and laying claim to the demon that by the time she reaches the end, Gaskell has managed to frighten herself, as she had frightened herself in *Ruth.* The end of the novel is therefore troubled. There are, in a sense, three separate endings, one a retraction by "Mrs. Gaskell," one the product of the conflict between "Mrs. Gaskell" and the demon, and the last one an escape for the demon into freedom.

"Mrs. Gaskell" brings the novel to a "religious" and "moral" conclusion. Sylvia, hoping to find some comfort after many years of pain, finally becomes a Quaker. Philip, who has now come home—although so altered in appearance that even Sylvia does not know him—also takes comfort in religion, becoming a Quaker once again. He lives a quiet, simple life until one day his daughter Bella, running into the waves of the sea, loses her footing and cries out for help. Philip is able to save her life, but in the process loses his own. Just before he dies, however, Sylvia arrives to thank the man who has saved her child from death, and in talking to him realizes that the man is her husband, Philip. All is forgiven, and Philip's last words, which are predictably "In heaven!" (6:528), seem to imply that they will be reunited in the hereafter.

On these last pages too, "Mrs. Gaskell" finally discredits Kinraid. The very last we hear about him, he has not only gone to seed, he has become a compulsive gambler who, to pay off his enormous debts, has married a wealthy older woman. This is, however, hard to believe. We might have believed—we had been prepared for it—that Kinraid had finally ended his days, although he had been true enough to return to Sylvia once, as a philanderer, breaking young hearts, even perhaps as an old rake. But it is very hard to believe that he becomes opportunistic. That is simply not his style. It may, however, be that Gaskell provides him with such an unlikely end because she intends us to disbelieve it. Her demon seems, in any case, to think that Kinraid, after all, might have been worthy of being trusted. The fact that he did not leave willingly, the fact that he came back when he could—becoming thus another sailor who disappears and returns in Gaskell—and that he wanted to marry Sylvia suggest that

Gaskell did believe him. Indeed, it is he who feels betrayed. The words we expect all through the novel to hear Sylvia say to him are words he actually says to her. When he returns, he says he had " 'trusted' " her but that she had proven " 'false' " (6:402). She should have waited, not married Philip. It is Philip, in fact, who lied. Perhaps it was he who could not be trusted. Before the reconciliation, before the forgiveness, before the end, Sylvia says very plainly to Philip " 'Our being wed were a great mistake' " (6:388).

But "Mrs. Gaskell" does not like to end a book on such a hopeless note. She does not like irremediability. It was not just because Unitarianism required her to be optimistic. It was because irremediable sorrow was simply too hard for her to bear. She needed to feel she could find a remedy or explain sorrow away. She knows that after Kinraid returns, Sylvia is right to say of Philip " 'he's just spoilt my life, and I'm not one and twenty yet' " (6:426), but she also knows this realization has come to Sylvia much too late. *Too Late,* according to A. W. Ward, was another of the titles Gaskell considered before she settled on *Sylvia's Lovers* (6:xiv–xv). "Too late" is always one of her themes, as well as one of her favorite phrases. When Peter in *Cranford* runs away, his parents follow him to the ship hoping they can persuade him to stay. But they arrive " 'too late . . . too late' " (2:68). Squire Osborne, in *Wives and Daughters,* wishes after Osborne dies he had been better friends with his son. " 'I know,' " he says, " 'better now; but it's too late—that's the sting of it—too late, too late!' " (8:661). So the knowledge comes too late to Sylvia that she should have waited. She is already "Mrs. Hepburn," just as Gaskell was "Mrs. Gaskell" when the knowledge came to her that she might have trusted her demon. That is why she called the novel "the saddest story I ever wrote" (6:xii).

Nothing can diminish the sadness. And yet the demon does escape. Sylvia's and Philip's daughter, Bella, when she grows up, moves to America. Her parents, by then, have long been dead, but they have entered into her. As Sylvia surrendered her quest to Philip, so, when he died to save her life, did Philip surrender it to Bella. Bella is thus the last of the relays. In moving therefore to America, Bella takes the family demon out of England, the land of women, to settle it in the home of the free.

XV

Nature Intended Me
for a Gypsy-Bachelor

FATHERS, BROTHERS, AND HUSBANDS, thus, act out the demon in Gaskell's fiction that women cannot act out for themselves. The women for whom they act are daemonic, and they continue to be daemonic, but something happens in this surrogacy. The demon, conveyed to a man for *doing,* becomes in the woman contained again. This is especially, although not exclusively, true in relationships between husbands and wives. On marrying Philip, Sylvia's feelings become, for instance, "concealed and latent" (6:362). In *North and South* Gaskell had tried to avoid this problem in Margaret and Thornton by letting the conflicts that had led them to the discovery of their love continue into their engagement and presumably into their marriage. Austen had done this in *Pride and Prejudice* and Charlotte Brontë in *Jane Eyre*. The playful antagonism, for instance, Jane establishes with Rochester places a space between their identities that lets her keep her own distinct. Gaskell envisions Margaret and Thornton too as playfully "antagonistic" (4:282–83). But, although the device had worked for Austen and for Charlotte Brontë, it simply does not work for Gaskell. Hard as she tries, she cannot manage to keep a woman daemonically equal. The moment she imagines a woman in a relationship with a man, she cannot resist the old compulsion to hide the demon that might "vex" him.

It is not men alone who intimidate Gaskell's demon into concealment, although it is they who do so most. It is—and this is the reason, of course, men become threats not only literally but metaphorically to Gaskell—the condition of "Mrs. Gaskell." Brontë, with her usual shrewdness, once asked Gaskell in a letter: "Do you, who have so many friends,—so large a circle of acquaintances,—find it easy, when you sit down to write, to isolate yourself from all those ties, and their sweet associations, so as to be your *own woman,* uninfluenced or swayed by the consciousness of how your work may affect other minds; what blame or sympathy it may call forth? Does no luminous cloud ever come between you and the severe Truth, as you know it in your own secret and clear-seeing soul? In a word, are you never tempted to make your characters more amiable than Life, by the inclination to assimilate your thought to the thoughts of those who always *feel* kindly, but sometimes fail to *see* justly? Don't answer the question; it is not intended to be answered" (*LCB*, pp. 450–51). Brontë focuses on the writing, but she is asking a larger question. What she is asking is whether Gaskell, in the midst of her family and friends, can tell what she thinks from what she believes others think she ought to be thinking, can tell what she feels from what she feels others think she ought to be feeling, or can even tell who she is not only apart from her relationships but without seeing herself reflected in the image she sees in their eyes.

On rare occasions Gaskell could, as, for example, when she remarked "I am myself and nobody else, and can't be bound by another's rules" (*L* 32). But all too often Gaskell could not continue to be herself with others. To be herself she needed solitude. "Mrs. Gaskell" found it hard to believe that Florence Nightingale not only could but in fact preferred to stand "perfectly alone" (*L* 217). But her demon understood. When Sylvia feels imprisoned by marriage, she longs for the "solitude" that is "freedom" (6:379). Similarly, Margaret Hale is relieved to hear at one point that her father is planning a journey. She has been taking care of her mother, who has just died, and now she feels "how great and long had been the pressure on her time and spirits. It was astonishing," she continues when she is at last alone, "to feel herself so much *at liberty*: no one depending on her for cheering care, if not for positive happiness; no invalid to plan and think for; she might be idle, and silent and forgetful—she might be unhappy if she liked. For months past all her own personal cares and troubles had had to be stuffed away into a dark cupboard, but now she had leisure to take them out" (4:410–11; italics mine). Gaskell too needed to have a time when she did not have to be cheerful. Once, while preparing the house for some guests, she wrote to Charles Eliot Norton "I am *very* fond of the people who are coming; but so worn-out that it is hard word [*sic*] to lash myself up into properly hospitable feelings. Marianne said yesterday, 'Oh! are not you tired of being agreeable! I do so want leisure to sulk and be silent in;' and really after long hard hot days at the Exhibition showing the same great pictures over & over again to visitors, who have only time to look superficially at the whole collection, one does want 'to sulk & be silent' in the evenings" (*L* 374). She treasured her rare moments of solitude. Returning from a vacation in Knutsford, where she had been alone a good deal, Gaskell once wrote: "I am so much better . . . partly air, partly quiet and partly being by myself a good piece of every day which is I am sure so essential to my health that I am going to preserve and enforce it here" (*L* 106).

When Gaskell speaks of being alone she does not always mean physical solitude, but solitude of the physical kind is often essential for her too, for, as Brontë had rightly guessed, as soon as she is with friends and family, she tends to become "Mrs. Gaskell" again. In her fiction, to keep her demon, to be really and fully herself, a woman must remain alone. She may have family and friends, although these must not be too close, but she must remain unmarried. Not every woman who is single is daemonic in Gaskell's fiction. There are single female types, Miss Matty, for example, in *Cranford*. But women, if they are daemonic, seem by nature single to Gaskell. Cynthia can stand as a paradigm case. Cynthia, as we have seen already, is very popular with men. Every man she meets falls in love with her, partly because she is so beautiful, but also because, although unconsciously, she works so hard at being alluring. And yet—or rather, perhaps, and therefore—Cynthia is, as Gaskell conceives her, really by nature a single type. When Mrs. Gibson at one point realizes that Cynthia has become entangled with a large number of men, she warns her that if she is not careful she will " 'end' " up as " 'an old maid.' " Cynthia replies, " 'I dare say I shall. . . . I sometimes think I'm the kind of person of which old maids are made' " (8:631). The Cynthia who makes men fall in love with her is the mirror of Molly Gibson after she has killed herself. The "real self," which is hidden—"shrouded"—remains in some ultimate way inaccessible. Cynthia is thus a virgin type, virginal not in the sexual sense but in the sense that, to preserve her demon against the encroachments of men, she has been required to make herself metaphorically impenetrable. Many characters of this sort are to be found in Gaskell's fiction. Some of them marry. Cynthia does. Some have been married in the past. Bridget the witch is the archetype here. But all in some ultimate sense are women who live within themselves, alone.

Most of Gaskell's virginal women never marry at all, in fact. The list of these characters is long. It includes such prototypical instances as Faith Benson and Sally in Ruth, Phoebe Browning in *Wives and Daughters,* Dixon in *North and South,* Susan Dixon in "Half a Lifetime Ago," Nest in "The Well of Pen Morfa," Miss Galindo in "My Lady Ludlow," Amante in "The Grey Woman," Victorine in "Crowley Castle," and the title character in "Libbie Marsh's Three Eras." Most are very hostile to marriage. When Faith receives the letter, for instance, from her brother about Ruth, she answers curtly " 'Nothing very romantic, I hope, Thurstan. Remember, I cannot stand much romance; I always distrust it' " (3:111). Miss Pole has no use for marriage in *Cranford,* and she congratulates herself on having so far escaped being married, "which she noticed always made people credulous to the last degree; indeed, it argues in her mind a great natural credulity in a woman if she cannot keep herself single" (2:127). Miss Browning observes in a similar way in *Wives and Daughters* to her guests, all of whom happen to be women, that she hopes she will not offend them if she admits that she is " 'inclined to look upon matrimony as a weakness' " (8:581). Sally in *Ruth* is even more hostile. She has only contempt for men. She tells at one point a very long story about a man with whom she kept company, although she really did not like him, until he offended her by proposing. Not only did she turn him down, she scolded him thoroughly for his conceit in thinking he had but to " 'ask and have' " (3:166–69). Dixon in *North and South* is the same. Deeply devoted to Mrs. Hale, as Sally is devoted to Benson, she despises Mr. Hale, whom she considers a "malignant giant" (4:20). And close to them, although not humorous, as Dixon and Sally often are, is Victorine in "Crowley Castle." If anyone in Gaskell's fiction is in earnest Amazonian it is characters such as these. Many happen to be servants, as are many of those named here. But unlike the servants in whom Gaskell embodies the image of ideal womanhood, servants like these are essentially male. The two are not unconnected, however. As female Bessys in her fiction are, as in the Mummers' Play, males who are disguised as women, so are many female servants in reality antithetical males.

Women who are born to be single are often women who whistle in Gaskell. Gaskell is thinking of the tradition that claims that whistling summons the devil. It is to this that she alludes when, in jest in *Wives and Daughters,* she speaks of whistling as a "sin" (8:500). The devil is, of course, the demon, as is made clear in "Lois the Witch," and it is their daemonic selves women summon when they whistle. Whistling is thus, being daemonic, associated in Gaskell's mind, as she remarks herself in *Ruth,* with "masculinity," with the male principle (3:111). Women who whistle are always male. In *Ruth* it is Faith Benson who whistles (3:111), in "My Lady Ludlow," Miss Galindo (5:143). Gaskell was a whistler herself. Her brother, facing contrary winds, teased her once by saying his progress had been impeded by her whistling.[1]

The business of the male principle is to keep itself from marriage. That is the point of a short story, "Mr. Harrison's Confessions." As many have noted, the story has much of the flavor in it of *Cranford.*[2] The setting, as Gérin suggests, is Knutsford[3]—it is called Duncombe in the story— and most of the characters, as in *Cranford,* are "women" "of a certain rank" (5:413–14). The plot concerns a surgeon named Harrison, who, on moving to Duncombe, finds that he is an object of interest to three women in the town, one a widow, Mrs. Rose, one a spinster, a Miss Bullock, and the third, a spinster too, the younger of the Tomkinson sisters. The last, Miss Caroline, first appears to be a kind of younger Miss Matty, but she is only playing a part. Her sister, however, the elder Miss Tomkinson, very much resembles Deborah. Like her, she is stern and fierce and of a military disposition. And she is virginal, a male type. Mr. Harrison describes her as a "masculine-looking woman, with an air of defiance about her" (5:414). Much of the humor of the story depends on the fact that each of the three convinces herself that Mr. Harrison has decided to marry her, spreading the news all over town and causing a good many misunderstandings. Mr. Harrison's task in the story is to escape being ensnared.

As in *Cranford,* Gaskell is writing not about sex here but about gender, and Mr. Harrison in the story is not so much a man as a male. In a town essentially female, he embodies the male principle. Gaskell so sets up the story as to make clear that if he marries he will cease to be a male. And when he marries, so he does. The story is a retrospective told by Mr. Harrison himself long after the events, and when we meet him at the beginning—married now to none of the three, but to a woman named Sophy—we see him sitting in his house with a friend who has come to visit him. The friend is male. He is active, "restless." He is a character who *does*. But Mr. Harrison has become so inactive by this time that he can no longer *do*. He is even, the narrator tells us, grown "too lazy" now to "talk" (5:405). Married, he has become a female who is content simply to *be*.

Women who want to keep their demons must often in Gaskell turn marriage down. This is what Susan Dixon does in "Half a Lifetime Ago." In "The Poor Clare," Gaskell shows that women who want to be loved and married—the narrator says he will marry Lucy as soon as she is free of her curse—must repudiate their demons. The choice in "Half a Lifetime Ago" is still the same—the demon or marriage—but here, instead of seeking love, Gaskell seeks to keep her demon. It is significant that Susan, who gets along well with her father, quarrels constantly with her mother. Generally, as we have seen, Gaskell idealizes mothers, and so do the children she creates. But sometimes there are terrible conflicts, as there are here, between mothers and daughters. These, however, seem confrontations less between individual characters than between the types they stand for, the single and the married woman. And this appears to be the case in "Half a Lifetime Ago." Mrs. Dixon is "Mrs. Gaskell." And this is what Susan refuses to be, as we discover when her lover, Michael Hurst, asks her to choose between marriage and her demon. Susan loves Michael as

Sylvia loves Charley, with a wild and passionate love. And Michael, being loved so passionately, proves inevitably unworthy. Charley, except at the very end, seems at worst lighthearted and casual. But Michael is calculating and cool and essentially materialistic. He likes Susan well enough, but what he really hopes to get is the farm she will inherit. Michael proposes and Susan accepts. But before they can be married, Mrs. Dixon falls ill and dies, not, however, until she has made Susan promise to take care of her younger brother, Willie, who is unable to care for himself. When Mr. Dixon also dies, Willie is left in Susan's charge. Willie's behavior is sometimes violent, and Michael does not want him around. He insists they institutionalize him. But Susan refuses. Michael thinks he will force her hand by telling her she must choose between them. And Susan does. She chooses Willie.

Most of those who have read this story, and not a great many people have, see Willie, as does Angus Easson, as a Wordsworthian idiot boy.[4] Some of the characters in the story who neither know nor understand him, call him an " 'idiot' " in derision (5:310), and it is true he is not " 'quick' " (5:283). But that is not Gaskell's point at all. The point is rather his wild behavior. It is on this that Gaskell dwells, inventing, we suspect, his slowness merely to explain the fact that he is impervious to reason. His outbursts and his rages indeed make him seem mad rather than witless, and this is what Gaskell suggests herself when Susan, as she wrestles with him—which she often has to do, sometimes only metaphorically but at other times quite literally—prays for strength so that she will not have to commit him to a "madhouse" (5:316). Daemonic single women in Gaskell often take mad people in. Nest, for example, in "The Well of Pen Morfa," a wild and vehement woman herself, takes a mad woman in to live with her after she loses the man she loves, and Libbie Marsh, a single woman whom Gaskell describes as "fierce and unwomanly" (1:488), takes in the mad Mrs. Hall. And these mad people, it is clear, are metaphorical externalizations of what Gaskell had in *Ruth* called the "sweet insanity within." As she so often does in her fiction, Gaskell is personifying the image, turning a mere figure of speech into a character in the plot. But the meaning is the same. Willie is Susan's "sweet insanity." He is her demon, and Gaskell says so when she remarks that, during those nights Susan has to struggle with him, passersby might hear the "sounds of knocking about of furniture, blows, and cries" as though there were someone within engaged in battle with "some tearing *demon*" (5:315; italics mine). When Susan, therefore, turns Michael down for the sake of keeping

Willie, she is turning down the role of the ideal "Mrs. Gaskell," choosing instead to live the single, the daemonic, life.

It is important to note explicitly what Gaskell makes implicit here, namely that a single woman, single in spirit as well as in fact, is transformed into a male. Gaskell thinks of Susan as male. A "strong" and "independent" woman (5:282), she seems to Gaskell "more of a man" (5:282). On the farm, Susan prefers the male activities to the female. Whenever she goes to market, for instance, she quickly disposes of the "more feminine articles" she has brought with her to sell and turns to "the man's side." And she is a "better judge," it would seem, "of a horse or a cow" than any man "in the country round" (5:318). Often Susan wishes in fact that she had been born a man (5:285). Gaskell thought of Marianne, because she was supremely competent in the practical details of life, in a very similar way. To Charles Eliot Norton, she wrote that " 'Marianne is as practical and humorous as ever. Her quick decision always makes me feel as if she was a kind of 'elder *son*' rather than daughter' " (*L* 418). Characters like Deborah Jenkyns, the elder Miss Browning in *Wives and Daughters* and the elder Miss Tomkinson in "Mr. Harrison's Confessions" are humorous versions of the type that is the single male woman. So is Miss Pole. Her manner in *Cranford* is curt and abrupt in a way that Gaskell always identifies as male. And her attempt to expose the magic show by using evidence and reason are, in Gaskell's imagination, a male attack on the female world. Her name, of course, is a phallic symbol.

The only women who are not single who remain daemonic in Gaskell are the ones who enter relationships, not as females, but as males. Most relationships in this category simulate a married couple, but only in an older pair is it a traditional marriage. In *Wives and Daughters,* for example, Lady Cumnor is a male, while her husband, weak and yielding, plays the traditional role of the female. A few of the simulated marriages also include a man as a female. This is the case with the Bensons in *Ruth*. I suggested earlier that Faith acts as a kind of "wife" to Benson. It would be more accurate to say that she assumes the part of his "husband." Lansbury is right to say that the two have exchanged roles.[5] Describing the pair, the narrator writes that "Miss Benson's excellent sense, perhaps, made her a more masculine character than her brother. He was often so much perplexed by the problems of life" (3:203). And that perplexity to Gaskell—women being unintellectual, undecided, and befuddled—makes of Mr. Benson a female.

Most of Gaskell's surrogate couples consist, however, of two women.

Sometimes, like a traditional family, the couple centers on a child. Thus, for example, Libbie Marsh becomes a kind of male protector to Mrs. Hall and her son Frankie, and even after the child dies, it is his memory that remains the primary bond between them. Many female couples are sisters. The Browning sisters in *Wives and Daughters* are a couple of this sort, as are the Jenkyns sisters in *Cranford* and the Tomkinsons in "Mr. Harrison's Confessions." "Morton Hall" has a pair of such sisters in Phillis and Ethelinda Morton (2:464–65). Sometimes couples of two women are related in other ways. Alice in "The Manchester Marriage" and her aunt are a kind of couple, although the aunt is a surrogate mother and a mother-in-law, in fact. Ellinor in "A Dark Night's Work" forms, with her governess, another couple, the two, now adults, living together but playing still the mother and child. None of these is a lesbian couple, as Lansbury thinks some are in Gaskell,[6] not in an ordinary sense at least. But in her reason for creating them, Gaskell anticipates Adrienne Rich, who writes that in a lesbian relationship a woman is given the "sense of desiring oneself; above all, of choosing oneself."[7] Gaskell would say of choosing the demon. For it is true that in each of her couples, one of the women plays the role of the feminine "Mrs. Gaskell," while the other, escaping the mold, creates a situation in which she can live the daemonic life.

The most significant couple of women is to be found in "The Grey Woman." The story, which is set in Germany, has as its heroine Anna Scherer, a very beautiful young woman wooed by many eligible men, one of whom she finally marries, a M. de la Tourelle. La Tourelle is a passionate man, and much like Alice in "The Manchester Marriage" in her relationship to Frank, Anna is "frightened" by "the excess of his demonstrations of love" (7:311). After they marry, Anna discovers that her husband is also violent. Suspecting that she has not been given some letters written to her by her family, Anna, one night while he is away, steals into her husband's study. But suddenly she hears a voice just outside the study door. Hiding quickly under a table, she sees her husband coming in with a band of men behind him, and from their conversation learns that he is a "chief of chauffeurs," a bloody band of thieves and murderers who plunder the countryside by night. They have a body with them, in fact, of a neighbor whom they have murdered. Also from their conversation, she learns that her husband was married before to a woman whom he murdered when she discovered his activities. There is no doubt she will be murdered if he finds her in the room, and the very thought of her danger causes her such terrible "fright" that her hair turns completely grey (7:303), making her "The Grey Woman" of the title.

M. de la Tourelle reminds us of the Squire in "The Squire's Story," and Anna reminds us of his wife, who also discovers after her marriage that her husband is a highwayman plundering the country at night. Tales such as this always fascinated Gaskell. On one of her many trips to Paris, Gaskell came across an account (in the very house she was staying in) of Mme. la Marquise de Gange, which she recorded in "French Life." In the essay, Gaskell reports that the marquise, before the wedding, believed that the man she intended to marry was a kind and gentle soul. As soon as they were married, however, he and his brothers conspired to kill her so that they could inherit her wealth. The story so appealed to Gaskell that she immediately determined to visit the house in which the marquise had allegedly been killed (7:664 ff.).

The fact that men seem only in Gaskell to reveal themselves at night has sexual implications, of course, and M. de la Tourelle has a name that, like Miss Pole's, makes an obvious phallic connection. But sexuality in Gaskell always represents the demon, and the narrator in due course does call la Tourelle a "demon" (7:364). He is Anna Scherer's demon. Like Frederick Hale in *North and South,* he is, in outward form, a woman, "effeminate," as he is called, both in "appearance" and in "manner" (7:313). Even his nocturnal activities, concealing the demon as they do under the secrecy of night, identify him as a woman who is required to hide her demon. The whole of his criminal career is Anna's demon acted out. M. de la Tourelle is thus one of the husbands in Gaskell's fiction who is assigned the task of *doing* what his wife only *is.* But yielding her demon to her husband has for Anna the usual consequences. Although her husband does not discover her hiding that night under the table, he does suspect she knows his secret, and he decides she must be "confined" (7:153). And when he locks her up in the castle, Anna becomes the typical woman, an angel imprisoned in her house.

It is precisely this "imprisonment" (7:319) she escapes when she proceeds to form a relationship with her servant and confidante, Amante. The fact that Amante's name has *love* at its etymological root might make a case for a lesbian couple, although it seems likely that Gaskell is thinking of sex imagistically again, not as something in their relationship but as a metaphor for the demon. Amante is a daemonic type. Being "Norman" (7:318), she is French, therefore of the demon's nation. And she is very much a male.[8] Daring, bold, aggressive, inventive, it is Amante who takes the initiative, plans the escape, and also executes it, meeting obstacles along the way in a cool and ready manner. And, if this is not enough to reveal her daemonic nature, Gaskell adds she is a whistler (7:346). Amante not only behaves like a man, she also, in fact, pretends to be one. To make it possible for them to escape and to function in the world, Amante disguises herself as a man, and she remains, for the rest of the story, always dressed in male attire. Once they are safe, they settle down in a small town and proceed to live in every way like a middle-class couple, Anna remaining at home with her child, which she has taken with her of course, and Amante going to work so as to be able to support them. At the end of "Half a Lifetime Ago," Susan takes on a similar role in relation to Eleanor Hurst, the widow of her lover, Michael. After rejecting Susan Dixon because she had kept her daemonic self, Michael had found and married Eleanor, a completely female woman. Eleanor, when he dies, is destitute, and Susan offers to take her in. Supporting and taking care of her, Susan becomes, as it were, her husband, even the father of her children, just as Amante is the father of the child she now shares with Anna. At the end of "The Grey Woman," we learn that Anna intends to remarry. Amante, however, as far as we know, is making no matrimonial plans. She remains single and a male.

In her own imagination, Gaskell too lived a single life. To her friend Eliza Fox, Gaskell once wrote these extraordinary words: "Nature intended me for a gypsy-bachelor; that *I* am sure of. Not an old maid for they are particular & fidgety, and tidy, and punctual,—but a gypsy-bachelor"(*L* 206). Gaskell is speaking partly in jest, but, as always, through her humor Gaskell tells a serious truth. The difference between an "old maid" and a "bachelor" is metaphorically the difference between a female and a male, between a Miss Matty who wanted to marry but did not happen to find a mate and an independent spirit who has escaped the snare of matrimony. Gaskell's words to Eliza Fox are especially astounding because they utterly annihilate the whole of "Mrs. Gaskell's" existence. A bachelor does not have a family. A gypsy does not have a home. Everything "Mrs. Gaskell" created—her house, her husband, and her children, her connection to the community and her standing in the world—everything is done away with. The image even changes her gender, for a bachelor is male. "Mrs. Gaskell" was a necessity, the price that Gaskell paid for love. Within that model of femininity there lived, however—detached from her family, unconnected to her friends, and indifferent to the world and the opinion it had of her—a male demon, solitary, free.

XVI

Freedom in Work

THE DEMON MAY BE EXPRESSED in Gaskell in a variety of ways, both in single and married women, but only in a single woman may it take the form of work. There are in Gaskell's fiction occasionally married women who also work. Gaskell was one of the first to record what was at the time the new phenomenon of women working outside the home. But Gaskell does not approve of these women. Only a single woman, in Gaskell, has her blessing if she works. This was the general Victorian view, even the view of the avant-garde, although not, obviously, of the feminists, and it is the view expressed in one of his essays by W. R. Greg. Greg does not object in principle to the idea of women working. "We are not at all disposed," he writes in "Why Are Women Redundant?" "to echo the cry of those who object to women and girls engaging in this or that industrial career." The argument that some have offered, namely that women will displace men who need these positions more because they have to support their families, is "founded," he says, on an "economical misconception. . . . It is a bequest from the days—now happily passing away—of surplus population, inadequate employment, and Malthusian terrors." It is understood that were it the case that women were displacing men, he would take a different position. Indeed, when he proceeds to say that not employing women is foolish, his point is that, since they are paid less, women are a cheap source of labor. It does not ever occur to Greg that women might actually want to work. He thinks that women who are "redundant"—women who are unmarried, that is, and are likely to remain so in a population in which women greatly outnumber men—"not having," he writes, "the natural duties and labours of wives and mothers," will "have to carve out artificial and painfully sought occupations for themselves." Some, who have no other income, might "have to earn their own living." But married women should not work. The "employment of married women," in fact, he considers a great "evil" because "it disables" women "from making their husbands' homes comfortable." And he considers the evil compounded if those married women are mothers.[1]

"Mrs. Gaskell's" official position is very similar to Greg's. Mrs. Wilson in *Mary Barton* observes, clearly speaking for Gaskell, that married women should not work. " 'I could reckon up' (counting with her fingers) 'ay, nine men I know, as has been driven to th' public-house by having wives as worked in factories: good folk, too, as thought there was no harm in putting their little ones out at nurse, and letting their house go all dirty, and their fires all out; and that was a place as was tempting for a husband to stay in, was it? He soon finds out gin-shops, where all is clean and bright, and where the fire blazes cheerily, and gives a man a welcome as it were.' " Her son, whom the heroine will actually marry as soon as she fulfills the image that he conceives of woman here, not only agrees with his mother completely but says that he would like to appeal to Prince Albert to make a law against the working of married women. How, he asks, would Prince Albert " 'like his missis to be from home when he comes in, tired and worn, and wanting some one to cheer him; and may be, her to come in by-and-by, just as tired and down in th' mouth; and how he'd like for her never to be at home to see to th' cleaning of his house, or to keep a bright fire in his grate. Let alone his meals being all hugger-mugger, and comfortless. I'd be bound, prince as he is, if his missis served him so, he'd be off to a gin-place, or summut o' the kind. So why can't he make a law again poor folks' wives working in factories?' " (1:137–38).

"Mrs. Gaskell" agrees with Greg about single women too. A single woman, like a married one, must take care of her family first. Gaskell is amazed and dismayed to learn from Lady Kay-Shuttleworth that women exist who, although they have "all the home duties of parents dependent upon them, brothers & sisters relying on them for companionship & comfort," are willing to "desert the post where God has placed them" so as to work, even if, as in the case Lady Kay-Shuttleworth has mentioned, the work is in a charitable institution (*L* 72). Only the women who are not needed by their parents or their siblings and who are "deprived" as well, Gaskell writes echoing Greg, "of their natural duties as wives & mothers," have, in Gaskell, to avoid the "feeling of *purposelessness,*" the right to seek out "other duties." But they will surely not enjoy the life of the single working woman. There must, she concludes, be a period "of great difficulty in the life of every woman who foresees and calmly accepts a single life" (*L* 72). Many women in Gaskell's fiction speak precisely in this way. Margaret, for instance, in *North and South,* says, after her father dies, as " 'I have neither husband nor child to give me natural duties, I must make myself some' " (4:498). Libbie in "Libbie Marsh's Three Eras," concluding that she will never marry, addresses herself in a similar manner. All the " 'more reason,' " she says, " 'as God has seen fit to keep me out of woman's natural work, I should try and find work for myself' " (1:484).

Gaskell's demon has, however, a very different view of the case. Work for the demon is liberation from its imprisonment in the wife. Before she had been brought to reiterate the orthodox views of "Mrs. Gaskell," Margaret Hale had conceived of working, in contrast to obeying authority, as the means of achieving "freedom" (4:497). Work was how Margaret imagined she could "take her life into her own hands" (4:497), the only way she could claim the "right to independence of action" (4:491). The single women who work in Gaskell, although they are often forced to do so simply to support themselves, nonetheless take pleasure in working and—despite "Mrs. Gaskell's" view that women have no intellectual ability, knowledge and reason being male—they do their work exceedingly well. Even a woman like Hester Rose, whose Quaker religion quiets her demon, finds a satisfaction in work. Most working women find much more. It is significant metaphorically that most of the women who "fall" in Gaskell do so somehow through their work. This is what happens to Lizzie Leigh, who is seduced by her employer. This is what happens as well to Esther, who is seduced in *Mary Barton* because her work has filled her head with idle dreams and vain illusions. Working and falling are the same. Both are expressions of the demon.

In one important and delightful instance, Miss Galindo in "My Lady Ludlow," Gaskell also makes it clear that working is the means through which a woman may live her life as a male. Finding herself without an income, Miss Galindo looks for work, which is no easy task in itself, and manages to find a position as a clerk to a Mr. Horner. The work has always been done by a man, and Miss Galindo feels called upon to make Mr. Horner forget she is a woman. " 'I do everything,' " she says, " 'as ship-shape as a masculine man-clerk. I see he can't find a fault—writing good, spelling correct, sums all right' " (5:143). As we see here, she has assumed, as part of her working personality, the clipped businesslike pattern of speech that Gaskell always attributes to men when she wants to stress their maleness. She takes on other male habits too. " 'I have stuck,' " she says, " 'my pen behind my ear; I have made him a bow instead of a curtsey' " (5:143). And she has even taken to whistling (5:143). One day a solicitor, Mr. Smithson, is brought in to look over the books. Smithson holds women in contempt, and when he hears that it is a woman who has prepared the ledgers before him, he mutters that he supposes it " 'was keeping a woman out of harm's way . . . to let her fancy herself useful.' " Much to his surprise, however, the books could not be in better order, and Smithson is so profoundly impressed he says he may have misjudged the sex. Enjoying her "victory," Miss Galindo, expressing her own contempt for men, remarks that she has been with Smithson " 'so curt, so abrupt, so abominably dull, that I'll answer for it he thinks me worthy to be a man' " (5:173 ff.). In Gaskell's metaphoric vocabulary, Miss Galindo is a man. By working, at least, she has become male.

What clerking is for Miss Galindo, writing was for Elizabeth Gaskell. The images in which she thinks of women working in her fiction are those in which she thinks of herself as the writer of her books.

Gaskell had no real theory of fiction, if theory means an abstract system. She did not even give much thought to the practical questions of her craft. Nor was she greatly concerned with technique,[2] although, if Angus Easson is right, she took more care in writing her stories than we have generally suspected.[3] But if we look carefully through her work, and especially her letters, we see there are comments here and there that, although they do not constitute a treatise on the novelist's art, stress a few fundamental principles.

Perhaps the most telling remarks she made on the subject of writing fiction are to be found in a letter she wrote to a young man named Herbert Grey who, being a great admirer, sent her his novel for her criticism. Gaskell does not like it much, and she offers advice she thinks might be of help to him in the future. Warning him first against introspection in a passage I quoted earlier, she adds that he ought to "observe what is *out* of you, instead of examining what is *in* you." She tells him to consider Defoe, who "sets *objects* not *feelings* before you." She suggests that he look at the men and women with whom he comes into contact at work and try to "imagine" in their lives "a complication of events" that "would form a good plot." She tells him to try to think of good incidents and outlines a method that will help him learn to describe them well and vividly: "imagine yourself," she writes, "a spectator & auditor of every scene & event! Work hard at this till it becomes a reality to you,—a thing you have to recollect & describe & report fully & accurately as it struck you, in order that your reader may have it equally before him." "Don't intrude yourself," she continues, "in your descriptions." "If you but think eagerly of your story till you see it in action, words, good simple strong words, will come" (*L* 420). In "Modern Greek Songs," she explains she admires those balladeers who do not rely on a mere "description of feeling" but who allow "the actions of the *dramatis personae*" to "tell plainly . . . how they felt" (3:490).

What Gaskell says about narrative here suggests a "dramatic" notion of fiction. The narrator is an "auditor," "spectator," to an "action" in his mind. His business is to imagine each "scene" until he can really "see it in action." The characters are "dramatis personae." Their thoughts and feelings must be enacted rather than described by the narrator. The reader too should be a spectator to the action of the narrative. He should be made to see it too. Gaskell had made this her own rule when she had started her first novel. Describing how she wrote *Mary Barton,* Gaskell explains to Eliza Fox, "I told the story according to a fancy of my own; to really SEE the scenes I tried to describe" (*L* 48). John McVeagh is right to argue that, as Gaskell gained experience in the handling of her narratives, she attempted more and more to externalize her "themes in the encounter and conflict of characters" and to make her "meaning" known through her "dialogue and action."4

Drama is *doing.* Etymologically, that is what the word, of course, means. Gaskell, as we have seen in *Cranford,* imagined that fiction came in genders, Dr. Johnson's being male and Charles Dickens's being female. As *doing,* dramatic fiction is male. The theater itself, the place of drama, was metaphorically male to Gaskell. When, for example, Jemima in *Ruth* says she wants to go to the theater, her brother, Richard, says their father would never let her do such a thing. " 'How do you go, then'?" she asks him. " 'Oh!' " Richard says, " 'Many things are right for men which are not for girls' " (3:211). This is an amusing exchange but, like most of Gaskell's humor, it is intended to make a point, the point that the theater is male territory.

Fiction was Gaskell's way of *doing.* It was a way for Gaskell to take, like Margaret, her life into her own hands. Margaret *does* by telling a lie. So does Philip in *Sylvia's Lovers.* And Gaskell makes it clear in *Ruth* that, as many have before her, she associates lying with fiction. The Bensons, when they choose to conceal Ruth's identity, we recall, decide they must make up a story to silence questions about her past, and Faith, repeating the made-up story to Mrs. Bradshaw who calls one day, finds herself tempted to embellish it. Gaskell's description of the event is important for its language. "Miss Benson," she writes, "accompanied Mrs. Bradshaw to the door; and in the passage gave her a long explanation of Ruth's (*fictious*) history. Mrs. Bradshaw looked so much interested and pleased, that Miss Benson enlarged a little more than was necessary, and rounded off her *invention* with one or two *imaginary* details." Thurstan, who has overheard her, asks her why she has conceived such a complicated tale, and Faith, defending herself, makes explicit the implications of the words that the narrator has used. " 'I do think,' " she says, " 'I've a talent for *fiction,* it is so pleasant to *invent,* and make the incidents dovetail together; and after all, if we are to tell a lie, we may as well do it thoroughly, or else it's of no use. . . .

And, Thurstan—it may be very wrong—but I believe—I am afraid I enjoy not being fettered by the truth' " (3:148–49; italics mine). Gaskell too spoke of fiction as lying. When, for instance, she discovered that the people she had mentioned in her biography of Charlotte Brontë were all complaining of the portraits presented of them in the book, she wrote in a letter that she intended henceforth to "confine myself to lies (*i.e.* fiction)" (*L* 358).

The lie in *Ruth,* it should be stressed, is Gaskell's lie as well as Faith's, not only in the obvious sense that everything in the book is Gaskell's, she having been its ultimate author, but in the narrower sense in which it is the indispensable means, as many have indeed observed, of achieving its destined end. "Mrs. Gaskell" would have claimed, and undoubtedly believed, that she had devised the lie to fulfill her moral purpose. But Gaskell could have invented a story in which a fallen woman was saved without anyone lying for her. Two years earlier, in "Lizzie Leigh," she had written just such a tale. Lizzie is saved by kindness alone. The fact that Gaskell cannot construct her story in *Ruth* without the lie makes it the creation less of the character in the book than of the author of the narrative.

Fiction is drama and drama is *doing* and *doing* is a male activity. It is no accident that in *Ruth* it is Faith who tells the lie and develops it into a fiction. Faith is a male. We are not surprised to learn that in "My Lady Ludlow" Miss Galindo had once considered becoming a writer of fiction herself (5:137–38). Looking for a male activity through which to express her demon, Gaskell found it in her art.

In this connection it is significant that Gaskell became a professional writer not only after the death of her son but in a sense also because of it. Gaskell had borne three daughters already when, in 1844, she gave birth to her son, William. He was to live only ten months. In the summer of 1845 he caught scarlet fever from Marianne. She recovered. He did not. Gaskell had lost a child already, her first, we recall, a stillborn daughter, and, as was clear in the poem she wrote on the third anniversary of her birth, her death brought back to her the memory of all the deaths she had known in childhood. When William died, she was utterly devastated. In April of 1848, she wrote to Anne Shaen "I have just been up to our room. There is a fire in it, and a smell of baking, and oddly enough the feelings and recollections of 3 years ago came over me strongly—when I used to sit up in the room so often in the evenings reading by the fire, and watching my darling *darling* Willie, who now sleeps sounder still in the dull, dreary chapel-yard at Warrington. That wound will never heal on earth, although hardly any one knows how it has changed me" (*L* 25a).

Like all the ghosts in Gaskell's mind, Willie is often recalled in her fiction. Countless characters lose their sons, and Gaskell seems to relive with each a different moment of Willie's death. In "Mr. Harrison's Confessions," she seems to remember his last hours as she describes "a look of terror on" the face of the vicar's son who is dying of the croup. "I have often," the narrator says, seen such a look "in young children smitten by a sudden and violent illness. It seems as if they recognised something infinite and invisible, at whose bidding the pain and the anguish come, from which no love can shield them" (5:434–35). With Owen in "The Doom of the Griffiths"—the child is sometimes lost by a man, although he is always a female man, as Owen has become at this point—she seems to relive the moment in which, looking down at Willie's bedside, she realized her son had died. "And there it was," the narrator writes as Owen looks down at his dead child, "the little clay image, that would never more gladden up at the sight of him, nor stretch forth to meet his embrace" (5:261). With Lizzie Leigh, who loses her daughter, she stares "with wild, glaring eyes" and utters a "a cry of wild despair" as she slowly becomes aware that her child is gone forever (2:232). And with Mrs. Holman she seems, in "Cousin Phillis," to try to "soothe herself with plaintive inarticulate sounds . . . for the aching sense of loss she would never get over in this world" (7:78).

It surely requires no explanation to understand why Gaskell mourned. But Willie's death had implications for Gaskell's career as a writer too. It was to help her survive his loss that she began to write *Mary Barton*. She had done some writing before. In adolescence, we recall, she had shown her brother, John, work in which he had encouraged her. At that time she had also written a piece that she later called "Sketch of Clopton House." With her husband she had written, early in 1837, a poem entitled "Sketches among the Poor," which appeared in *Blackwood's Magazine*. And she had written three short stories, which appeared in *Howitt's Journal* from the summer of 1847 through New Year's Day in 1848: "Libbie Marsh's Three Eras," "The Sexton's Hero," and "Christmas Storms and Sunshine."

The stories she must have begun to write a year or so after Willie's death and therefore also perhaps because she needed something to distract her, to the extent that anything could. That was certainly the reason she began to write *Mary Barton*. As she explained to Mrs. Greg, "The tale was formed, and the greater part of the first volume was written when I was obliged to lie down constantly on the sofa, and when I took refuge in the invention to exclude the memory of painful scenes which would force

themselves upon my remembrance" (*L* 42). Gaskell alludes to the novel's
genesis in the text of the book itself, first in the opening words of the
Preface in which she writes "Three years ago I became anxious (from
circumstances that need not be more fully alluded to) to employ myself in
writing a work of fiction," and then in the body of the text, in which she
interrupts the narrator to comment on the land of dreams "where alone I
may see, while yet I tarry here, the sweet looks of my dead child" (1:311).
Even the plot and the resolution of the novel recall Willie. It is the murder
of his son that makes Carson understand what it is John Barton suffered
when his own child died of hunger. The death of a son is thus the point on
which the plot of the novel turns. Gaskell, in fact, is said to have told her
Manchester friend Travers Madge that she decided to write *Mary Barton*
when, as part of the charitable activities she had undertaken in Manchester,
she had visited the hovel of a laborer who was destitute. He had suddenly
grabbed her arm and asked whether she had ever seen a child of hers
" 'clemmed to death.' "5 Of course, she had not, but losing Willie, she
knew what it meant for a child to die.

Thus, in a very real sense, Willie's death inspired the book. But the
connection was closer yet between Willie and Gaskell's fiction. Whatever
in other ways the relationship may be between a mother and son, it is
always the case in Gaskell that there is something sexual in it. Mothers are
almost always possessive, sometimes in a cloying way. Mrs. Hamley in
Wives and Daughters dotes on Osborne, whom, indeed, she considers a
fitter mate than her sometimes boorish husband. Mrs. Browne in "The
Moorland Cottage" dotes in a similar way on her son, to whom she almost
looks in fact, being a widow, as a surrogate husband. Most of the mothers
Gaskell conceives are fiercely jealous of the women whom their sons
intend to marry. Mrs. Wilson in *Mary Barton* suffers from "jealousy" at the
thought of "being supplanted" by Mary Barton "in the affections of" her
"son." She talks like a deserted lover. " 'Thou'rt old enough to please
thysel,' " she "coldly" addresses her son one evening when she realizes
how he feels. " 'Old mothers are cast aside, and what they've borne
forgotten as soon as a pretty face comes along' " (1:397). Mme. de Créquy
in "My Lady Ludlow"—when her son sets sail for France, hoping to save
the woman he loves from the guillotine—cries out, like an abandoned
wife, " 'He has left me for her!' " (5:79).

In *Ruth* Gaskell allows the son to become metaphorically the lover.
Ruth has another possessive mother, Bellingham's, who appears in Wales
to take her son away from Ruth. But the more revealing relationship is to
be found between Leonard and Ruth. It might be possible to pass over the

fact that Leonard and Ruth in the novel are constantly fondling one another, for this, although to a lesser degree than Gaskell makes it happen in *Ruth,* was a common Victorian practice. It might be possible too to pass over the fact that Gaskell makes sure we know that Leonard looks exactly like Bellingham (3:261), like the man Ruth loves, that is, since, after all, he is Bellingham's son. But we cannot ignore the fact that Gaskell, describing Ruth and Leonard together, frequently uses the same metaphors she had used to describe the relationships between Bellingham and Ruth. Sitting one day in the garden, for instance, Ruth begins to pelt Leonard with petals from a flower she has picked (3:190), duplicating, thus, the scene in which Ruth, in a sexual dream, imagined Bellingham presenting her with one flower after another. Metaphorically, Gaskell, in fact, imagines Leonard seducing Ruth. The night of the day on which he is born, Ruth has one of her many dreams. She dreams that "the innocent babe that lay by her side in soft ruddy slumber, had started up into man's growth, and, instead of the pure and noble being whom she had prayed to present as her child to "Our Father in heaven,' he was a repetition of his father; and, like him, lured some maiden (who in her dream seemed strangely like herself, only more utterly sad and desolate even than she) into sin, and left her there to even a worse fate than that of suicide" (3:162). Ruth had often dreamed of Bellingham. Now she is always dreaming of Leonard. And he in turn often dreams of her. In one such dream, Leonard imagines that Ruth stands by his bed as he sleeps. He dreams that he has awakened to find his mother bending down to kiss him. Then she "spread out her large, soft, white-feathered wings (which in no way surprised her child—he seemed to have known they were there all along), and sailed away through the open window far into the blue sky of a summer's day" (3:256). Ruth enclosing Leonard with wings that raise both of them into flight is an obvious sexual metaphor. Finally, there is Leonard's name. Old Thomas, the old family friend, had tried, earlier in the novel, to warn Ruth against temptation by quoting to her the biblical text: "Remember the devil goeth about as a roaring lion, seeking whom he may devour." Ruth had heard this verse as a child, and she had always "imagined" then "a lion's head with glaring eyes peering out of the bushes in a dark shady part of the wood, which, for this reason, she had always avoided, and even now could hardly think of without a shudder" (3:50). The lion peering out of the bushes is a very suggestive image. The bushes are surely pubic hair, and the lion peering out is an image of sexual intercourse. The "shudder" is a sexual shudder. It is significant that old Thomas, although he is referring to Bellingham, does not actually name him by name. Gaskell is certainly thinking of Bellingham but simultaneously of Leonard, whom, by his very name, she identifies as the lion in the bush.

The son has thus become the lover. It would not be an error to see something Oedipal in all this, but, as always in Gaskell's fiction, sexuality is an attribute that identifies the demon. Gaskell makes it very clear she is thinking of the demon. The biblical passage old Thomas quotes speaks of the lion as the form in which the devil likes to appear, and the devil, as we know from such stories as "Lois the Witch," is one of the shapes the demon takes. Leonard is a lover like Charley, an embodiment of the demon, and like Charley he is a proxy for the heroine's male self. It is, in modern psychology, a commonplace that women who have no other channel through which to express those characteristics that Gaskell considered her male self project their identities into their sons. Gaskell did as her heroines do. Willie, transformed in Gaskell's mind as so many others had been, to function in her private drama, became another male self. It is no accident that she gave, even to its diminutive form, the name of her son to Susan's mad brother in "Half a Lifetime Ago."

Leonard in *Ruth* is the male who *does* what his mother had *done* in Wales but what in Eccleston she must be satisfied to merely *be*. As Ruth had been "naughty," to use the word the boy had used who had slapped her face, Leonard is "For ever in mischief" (3:200). It is significant that the mischief generally takes the form of lying (3:200). Gaskell intends a "moral" point. Lying, she wants to say, is contagious. The Bensons, by telling a lie, have created a moral atmosphere that inevitably makes a liar out of Leonard. But there is something not quite right here. The Bensons have told only one lie, the lie that Faith has called her fiction, and Leonard fully believes this story. Only at the end of the novel does he learn the truth, in fact (3:357). It cannot, therefore, be the case that the Bensons' bad example is what turned him into a liar. But Gaskell, as always, knows what she means. The real connection in her mind between Faith's story and Leonard's lying is not textual but subtextual. Both Faith and Leonard are makers of fictions, one, namely Faith, a surrogate self who spins in the novel the very story that Gaskell is spinning through her book, the other, Leonard, a maker of fiction in the sense that Gaskell projected in him the son in whom she had invested the demon that had made her art.

The demon, "shrouded," had been transformed into memories and dreams. These had in turn been transformed into fiction. The fiction was Gaskell's male self. Gaskell projected that male self into her fiction in various ways: in her attitudes, in her views, in the many manifestations of her various daemonic images: subjects, characters, figures of speech, incidents, plots, and a number of others. But sometimes this was not enough. Once in a while, Gaskell needed to see herself in her fiction reflected not just as a male but as a man. A man, we know, is not always male, but, there being a connection on the face of it between them, Gaskell tends, all things being equal, to think of a man as the natural form that the male demon will choose. And just as she provides for Philip a woman's mirror so he can see himself as the female he really is, Gaskell creates in her fiction men to act as reflections of the male demon in his role as the maker of fiction.

As a narrator, that is, she assumes a male voice. Women had done so before, of course. Maria Edgeworth, for example, had told the story of *Castle Rackrent* as a first-person narrative of a male character in the book. But it was not a common thing, and Gaskell would not have thought to do it had she not felt a particular need to envision herself as a male. She assumed a male voice in a great many stories. A partial list includes such narratives as "The Sexton's Hero," "The Heart of John Middleton," "Mr. Harrison's Confessions," "The Schah's English Garden," "The Poor Clare," "Curious if True," "Six Weeks at Heppenheim," and "Cousin Phillis." She does not always succeed in finding a male identity in this way. Sometimes, even as she writes, the male is transformed into a female. This, as we have seen, occurs in "Mr. Harrison's Confessions." A similar permutation occurs in the story "Six Weeks at Heppenheim." The narrator here, on a trip to Germany, a female nation we recall, no sooner arrives than, falling ill, takes to his bed, becoming, inactivated thus, no longer a *doer* but a *be-er*. But sometimes Gaskell does succeed, through the male narrators of her stories, in becoming a true male. Sometimes she even manages to comment through these males on her female self. This is the case in "The Poor Clare," in which the narrator is the man who falls in love with the perfect Lucy. As her lover, he is eager to do away with Lucy's demon so she will be an ideal type. But as the narrator, he observes, seeing how Lucy handles her demon, that she seems to him "too patient," "too resigned," and "over-passive" (5:375). As a character, the narrator is just another of Gaskell's men rejecting the daemonic woman. As a narrator, he is a male expressing the daemonic point of view.

Sometimes a male creates in Gaskell a distinctly male personality as the narrative voice of the story. He speaks in a manner, he assumes an attitude, he suggests a quality of mind that is, in Gaskell's sense of the word, unambiguously male. And this is often conveyed in the style Gaskell always imagines as male, the style she had used with Miss Galindo: curt, abrupt, direct, unadorned. Perhaps what is most important, however, in the style that Gaskell adopts when she writes in the voice of a male, is that she uses many more first-person singular pronouns and makes greater use of verbs. As a man she has an identity, and she is able to *do*. A typical passage can be found in "The Heart of John Middleton." Here the narrator, the title character, recounts the moment in his life when his wife was taken ill just at the time he lost his job. One of his neighbors has kindly brought supplies to help him in his crisis. "I was not proud," he says. "I was most thankful. I took the meat, and boiled some broth for my poor Nelly. She was in a sleep, or in a faint, I know not which; but I roused her, and held her up in bed, and fed her with a teaspoon, and the light came back to her eyes, and the faint moonlight smile to her lips; and when she had ended, she said her innocent grace, and fell asleep, with her baby on her breast. I sat over the fire, and listened to the bells, as they swept past my cottage on the gusts of the wind" (2:397).

One of the most significant uses Gaskell makes of a male narrator is to be found in "Cousin Phillis." This story is a general favorite with those who love "Mrs. Gaskell's" fiction, and many elements in it remind us of *Wives and Daughters* and of *Cranford*. The setting, an idealized Knutsford, makes the story seem a pastoral, and to some extent it is, especially in its use of seasons to suggest the progress of time. But if we look at this story closely, we see that Phillis is a young girl who wants to break out of her female world and to embody herself as a male. A male, as Gaskell makes sure we realize, is from the first concealed in Phillis. She is—and both define her as male—an extremely intelligent woman and a scholar of sorts as well. Her learning, at least, by far surpasses that of ordinary men, since, as we recall, she reads writers like Dante in the original (7:27–28). Also manly is the fact that Phillis is extremely tall, taller by half a head than Paul Manning (7:28), the cousin who is the story's narrator. Phillis, however, is not allowed to express her male identity. Like Molly Gibson, she is kept prepubescent by her father. Although at the time the story opens she is already well into her teens, her father still wants to dress her in pinafores. Her sexuality, which is her demon, is thus not permitted to express itself. Like many of Gaskell's heroines, therefore, Phillis, as the story begins, finds herself a daemonic male imprisoned in a female form. And, like others in her condition, she is divided between two men. One is Holdsworth, whom she loves and who is an engineer with the railroad. The railroad here, as it was in *Cranford*, is the male principle that intrudes into a world essentially female. In *Cranford* the railroad had killed Mr. Brown, proving he was really female. Holdsworth is not killed by the railroad, proving he is really male. He is the very male demon, in fact, Phillis is

seeking to possess. The name that Gaskell gives him tells us that Holdsworth is well worth the holding. But Phillis finds she cannot hold him.
Being a male, he is naturally free, and being free, he gets away. Indeed, not
only does he escape, he moves to America, to Canada, taking up his
residence, thus, in the very home of the free. Like Sylvia, therefore, in
Sylvia's Lovers, Phillis cannot possess her demon, and, just as in the novel
the quest is transferred from Sylvia to Philip, so in the story it passes to
Paul, the second of the story's two men. But Paul, unlike Philip, is a male.
Not only does he work on the railroad, both his names suggest his gender.
His last identifies him as a man, and his first seems an allusion, like
Charlotte Brontë's in *Villette* in the character Paul Emanuel, to the masculine point of view often associated with St. Paul. Holdsworth, when he
reaches Canada, quickly marries, it turns out, thus becoming, as Charley
was, a demon that is itself ensnared. Paul, however, escapes matrimony.
When he arrives to visit the Holmans, it is generally assumed that he will
want to marry Phillis. He himself toys with the thought. But, put off both
by her height and by her excessive erudition, Paul decides he would rather
not. Instead he becomes to her a brother, a brother who *does* what his sister
is. As she sends Philip after Kinraid, Gaskell sends Paul now after Holdsworth. And there we leave him, living unmarried, working for the railroad still, and having, in a surrogate way, achieved the freedom Phillis
sought. There are, however, several differences between this story and
Sylvia's Lovers. One is that Paul, once he is free, is not imprisoned again
like Philip. Another is that, while in the novel the quest for the demon is
only passed from one character to another, in the story it is passed to the
narrator himself. In her male voice, Gaskell is able through her narrator to
become the surrogate self through whom the demon can be finally possessed.

Gaskell never wrote a novel in which the narrator is a male. Perhaps it
would have been too difficult to sustain a male identity for the length of a
whole book. But even in her longer works Gaskell does manage, surrep-
titiously, to introduce a male voice by allowing her male characters sometimes to take over the narrative. In *Sylvia's Lovers,* for example, although
she cannot let Kinraid become the teller of the tale, when she lets him spin
his yarns she does allow him for a moment to become her narrative voice.

Like the young man, then, in "Modern Greek Songs," whose song of
sorrow at being unwanted moved his hard-hearted mother to love him
and to call him back, Gaskell found a way through her fiction not only to
express her demon but, through her readers, to make the "world" accept
and honor her daemonic self.

XVII

"Mrs. Gaskell"
and Currer Bell

GASKELL HAD TURNED HERSELF into a novelist. But did she have, she seemed to ask herself, the courage to live the life of an artist, the life, that is, of a daemonic male? This is the question she set out to answer in *The Life of Charlotte Brontë,* a book she began in midsummer in 1855 and which she published in February of 1857. Most of Gaskell's readers believe she was moved to write the biography because she was Charlotte Brontë's friend. Gaskell does, in one of her letters, call Charlotte Brontë "my dear friend" (*LCB,* p. 22), but, since they only met five times as they visited back and forth, their friendship may have been exaggerated. Sanders may err on the other side when he remarks that their connection was more literary than personal,[1] but it was not just their relationship that inspired Gaskell to write the *Life.*

What really inspired her to the project was that in this woman artist she saw a reflection of herself. *The Life of Charlotte Brontë* is less a biography than an autobiography. Gaskell's and Brontë's lives were not identical in a factual way, although even factually there were parallels that would have been important to Gaskell. Brontë's father was a minister, as Gaskell's own had been at one point. Both had early lost their mothers and both had been brought up by aunts, although in Brontë's case the aunt had come to live with the family at Haworth. Both eventually married ministers, although at the time that Gaskell met her, Brontë had not yet married Nicholls. What Gaskell responded to, however, in Charlotte Brontë was something else. Whether she actually saw it in Brontë or whether she only believed she saw it—and it was probably a little of both—Gaskell perceived in Brontë's life a dramatization of the images she was projecting in her fiction. Brontë was actually in her life living the conflict in Gaskell's mind. A chance to write Charlotte Brontë's biography gave her a chance to write her own and to do it without knowing that she was writing about herself.

Gaskell projects herself in the *Life* exactly as she does in her fiction. The *Life* is not only novelistic, as Edgar Wright has rightly remarked,[2] it reads like one of Gaskell's novels. Charlotte Brontë is presented as a typical daemonic heroine. Brontë was a passionate woman, and Gaskell allows her to show her passion by quoting extensively from her letters. Her theory is in any case, which she explains in the text itself, that it is best to let the subject speak for herself as much as possible (*LCB,* p. 242). The letters are dramatic soliloquies in the drama of Brontë's life. The ones that Gaskell chooses to quote are the most passionate she can find, those that most reveal the demon. Thus, for example, she quotes from a letter in which we find the following passages: " 'If Christian perfection be necessary to salvation, I shall never be saved; my heart is a very hot-bed for sinful thoughts, and when I decide on an action I scarcely remember to look to my Redeemer for direction.' " " 'I hope, I trust, I might one day become better, far better than my evil, wandering thoughts, my corrupt heart, cold to the spirit and warm to the flesh, will now permit me to be' " (*LCB,* p. 134).

The Brontës were all daemonic to Gaskell, except perhaps for gentle Anne. Gaskell often calls them wild, one of her favorite words, we recall, in *Sylvia's Lovers* for the demon. They were, she says, describing the ritual in which, when all had gone to bed, the sisters paced "up and down . . . in the parlour," just "like restless wild animals" (*LCB,* p. 155). The setting too seems "wild" to Gaskell (e.g., *LCB,* p. 23), as it had in *Sylvia's Lovers.* Gaskell devotes a good many pages at the beginning of the biography to a description of the land and a history of its people, on the theory that we must know how life was lived on these lonely moors to understand what Brontë was (*LCB,* p. 22), and the picture she projects, both through descriptions of the terrain and through stories of its inhabitants, is of a fierce, daemonic place. The people, she tells us, are "distinguished by their spirit of independence," by the fact that they are ever "ready . . . to resist authority" (*LCB,* p. 25). They are even, like the people of Milton-Northern in *North and South,* little altered from their "Norse ancestors" (*LCB,* pp. 23, 33).

Gaskell recognizes in Brontë, as she recognized in her heroines, a desire to escape the prison that confines the female. Brontë, she writes in the biography, wanted "release" from domestic life (*LCB,* p. 260). She quotes a letter in which Brontë writes that she "can hardly tell you how time gets on at Haworth. There is no event to mark its progress. One day resembles another; and all have heavy, lifeless physiognomies. Sunday, baking-day, and Saturday, the only ones that have any distinctive mark" (*LCB,* p. 229). She wanted to be released as well from her imprisonment as a governess. In another letter Gaskell reproduces at some length, Brontë, receiving a note from friends who are traveling abroad while she is working as a governess, alludes to her "impatience of restraint." In an image Gaskell herself often used to describe her condition, Brontë yearns for "wings" to escape (*LCB*, p. 171).

Charlotte Brontë seems to Gaskell by her nature a single woman. None of the Brontë sisters to Gaskell appears to be made to be a wife. Two of the sisters never married, and Charlotte married at thirty-nine, only nine months before her death. To all intents and purposes, therefore, Charlotte had lived a single life. "Matrimony," Gaskell writes, "did not enter into the scheme of her life" (*LCB*, p. 140). Sometimes Brontë sounds indeed like one of Gaskell's fictional virgins. " 'You ask me,' " Charlotte writes for instance in yet another of the letters Gaskell chooses to quote at length, " 'if I do not think that men are strange beings? I do, indeed. I have often thought so' " (*LCB*, pp. 243–44). Brontë is not a mother either. None of the sisters seemed to Gaskell to be "naturally fond of children" (*LCB*, p. 140). Charlotte did, on one of her visits, exhibit—or pretend to feel—a fondness for "Mrs. Gaskell's" children, and Gaskell takes a mother's pride that her offsprings were an exception. But she concedes that on the whole Brontë felt children were merely "troublesome" (*LCB*, p. 166).

She thinks of Brontë as a male. In another instance in which her fiction influenced the *Life*, Gaskell returns to "The Moorland Cottage," in which she had first suggested the difference between the female and the male as a difference between *being* and *doing*, to distinguish, in a passage I quoted earlier in another connection, between his sisters and Branwell Brontë by saying that he was expected to *do*, while they were only expected to *be* (*LCB*, p. 153). She knows that Brontë wants to *do*. She likes to quote from Brontë's letters passages such as the one in which Brontë says " 'I long to travel; to work; to live a life of action' " (*LCB*, p. 229).

Gaskell is aware, moreover, that Brontë is an ambitious woman. In one of the letters from which she quotes, Brontë bitterly reflects that she will soon reach the age of thirty, "and I have done nothing yet' " (*LCB*, p. 229). Brontë is conscious, as Gaskell knows, that her talent is being wasted. She quotes her as saying she is " 'tantalised by the consciousness of faculties unexercised' " (*LCB*, p. 171). She sees that Brontë wants to work. If marriage, she writes, did not enter into her scheme, "good, sound, earnest labour did" (*LCB*, p. 140). Brontë, Gaskell reports, believed there was " 'no more respectable character on earth than an unmarried woman, who makes her own way through life, quietly, perseveringly, without support of husband or brother' " (*LCB*, p. 244).

But having given the demon a voice, "Mrs. Gaskell" frightens herself. She panics just as she had in *Ruth*. No one, to my knowledge, has noticed how much the biography resembles *Ruth*. Gaskell is not only repeating a pattern she has established before, she sees in the daemonic Brontë a woman very much like Ruth, one who in her daemonic life is living the life Ruth lived in Wales. And just as she had quieted Ruth, she needs to quiet Brontë now. As soon as she appears on the scene, "Mrs. Gaskell" refuses to hear Charlotte Brontë's daemonic voice. One of the reasons Gaskell prefers to let Charlotte Brontë speak through her letters is that quotations do not require "Mrs. Gaskell" to acknowledge or to acquiesce in the demon. In many instances, "Mrs. Gaskell" simply ignores the daemonic content and fastens on something else instead, usually something wholly extraneous or inappropriate in the extreme. Brontë, for example, writes: " 'If you knew my thoughts, the dreams that absorb me, and the fiery imagination that at times eats me up, and makes me feel society, as it is, wretchedly insipid, you would pity and I dare say despise me. But I know the treasures of the *Bible:* I love and adore them. I can see the Well of Life in all its clearness and brightness; but when I step down to drink of the pure waters, they fly from my lips as if I were Tantalus.' " Brontë is in agony here. Her imagery says she is in hell. But all "Mrs. Gaskell" is willing to say is that sometimes "there is a despondency in some of her expressions, that too sadly reminds one of some of Cowper's letters" (*LCB,* pp. 118–19).

This is also the reason Gaskell did not deal with the juvenilia. Most have believed that she was blind to the importance of these writings, but this is not, I think, the case. Gaskell knew very well what they were, as she suggests herself when she calls them, in images that she always used as embodiments of her demon, "the wildest & most incoherent things," demonstrating a "creative power carried to the verge of insanity" (*L* 297). It was not because she did not know the implications of these writings that Gaskell ignored them in her book. It was because "Mrs. Gaskell" refused to acknowledge what she knew.

And it was for this reason too that she concealed what she had uncovered of Brontë's relationship with Heger. No one knows precisely what happened between Brontë and Heger, but Brontë, having gone to Belgium, first with Emily and then alone, so as to learn enough French to start a school for young girls in Yorkshire, fell in love with Constantin Heger, one of the professors at the Athénée. Heger, who had a wife and family, did not return Brontë's affection but he did not discourage it either. Later, Brontë used her passion in the creation of her books. To an extent,

Heger became the title character in *The Professor,* a novel Gaskell had undertaken to help Arthur Nicholls publish, and Paul Emanuel in *Villette.* Gaskell certainly knew the story of Brontë's relationship with Heger, much of it from Heger himself, whom she had traveled to Brussels to interview. Heger not only told her the tale, he showed her the passionate, anguished love letters Brontë had written him from England after she had returned home. But Gaskell never used this material. Not only did she not tell the tale, she lived in terror that others would tell it. She thought Heger would not himself want to make the matter public,[3] but his friends might let it out. "I cannot tell you," she wrote to George Smith, the thought preying on her mind, "how I should deprecate anything leading to the publication of those letters" (*L* 299). She thought that Charlotte had already confessed too much of her passion in *Villette* (*L* 299), and she was worried that *The Professor* would be seen as another confession (*L* 308).

Most nineteenth-century biographers would have concealed the "affair" with Heger. Until Lytton Strachey, Victorian biographers did not believe it was their function to strip their subjects utterly bare. Most acknowledged private precincts into which they did not pry. In his obituary for Gaskell, David Masson, we recall, writes, in summarizing her history, that of her "private life it would . . . be unfitting to speak."[4] Brontë's biography, moreover, had been requested by her friends and family, and it was, if not an official, at least a kind of authorized, life. Gaskell did not have to write a eulogy, but it was customary to praise. The fact indeed that Brontë's husband and her father were still alive would have made it hard for Gaskell, kind and thoughtful as she was, to reveal a painful truth. Shortly after Brontë's death, Gaskell had written to Smith, in fact, that she might one day want to write a biography of Charlotte Brontë, but that she would not want to do it until "no one is living whom such a publication would hurt" (*L* 241). As it turned out, she wrote it much sooner, but she continued to feel it her duty, if she could help it, not to hurt anyone.

Smith, who was going to publish the volume, having been Brontë's and Gaskell's publisher, would have, in any case, shied away from any material that might be libelous. Gaskell had to assure him at one point that she intended to delete from the final copy of the manuscript parts of a "very graphic" letter (*L* 326). Smith was not being overly cautious. In fact, he had not been cautious enough. Despite all that the book left out, it became, the moment it was published, an "apple of discord," as Gaskell called it (*L* 382). Complaints poured in from every quarter, including from the Brontë servants, who objected to the fact that Gaskell had observed in passing that there had been great waste at Haworth (*L* 365, 366). "It is 'anything for a quiet life,' " Gaskell wrote to George Smith, ready to yield on virtually everything; "if anybody objects to anything I am ready to take it out" (*L* 366). She came eventually to call the *Life* her "unlucky book" (*L* 365) and wrote a preface for the third edition that she did not dare to print but that, wishing to put it on record, she copied out in one of her letters: "If anybody is displeased with any statement in this book, they are requested to believe it withdrawn, and my deep regret expressed for its insertion, as truth is too expensive an article to be laid before the British public" (*L* 385). Indeed, as we shall shortly see, she was even threatened with a lawsuit.

But it was not, although they were important considerations certainly, any of these that was the reason Gaskell decided not to discuss Charlotte's attachment to Heger. What really determined her decision was that she wished to save Charlotte Brontë precisely as she had saved Ruth. The affair with Heger had in Gaskell's mind made Charlotte Brontë a fallen woman. At least it had made her a falling woman. But she was, no less than Ruth, capable of being redeemed. Gaskell did not, in any case, believe that it was the real Charlotte Brontë who had been in love with Heger. She was not lying, in a sense, when she wrote that, having considered carefully what to include and exclude, she "came to the resolution of writing truly, if I wrote at all" (*LCB,* p. 436). Just as she, in her fiction, distinguished between the French and English girls—Cynthia and Molly, Erminia and Maggie, Theresa and Bessy—so she distinguishes in the *Life* between the French and English Brontë. Brontë in Brussels had become passionate, Brussels being, like France, daemonic. In Gaskell's metaphoric vocabulary, Brontë had become French, in fact. Gaskell offers us, in the biography, a picture of what a French woman is by describing one French woman Brontë met at the Athénée. This woman, whom Gaskell calls the "Frenchwoman" so as to fix her nationality, was "more profligate, more steeped in a kind of cold, systematic sensuality, than" Charlotte "had before imagined it possible for a human being to be" (*LCB,* p. 214). We are presumably to assume that this behavior had, in Belgium, somehow rubbed off on Charlotte Brontë. But Brontë in Belgium was not the real Brontë. The real Charlotte Brontë to Gaskell was English. Over and over again in the *Life,* to distinguish her from the "Frenchwoman," Gaskell calls Brontë the "Englishwoman." Not only did Brontë come home eventually to live in England where she belonged, even in Brussels, Gaskell insists, she did not visit with the Belgians. She visited only an English family, where "she felt herself more at ease" (*LCB,* p. 196). "Mrs. Gaskell" was going to write the life of the English Charlotte Brontë. And just as she had expressed to Dickens her hope that Miss Pasley's past could be hidden so she could start a new life abroad with a "free and unbranded character," just as she had allowed in *Ruth* the Bensons to lie about Ruth's past, so she wanted to conceal, in her biography of the English, the life of Charlotte Brontë in Belgium. Brontë herself, since she was dead when Gaskell undertook her biography, could not be saved like Miss Pasley and Ruth. But on the pages of the *Life* her "character" could be made "free and unbranded."

In silencing what was French in Brontë, Gaskell of course had, in her own mind, silenced Charlotte Brontë's demon, and having done so she was compelled, just as she was compelled in her fiction to dispel in daemonic doubles the selves her heroines deny, to find among the people in Haworth a daemonic double for Charlotte. As it happened, Haworth was full of people ready to play that part. One of these was Branwell Brontë. He was a demon ready-made, especially in his illicit relationship with Mrs. Edmund Robinson. Edmund Robinson, a minister, had hired Anne to tutor his daughters, and it was on the strength of her word that, needing a tutor for his son, he had made an offer to Branwell. Branwell accepted and moved in. He lived in the house three years and a half, during which time he carried on an affair with Mrs. Robinson. When her husband at last discovered what had been going on in his house, Branwell, of course, was summarily dismissed.

Branwell's relationship with Mrs. Robinson resembles, in almost every particular, Charlotte's relationship with Heger. One becomes, for "Mrs. Gaskell," the natural proxy for the other. Branwell and Charlotte fit as well into another of Gaskell's patterns. Branwell is an idolized son at the expense of neglected daughters. Just as in "The Doom of the Griffiths" Angharad becomes, as Gaskell writes, "accustomed to give way" to Owen (5:242), so the Brontë sisters become accustomed to give way to Branwell. Gaskell describes a summer's day in 1835 when the Brontës all sat down to make plans for Branwell's future. There, after a long discussion, it was agreed he would study art while the girls would do what was necessary to help finance his education. He was to be their surrogate self. Whatever he did, he would do for all of them. The sisters consented. They "hardly recognized," Gaskell remarks, "their own, or each other's powers, but they knew his" (*LCB*, p. 111). Gaskell does not imagine the girls resenting or resisting the plan. She thinks the girls thought it fair. And it seems fair to her as well. Branwell was to fail in this enterprise, as he failed in every other, and Gaskell regrets the Brontë girls suffered thus a useless martyrdom. But she does not regret the martyrdom. "These are not," she later comments, "the first sisters who had laid their lives as a sacrifice before their brother's idolized wish. Would to God they might be the last"—and here is the point at which we wish Gaskell had actually stopped her sentence; but she goes on. She does not mean she wishes the girls had been the last to make such a sacrifice, but only the last whose sacrifice would meet "with such a miserable return!" (*LCB*, p. 114). It is in this connection that Gaskell writes the passage in which she says that men are required to *do* while women are required to *be*. And it is no surprise to her that an adulterous affair should be one of Branwell's *doings*. The sisters, Gaskell writes in the *Life,* knew that Branwell had been guilty of some sexual peccadillos but "such coarseness" seemed to them only a natural "part of manliness" (*LCB*, p. 153). Gaskell thinks it is manly too. Sexuality is daemonic, and the demon is a male. Brontë could not be saved from the demon unless the affair with Heger was silenced. But, as in *Ruth* and *North and South* brothers act out their sisters' demons, so in the *Life* Gaskell uses Branwell to *do* what his sister *is*.

Branwell had acted out the demon, but it was, in Gaskell's mind, Mrs. Robinson who had fallen. Gaskell is, as many have noticed, irrational in assessing the evidence against Mrs. Robinson in the biography and compulsive in her desire to make her seem entirely to blame. She admits that Branwell, having been idolized, has become selfish and self-indulgent (*LCB*, p. 153). But it is Mrs. Robinson still who is responsible for the affair as well as for Branwell's ruin and death. "The case," she writes, "presents the reverse of the usual features; the man became the victim; the man's life was blighted, and crushed out of him by suffering, and guilt entailed by guilt" (*LCB*, p. 234). Mrs. Robinson is the aggressor, tempting Branwell by gifts and promises but letting him go at her husband's request and even jilting him for another after her husband's death. Let her, Gaskell cries at one point, turning to a kind of rhetoric that she is not accustomed to using, "live and flourish!" "He died, his pockets filled with her letters, which he carried perpetually about his person. . . . He lies dead; and his doom is only known to God's mercy" (*LCB*, pp. 236–37). Gaskell is perfectly well aware that Branwell died of his own dissipation. But even for this it is Mrs. Robinson who is ultimately responsible. "For the last three years of Branwell's life, he took opium habitually, by way of stunning his conscience; he drank, moreover, whenever he could get the opportunity" (*LCB*, pp. 236–37). When the biography appeared, Mrs. Robinson threatened to sue. Although she had not been mentioned by name, having married Sir Edward Scott shortly after the death of her husband, she had become a prominent member of society in London, and Gaskell's hints had clearly identified her to nearly everyone she knew. Gaskell was away at the time but, learning of the threatened lawsuit, Smith and William Gaskell agreed on her behalf to make a retraction.

If Branwell plays for Gaskell the role that Richard Bradshaw plays in *Ruth*, the role of Jemima is assumed in the biography by Emily. Emily was already dead when Gaskell first met Charlotte Brontë, but she was, it would appear, often the subject of their discussions. For Charlotte "never tired of talking" or she of "listening," Gaskell writes, to the stories about Emily (*LCB*, p. 453). Brontë perhaps embellished her stories, but there was nothing she could say that Gaskell did not believe already. To Gaskell Emily had become the embodiment of the moors. Emily, she writes as though invoking a wild force of nature, "never happy nor well but on the sweeping moors that gathered round her home" (*LCB*, p. 123). Emily is the soul of Yorkshire, an independent spirit, free. "Emily," she apostrophizes her, "that free, wild, untameable spirit" (*LCB*, p. 123). Emily has her own identity. She had spent some time in Belgium with Charlotte at the Athénée, and although she had grown homesick and returned to the Yorkshire moors, she had been long enough in Brussels for Heger to form an opinion of her intellect and character. Whether he was right or not— and he very probably was—Gaskell agrees with his conclusions. She does not question Charlotte Brontë, who says that Emily was " 'good' " (*LCB*, p. 329), but she also believes Heger, who says that Emily was " 'selfish' " (*LCB*, p. 185). If she was selfish, in Gaskell's vocabulary, she had succeeded in retaining her self. Females, like Edith in *North and South*, have, as we know, no will of their own. But Emily, as Heger remarks, had " 'a stubborn tenacity of will' " (*LCB*, p. 185). Looking at Emily in the portrait Branwell painted of the sisters, Gaskell sees what she had seen in the men of *North and South*, someone who is imbued with "power" (*LCB*, p. 113). Heger is using the very words Gaskell would have used herself when he remarks that in his view Emily " 'should have been a man' " (*LCB*, p. 185). As Florence Nightingale had seemed "a creature of another race" (*L* 211), Emily Brontë "must have been a remnant," Gaskell writes, "of the Titans,—great-grand-daughter of the giants who used to inhabit the earth" (*LCB*, p. 453). Emily had become, thus, mythic. She was the archetype of the demon, Charlotte Brontë's daemonic self.

She was Charlotte Brontë's double. And she was Gaskell's double too. If Gaskell saw in Charlotte Brontë a reflection of "Mrs. Gaskell," she saw in Emily the double of her own daemonic self. Charlotte Brontë had herself recognized a similarity between Gaskell and her sister. To her publisher she had written, " 'In Mrs. Gaskell's nature it mournfully pleases me to fancy a remote affinity to my sister Emily.' "[5]

But in saving her from her demon, "Mrs. Gaskell" had, however, made it necessary for her to save Charlotte Brontë from her art.

When Gaskell decided to write the *Life,* long before she thought she would write it, she did so in response to an article that had appeared about Charlotte Brontë in *Sharpe's London Magazine of Entertainment and Instruction* in June of 1855, just three months after her death. The article, which was entitled "A Few Words about 'Jane Eyre,'" is not as hostile or as condemnatory as Brontë's friends and family felt or as subsequent readers have thought. Its author appreciates Brontë's talent and even admires some of her work. He does, however, imply that her fiction has something in it that is coarse. Leveled against a woman especially, this was, in the nineteenth century, a very serious accusation. To be called coarse was to be called vulgar, gross, indecent, obscene. Brontë's frank portrayal of passion, in women almost as much as in men, and the candid language she used had made her a target before of such charges, but coming so close now on her death, the article outraged Ellen Nussey, who urged Patrick Brontë and Arthur Nicholls to ask Gaskell to respond.

Gaskell agreed to do so immediately. She might have done it in many ways. She might have defended Brontë's fiction as reaching new frontiers of realism. She might have argued that an artist has the right to speak her mind. She might have simply pointed out that what had been called Charlotte Brontë's coarseness was only a very small part of her work. But Gaskell did not do any of these. "Mrs. Gaskell" could not, in fact, defend Charlotte Brontë's fiction at all. She herself thought it was coarse. She tries not to say so in the *Life,* although even here she is forced to grant "the existence of coarseness here and there" (*LCB,* p. 441). But she does not equivocate in her letters. To Emily Shaen she writes, for example, that *The Professor,* in her view, is seriously "disfigured" by "coarseness" (*L* 308). She writes to George Smith that she hopes Arthur Nicholls will "expunge some expressions & phrases" before *The Professor* goes to print (*L* 303). Nicholls did expunge a good deal but not enough to satisfy Gaskell. Hearing from Smith what Nicholls had done, she writes again to say that she wishes he had "altered more! I fear from what you say he has left many little things *you* would & should have taken out" as not "essential to the characters or the story, & as likely to make her misunderstood. For I would not, if I could help it, have another syllable that could be called coarse to be associated with her name" (*L* 314).

Seeing Brontë's fiction as coarse, Gaskell inevitably saw it as a projection of her demon. Writing once to Lady Kay-Shuttleworth, Gaskell explains what she considers the difference between herself and Brontë. The "difference," she says, "is that she puts all her naughtiness into her books, and I put all my goodness" (*L* 154). "Naughtiness" is an interesting word for Gaskell to use in this connection. She had, as it happened, just published *Ruth* when she sat down to write this letter, and *naughty* was the word in *Ruth* that she had put in the mouth of the child who first accuses Ruth of sinning. Ruth had committed a sexual sin, but so in a sense had Charlotte Brontë, since her fiction, being "coarse," was vulgar, gross, indecent, obscene. Charlotte in Brussels with Heger had almost become a fallen woman. The fall she had failed to achieve in her life she had achieved in her novels instead. Ruth had lived her passion in Wales. Brontë had lived hers in her fiction.

The fiction is what fascinated Gaskell. It was not the woman in Haworth who first attracted Gaskell's attention. It was the woman in her books. Hearing, for instance, that Charlotte Brontë, only known to her at the time through her novels *Jane Eyre* and *Shirley,* had paid a visit to Lady Kay-Shuttleworth, Gaskell writes to hint that she would welcome an introduction to her. "I have been so much interested," she adds, "in what she has written. I don't mean merely in the story and mode of narration . . . but in the glimpses one gets of *her,* and her modes of thought. . . . I should like very much indeed to know her" (*L* 72). The woman Gaskell wants to know is the demon of the fiction. The fiction, however, is also what threatens her. Never did Gaskell speak unequivocally well of any of Brontë's books. About *The Professor,* as we have seen, she writes it is "disfigured" by "coarseness." About *Jane Eyre* she writes "I don't know if I like or dislike it" (*L* 25a). She knows she "disliked a good deal" in *Shirley* (*L* 72). And she does not care, it seems, very much for *Villette* either since she dislikes Lucy Snowe (*L* 167), who is not only the novel's heroine but its ever-present narrator.

For Gaskell there was only one way, therefore, to defend Charlotte Brontë against the charge that had appeared in *Sharpe's London Magazine,* and it was the very same way she had defended the heroine in *Ruth* against the accusing eyes of the world. It was to disengage the woman from her offending daemonic self. In Gaskell's mind, Brontë herself had already done half the work. By working her naughtiness into her fiction, she had worked it out of her life. To prove that she was really good, Gaskell had only now to detach Charlotte Brontë from her fiction. She would admit the writer was naughty. But, she would argue, the woman was good. In "The Poor Clare," which she published while she was working on the biography, Gaskell was repeating this pattern. Lucy's "wanton," "voluptuous" demon wanders about doing and saying things that might be considered "coarse." But Lucy—Gaskell makes a point of this—remains uncorrupted by her demon. "'Her holy nature,'" the narrator says, "'dwells apart, and cannot be defiled or stained by all the devilish arts in the whole world'" (5:366). Gaskell writes about Charlotte Brontë in precisely the same way, even in the same language. She pleads with the reader not to "censure her"; "circumstances forced her to touch pitch"; but if "by it her hand was for a moment defiled," it was "but skin-deep. Every change in her life was purifying her" (*LCB*, p. 441). Coarse as her fiction may therefore have been, Charlotte Brontë was herself, Gaskell says that she will prove, a "noble, true, and tender woman" (*LCB*, p. 436). And the emphasis is here not on the adjectives but on the noun.

Gaskell thus divides Brontë in two. And having done so, she proceeds to divide the narrative with her. *Ruth* had been divided similarly, one part recording Ruth's life in Wales, the other her salvation in Eccleston. The *Life* is divided into two tales not sequentially but simultaneously, one recording the life of the woman and the other of the writer. Not only is Brontë thus divided, each of her wholly distinct identities is provided a different name. Gaskell had given Ruth a new name when she had moved her from Wales to Eccleston. In the biography Brontë the woman is referred to as Charlotte Brontë and the writer as Currer Bell. And as she reports the progress first of one and then the other, Gaskell moves back and forth between them as though they were really two separate people. Ending one section and starting another, she writes, for example, "Let us turn from Currer Bell to Charlotte Brontë" (*LCB*, p. 290). Bell and Brontë may share a body, but they are otherwise not alike. Currer Bell is bold and passionate, intellectual and ambitious. Charlotte Brontë is domestic. Whenever we move from one to the other, this is the contrast Gaskell emphasizes. Having reported at some length what Currer Bell, for instance, thinks of John Ruskin's *Stones of Venice*, Gaskell says she will now turn "from the literary opinions of the author to the domestic interests of the woman" (*LCB*, p. 391). The author has no domestic interests and the woman no literary thoughts.

This sets the stage for Gaskell to ask the central question on her mind. To what extent and in what way must the artist yield to the woman? "There were," she writes on one occasion,

> *separate duties belonging to each character—not opposing each other; not impossible to be reconciled. When a man becomes an author, it is probably merely a change of employment for him. He takes a portion of that time which has hitherto been devoted to some other study or pursuit; he gives up something of the legal or medical profession, in which he has hitherto*

endeavoured to serve others, or relinquishes part of the trade or business by which he has been striving to gain a livelihood; and another merchant or lawyer, or doctor, steps into his vacant place, and probably does as well as he. But no other can take up the quiet, regular duties of the daughter, the wife, or the mother as well as she whom God has appointed to fill that particular place: a woman's principal work in life is hardly left to her own choice; nor can she drop the domestic charges devolving on her as an individual, for the exercise of the most splendid talents that were ever bestowed. And yet she must not shrink from the extra responsibility implied by the very fact of her possessing such talents. She must not hide her gift in a napkin; it was meant for use and service of others. In an humble and faithful spirit must she labour to do what is not impossible, or God would not have set her to do it.

Gaskell has begun this passage thinking about Charlotte Brontë. At the end she is, however, clearly thinking of herself. We can even see the sentence in which the shift is taking place. It is the sentence in which she speaks of the duties of a woman as a daughter, wife, and mother. Charlotte Brontë was a daughter but when she became a writer she had not yet become a wife. And she was never to be a mother. It was Gaskell who was all three. Gaskell is aware herself of her personal involvement. "I put into words," she writes self-consciously, trying to distance herself again, "what Charlotte Brontë put into actions" (*LCB*, pp. 284–85).

Up to a point, a considerable point, Charlotte Brontë was a feminist, and Gaskell, although she does not always actually say that she agrees, seems, by quoting her, implicitly to endorse her feminist views. She quotes, for instance, from one letter in which Charlotte Brontë writes that she is happy to see the author of a recently published essay in the *Westminster Review* urge the enfranchisement of women (*LCB*, pp. 371–72). In the same spirit, she repeats Brontë's feminist views on literature. Brontë did not believe that fiction should be a vehicle for causes, but she believed it should tell the truth and one of the truths she thought it should tell concerned the characterization of women. Gaskell lets Brontë, in the *Life*, take to task a number of novelists for the women they created (*LCB*, pp. 415–16, 420), and she lets her scold her sisters who, she believed, were " 'morally wrong' " to create heroines who were "beautiful" (*LCB*, p. 259). She herself, Gaskell explains, was "determined to make her heroine" in *Jane Eyre* "plain, small, and unattractive, in defiance of the accepted canon" (*LCB*, pp. 258–59).

Inspired by some of Brontë's views, Gaskell becomes more radical too in her views on the status of women. There had always been in Gaskell little surges of feminist thought. Some had erupted in her letters. Thus, for example, when she had sent Anne Shaen a copy of "Lizzie Lindsay," an old Irish air whose lyrics upbraid a young woman for not showing the proper submission to her lover, Gaskell had urged her not to smile at this "glorious specimen of man monarchy." In place of the lyrics that it came with, she had even suggested to Shaen that she "adopt" "a sentence" perhaps "out of Mary Wollstonecraft" (*L* 25a). When her Unitarian friends were sending a petition around to urge legislation that would allow married women to keep their properties, Gaskell not only signed her name, she wrote to Eliza Fox to say that while she doubted legislation could do much to offset domestic intimidation, a "husband," having always in her view the power to "coax, wheedle, beat or tyrannize his wife out of something," still she was willing to support those who wanted to make the law because "our sex is badly used and legislated *against,* there's no doubt of *that*" (*L* 276). In *Sylvia's Lovers,* Gaskell had even, although very quietly, lodged a protest against a professional inequity. When the Fosters, who own the store in which Philip Hepburn works, decide to retire, they leave their property, having no family, to their workers, or, at least, to two of their workers, Philip and William. Hester Rose, who has worked as long as they in the store and just as hard, is not included in the bequest. Had she been " 'a lad,' " they say, they would have given her " 'a third,' " but there was no point in " 'troubling' " a woman by including her in the " 'partnership' " (6:185).

Writing about Charlotte Brontë emboldened Gaskell even more. Indeed, as she was writing the *Life,* Gaskell must have, at some point, intended to make it a feminist battle cry, for on its title page she put these stirring lines from Elizabeth Barrett's feminist poem "Aurora Leigh":

> Oh my God,
> ————————————————Thou hast knowledge, only Thou,
> How dreary 'tis for women to sit still
> On winter nights by solitary fires
> And hear the nations praising them far off.

But Brontë was not a feminist always nor entirely at any time. She herself, in trying to answer the question of her right to work, could not escape the view that women, whatever else they chose to do, were required to accept still their roles as domestic angels. When Southey, on receiving some poems Brontë had sent him at nineteen hoping he would encourage her work, had written in answer " 'Literature cannot be the business of a woman's life, and it ought not to be. The more she is engaged in her proper duties, the less leisure will she have for it, even as an accomplishment and a recreation. To those duties you have not yet been called, and when you are you will be less eager for celebrity' " (*LCB,* pp. 129–30), Brontë did not, in her reply, question the premise of Southey's comments. On the contrary, she agreed with them, and attempted to convince him that she was trying to live by them (*LCB,* pp. 131–32). She was, it is true, very young at this time, but she herself, a decade later, offers almost the same advice to a young woman who is uncertain as to which of two roads to take: " 'the right path,' " she says, " 'is that which necessitates the greatest sacrifice of self-interest.' " " 'I recommend,' " she ends her letter, " 'you to do what I am trying to do myself' " (*LCB,* pp. 249–50).

Gaskell too, who, as we know, did not like married women to work, and even single ones if someone wanted them for something at home, cannot bring herself to say, however bold she is at moments when the feminist spirit is on her, that the artist has a right to take precedence over the woman. This is something she had never been able to bring herself to say. A letter she wrote once to a woman who had written to her to tell her she wanted to become a novelist offers us an interesting glimpse into Gaskell's thoughts on this subject. The woman, in her letter, asks for advice on how to balance the demands of her home duties and the requirements of her art. Gaskell tells her, in reply, that she must learn, in her "household labors" "to oeconomize" her "strength," and she provides some household tips on how to do her washing and ironing, her sewing and mending, so efficiently that she will have time to write. If she does not succeed, however, Gaskell suggests she consider postponing her writing until her children are grown. Meanwhile, she says, she might begin to think of her duties at home as having a certain kind of "poetry." Homer himself, she reminds the woman, did not disdain to give a description of "the Greek princesses" as they "washed their clothes" (*L* 515). The aspiring young woman had written to Gaskell to ask how she might become a Homer. Gaskell tells her she must be satisfied to function in the role of Nausicaa.

If Gaskell seems to have in mind a woman here, a pen in one hand and a ladle in the other, writing as she stirs the soup, she is virtually describing how she actually wrote herself. The artist was required always to be subordinate to the woman. She felt it necessary, for instance, to work where she could keep an eye on the household and the children. Although she would have much preferred to "shut" herself "up" where she could be "secure from" any "interruption," she chose to write in the downstairs parlor because it was the hub of the house. It was extremely difficult there for her "to get," as she wrote in one letter, as much as "an uninterrupted 5 minutes." (*L* 480). Knowing that she is available, everyone, she writes in another, "comes to me perpetually." To give an example of what she means, she says that in the preceding hour, she has "had to decide on the following variety of important questions. Boiled beef—how long to boil? What perennials will do in Manchester smoke, & what colours our garden wants? Length of skirt for a gown? Salary of a nursery governess, & stipulations for a certain quantity of time to be left to herself.—Read letters on the state of Indian army—lent me by a very agreeable neighbour & return them, with a proper note, & as many wise remarks as would come in a hurry. Settle 20 questions of dress for the girls, who are going out for the day; & want to look nice & yet not spoil their gowns with the mud &c &c—See a lady about an MS story of hers, & give her disheartening but very good advice. Arrange about selling two poor cows for one good one,—see purchasers, & show myself up to cattle questions, keep, & prices,—and it's not 1/2 past 10 yet!" (*L* 384). We hardly ever hear of her work without hearing of household affairs that she must simultaneously deal with. "What with a new end to my book," she writes in one letter, "new flannel petticoats, & bad tides I'm altogether in a maze" (*L* 226). She often writes letters while she eats. "I am getting my lunch," she writes at one time, "(or rather dinner) while I write. . . . Ham sandwiches and beer if you wish to know" (*L* 199). She is always racing the clock. "I know you will excuse my bad writing," she apologizes to George Smith, "I *am* in such a hurry" (*L* 336). "In a hurry" might be used as the title of her letters. "In haste," she ends one letter, for instance, "as I think I am always in at home" (*L* 224). "I am writing in a terrible hurry as usual" (*L* 322). "Somehow I am always in a hurry" (*L* 315). Gaskell knew her work was suffering because of the many interruptions, because she was always writing in haste. "Expecting an interruption every instant is not a good time for telling all one thinks and feels," she explains to one of her sisters-in-law. "One is thankful to get in bare facts" (*L* 13). It is no wonder she describes herself as "swallowed up by small household cares" (*L* 421). How she got anything done is a mystery. According to Margaret Shaen, their niece, Catherine and Susanna Winkworth believed that what Gaskell "had actually published was a mere fraction of what she might have written, had her life been a less many-sided one."[6]

Virginia Woolf would have said of Gaskell that she asked for no room of her own. And the fact is she did not, not metaphorically and not literally. She wrote once to Norton, "If I had a library like yours, all

undisturbed for hours, how I would write!" (*L* 384). But the only study in
the house was, of course, given to William, who had sermons and lectures
to prepare and parish business to attend to. Gaskell felt it was his by right.
She could not imagine she herself had as good a right as William to a study
of her own. One of her remarks in the letter she wrote to the aspiring
young woman tells us something very important about how Gaskell saw
herself. In that letter she suggests, as we have seen, the woman wait until
her children are grown to write. But Gaskell herself was writing fiction
long before her children were grown. When she published *Mary Barton,*
Marianne was fourteen, Meta eleven, Florence six, and Julia two. Yet
Gaskell is not being hypocritical. She simply cannot imagine a woman,
defined as a woman is in her mind, doing the things that, in reality, she has
been able to do herself. And just as the picture in her mind, rather than her
own experiences, determines the advice she gives, so it determines how
she regards herself. Seeing herself in the role of "woman," she cannot
imagine herself an "artist." Art for a woman is not a vocation but, at most,
an avocation. A woman may write, a woman may paint, but to be a
professional artist claiming professional rights and privileges was something only a man could do.

Gaskell did once make an exception in the case of her daughter Meta.
Meta had, at an early age, shown a talent for drawing and painting, and
Gaskell had not only encouraged her but arranged for her to receive
private lessons from John Ruskin. When Meta announced, at twenty-
three, she wanted to be a professional artist, Gaskell was almost prepared
for the news. Although she confided to Charles Eliot Norton that it would
be "a silent trial to" her, she said nonetheless that she thought if Meta
"really & truly . . . wished it," "at her age, I should think it right to yield,
for I believe she has great genius for it; and as, if she had married her life
would have been apart & separate from mine, so I think she has a *right* to
make it now" (*L* 476).

But she was never as courageous when she was writing about herself.
About herself she always wavers. Writing, for instance, to Eliza Fox, she
says it is a terrible "puzzle" to which she can offer no "solution" "where
and when," in a woman's conflict between "home duties and individual
life," one must "give place to the other" (*L* 68). The history of her writing
career leaves no doubt that Gaskell saw herself merely as a woman who
wrote, not as a professional writer. There is no question that every year
Gaskell learned more about her craft and acquired greater confidence both
in her talent and her judgments. Her correspondence with Dickens especially implies, as she begins to resist his suggestions about her fiction and

even his editorial demands, that she came to trust herself even against such a formidable critic.[7] But she could never cross that line between the amateur and the professional. Whenever she finished a particular work, she never believed she would write another. "I have nothing else to say," she wrote after finishing *Mary Barton* (L 41). "I do not at present look forward," she wrote, having finished *Cranford* and *Ruth,* "to ever writing again for publication, having literally nothing to write about" (L 167a). In the spring of 1855, just before she began the biography, she wrote "I doubt if I shall ever write again for publication" (L 237). Although she continued to write, in fact, to the very day she died, she never envisioned herself a woman for whom her art was a career.

She could not therefore imagine Brontë as a professional writer either. Brontë, although she had moments of doubt, did consider herself an artist, so much so that she insisted no one, in reviewing her work, take her sex into account. Writing, for instance, to George Henry Lewes— whom she had begged, on being told that he was planning to review *Shirley,* not to judge her " 'by some standard' " he thought " 'becoming to my sex' " (*LCB,* p. 336)—Brontë writes to say she was " 'grieved' " and " 'indignant' " to discover that he had not complied with her wishes. She cannot imagine why the " 'critics' " find it so difficult to " 'judge' " her " 'not as a woman' " but " 'as an author' " (*LCB,* p. 348). It was to avoid such reviews as Lewes's that Charlotte Brontë and her sisters had, on first going into print, chosen to use the genderless pseudonyms Acton, Currer, and Ellis Bell. Gaskell herself had used a pseudonym that had camouflaged her sex when she had published her early stories under the name Cotton Mather Mills and had been ready to sign *Mary Barton* with the pen name Stephen Berwick. But hearing the position explained, as Brontë does in one of her letters, in a theoretic way, Gaskell, "Mrs. Gaskell," is threatened. "Whether right or wrong," she remarks, afraid to commit herself to a position, "her feeling was strong on this point" (*LCB,* p. 347). The woman in Gaskell cannot allow the artist in Brontë to prevail.

Gaskell herself was praised when she died for never having allowed her work to interfere with her womanly duties. G. B. Smith, we recall, had concluded his summation of her life by observing that, although her work proved a woman could do more than was generally allowed her, Gaskell "lacked none of those virtues which make home 'the earthly paradise.' " Emily Shaen, who had herself seen firsthand how difficult it had been for Gaskell, in the midst of household chores, to find a moment for her writing, praises Gaskell nevertheless because her "books were only written when all possible domestic and social claims had been satisfied."

Even Marianne is reported to have said of her mother that it was wonderful " 'how her writing never interfered with her social or domestic duties.' "[8]

In the same way, Gaskell herself praises Brontë in the biography for never sacrificing her duties to the demands of her art. Even when Brontë felt she was in the " 'possession' " of some power beyond herself—so much "more present to her mind" was the fictional world than "her actual life"—even then, it was "her care" "to discharge her household and filial duties" before she felt she could allow herself the "leisure to sit down and write" (*LCB,* p. 257). Nor did she, Gaskell continues, object to "breaking off in the full flow of interest and inspiration in her writing" if the time came when it was her turn to "cut the specks in the potatoes" (*LCB,* p. 257). Those "who survive," Gaskell assures us, "of her daily and household companions, are clear in their testimony, that never was the claim of any duty, never the call of another for help, neglected for an instant" (*LCB,* p. 257).

If Gaskell, then, began the biography hoping to find through Charlotte Brontë the strength to assert that, although a woman, she had the right to be an artist, she did not succeed in convincing herself. Instead, she managed to turn Charlotte Brontë into an image of "Mrs. Gaskell." And that transformation in Gaskell's mind became complete when Brontë married. "Mrs. Gaskell" always required the heroines of her fiction to marry if they found themselves in situations that paralleled her own early life. And Charlotte Brontë, as Gaskell saw her, satisfied some crucial criteria. Her mother had died when she was a child and so had her two older sisters. Later, her brother had died as well and also her two younger sisters. Her father was still alive, of course, but he—although in fact he outlived her—growing increasingly old and infirm, did not seem likely to last very long. To all intents and purposes, therefore, Charlotte was Alone! Alone! And just as "Mrs. Gaskell" arranges for her heroines to marry when they find themselves alone, she felt a psychological need to see Charlotte Brontë married too.

She felt it not only in the biography. She actually felt it in real life. Gérin is undoubtedly right to conclude that it was Gaskell who made the circumstances possible for the marriage to take place between Brontë and Arthur Nicholls and who actually brought it about.[9] What is amazing is that Gaskell was aware that Charlotte Brontë did not want to marry Nicholls. Charlotte herself had told her in Haworth that she did not find Nicholls attractive, by which Charlotte had certainly meant not only physically but psychologically. Nicholls—as is perfectly obvious from every detail that we know of him—while a decent, hardworking man, was hardly a suitable mate for Brontë, caring nothing, as he did, for any of the things she cared for and indifferent, as he was, to the books that she had written and that she still hoped to write. Brontë knew his limitations, and Gaskell must have known them too from her discussions of him with Brontë. There is no question that she knew Nicholls had proposed already and that Charlotte had turned him down. But none of this mattered, it seems, to Gaskell. Deciding that Charlotte had to marry and finding no other available candidate, she managed, first, to arrange through a friend for Nicholls to receive a pension that would provide him with an income on which he would be able to marry, then, since Nicholls had left Haworth when his proposal had been turned down, to bring the two together in London. It may be true, as Gérin thinks, that, by the time Gaskell interfered, Brontë had reconsidered the match.[10] She must have been willing to see Nicholls again, or she would not have gone to meet him. But it is not with any enthusiasm that she contemplates this marriage. Reporting to Gaskell a little later, and unaware of Gaskell's part in the events that have transpired, Brontë, for example, writes: "Things have progressed I don't know how. It is of no use going into detail. After various visits and as the result of perseverence in one quarter and a gradual change of feeling in others, I find myself what people call 'engaged.' "[11] Brontë's tone is weary here, and the marriage not a prospect to which she is looking forward, more a trial she must endure. In her juvenilia, Charlotte dreamed of marrying the equivalent of what in Gaskell's imagination was to become a Charley Kinraid. Gaskell had given her Philip Hepburn.

Brontë's marriage is, like Sylvia's, the final step in Gaskell's mind in the silencing of the demon. It is the final transformation of the artist Currer Bell into the "true and tender" woman. Gaskell could not have known that Brontë would not be able to go on writing after she had married Nicholls, but she certainly knew what it was to be a busy minister's wife. Although she made a number of efforts, Brontë did not, once she was married, manage to produce very much. In her letters she explains why. "My time is not my own," she writes; "somebody else wants a good portion of it, and says 'we must *do* so and so.' We do so and so, accordingly; and it generally seems the right thing" (*LCB,* p. 465). "Of course, he often," she writes again, "finds a little work for his wife to do, and I hope she is not sorry to help him. I believe it is not bad for me that his bent should be so wholly towards matters of life and active usefulness; so little inclined to the literary and contemplative" (*LCB,* p. 466). It is not difficult to imagine the passionate conflicts, the self-control, and the agonies of self-repression that have gone into these simple sentences. But "Mrs. Gaskell" refuses to hear anything but "Mrs. Nicholls." Brontë, she insists, is blissful. Commenting on these very letters, she speaks of "the low murmurs of happiness" that those who "listened" to Charlotte "heard" (*LCB,* p. 465).

Gaskell had thus saved Charlotte Brontë, saved her not only from her detractors, as she had been asked to do, but, since she in fact agreed with them, from the self that had produced the fiction they considered coarse. But saving her meant killing her too, just as it had done with Ruth. "Mrs. Gaskell" ends the *Life* on what she feels is a happy note, the thought that there are readers who, forgiving Brontë's "faults and errors," will be able, "with warm hearts," to feel "reverence" for the "virtue" that was present in the woman (*LCB,* p. 472). But the demon, well aware that "Mrs. Gaskell" intends to bury her, opens the *Life,* not with Brontë's birth, as most biographies would have done, but with her grave in the family cemetery. In an almost aerial descent, we find ourselves, at the beginning, circling down to the Yorkshire moors and closing in on the Haworth parsonage. Gaskell was to use this technique once again in *Wives and Daughters,* in which the narrator opens the story by circling slowly down to Hollingford and making his way to the Gibson house. Here the house into which we are taken is literally the house of the dead. Gaskell walks us through the "graveyard" pointing out the "upright tombstones" as, on a tour of a family mansion, one might point to different rooms (*LCB,* p. 18). And just as in an ordinary biography we would be introduced to the family, here we are asked in turn to meet every "dead member of the household." They followed one "another fast," Gaskell tells us, "to the grave." She reproduces the inscriptions on the gravestones one by one: Maria Brontë, Charlotte's mother; Maria Brontë, her oldest sister; Elizabeth Brontë, the second child of Maria and Patrick Brontë; Branwell; Emily; and Anne. Finally, we reach the last:

> *Adjoining Lie the Remains of*
> CHARLOTTE, WIFE
> *of the*
> *Rev. Arthur Bell Nicholls, A.B.,*
> *And Daughter of the Rev. P. Brontë, A.B., Incumbent.*
> *She Died March 31st, 1855, in the 39th*
> *Year of Her Age.*

Like "Mrs. Gaskell's" memorial plaque at the Cross Street Chapel in Manchester, which praises her as a wife and mother and for her community work, but does not say, at least directly, that she was a writer of fiction, the tombstone here identifies Charlotte by giving the names of her father and husband, but says not a word about the fact that she was a novelist too. A tombstone is not perhaps required to. But Gaskell, by denying the artist so that she could praise the woman, turned *The Life of Charlotte Brontë* into the tomb of Currer Bell.

XVIII

The Witch Who Sits on the Seven Hills

IN HER BIOGRAPHY of Charlotte Brontë "Mrs. Gaskell" had understood that she would have to bury the artist if she wanted to save the woman. Gaskell's demon knew, conversely, that it would have to bury the woman if the artist was to be saved. This is the subtextual theme of the short piece called "Sketch of Clopton House." The date of the piece is somewhat uncertain. Gaskell was probably still in her teens and a pupil at the Miss Byerleys' when she heard, at the Anglican Church that she attended in Stratford-on-Avon, the "fearful . . . legend" of Charlotte Clopton, which was to become its core (1:506). And it was probably during those years that she visited the house. She must have written something down very shortly after her visit, for the vividness of the detail suggests a recent recollection, although it was only in 1840 that William and Mary Howitt published the "Sketch" in *Visits to Remarkable Places*.

The piece is short and mostly devoted to a tour of the house itself. In it, however, lies embedded what in effect is a short story about the death of Charlotte Clopton. The story is set in the time of a plague. The fear of contagion was so great, Gaskell writes, that many people were sent in "fearful haste" to their graves. Charlotte Clopton was one of these. One of the first to be infected, Charlotte had been taken for dead and entombed in the family vault. Only when the vault was opened to admit another Clopton did the family, to its horror, realize what it had done. Finding her standing "in her grave-clothes," "leaning against the wall" of the vault, they saw that she had not only recovered but had risen from her coffin. And she had not died, it seemed, until, "in the agonies of despair and hunger, she had bitten a piece from her white round shoulder!" "Of course," Gaskell adds, "she had *walked* ever since" (1:506).

As it happens, all this occurred in the year 1564,[1] which was the year of Shakespeare's birth, and since it also occurred in his birthplace, a fact of which Gaskell is keenly aware, the context here is part of the text and makes a subtextual contrast. Gaskell could not have known the importance the contrast was to have to her life when she first heard the Clopton legend, but she must have begun to suspect something of its relevance to her when she rewrote the piece for the Howitts. The juxtaposition of the two figures makes of this part of the sketch a story in which the artist—in England, in fact, the very embodiment of art—is born in the very time and place in which the woman is not only buried but, as it always occurs in Gaskell in a metaphoric way, buried literally alive.

Developed in significant ways, this is the theme of "A Dark Night's Work." The heroine, Ellinor, who is daemonic—she is called a "bewitching" young woman (7:456) in whom a "wild spirit" "lurked" (7:428)—not only shares, as we have seen on a number of occasions, many parts of Gaskell's history, but so much resembles Gaskell both in character and personality that Charles Dickens, who published the story and with whom Gaskell was just then at odds, wrote to his editor that he wished "'the fair Ellinor were not so horribly like Mrs. Gaskell!'"[2] Ellinor's father, a daemonic surrogate in the style of Barton and Robson (although there are parts of him that seem a surrogate brother and husband too), commits a murder one night in rage, when he kills his assistant, Dunstan. Dixon, his servant, suggests that the two conceal the crime and bury the body, which under cover of night, they do (7:464), providing Gaskell with her title. And in a variation of the events that reveal to Anna Scherer in "The Grey Woman" that her husband is a chief of chauffeurs, Ellinor, waiting to speak to her father in the next room at the time of the murder, hears it all and thus becomes, like so many characters in Gaskell, by sharing the secret, its secret sharer. She helps, in fact, to bury the body, thus becoming a sharer too in the concealment of the crime. And when her father dies soon after, the secret in effect becomes hers, for, as children do in Gaskell, Ellinor is made to "'bear,'" as someone actually says in the story, "'the sins of thy father'" (7:510). The secret weighs heavily on Ellinor, so much so it makes her ill, and, receiving an invitation to accompany friends to Rome, she accepts, being persuaded a change of scene will do her good. But as soon as she reaches Rome, Ellinor is informed by letter that the crime has been discovered, Dunstan's body having been found by men who were digging to build a railroad (7:552). The body, of course, is discovered in England but, as the narrative is constructed, the crime only comes out in Rome, since it is there that Ellinor hears of it. Indeed, in that magical way that metaphors always work in Gaskell's mind, Rome has caused it to come out, the body being still concealed when Ellinor sets sail from England but turning out to be revealed as soon as she arrives in Rome.

But something else comes out as well as soon as Ellinor reaches

Rome, and that is her "latent . . . artistic temperament" (7:548). The narrator makes this remark as Ellinor, looking around when she arrives, finds herself responding intensely to every shape and color and line that she sees in the luscious countryside and to every vivid impression of the vibrant city streets. England had nothing like this to offer and the artistic sensibility that had been merely dormant in England is, we are obviously meant to see, aroused by the splendid sights of Italy. It is no accident, however, that the latent artistic temperament and the crime come out together and in the identical place. They are connected in Gaskell's mind. *Latent,* as we have often seen, is one of Gaskell's favorite words. Barton's anger at the masters lights a "latent fire in his eyes" (1:8), Margaret Hale hides a "latent Vashti" (4:446), Frederick Hale hides a "latent passion" (4:293), and Sylvia, when she marries Philip, is required to veil her passion, therefore making it "latent" too (6:362). Latency is a common element, furthermore, in Gaskell's plots, in which it is often the case that characters are literally hidden. Frederick, for instance, in *North and South* and Osborne's wife in *Wives and Daughters* both must hide themselves in England, Frederick because the authorities want him and Aimée because her husband fears to tell his parents of their marriage. In *Cranford* it is men who are hidden, not in the town, as it is thought, but in the minds of the Cranford ladies. Frequently it is not the character but the relationship that is hidden. So, for example, in *Wives and Daughters,* is Cynthia's relationship to Preston. People are hidden in other ways too. Charlie Kinraid is hidden, for instance, when Philip conceals what has happened to him. Sometimes even the dead are hidden, not only, as in "A Dark Night's Work," when bodies are concealed by murderers because they wish to escape detection but when the demon must be protected and therefore hidden in the grave, hidden literally, as in the case of Gregory in "The Half-Brothers," or metaphorically, as in Cynthia, in whom the "real self" is "shrouded." Sin is often latent too. Thus, for example, Ruth's past is hidden when she is brought to be saved in Eccleston, even as the " 'earth' " in winter is " 'hiding' " its guilty front with snow (3:159). Similarly, crime is hidden. A theft is concealed in "The Crooked Branch" and frauds and forgeries in *Ruth,* "Right at Last," and "The Moorland Cottage." In England, Frederick, concealing himself, had also concealed his crime, his mutiny. In "The Grey Woman" and "The Squire's Story" the bloody deeds of the husbands are hidden as well as the bodies they drag home. All these latencies are different, but they are variants of one thing. In every instance of concealment, it is the demon that is hidden, as Gaskell herself had hidden hers.[3]

In the light of all these latencies, it is revealing that, while discussing the subject of art with Eliza Fox as it is related to women, Gaskell in a letter writes "I am sure it is healthy for" women "to have the refuge of the *hidden* world of Art to *shelter* themselves in when too much pressed upon by daily small Lilliputian arrows of peddling [*sic*] cares; it keeps them from being morbid as you say; and takes them into the land where King Arthur lies *hidden,* and soothes them with its peace. I have felt this in writing, I see others feel it in music, you in painting" (*L* 68; italics mine). Gaskell came, as we have seen, to think of fiction as the means through which she could express her demon. Here she tells us she thinks of art as rooted in her hidden life.

The logic therefore of the fact that in "A Dark Night's Work" the crime as well as the artistic temperament come out together and both in Rome seems to be simply that the demon, which had been a crime in England and had therefore to be buried, has been liberated in Rome to take its natural form as art. In a metaphoric sense, it had been Ellinor herself who had been killed and buried in England. Acting on behalf of his daughter, like John Barton and Daniel Robson, Wilkins had, in killing Dunstan, *done* what his daughter *is.* But in letting her father act for her, Ellinor had, like Mary and Sylvia, been compelled to bury her demon, bury it literally, in her case. For in a sense it is her demon that lies buried in Dunstan's grave. Gaskell makes a point of telling us that her lover, reading the letters Ellinor sends him after the murder, feels, although he has no knowledge of the events that have transpired, that she is "subdued," "repressed," in her expressions of love to him, that she is making an effort at something that he rightly describes as "concealment" (7:445). The demon indeed has been concealed, shrouded, like Cynthia's, in the grave. Gaskell also lets us know that Dunstan's death is somehow Ellinor's. Dixon, for instance, remarks that the secret " 'will be the death' " of both of them (7:480), and Ellinor is so despondent after the murder has been committed that "she would fain have died" herself (7:477). Imagistically, she has died. But she is resurrected in Rome. As the witch comes out in "Lois" when Lois reaches the land of the free, so does the crime come out in Ellinor the moment she sets foot in Rome, and with the crime, her artistic temperament.

Gaskell once visited Rome herself. Although in one letter to Catherine Winkworth she said she did not care for travel (*L* 211), the fact is she traveled a good deal. As indeed the years went by, her trips grew longer and more frequent. In the early days of her marriage, she traveled most of the time with William. Later she traveled mostly without him, although she almost always took one or more of the girls along. Sometimes she

traveled for her work. Research, for instance, for *Sylvia's Lovers* sent her
for a time to Whitby. For the *Life* it sent her to Haworth to talk to Brontë's
father and husband, then to Belgium to talk with Heger. Sometimes she
traveled for her health, to get away from the smoke of Manchester or to
rest from her busy life. Vacations like these often took her to Knutsford or
to the Lake District, which she loved. But most of the time she traveled
elsewhere and not for any of these reasons. Most of the time she traveled to
places in which her demon could be free. Her travels were flights of the
caged bird, adventures of the gypsy-bachelor. Much of the time Gaskell
traveled abroad. She made three trips, for instance, to Germany, one with
William, two without him. She made six separate trips to France, the first
with William once again, four with one or more of her daughters, and the
last one all alone. And she made two trips to Italy, the first of which was
her trip to Rome.

Gaskell had wanted to leave for this journey as soon as she had
completed the *Life,* the very day the book was finished (*L* 329) in February
of 1857, and while she did not manage to do so, she did get away a few
days later. Much of Gaskell's Roman adventure is relayed in "A Dark
Night's Work." Although she did not write its conclusion until 1862,
Gaskell, as she reports to George Smith, had started the story four years
earlier (*L* 517), shortly after she had returned from her trip to Rome, that
is. There are a great many actual parallels between her own and Ellinor's
journey. Even the fact that the boiler exploded on Gaskell's ship as she
sailed from Marseilles is included in the narrative. But these are only hints
that the story contains the psychological parallels that we have come to
expect from her work.

Gaskell was brought to Rome at that moment by the same things that
were to bring Ellinor. Writing to her friends, she said she needed a change
of scene to recuperate. She said that she had been exhausted in the writing
of the biography. And she very probably had, not only because it had been
such hard work and forced her to deal with so many people, each of whom
had a fear about something that she might reveal in the *Life,* but chiefly, for
she could have survived easily the rest of her difficulties, because she had
been, in the writing of it, in such conflict with herself. She had had to
confront her demon. She had grappled with it and lost. Like Ellinor, she
had kept the secret, not only of Brontë's affair with Heger but the far more
important secret that Charlotte Brontë was an artist. Burying Brontë in
the biography, she had buried herself as well, just as Ellinor, burying
Dunstan, really places herself in the grave. What Gaskell needed more than

anything was to find a place, like Ellinor, in which to let her secret out. It is significant that in the letter in which she speaks of art as "hidden," Gaskell says that it is "healthy" for women to have the refuge of art. Health is what Ellinor seeks in Rome. And health is also what she finds there. In Rome, the narrator explains, Ellinor "forgot her despondency," "as if by magic," "her ill-health disappeared" (7:548). Gaskell at one point remarks that Ellinor was led to Rome by her "instinct for self-preservation" (7:523). Gaskell uses identical words to describe the impulse that leads Philip Hepburn to seek an escape for his demon as Stephen Freeman (6:411). What Ellinor goes to Rome to do is to "preserve" her daemonic "self." And that is what Gaskell went to do. The health she went to seek in Rome was the possession of her demon.

Gaskell had not been to Rome before, but she had often thought about it and in her mind she had transformed it—all of Italy, in fact, and the whole Mediterranean—into one of her central images.[4] She writes to Eliza Fox, for example, in 1853, "oh how I should like to be wafted out of this England" for "a long sail along the Mediterranean, slowly and lazily floating" (L 151). In *North and South,* the Mediterranean, where Edith is living for a time, seems to Gaskell "glad and pleasure-seeking" (4:75). The sybaritic self in Gaskell, one of her several "warring members," had, we recall, a "taste for beauty." That was one of the selves she imagined that the Mediterranean released. It was also a place of freedom. Reading the letters her cousin sends her, Margaret feels that Edith is living a life that is "free— utterly free" (4:76). And it is to the Mediterranean that Philip goes to become Stephen Freeman. Edith happens to be in Corfu and Philip happens to be in Palestine, but Gaskell sweeps into one metaphor all the places that girt the sea. Italy she describes very similarly. The narrator in "My Lady Ludlow" speaks of the "life they lead in Italy" as being both "beautiful" and "free" (5:190). Rome to Gaskell is also free. In "A Dark Night's Work" she writes that Ellinor comes to Rome to find a "dwelling" that is "unhaunted," in "a free . . . country" (7:523). And Gaskell makes clear in one of her letters that the freedom of which she is thinking is the freedom of the demon. Writing to her friends the Storys, she describes the city of Rome as "the great witch who sits . . . upon her seven hills" (L 482). Like Bridget and Lois, Rome is a witch. As Paris and France came to embody for Gaskell the demon in its passionate form, Rome embodied the demon as art. When Gaskell in "My Lady Ludlow" writes of the freedom and beauty of Italy, she adds that Sir Lawrence, a minor character who had moved from England to Italy, was "a man of . . . artistic taste" (5:190). Sir

Lawrence is of little significance in the development of the narrative. His tastes are of no interest to us. But Gaskell cannot think of Italy without simultaneously thinking of art.

Gaskell's journey to Rome would have been important in her imagination even if nothing at all had occurred there, simply because she was acting out one of the metaphors in her mind. But something did occur on this journey. She met Charles Eliot Norton. Gaskell's biographers have long debated what, if anything, happened with Norton, and to this question there are, I think, two entirely opposite answers, both of which are, however, true. From one perspective, nothing happened. From another, everything happened. I think we can be fairly certain that they did not have an "affair." Gaskell was not the kind of woman who would have been sexually unfaithful. She could not have written the letters to Norton that she did on her return had she been guilty of adultery, even adultery in her heart. There is no doubt that something in each was attractive to the other. They shared many things: religious beliefs, political views, social attitudes, moral convictions, and a host of general interests. Even more, they were brought together by their warmth, their youthful enthusiasm, their humor, their candor, their sincerity, and the delight they took in experience. And the fact that Norton was younger—Gaskell was forty-six already, and Norton had only just turned thirty—would not have stood in the way on her part, liking the young as she always did.

But this, although it became the basis of the lasting friendship they formed, was not the magic of the moment that Gaskell shared with Norton in Rome. Gaskell had met Norton before, seven years earlier in London, but there had been no magic in it. Five years after that first meeting, and two before their meeting in Rome, Norton had written to Gaskell to tell her how much the meeting had meant to him. "It has probably," he wrote, "long passed from your remembrance that one evening in June (I think) 1850 a young American was introduced to you at Mr. Proctor's in London. It was an occasion not to be forgotten by him, however—, and that evening affords one of the pleasantest recollections of a time which has left none but pleasant memories."[5] Norton had remembered their meeting. Gaskell, however, had forgotten it. She had completely forgotten him. When she saw him again in Rome, she was entirely unaware that she had met him once already.

The magic was not Norton at all. The magic occurred because for Gaskell Norton came to be associated, another image in her mind, with the release of her artistic demon. It happened, in one of those extraordinary accidents that seem to turn life itself into fiction, that Gaskell, arriving on February 23, reached the city on the eve of Shrove Tuesday. Burying Charlotte Brontë in England and fleeing to Italy for release, she found herself, on reaching Rome, in a city wild with excitement as it prepared for the period of Lent by making the most of its last day of freedom in a mad and frenzied carnival. The Storys had prepared for her visit by renting a balcony on the Corso so as to have a good view of the carnival and Gaskell describes in "A Dark Night's Work" the scene that she had first looked down on. "Lent," she writes, "was late that year. The great nosegays of violets and camellias were for sale at the corner of the Condotti, and the revellers had no difficulty in procuring much rarer flowers for the belles of the Corso. The embassies had their balconies; the attachés of the Russian Embassy threw their light and lovely presents at every pretty girl, or suspicion of a pretty girl, who passed slowly in her carriage, covered over with her white domino, and holding her wire mask as a protection to her face from the showers of *confetti,* which otherwise would have been enough to blind her." The woman with whom Ellinor is staying has, like the Storys, "her own . . . balcony." And, in a scene that recalls the dream that Ruth had had about her son, the girls, the daughters of Ellinor's friend, have provided themselves with

(7:548–49)   *a great basket, full of bouquets with which to pelt their friends in the crowd below; a store of* maccoletti *lay piled on the table behind, for it was the last day of Carnival, and as soon as dusk came on the tapers were to be lighted, to be as quickly extinguished by every means in every one's power. The crowd below was at its wildest pitch; the rows of stately* contadini *alone sitting immovable as their possible ancestors, the senators who received Brennus and his Gauls. Masks and white dominoes, foreign gentlemen, and the riff-raff of the city, slow-driving carriages, showers of flowers, most of them faded by this time, every one shouting and struggling at that wild pitch of excitement which may so soon turn into fury.*

It was just as she was looking down from the balcony on that crowd that Gaskell spotted Charles Eliot Norton. Meta, in a letter to Norton, recalls the moment the two met. "I can see," she writes, "your face and smile now (as distinctly as if I were only just turning away from them) when you caught at some confetti that Mama was dangling on a long stick from the balcony—and Mama said 'Oh look what a charming face!' and Mr. Story (I think it was) said 'Oh, that's Charles Norton,' and then there was a chorus of welcome and bidding you come up."[6] For Gaskell it was as though the enthusiasm of the wild crowd below had materialized in the face of the young man. He was the spirit of the carnival. Had the "charming face" she saw not belonged—another accident turning Gaskell's life into fiction—to someone whom the Storys knew, Gaskell might have quickly forgotten it. But since it did, in fact, belong to an acquaintance of the Storys, it became to her a symbol of the excitement of that day.

But there was yet another coincidence that lay in store for Gaskell in Norton. It happened that he himself was endowed with the talent that was the secret she had come to Rome to let out. Norton, later to become a leading historian of art at Harvard, was already, when Gaskell met him, an authority on art. One of the attractions of Italy was, of course, its artistic wealth, and Gaskell's sybaritic self must have taken enormous pleasure in the sensory world of art. This is not to be underestimated even in its simplest form, for Gaskell's "social" and "Christian" selves did not allow her, as we have seen, to indulge herself too much in the enjoyment of her senses. Italy must have seemed a feast after sensory deprivation. But Gaskell relished Italian art in a deeper sense as well. The sensory, sybaritic "me" was in Elizabeth Gaskell the basis of her aesthetic sensibility. And her aesthetic appreciation took as much pleasure in seeing the painting and the sculpture she found in Italy as it took in reading literature. She was, we recall, extremely visual, even in her literary descriptions. And she had graphic talent as well. It was from her that her daughter Meta inherited her graphic gift. Although it was a literary secret, therefore, that Gaskell had buried in England, it made no difference that in Rome it came out in a graphic form. One was a surrogate for the other.

Norton, thus, who had become for Gaskell first the incarnation of the wild pre-Lenten carnival, also became, by being her guide through the museums and piazzas of Italy, the embodiment of art. That was the real attraction of Norton. Together in Rome they lived what Gaskell had called the hidden world of art. In Rome, they were together constantly, although they were almost always accompanied by Marianne or Meta or both. Gaskell had brought them both to Rome, Marianne mostly for the adventure and Meta to improve her craft. Day after day Gaskell and Norton took long tours around the city. Gaskell was fascinated by Rome. Everything, she writes about Ellinor in "A Dark Night's Work," "was a picture and a delight" to her; "the merest group in the street, a Roman facchino, with his cloak draped over his shoulder, a girl going to market carrying her pitcher back from the fountain, everything and every person that presented it or himself to her senses, gave them a delicious shock, as if it were something strangely familiar from Pinello, but unseen by her mortal eyes before" (7:548). Daily they toured the museums and galleries. In the evenings they would return sometimes to the Storys' apartment on the Via San Isidoro and other times to Norton's rooms. In Rome, they spent seven weeks together. Then they discovered they had planned, by yet another amazing coincidence, to leave Rome at the very same time and to travel in the same direction. They had enjoyed one another so much, they saw no reason not to continue as long as they could in each other's company. They left Rome together on April 12, Gaskell bringing Marianne and Meta and Norton a friend, the painter Hamilton Wild, and set out on a tour of Italy that was to last another month. From Rome to Venice, the group made its way slowly through the Italian countryside, stopping many times on the way. In Venice, they parted. They corresponded for eight years, until the time of Gaskell's death, but they only met once more, when, on his journey home to America, Norton stopped to see her in Manchester. By then the adventure had come to an end. They met in England simply as friends. The romance of Rome could not be continued in the sober land of England.

The first full-length novel Gaskell wrote after she returned from Italy, although it was after a number of years, was *Sylvia's Lovers.* When she published it, she dedicated the English edition to her husband and the American to Norton. She had never before in her life dedicated anything to anyone, and she was never to do so again. The fact that she provided not one but two dedications for *Sylvia's Lovers* has, understandably, puzzled her readers. Many, speculating on possibilities, have hazarded various explanations. Lucy Stebbins has, for example, suggested that it was *Sylvia's Lovers,* not *Mary Barton,* that Gaskell began to write after Willie's death. The dedication to William, thus, was an acknowledgment that the novel commemorated a common loss. Gérin believes that, since *Sylvia's Lovers* implies that the bonds of marriage are precarious, Gaskell dedicated the novel to William as a way of reassuring him.[7] The dedication itself, which states "This book is dedicated to my dear husband by her who best knows his value," might perhaps be read in this way. But Gaskell had often implied much worse than she did in *Sylvia's Lovers,* and it had never before occurred to her that William needed to be reassured. Some have thought the American dedication was Gaskell's way of telling Norton, as the Civil War was raging, that she shared his Northern sympathies. Gaskell does allude to the war in the American dedication. "This book," she writes, "is Dedicated To all my Northern Friends with the truest sympathy of an English Woman; and in an especial manner to my dear Friend Charles Eliot Norton and to his Wife Who though personally unknown to me is yet dear to me for his sake." "Mrs. Gaskell" may well have had reasons such as the latter two—Lucy Stebbins's seems unlikely—for the double dedication, but the demon had perhaps something very different in mind. Returning to England, Gaskell may have seen herself as having two lovers, as her heroines do in her fiction. She herself was split in two, and each of her halves had its own mate: the English "Mrs. Gaskell" had William, and the demon, Charles Eliot Norton.

It is not easy to understand Gaskell's relationship to William. The evidence is very scanty, especially since the letters are lost they must have written to one another. The comments in her letters on William, which are rare and superficial, give us very little sense of what Gaskell felt about him. And those of their friends who went into print, as many did on various subjects, said very little about their relationship. Gaskell herself, in the Brontë biography, closes the door on Brontë's life when Brontë marries Arthur Nicholls, saying, on bringing them back from their honeymoon, "Henceforward the sacred doors of home are closed upon her married life" (*LCB*, p. 465). This was the nineteenth-century view, and Gaskell's own friends seem to have felt the door should be closed on her marriage also.

Gaskell warns us, in her own fiction, not to indulge in easy inferences about relationships between husbands and wives. When Mrs. Browne in "The Moorland Cottage" leaves the Buxtons, for example, thinking Mr. Buxton must be unhappy caring for an invalid wife, the narrator interrupts to say: "If she had been a clairvoyante at that moment, she might have seen Mr. Buxton tenderly chafing his wife's hands, and feeling in his innermost soul a wonder how one so saint-like could ever have learnt to love such a boor as he was; it was the wonderful mysterious blessing of his life. So little do we know of the inner truths of the households, where we come and go like intimate guests" (2:287–88). Similarly, in *Wives and Daughters,* speaking of the Cumnors, the narrator says that, although "it was one of those perplexing marriages of which one cannot understand the reasons," they were happy nonetheless (8:44–45). But Gaskell also sometimes marvels at the misery of marriage. Writing about Philip and Sylvia, Gaskell remarks in *Sylvia's Lovers* that to "an onlooker, the course of married life, which should lead to perfect happiness, seemed so plain! . . . the resisting forces which make all such harmony and delight impossible are not recognised by the bystanders, hardly by the actors" (6:417).

There is no doubt that Elizabeth Stevenson and William Gaskell married for love. They met at the home of the Reverend John Gooch Robberds, the minister then at the Cross Street Chapel. William, who was to succeed him later, was his assistant at that time. They seem to have fallen in love immediately. Within a few months they were engaged. In a few more they were married. But love, in that sense, is not the question. When Gaskell writes in *Sylvia's Lovers* "love . . . will make all things right in heaven" (6:417), she means to imply that here on earth love is certainly not enough. The question in the Gaskells' marriage is considerably more complex. It is a matter, first, of whether William met "Mrs. Gaskell's" needs. Gaskell had married so as to find the love and the family she had lost. She came to the marriage with great demands, which William was expected to satisfy. But even more important than that is the question of whether anything that could satisfy "Mrs. Gaskell" was not, by its very nature, designed to dissatisfy the demon.

William very probably did meet some of "Mrs. Gaskell's" needs. Deprived of a father for whose love she had never ceased to long, Gaskell needed a fatherly husband, and William, although just five years older, was—sober, serious, and authoritative—decades older in personality. "Mrs. Gaskell" had been the victim of behavior that had seemed to her arbitrary and irresponsible. She needed a husband who would be solid, steady, and reliable. William was absolutely dependable. "Mrs. Gaskell" was not weak, but she wanted someone to lean on. William was strong and liked to be leaned on. And if "Mrs. Gaskell" was undecided and lacked confidence in herself, William was self-assured, secure, and never uncertain about his opinions. He liked, moreover, to take charge, to assume responsibility, as "Mrs. Gaskell" never did. And he enjoyed helping his wife, guiding her, and even teaching her, all of which "Mrs. Gaskell" needed. Gaskell, for instance, always liked William to look her manuscripts over before she sent them to her publisher, since she did not trust herself to spot her mistakes in spelling and grammar. The fact that William had, by chance, the very name that had been her father's must have made "Mrs. Gaskell" feel, tending as she always did not only to fuse people in her mind but to turn them into metaphors, that in William she had found, as in the houses of her fiction, a restitution for her past.

But, as many have remarked, they were temperamentally different. Gaskell was warm, romantic, exuberant. William was quiet, cool, and reserved. Gaskell was sociable. She liked people. William was solitary, detached, and almost entirely self-sufficient. Gaskell approached the world emotionally, enthusiastically, impulsively. William had a logical mind and an inner need for order. In their early years together, these differences were not as pronounced. Writing to his sister Elizabeth, William appears, like any young man doting on his prospective bride, warm, affectionate, even silly. "You can't imagine," he writes, "how lonely I feel without her. I must get over to K– again next week, for one day at least. I am now writing with her rings on my fingers" and "with her likeness lying before me, if likeness it can be called."[8] To his sister Elizabeth again, on his honeymoon he writes "My bonny wee wifee—*My* bonny wee wife—grows I do think more bonny than ever."[9] When they were small, he enjoyed the children. In a letter to Marianne, Gaskell, for example, reports that "Papa is 'taking the little ones to walk with him in the Park, & make snowballs' " (*L* 175). Sometimes he seems to have joined in the fun Gaskell herself had with the children. Writing to thank George Smith for a box that had just arrived with gifts, Gaskell says that William joined her and Julia in fits of "screaming & laughing" as they opened the presents (*L* 442). The Winkworth sisters remember Gaskell boasting that William was very "good" "to the children" and that he made a very "good" "sick nurse" during the children's various illnesses.[10] But even in relation to them, and even in those early days, he was never as demonstrative as Gaskell wanted him to be. To Anne Robson, Gaskell writes in 1841—there were two children at this time, Marianne, seven, and Meta, three—that although she expects William was feeling "most kindly towards his children," he was "yet most reserved in *expressions* of either affection or sympathy" (*L* 16).

Whatever was wrong with the relationship seemed to get worse as the years progressed. For one thing, each became increasingly absorbed in his or her work. William was certainly very busy, adding to his ministerial duties many services to the community as well as work in writing and teaching. Gaskell was very busy too, first with the house and the growing family, and then with her writing. Her writing, in fact, may have had an effect on her marriage. Geraldine Jewsbury seemed to think so. In a letter to Jane Carlyle, written in December of 1850, just as *Mary Barton* was beginning to enjoy its enormous success, Jewsbury, reporting the prevailing opinion in Manchester, remarks "The people here are beginning mildly to be pained for Mr. 'Mary Barton.' And one lady said to me the other day, 'I don't think authoresses ought ever to marry.' "[11] William continued to encourage and to help Gaskell in her work. But something in him may have resented it. Whatever the reason, as the years passed, William grew increasingly cool. Gaskell had had a rejecting father. William's coolness must have made her feel rejected all over again. William had even, it would seem, grown a little cool to his daughters. Writing about him to the Storys in 1861, Gaskell remarks that he is "very fond of children, playing with them all the day long" but "not caring for them so much when they are grown up" (*L* 490).

The fact that they chose to travel alone after their first few years together may not in itself be a sign that there were difficulties in their marriage, although it seems to point that way. But their travel arrangements occasioned several letters that betray some serious problems in their relationship. One of the reasons, it would appear, that they did not travel together is that William did not enjoy going on journeys with his family. Gaskell sounds hurt as she attempts, writing once again to the Storys, to explain why William may travel to visit them in Rome alone: "he can find no one to go with him, but the women of his family, and he says he feels so much the entire want of *change,* and the desirableness of having no *responsibility* that he would rather not feel that he had any one dependent on him" (*L* 489; see also *L* 490). She writes the identical thing to Anne Robson. "He does not like any of us to go with him when he goes from home," she remarks, more to convince herself perhaps, "saying it does not give him so much change; & with us he does not make so many acquaintances certainly. . . . I had got money enough (from writing) both to pay for *his* going, & for Meta's *or* mine, *or* both of us, *with* him but he quite declined it, giving the reason as above, —" (*L* 570). Sometimes, like Gaskell, when he traveled, William went to stay with friends. Among his friends were the Edmund Potters, who always invited William to join them in the house they usually rented. And never did Gaskell record a sadder or a more revealing fact about the status of her marriage than when she wrote, again to Anne Robson, that "Mrs. Potter says she has often asked me (in her letters to him,) to accompany him; but if she has, he has never told me of it" (*L* 570). Gaskell, of course, also traveled alone. The gypsy-bachelor enjoyed solitude. But "Mrs. Gaskell," we can be sure, would have joined William at the Potters.

Gaskell often complains of loneliness when William is away from home (e.g., *L* 35). But often, when he is at home, "Mrs. Gaskell" is just as lonely. For William spends most of his time in his study. How frequently Gaskell in her letters writes to someone to complain that William is in his study "again." His study, as she remarks in one letter, is for William the "room" "out of which," "by his own free will he would never stir" (*L* 418). In one long letter to Anne Robson in which she lists William's activities, explaining that every hour of the day is devoted to one of his interests, Gaskell observes that on those occasions, and even these seem very rare, "when he is at home, we only see him at meal-times" (*L* 570).

Most accounts of the Gaskells' marriage see no specific rift between them, but once or twice we come across hints that William may not have been altogether faithful to Gaskell. Replying to Elizabeth Haldane, who, while gathering materials for *Mrs. Gaskell and Her Friends,* had written to ask for information, Margaret Shaen, in one of her letters, made the following remark: " 'I wonder whether you will wish to say much about *Mr.* Gaskell—I cd in talk tell you a good deal about him, more than I cd write. Those sheets & sheets of love affairs are now all safely burnt—pitiful—I shd have burnt them on receipt!' "[12] Although her meaning is not clear, the words are certainly suggestive. Suggestive too are her remarks about Susanna Winkworth and William. We know that Susanna, William's pupil, admired him greatly as a teacher. But she may also have taken a fancy to him. William thought so, it would seem. Writing to Haldane again, Margaret Shaen implies that William conceived the idea that she wanted to marry him. Shaen suggests it was his vanity that put such a thought into his head,[13] but Gaskell at one point thought so too. She writes to Eliza Fox, for instance, in May of 1852, that Susanna "snubs me so, and makes such love to William he says 'my life is the only protection he has—else he knows she would marry him.' I wish you could hear him speaking thus in a meek fatalistic kind of way, and I believe she *would* too. *Can't* you marry her to Mr. Forster; then I *cd* die in peace feeling that my husband was in safety" (*L* 124). Although she pretends to make light of the matter, Gaskell may have felt more than she said. She was a very jealous woman, although William never knew it. "William," Gaskell once wrote in her "Diary," "told me the other day I was not of a jealous disposition. I do not think he knows me" (p. 16).

Anyone who knew her history should have known she would be jealous. How could she not be, prizing like Ruth every symptom of regard? The fact that William did not know it raises another important question, namely, whether he understood her. Many have thought that, being so different, they did not understand each other.[14] Sometimes it seems they were not as open with one another as they might have been. To her sister-in-law Elizabeth, Gaskell confided that she thought she was more open with William's brother than she felt she could be with William (*L* 13). Especially in the early years, but to some extent even later, William inhibits and intimidates her. Reporting, again to Elizabeth Gaskell that William considered her last letter "*slip-shod,*" Gaskell says that, as she writes, "the consciousness that Wm may any time and does generally see my letters makes me not write so naturally & heartily as I think I should do" (*L* 13). Gaskell frequently felt she could not discuss anxieties with her husband. To his sister Anne she writes that William "won't allow me ever to talk to him about anxieties." "I dare say kindly," she then adds as though trying to excuse him. But, she cannot help adding too, and moreover in capital letters, that "it would be SUCH A RELIEF" if she could only share her fears with him (*L* 16). The fact, however, is she cannot. That is indeed why she begs Anne to "let me open my heart sometimes to you . . . with reliance on your sympathy and secrecy" (*L* 16). All of these are early letters, but in May of 1865, just half a year before her death, Gaskell is still writing that William "does rather hate facing anxiety," being "so very anxious when he is anxious" (*L* 570).

Gaskell always claimed she was happy. To Elizabeth Gaskell once more, she writes, at an early point in her marriage, interrupting herself in the middle of a long list of household chores that, she reports, have been keeping her busy, "However I hope I am not complaining, for I *am* very happy" (*L* 13). The feeling seems genuine, but whether it lasted it is very hard to say.

But none of this, although important, was the real problem with William. The real problem was that William was the husband of "Mrs. Gaskell," and the more he met her needs, the more did he imprison her demon.

We have no reason to believe that in the marriages of her fiction Gaskell was mirroring her own, although it is an interesting fact that, while there are many unhappy marriages and many that Gaskell argues are happy, as we have seen on many occasions, although they do not seem so to us, there is not one that seems self-evidently the happy union of a well-matched pair, and very few that even approximate it. The closest that Gaskell comes to illustrating something like a good relationship is in the Browns in "Right at Last." They at least are able to talk to one another in an adult and intelligent manner. But the fact that we have to look so far into the minor fiction to find one—there is not a single one in the novels; Margaret and Thornton in *North and South* will, we suspect, have a good marriage, but it is not a marriage we see; it is only one projected beyond the conclusion of the book—suggests perhaps that Gaskell could not envision happy marriages easily. It is significant that while Gaskell persists in *Wives and Daughters* in claiming that the Hamleys are really happy, theirs being "one of those perplexing marriages of which one cannot understand the reasons" (8:44–45), she also tells us that Mrs. Hamley, who "had a fresh nosegay every day from her husband," had to have "a draught" as well "of medicine every three hours brought by her maid" (8:47). And Gaskell is perfectly well aware why the medication is necessary. She "would not," the narrator writes, "have sunk into the condition of a chronic invalid if her husband had cared a little more for her various tastes, or allowed her the companionship of those who did" (8:45). Happy as Gaskell says it is, the marriage has made Mrs. Hamley ill.

We have no reason to believe that Gaskell intends to represent William in the ministers of her fiction, although it is a curious fact that there are very few in her fiction of this vocation whom we admire. Some, like Mr. Hale and Benson, are very kind and decent men. But even they have serious failings. Hale and Benson, for instance, are weak. Some are caricatures very much in the literary tradition. Thus, Mr. Mountfort in "My Lady Ludlow" is a pleasant fellow enough, but his chief concern in life is not religion but hunting and politics (5:20–25). A similar literary caricature is Mr. Ashton in *Wives and Daughters,* an "indolent" man who, although kindly, is not very bright, not very eager, and not very willing to exert himself in the service of his church (8:41–43). Also a literary convention but a very different type is, in *Cranford,* Mr. Jenkyns. Stiff and self-important and pompous, he is in a line of descent from Mr. Collins in *Pride and Prejudice.* Clergymen like Mr. Hale recall Mr. Stevenson, as we know, as does the clergyman in "Lois" who is the father of the heroine. But some of Gaskell's religious figures are meant to embody in her mind not the place she gives to fathers but to lovers and to husbands. Ellinor in "A Dark Night's Work" ends up marrying such a minister after she is betrayed by Ralph, who is the man she really loves. The minister, Livingstone, is not appealing, and Gaskell does not intend him to be. The description we have of the thoughts that bring him finally to propose is amusing until we remember that Ellinor intends to accept him. Imagining himself married to her, Livingstone pictures Ellinor's "face listening with admiring interest to his sermons, her arm passed into his as they went together round the parish; her sweet voice instructing classes in his schools—turn where he would, in his imagination Ellinor's presence rose up before him" (7:456).

Gaskell may not have seemed to herself as ludicrous or as sad a figure in the role of the minister's wife as she makes Ellinor look to us here, but it is significant again that ministers' wives in Gaskell's fiction are seldom suited for their roles. Mrs. Hale in *North and South* whines so much about her husband that she appears to be a caricature, but she is typical of her class in the fact that she takes no interest in the affairs of her husband's parish and dislikes the interruptions to her life of his parish duties (4:18–19). Gaskell herself, although always humorously, comments continually in her letters on the little gaffs she makes in her role as the minister's wife. "Oh dear!" she writes to Catherine Winkworth, "I envy you the *Times:*— it's very unprincipled and all that, but the most satisfactory newspaper going. Now is not that sentence unbecoming in a minister's wife?" (*L* 29). Sometimes she catches herself in activities that scandalize her coparishioners. Thus she explains in a letter, for instance, that she thinks she is "in a scrape" because she has happened, in the presence of a fellow-Unitarian who was "shocked" to hear her choose "such a subject of conversation on a *Sunday,*" to discuss with one of her pupils in her Sunday school class a novel by Sir Walter Scott (*L* 32). The image has so long persisted of "Mrs. Gaskell" as a woman tailor-made to be the wife of a Dissenting English clergyman that it is difficult to imagine anyone doubting her in that role. But, as she once told Mary Howitt, someone she had known as a child had been "dreadfully shocked" to learn that she had "married a *Unitarian* minister" (*L* 616).

Whatever the actual facts of the case, Gaskell's fiction makes us wonder whether Gaskell did not feel, in her marriage to William Gaskell, what Sylvia feels in her marriage to Philip. We need not succumb to simple equations to notice that Philip has a good deal in common with William. They even look alike, in fact. Both are very tall and lean. William, although one cannot be sure looking only at drawings and photographs, may even have had that "long upper lip" that Gaskell describes Philip Hepburn as having, saying it gave "a disagreeable aspect to a face that might otherwise have been good-looking" (6:26). Philip is like William too in being quiet, sedate, reserved. He is serious. He is reliable. And like William, he is erudite, taking on, as William did, the role of a teacher to his wife. And he embodies, as William did too, the religious point of view. It might be an accident but it might not that Philip's best friend and business associate, and eventually his partner, is a man named *William* Coulson. William was a popular name, but so were any number of others that Gaskell might have chosen instead. Working through relays perhaps again, Gaskell may be transferring here to a surrogate the name she cannot let herself give Philip lest she make her point so obvious that she has to see it herself.

Rome was the witch on the seven hills, and Gaskell in Rome had lived the life of the daemonic gypsy-bachelor. Returning to England she had become the ideal "Mrs. Gaskell" again. Gaskell never got over Rome. Sending a letter to say she was coming, Gaskell had written the Storys in words wild with joyous anticipation. "We are really truly coming to Rome!!!!!!" she writes, exploding into exclamation points (*L* 342). "And are we really," she writes again, "coming, and shall we truly see Rome? I don't believe it. It is a dream! I shall never believe it, and shall have to keep pinching myself!" (*L* 342). Looking back on her return, she is wild with excitement again. "Oh!" she interrupts a letter she is writing to Eliza Fox, "is not Rome above every place you imagined?" (*L* 421). Her thoughts go back to Rome continually. "Oh!" she exclaims in another letter, "the delicious quiet & dolce far niente of Italy!" (*L* 349). Rome is still so alive in her mind that the memory of it pains her. "I sometimes think I would almost rather never have been there than have this ache of yearning for" it (*L* 482). Rome was the highlight of her life. "It was," she writes in a letter to the Storys, "in those charming Roman days that my life, at any rate, culminated." She knows that she can never again recapture that moment she had with Norton. "I shall never," she continues, "be so happy again. I don't think I was ever so happy before. My eyes fill with tears when I think of those days. . . . The girls may see happier ones—I never shall" (*L* 375). Life, she later wrote to Norton, "never flows Back—we shall never again have the old happy days in Rome, shall we?" (*L* 583).

Gaskell once returned to Italy. Taking Meta, Flossy, and Julia, she went back in 1863. But that was just a trip to Italy. Rome with Norton had been a journey in the geography of her mind. She could never relive those days. But she could transform the experience. As Ruth transforms her honeymoon in Wales into her dream life in Eccleston, Gaskell transformed into a dream her memory of her days in Rome. When Marianne goes off to Rome, Gaskell writes to Norton to tell him that she intends to go along with her in her "imagination" (*L* 497). When Eliza Fox gets married to the painter Frederick Lee Bridell, Gaskell writes to her in Rome, asking her, as though they could carry her to the required spot in their thoughts, to think of her if they go to the Medici gardens at Albano (*L* 421). In Gaskell's imagination, Rome becomes the site of imagined events. "Only the other night, I dreamed," she writes to the Storys, "of a breakfast, not a past breakfast, but some mysterious breakfast which neither had been nor, alas! would be—in the Via Sant' Isidoro dining-room, with the amber sunlight streaming on the gold-grey Roman roofs and the Sabine hills on one side and the Vatican on the other" (*L* 482).

Rome had become for her internalized. Norton had been internalized too. He had become her daemonic lover. The English edition of *Sylvia's Lovers* required a dedication to William because it was he who was the husband of the English "Mrs. Gaskell." But Norton in Rome had been the soulmate of the gypsy-bachelor. To him she dedicates the edition published in the land of the free. Like all of Gaskell's surrogate selves, Norton had found a place in her fiction. Gaskell herself did not know probably what precisely the parallels were between Norton and Kinraid. But even "Mrs. Gaskell" knew enough of what she had had with Norton to give her hero his first name. It is no accident that at the end, in the last of the novel's relays, Bella is sent to live in America. To Gaskell, America looks like Rome. Gaskell had never seen America. Although, like the daughters of her fiction, she had always wanted to go, she had never been able to do it.

She has no basis in fact to assume that it resembles the city in Italy. But the truth is that the city does not resemble in her mind the city she had actually seen. Both are only metaphors now, and she thinks they look alike because they both embody her demon. "Sometimes," she writes to Charles Eliot Norton in January of 1860, "I dream I am in America, but it always looks like Rome, whh I know it is not" (*L* 453).

A. B. Hopkins may have been right to suspect, on the basis of a letter in which she describes her daughters to Norton as though presenting them for inspection (see *L* 418), that Gaskell hoped he would marry one of them.[15] A daughter married to Charles Eliot Norton would not only, through a relay, manage to possess her demon, it would enable her to live, as Sylvia does at last through Bella, vicariously in the land of the free.

XIX

Whole Again and with Her Demon

GASKELL HAD RETURNED from Rome in a hopeful frame of mind, and she explained the reason for it in the story that appeared under the title "The Sin of a Father." Gaskell must have written this story not long after her return. She published it in the following year. In this story Gaskell projects herself in the hero, Dr. Brown, who, being weak and indecisive, is more a female than a male. Many of Gaskell's perennial themes make their way into this story. As the title suggests, for instance, Brown must pay for the sin of his father. And, as in "A Dark Night's Work," which Gaskell must also have begun shortly after her return, the sin is the commission of a crime. The father, moreover, having committed it, seeks to keep his crime a secret, and the child, who shares his secret, thus becomes his secret sharer. Gaskell implies in other ways too that it is Dr. Brown himself who is the criminal in her mind. Not only does he share the secret, he fears that, taking after his father, he will commit a crime like him. " 'I sometimes fear,' " he tells his fiancée, " 'that crime is hereditary' " (7:296). The crime is, of course, a daemonic expression, and having committed it metaphorically, Dr. Brown behaves precisely as all of Gaskell's females do who conceal a secret demon. He fears to be seen by the eyes of the world. As he also tells his fiancée, he is haunted by the thought that if the world knew the crime it would " 'look askance' " at him (7:297). He is prepared to suffer anything rather than let the secret out. His life is, therefore, one long vigil. " 'I have spent,' " he says, " 'all my life in fearing' " the crime would one day come out (7:297).

The crime his father has committed is, not surprisingly, a forgery (7:297), and the fact that in her mind Dr. Brown has committed it too tells us that Gaskell is thinking of him, as she does of Richard in *Ruth,* as living in a forged identity. One day his servant, who shares his secret and is ready to act it out—he is thus a combination of Dixon in "A Dark Night's Work" and Victorine in "Crowley Castle"—threatens to reveal the crime unless he is paid a sum of money. Dr. Brown at first is terrified, but, emboldened by his fiancée, who has now become his wife and who is more male than

he is, he decides to tell his servant to " 'Let the world know the truth' "
(7:298). "All the consequences took place," Gaskell concludes, "which he
had anticipated" (7:299). His practice falls off, he has no income, he loses
everything, they have to move, and for a time he is forced to live in the
very direst circumstances. Eventually he prospers again, but for many
years he pays for having let the secret out. Yet Gaskell says he did well to
do it. She had not said so before in *Ruth* or in *The Life of Charlotte Brontë*.
But having, in her Roman adventure, let her own secret out at last, Gaskell
returned with the courage to write a story in which her surrogate self has
escaped the ancestral curse. The truth has set Dr. Brown, she says,
" 'free' " (7:298). When Gaskell later reprinted this tale in a collection of her
short fiction, she renamed it "Right at Last."

It was the confidence she brought back with her that made it possible
for Gaskell to wonder whether, in *Sylvia's Lovers,* she might be able to trust
Kinraid. Never before had she trusted her demon. She does not finally
trust it now. But there are moments, as we have seen, when she is almost
able to trust it. Yet, as in one alternative title she had considered for the
novel, she had come to trust it too late. She had been formed. She was
what she was. She could not escape being "Mrs. Gaskell" any more than
Sylvia could escape becoming "Mrs. Hepburn." The only thing that had
changed for her was that she had become aware—if not quite consciously
yet more so than she had ever been before—that her life as "Mrs. Gaskell"
was an utter fabrication. When Ellinor in "A Dark Night's Work" returns
from her Roman adventure to England and resolves henceforth to lead
what she calls a model life, she wonders whether God will watch over
someone "whose life hereafter must seem based upon a lie." The narrator
says it is "the Tempter" who prompts her to ask this terrible question
(7:477). But we have met this "Tempter" before. His were the thoughts
that were articulated by Lucy Gisborne's daemonic double.

This, then, was Gaskell's frame of mind when, having finished *Sylvia's Lovers,* she turned to the writing of *Wives and Daughters* in the fall of
1863. She was still at work on this novel when the idea occurred to her, in
the summer of 1865, that she would buy a house to which William would
be able to retire and in which her unmarried daughters would be able to
live when she died. Only one daughter had married so far, Florence in
September two years earlier. The other three were still at home, although
Marianne was already engaged to E. Thurstan Holland, her second cousin, whom she was indeed to marry a year after her mother's death. Meta
and Julia never married. The girls were to be told of the purchase. For
William it was to be a surprise. In September of 1865, just two months

before her death, she writes to tell Norton what she has done. "And then I did a terribly grand thing! and a secret thing too! . . . I bought a house and 4 acres of land in Hampshire,—near Alton,—for Mr Gaskell to retire to & for a home for my unmarried daughters. That's to say I had not money enough to pay the whole £ 2,666; but my publisher (*Smith* & Elder) advanced the £ 1000, on an 'equitable mortgage.' And I hope to pay him off by degrees. Mr Gaskell is *not to know till then*" (*L* 583).

Gaskell had always worried about William. Her letters are a constant lament that William is not, as she writes to Anne Holland in 1854, for instance, getting enough "rest & quiet, things impossible to be procured in our busy busy place" (*L* 221). She says nothing about herself, although she reports, in the very next letter, which she writes to Eliza Fox, "I've been as nearly dazed and crazed with hits c——,d——be h——to it, story as can be. I've been sick of writing, and everything connected with literature or improvement of the mind; to say nothing of deep hatred to my species about whom I was obliged to write as if I love'em. Moreover I have had to write so hard that I have spoilt my hand, and forgotten all my spelling. Seriously it has been a terrible weight on me and has made me have some of the most felling headaches I ever had in my life" (*L* 222). She needed to rest as much as William, but her thoughts were all for him. She worried about her daughters too, especially since, if they did not marry, they would have to fend for themselves. She wanted to know they would have an income and a suitable place to live. The house was thus to be a gift to the family from "Mrs. Gaskell."

But just as she was making arrangements for the house and for its furnishings, Gaskell began to experience difficulties with the progress of her book. Most of her readers have assumed it was the house that impeded her progress. And it is true that buying the house as well as the furnishings it required took a good deal of her time. It is also true that Gaskell was worried about the expenses she had incurred. Smith had given her an advance, but how would she ever pay him back? She planned to earn the money by writing, but, she confides to Marianne, she is "afraid" she will "never" be able to "write up the money for the house" (*L* 575a). Gaskell herself believed that the house had caused her her problems with the novel. In August of 1865, less than three months before she died, Gaskell wrote to Marianne, "I *am* so badly behindhand in Wives & Daughters. All these worries about Alton do so incapacitate me from writing" (*L* 575a).

The work and the worry exacted their toll, but it was not the house that prevented Gaskell from completing the novel. The composition of *Wives and Daughters* suggests that the work went on very well, smoothly and rapidly,[1] up to the moment at which the narrative had to be turned toward its inevitable conclusion. It is the conclusion that stood in the way. This is especially clear in the fact that when she died, on November 12, virtually all that remained to be done was for the chapter to be written in which the hero and heroine marry. As Frederick Greenwood, then the editor of the *Cornhill Magazine,* which was serializing the book, was to comment in the "Conclusion" he wrote to bring the story to a close, "if the work is not quite complete, little remains to be added to it. . . . We know that Roger Hamley will marry Molly, and that is what we are most concerned about. Indeed, there was little else to tell" (8:756). Greenwood was right. All that was left was for Molly to marry Roger, and this, had nothing interfered, would undoubtedly have been the easiest part of the book to write. Gaskell had already, in fact, sketched an outline for the chapter. It was on this outline that Greenwood based the "Conclusion" he wrote for the book. Had there been no other impediment, Gaskell could have written this chapter without much effort in an afternoon. Gaskell herself, going to Alton at the very end of October and planning not to stay too long, wrote to Marianne she was sure she could finish the novel there (*L* 588). And yet when she died on November 12, still at Alton, she had not finished it. The reason seems obvious. She did not want to. She did not want to make Molly Gibson end by marrying Roger Hamley. "Mrs. Gaskell" required the marriage, but Gaskell's demon understood that to let Molly marry Roger was to acquiesce in her suicide.

There was a marriage that the demon did very much want to bring about but which "Mrs. Gaskell" prevented, and that was the marriage of Cynthia to Preston. Preston had, we recall, extracted a promise from Cynthia that she would marry him when he had lent her money once (8:543 ff.). To "Mrs. Gaskell" he is a villain. Her demon, however, has a different view. Her demon recognizes Preston as another daemonic character. Cynthia, describing him, says at one point that he is "cruel in his very soul—tigerish, with his beautiful striped skin and relentless heart" (8:550). Gaskell had used the tiger image in her fiction once before, when Anna Scherer in "The Grey Woman" had prayed for a daughter and not a son, fearing that a boy would inherit the "tiger nature" of his father (7:355). M. de la Tourelle had been Anna's daemonic self in the story, and Preston is Cynthia's demon here. Since Cynthia conceals her relationship to him, he is, in fact, her hidden demon. Like Frederick Hale and Charlie Kinraid, he is Cynthia's hidden self.

A marriage between Cynthia and Preston is the only possibility in the novel's daemonic subtext. Cynthia is the only woman who has preserved her daemonic identity, and Preston is the only man who can love her for her demon. He alone of all the men who fall in love with and propose to Cynthia knows who Cynthia really is. All the other men in the novel love, not individual women, but women as representative types, either the seductive type of the second Mrs. Gibson or the type of the ideal, which is what Molly has become. Preston alone, knowing her demon, understands Cynthia as an individual. For the other men in the novel, women are virtually interchangeable. For Preston, no one but Cynthia will do. Although she rejects him, he goes on loving her, not because she is good or worthy but because she is who she is. Metaphorically, of course, that is the point of his lending her money. As always in Gaskell, the money is love, and Preston loves Cynthia as no other man in all of her fiction loves a woman. "Cynthia was Cynthia," the narrator says, describing Preston's thoughts about her, "and not Venus herself could have been her substitute." Gaskell's demon knows what this means and appreciates its value. In his constancy, she writes, "Mr. Preston was more really true than many worthy men" (8:558). Preston thus would offer Cynthia the freedom to be her daemonic self. Gaskell's demon wants this to happen, and she toys with the possibility. Cynthia, for instance, tells Molly one day that she has " 'once or twice . . . thought' " she " 'would marry Mr. Preston.' " "Mrs. Gaskell" pretends the reason is that Cynthia wants " 'revenge.' " Marrying Preston, Cynthia says, would put " 'him for ever in my power' " (8:550). The truth, however, is something else, and Gaskell herself knows what it is, as she implies when Cynthia, explaining why she is thinking of marrying Preston, inquires of Molly whether she has "never heard of strong wills mesmerizing weaker ones into submission" (8:474). Submitting to Preston would be for Cynthia a submission to her demon. "Mrs. Gaskell," however, resists. The very thought of it, indeed, drives her to the other extreme. She tries to marry Cynthia to Roger. But this is something Cynthia herself will not let "Mrs. Gaskell" do. They get engaged, but Cynthia, realizing that Roger expects her to be "good," very soon breaks off the relationship. We know what "good" means in this novel. Roger himself had defined it to Molly. Cynthia knows it without being told. " 'I'm afraid,' " she says, " 'he'll expect me always to be as good as he fancies me now, and I shall have to walk on tiptoe all the rest of my life' " (8:508). It is significant that Cynthia, once released from her engagement, feels an enormous sense of " 'relief.' " She feels that she is " 'free again' " (8:636).

Cynthia thus escapes the destiny of the angel in the house. But it is, therefore, all the more necessary that Molly Gibson take her place. Consciously, Gaskell still insists that the union is ideal. But she cannot write the chapter. Gaskell had had this problem before. In *Sylvia's Lovers,* "Mrs. Gaskell" had wanted Sylvia to marry Philip, but the demon had protested and delayed her for eight months. During those months, she had fled to Paris, hoping that in the demon's land she could escape "Mrs. Gaskell's" intentions. Trying now to escape the marriage "Mrs. Gaskell" has planned for Molly, Gaskell flees to Paris again. Officially, she explains her trip by saying that she hopes in Paris to find the uninterrupted time that she needs to finish the novel. In fact, she goes to Paris to find the strength to avoid putting on paper the ending "Mrs. Gaskell" wants. In Paris Gaskell stayed with the Mohls, where she had often stayed before. Her work had often gone very well there. This time it did not go well at all. It would undoubtedly have gone better had she been planning a different conclusion. But this "Mrs. Gaskell" could not do. The only alternative for Gaskell was not to finish the book at all. And the only way not to finish it was to die before the end.

In a sense, she willed her death. When she died, she was fifty-five, an age that was, in the nineteenth century, not as young as it is today, but that was not very old either. No one knows what precisely she died of. In the letter he wrote to Norton to let him know of Gaskell's death, E. Thurstan Holland said the physician called in when she collapsed at Alton believed she had died of "disease of" the "heart" (*L*, p. 971). A great many circumstances could have contributed to her death and probably did. The work on the novel and the house, as well as the tension that pulled her between them, may, as many believe, have exhausted her and made her susceptible to a heart attack.[2] Her efforts in 1862 during the great Distress in Manchester—day after day and month after month of feeding and nursing and teaching and worrying—had certainly undermined her health. Her health had, in any case, never been good. She had not inherited a strong constitution. In Paris with Mme. Mohl in the spring, she had suffered an unnamed illness. It may have been, as Gérin suggests, a warning of what was soon to come.[3] But in that letter he wrote to Norton, Holland reported that Gaskell said, virtually moments before she died, that she was feeling better, healthier, than she had felt in many years. It could be that she simply was not subjectively aware of her danger. It could, however, be ill health was not the ultimate cause of her death.

Gaskell in her last few months began, in her letters, to be haunted strangely by metaphors of death. On August 31, for instance, two and a half months before the end, Gaskell wrote to Marianne that, having spent the day on details concerning the house, she is "*dead-beat* (*L* 580; the italics are Gaskell's). A letter she wrote on September 2, once again to Marianne, is a series of such metaphors: she has spent another "*crazing*" day of shopping for furnishings for the house and has returned "nearly dead," she says, "for want of food & rest." "Oh dear!" she interrupts herself, "I *am* nearly *killed*" by the "*stress*." The letter ends, not with her usual affectionate and playful farewell, but with the extraordinary remark "oh *how* dead I feel!" (*L* 582; the italics once again are Gaskell's). Gaskell's body may have been warning her of a physical problem. But she may have, like the character she describes in *Mary Barton,* had the kind of intuition "by which almost" her "body thought" (1:92), and her metaphors may not be a warning here of a disease but the physical manifestations of the thoughts she was then thinking. For if it is true (and it is difficult not to believe what we learn every day about the connection between mind and body) that—especially in those in whom the two are virtually fused, as we have seen they were in Gaskell, and for whom the inner life is more vital than the outer—the mind really does control the body more than we have yet understood, Gaskell really did will her death. It was as though she had decided that she would rather die herself than kill her surrogate in the novel.

The choice, as for Lois the witch, for Gaskell was of one death or another, the death of the demon in Molly's suicide that would win her the love of the world or a dying to the world to become one again with her demon. "Mrs. Gaskell" had killed herself in the way of Molly Gibson, but something in her had all her life tried to withdraw to that inner world where the demon dwelt intact. That turning inward is what accounts for the morbidity in Gaskell that many of her readers have noted.[4] Gaskell often writes of morbidity, and she often uses the word. Benson in *Ruth* has become "morbid" as a result of his childhood injury. A woman in "Christmas Storms and Sunshine" is made "morbid" by her experiences (2:200). Susan in "Half a Lifetime Ago," after Willie dies, turns "morbid" (5:318). In different ways, each of these characters has been turned inward by some circumstance, and inward thoughts in Gaskell's view invariably end in such morbidity. Writing to Herbert Grey, we recall, to tell him to avoid introspection, she had explained that if he did not, he was likely to become "morbid" (*L* 420). And those who turn inward are always in Gaskell those in whom a demon dwells. In "Right at Last" Dr. Brown is morbid, and Gaskell here says just what she means when his wife remarks to him " 'You have been rendered morbid . . . by having something all your life to conceal' " (7:298). Only by revealing the secret can morbidity be avoided. In the letter to Eliza Fox in which she had spoken of art as "hidden,"

Gaskell had also said that art—expressing the demon as it did—was what kept women from becoming "morbid" (*L* 68). Gaskell is using the word with an eye to its etymological meaning. The price of keeping a secret is death. Even in her sunniest moments, Gaskell shows her morbid tendency. If we wanted to paint her portrait as Lily Briscoe paints Mrs. Ramsey's in Virginia Woolf's *To the Lighthouse,* not by conveying her physical appearance, but by projecting her inner soul, we could not do better than to use the description Gaskell herself provides, in "Half a Lifetime Ago," of Susan Dixon's farm. Taking us on a tour of the farm, the narrator points to a green pasture "in the midst of which," she writes, "stands a mighty, funereal umbrageous yew, making a solemn shadow, as of death, in the very heart and center of the light and heat of the brightest summer day" (5:278). Although on the surface bright and sunny, there is, at the heart of Elizabeth Gaskell, always the solemn shadow of death.

But Gaskell's morbidity, in contrast to the killing of the demon, is a relatively cheerful thing. Death, in and of itself, is seldom unpleasant in Gaskell. Some individual deaths distress her, the deaths in *Mary Barton,* for instance, about which she is morally outraged. The deaths of children always pain her. And part of her is always aware—that part of her that lives in the moment and treasures only the present joy—that death is a terrible annihilation. Commenting on the fact that Cynthia uses "a euphemism" for death, the narrator says "most people do (it is an ugly word to speak plain out in the midst of life)" (8:479). But death in general is almost never spoken ill of in Gaskell's work. In one remarkable scene, in fact, Gaskell seems, in *Sylvia's Lovers,* to relish death in a sensory way. As Philip nears the moment of death, the narrator writes "But now there was the new feeling—the last new feeling which we shall any of us experience in this world—that death was not only close at hand but inevitable" (6:526). Gaskell herself once wrote to Anne Robson, we remember, "As for death, I have I think remarkably little constitutional dread of it—I often fear I do not look forward to it with sufficient awe, considering the futurity which *must* follow" (*L* 16). Most of the characters in her fiction actually look forward to dying. Margaret Hale in *North and South* "shrank from death with all the clinging to life so natural to the young and healthy" (6:103), but when she inquires of Bessy Higgins whether she is afraid of death, Bessy replies that when she considers all the sorrow she would have to face if she were to live out her life, she is " 'glad enough' " to know that she will not survive the winter (4:103).

Gaskell is very clear in her fiction about the things that make dying attractive. Many seem at first clichés until we remember her peculiar history. One is that we are in death reunited with those we love. A traditional comfort to the dying, to Gaskell this must have been a thought that made of death, if only imaginatively, a means of repossessing the past. Many characters in her fiction look forward in their dying moments to seeing their loved ones again in heaven, and that subject is the theme of a poem, titled "Night Fancies," that Gaskell's great-granddaughter, Mrs. Trevor Jones, believed her great-grandmother had written (*L*, pp. 967–68).

Even more powerful than the hope of being reunited with loved ones is for Gaskell the thought that death is a release from pain and sorrow. Job remarking on Barton's death says that " 'God has heard that man's prayer. He has comforted him' " (1:432). When Davenport in *Mary Barton* dies of hunger and cold, his last words are " 'Oh Lord God! I thank thee, that the hard struggle of living is over' " (1:79). The narrator in a similar way comments on the death of Ruth's father by saying that " 'God in His mercy knew the sure balm, and sent the Beautiful Messenger to take the weary one home' " (3:37). The fact that Gaskell calls death a "home" is significant in itself. Yearning all her life for a home, Gaskell conceived of death as able to provide an ultimate home.

Of those who look forward to dying in Gaskell, itself a class that is very large, one of the largest groups consists of characters who conceal a secret. Not only would Ellinor, as we have seen, "fain have died" in "A Dark Night's Work" after she learns her father's secret, making it in this way her own (7:477), but Dixon, the servant who shares it as well and who is convicted for it, says, when he is told his death sentence has been commuted to life imprisonment, " 'I think I'd as lief be with God as with men' " (7:574–75).

Many of those who conceal a secret and wish they were dead or want to die contemplate suicide or commit it. Ruth thinks twice of killing herself, once in the waters of a "deep black pool" when she is first abandoned by Bellingham (3:101), and once in Eccleston in the sea, after she herself decides she must send Bellingham away (3:332–33). Each of these is a time, of course, she has been forced to give up her demon. At a precisely similar moment, when she has given up Kinraid, Sylvia also considers leaping into the waters of a stream (6:399). And to add just one more example, although there are dozens more to be had, Manasseh, also concealing his demon that is contained by his religion, is altogether suicidal and has actually tried to kill himself (7:156). Manasseh fails, but many succeed. On rare occasions, the cause of the suicide is something practical and external. Boucher, for instance, in *North and South,* kills himself because his poverty has brought him to a pitch of distress that, being weak, he just cannot deal with. He drowns himself in a little stream (4:358). But most, like the attempted suicides, kill themselves on losing their demons. Thus, Frank Wilson hurls himself into the Thames in "The Manchester Marriage" when he loses Alice to Openshaw (5:520–21), Morin in "My Lady Ludlow" shoots himself when he loses Virginie (5:124), and Mary Fitzgerald, Lucy's mother, drowns herself when Gisborne abandons her (7:366). And it is important to note here that in every single case of a suicide or a near suicide—except for one instance in *Sylvia's Lovers* in which "Mrs. Gaskell's" voice is heard, although it is in a subordinate clause (6:414)—Gaskell never condemns the suicide or tries to tell us it is a sin.

Even those who do not kill themselves or attempt to do so in Gaskell often, if they conceal a demon, wait impatiently for death. In "Half a Lifetime Ago," for instance, the comfort Gaskell offers Susan, after she sends Michael away, are the words of Peggy, the servant, who tells her " 'It is not long to bide, and then the end will come' " (5:311). Susan is so eager to die she cannot even imagine waiting. " 'But you are very old,' " she says, thinking of the years ahead. Peggy's reply is characteristic of such situations in Gaskell: " 'It is but a day sin' I were young' " (5:312). Susan at the end of her life acknowledges Peggy had been right. "It seemed but yesterday since all the love of her being had been poured out, and run to waste. The intervening years—the long monotonous years that had turned her into an old woman before her time—were but a dream" (5:323). Hurrying as they are toward death, life seems slow to Gaskell's characters. When they are near their end, however, the life they look back on appears so empty that it seems to have rushed by.

When Gaskell in "Half a Lifetime Ago," in the passage I quoted above, speaks of life passing as in a "dream," she uses the word, not in her own sense, but in the common sense of "unreal." Life is unreal without the demon. For those who live without the demon, the only reality is death. Molly Gibson actually says so. Thinking about the day her father told her that he planned to remarry, Molly asks herself "Could she ever be so passionately unhappy again? Was it goodness, or was it numbness, that made her feel as though life was too short to be troubled much about anything? Death seemed the only reality" (8:239).

Death is real, as life is not, because it is a return to the demon. If, as in Cynthia, the "real self" is "shrouded," if, as in Gregory, it lies in the grave, only in death does a reunion become possible with the demon. It is significant that in Gaskell suicides and attempted suicides, as well as many of those who die not ostensibly by choice, in the preponderance of cases seek and find their end in water. Sylvia wants, for instance, to drown herself after she has married Philip when she happens to think of Kinraid (6:399), and Philip, sent away by Sylvia, feels the "luring power" of water as he leaves on his quest as Freeman (6:409–10). Owen in "The Doom of the Griffiths," rowing on a lake one day, is possessed by a "half longing to fall into the dark waters" (5:270). And Ruth longs twice to drown herself. Many characters actually do. Frank Wilson in "The Manchester Marriage" as well as Boucher in *North and South* and, of course, of special importance, Mary Fitzgerald in "The Poor Clare" (5:366). Philip Hepburn, when he dies supposedly not by his own hand, dies by drowning in the sea. Even when characters die in other ways, Gaskell uses water imagery in her descriptions of their deaths. When Mrs. Hamley dies, for instance, although she dies at home in her bed, the narrator depicts her passing by saying the "quiet waves closed over her" (8:251). Gaskell used water imagery herself when she wrote to Eliza Fox that she would attempt to resolve the conflict among her "warring members" by trying to "drown" her "Christian" "me" (*L* 69). Water we know, as from *Sylvia's Lovers,* is to Gaskell a daemonic element. Dying to their deadened selves, all these characters through water find their daemonic identities again.

Death to Gaskell is thus salvation. As she makes very clear in *Ruth,* it is a salvation from salvation, from the condition of being "good," from the image of "Mrs. Gaskell." For Ruth, who is turned into "Mrs. Gaskell," physical death is a release from her living death in Eccleston. On her deathbed, we recall, Ruth is said to have returned to the "sweet . . . insanity within" (3:444). In that insanity she is able once again to live in Wales. Before she had left, she had, we remember, committed the sights of Wales to memory, and she had never, even in Eccleston, let these recollections go. But she had been divided in Eccleston from her daemonic, her Welsh, self. Like Lucy Gisborne, she had been doubled. The inner insanity is sweet because it is a reintegration. Going double like Hannah in "Lois," Ruth can escape being doubled like Lucy. She is Bridget the witch again. Even before she had left for Eccleston, Gaskell had predicted that Ruth would hear the running waters of Wales when she was lying on her deathbed (3:130). Ruth can no longer, on her deathbed, recognize those she knew in Eccleston. She has returned to Wales, in fact. In her death she is made whole. Dying, she has returned to her demon.

Gaskell had often in her fiction literalized her daemonic metaphors. Images that were figures of speech had been transformed into characters, plots, incidents, narrators, and structures. The demon itself had been such an image, and the ideal Lucy another. And these images she had also actualized in her own life. The image of the gypsy-bachelor had sent her on a good many journeys, and her destinations had each had a significance in her mind. In the end, she chose to realize one more image in her death. She had always seen the demon as existing in the grave, she had always thought of death as the means of passing to it. Writing the end of *Wives and Daughters* entailed allowing Molly Gibson to marry the man who had advised her that if she wanted to be loved she would have to kill herself, kill the self that was the demon. It meant she would have to reenact the moment in which she had killed her own. She had so often done it before. Over and over again in her fiction she had relived that deadening moment in which she had split herself in two. At last, she would not do it again. E. Thurstan Holland reports that Gaskell died without "any struggle" (*L*, p. 971). Rather than letting herself be doubled in her fiction one more time, she chose to join her demon instead. She had lived as Lucy Gisborne. But she died as Bridget the witch.

Notes

Chapter 1

1. Winifred Gérin, *Elizabeth Gaskell: A Biography* (Oxford: At the Clarendon Press, 1976).

2. Aina Rubenius, *The Woman Question in Mrs. Gaskell's Life and Works,* The English Institute in the University of Upsala: Essays and Studies on English Language and Literature (Upsala: Almqvist & Wiksells Boktryckeri Ab, 1950); Elaine Showalter, *A Literature of Their Own: British Women Novelists from Brontë to Lessing* (Princeton, N.J.: Princeton University Press, 1977).

3. G. B. Smith, "Mrs. Gaskell and Her Novels," *Cornhill Magazine* 29 (1874): 192–93; Lord David Cecil, *Victorian Novelists: Essays in Revaluation* (1935; Chicago: University of Chicago Press, 1958), pp. 183–84; Arthur Pollard, *Mrs. Gaskell: Novelist and Biographer* (Cambridge, Mass.: Harvard University Press, 1965), p. 250.

4. J. A. V. Chapple and Arthur Pollard, eds., *The Letters of Mrs. Gaskell* (Cambridge, Mass.: Harvard University Press, 1967), letter no. 571. (Letters are numbered in this volume in a chronological sequence.) To this excellent edition of Elizabeth Gaskell's letters, Chapple and Pollard add a good introduction and some important information on the history of the letters. Subsequent references to this volume will appear, in abbreviated form, in parentheses in the text (*L*) and, unless indicated otherwise, will refer, not to the page, but to the number of the letter.

5. G. A. Payne, *Mrs. Gaskell: A Brief Biography* (Manchester: Sherratt & Hughes, 1929), p. 14.

6. All references to Gaskell's works, except for *The Life of Charlotte Brontë,* which was not included in this edition, and "My Diary," which was printed privately, will be to *The Knutsford Edition of the Works of Mrs. Gaskell,* ed. A. W. Ward. 8 vols. (1906; rpt. New York: AMS Press, 1972).

7. Gaskell enjoyed, for many years, a close professional association with Dickens, who published many of her stories in *Household Words* and *All the Year Round.* In the former he also serialized two of her novels, *Cranford* and *North and South.*

8. David Masson, "Mrs. Gaskell," *Macmillan's Magazine* 74 (1865): 154.

9. Anne Thackeray Ritchie, "Mrs. Gaskell," in her *Blackstick Papers* (London: Smith, Elder, & Co., 1908), pp. 217–18. In this connection see also H. P. Collins— "The Naked Sensibility: Elizabeth Gaskell," *Essays in Criticism* 3 (1953): 60–72— who argues that Gaskell could not transmute experience into a fictional world that was, like George Eliot's for instance in *Middlemarch,* fully objective and self-contained.

10. Masson, "Mrs. Gaskell"; Miriam Allott, *Elizabeth Gaskell* (London:

Longmans, Green & Co., 1960); John McVeagh, *Elizabeth Gaskell* (New York: Humanities Press, 1970); Margaret Ganz, *Elizabeth Gaskell: The Artist in Conflict* (New York: Twayne, 1969).

11. For example, Sandra M. Gilbert and Susan Gubar, *The Madwoman in the Attic: The Woman Writer and the Nineteenth-Century Literary Imagination* (New Haven: Yale University Press, 1979), p. 151, and Ellen Moers, *Literary Women: The Great Writers* (Garden City, N. Y.: Doubleday: Anchor Press, 1977), p. 27.

12. Patsy Stoneman, *Elizabeth Gaskell* (Brighton, Sussex: Harvester Press, 1987); Jenni Calder, *Women and Marriage in Victorian Fiction* (London: Thomas & Hudson, 1976); Nina Auerbach, *Communities of Women: An Idea in Fiction* (Cambridge, Mass.: Harvard University Press, 1978); Maureen Reddy, "Gaskell's 'The Grey Woman': A Feminist Palimpsest," *Journal of Narrative Technique* 15 (1985): 183–193; Coral Lansbury, *Elizabeth Gaskell: The Novel of Social Crisis* (New York: Barnes & Noble, 1975), and *Elizabeth Gaskell* (Boston: Twayne Publishers, 1984). (The second volume is essentially a revision of the first, but the first is a better book: more original, more incisive.)

13. J. G. Sharps, *Mrs. Gaskell's Observation and Invention: A Study of Her Non-Biographic Works* (London: Linden Press, 1970).

14. Edna Lyall, "Mrs. Gaskell," in *Women Novelists of Queen Victoria's Reign: A Book of Appreciations by Mrs. Oliphant et al.* (London: Hurst & Blackett, 1897), p. 144. See also Mrs. Ellis H. Chadwick, *Mrs. Gaskell: Haunts, Homes, and Stories* (London: Sir Isaac Pitman and Sons, 1910), p. 25.

15. See Angus Easson, *Elizabeth Gaskell* (London: Routledge & Kegan Paul, 1979), p. 184.

16. Yvonne ffrench, *Mrs. Gaskell* (London: Home & Van Thal, 1949), p. 45.

17. Lansbury, *The Novel of Social Crisis,* pp. 210–11.

18. Kathleen Tillotson, *Novels of the Eighteen-Forties* (1954; rpt. London: Oxford University Press, 1962), pp. 205–6.

19. Sigmund Freud, *The Interpretation of Dreams,* trans. and ed. James Strachey (New York: Avon Books, 1965), pp. 311–12.

20. As Ira Bruce Nadel suggests, in a fascinating study of the biographical form and of innovative trends in the writing of biography—*Biography: Fiction, Fact, and Form* (New York: St. Martin's Press, 1984)—the question of the degree to which a biography is fact or fiction is becoming a central question in the practice of the art (see especially his ch. 6).

21. Richard B. Sewall, *The Life of Emily Dickinson,* 2 vols. (New York: Farrar, Straus and Giroux, 1974), 1:83.

Chapter 2

1. "My Diary: The Early Years of My Daughter Marianne" (London: privately printed by Clement Shorter, 1923), p. 13. Gaskell began to keep this diary on March 10, 1835, when Marianne was six months old. In one of her very earliest entries, she says she is sorry she did not begin sooner (p. 5). She continued to record Marianne's childhood for some time, and Meta's as well when she was born on February 5, 1837, although at very irregular intervals. At one point it seems that a year has passed without her having made an entry (p. 28). She was obviously

beginning to find it hard to put aside the time to make entries in the "Diary," and on October 28, 1838, she stopped. Subsequent references to this work will appear in the text itself.

2. The original of this letter appears to be no longer in existence. Winifred Gérin, who refers to it in her biography (*Elizabeth Gaskell*, pp. 6–7), quotes from a copy in The Brotherton Collection, Leeds University Library, from which, with its kind permission, I am quoting here as well.

3. For example, Gerald DeWitt Sanders, *Elizabeth Gaskell* (1929; rpt. New York: Russell & Russell, 1971), p. 34;, Pollard, *Mrs. Gaskell*, p. 188; Easson, *Elizabeth Gaskell*, p. 184; and Charles Algernon Swinburne, *A Note on Charlotte Brontë* (London: Chatto & Windus, 1877), p. 31.

4. Anne Thackeray Ritchie, Preface to *Cranford* (London: Macmillan and Co., 1891), p. xii.

5. Françoise Basch, *Relative Creatures: Victorian Women in Society and the Novel*, trans. Anthony Rudolf (New York: Schocken Books, 1974), p. 65.

6. This letter too appears to be no longer in existence in the original. With its kind permission I quote from a copy to be found in The Brotherton Collection, Leeds University Library, as does Gérin in her biography (*Elizabeth Gaskell*, p. 38).

7. Two leaves of this letter, which is quoted both by Gérin (*Elizabeth Gaskell*, pp. 15–16) and by Sharps (*Mrs. Gaskell's Observation and Invention*, p. 17, n. 1, and p. 120), are in Sharps's possession currently, and I am deeply indebted to him for allowing me to quote from them.

Chapter 3

1. Lansbury, *The Novel of Social Crisis*, ch. 1.

2. Chadwick, *Mrs. Gaskell*, pp. 402–4.

3. W. R. Greg, "Why Are Women Redundant?" in his *Literary and Social Judgments* (New York: Henry Holt and Company, 1876), p. 303.

4. Ritchie, Preface to *Cranford*, p. xvii.

5. Greg, "Why Are Women Redundant?" p. 280.

6. Walter Allen, *The English Novel: A Short Critical History* (New York: E. P. Dutton & Co., 1958), p. 209.

Chapter 4

1. Chadwick, *Mrs. Gaskell*, p. 200; Gérin, *Elizabeth Gaskell*, p. 122; Moers, *Literary Women*, ch. 7.

2. As far as I know, K. L. Montgomery—"Elizabeth Cleghorn Gaskell," *Fortnightly Review*, n.s. 75 (1910): 450–63—was the first to call attention to the similarity between the two stories.

3. Gilbert and Gubar, *The Madwoman in the Attic*, p. 78.

4. For a general discussion of the image of the demon in the fiction of nineteenth-century women writers see Nina Auerbach, *Woman and the Demon: The Life of a Victorian Myth* (Cambridge, Mass.: Harvard University Press, 1982). Gaskell's story is not, however, included in Auerbach's discussion.

5. See the Index entry "Woman as Witch" in Gilbert and Gubar, *The Madwoman in the Attic.*

6. Ellen M. Laun, "A Missing Gaskell Tale Found," *Studies in Short Fiction* 15 (1978): 177–83.

7. For a general discussion of the image of the fallen woman in the fiction of nineteenth-century women writers, see Nina Auerbach, *Woman and the Demon,* especially ch. 5.

Chapter 5

1. But see Gérin, who disagrees (*Elizabeth Gaskell,* pp. 276–78).

2. The character was called Augharad for years, but Sharps is obviously right to suggest that this was due to a misreading of Gaskell's handwriting in the manuscript, Augharad not being a name at all and Angharad a popular one in Wales (*Mrs. Gaskell's Observation and Invention,* p. 268).

3. *The Life of Charlotte Brontë* (1857; rpt. New York: Doubleday & Company, n.d.), p. 196. Subsequent references to this text will appear in parentheses in the text as *LCB.*

Chapter 6

1. Basch, *Relative Creatures,* ch. 3.

2. Long neglected, *Ruth* has recently begun to stir some interest again. See, for example, Hervé Abalain, "Le Refus de la marginalité: Le Combat d'Elizabeth Gaskell pour la réisertion et la réhabilitation de la *femme déchue* dans la société," in *La Marginalité dans la littérature et la pensé anglaises,* ed. N.-J. Rigaud (Aix-en-Provence: Université de Provence, 1983), pp. 105–23; A. J. Shelston, "Ruth: Mrs. Gaskell's Neglected Novel," *Bulletin of the John Rylands University Library of Manchester* 58 (1975): 173–92; and, most especially, Michael D. Wheeler, "The Sinner as Heroine: A Study of Mrs. Gaskell's *Ruth* and the Bible," *Durham University Journal* 37 (1976): 148–61.

3. Sanders, *Elizabeth Gaskell,* pp. 48–49.

4. Tillotson, *Novels of the Eighteen-Forties,* p. 58.

5. For example, Sanders, *Elizabeth Gaskell,* p. 57, and A. Stanton Whitfield, *Mrs. Gaskell: Her Life and Work* (London: George Routledge & Sons, 1929), pp. 142, 151.

Chapter 7

1. A good discussion of the Unitarianism practiced in Manchester in Gaskell's time, and in fact in Gaskell's circle, is to be found in the third chapter of R. K. Webb's excellent study *Harriet Martineau: A Radical Victorian* (New York: Columbia University Press, 1960).

2. Collins, "The Naked Sensibility," p. 63.

3. Gérin, *Elizabeth Gaskell,* p. 54.

4. ffrench, *Mrs. Gaskell,* pp. 66, 133.

5. Gérin, *Elizabeth Gaskell,* pp. 223–24.

6. See Sara Norton and M. H. DeWolfe Howe, eds., *Letters of Charles Eliot Norton*, 2 vols. (Boston: Houghton Mifflin, 1913), 1:xx.

7. Catherine Winkworth quoted in Vera Wheatley, *The Life and Work of Harriet Martineau* (Fair Lawn, N.J.: Essential Books, 1957), p. 303.

8. For a different view of Gaskell's relationship to Calvinism see Lansbury, *The Novel of Social Crisis*, pp. 156 ff.

9. But see Sharps, who thinks this is probably a reference to "A Dark Night's Work" (*Mrs. Gaskell's Observation and Invention*, p. 355 n. 10).

10. Gérin, *Elizabeth Gaskell*, p. 27.

Chapter 8

1. Graham Storey and Kathleen Tillotson, eds., *The Pilgrim Edition of the Letters of Charles Dickens*, vol. 6 (Oxford: At the Clarendon Press, 1988), p. 231.

2. Many assume that it was Dickens who persuaded Gaskell to let Lizzie live, but the evidence usually cited does not support such a conclusion. On February 27, 1850, having received the first installment of the story, Dickens writes to ask whether Gaskell intends to kill Lizzie. On March 14, having obviously received a reply (of which we have no record, unfortunately), he makes a suggestion for the story that can only be based on his having been told that Lizzie was intended to live. Nowhere in the correspondence does he make even a suggestion as to what should be done with Lizzie. Her fate was obviously Gaskell's choice. See Storey and Tillotson, eds., *The Pilgrim Edition of the Letters of Charles Dickens*, 6:48, 65.

3. Charlotte Brontë and Elizabeth Barrett Browning in R. D. Waller, ed., "Letters Addressed to Mrs. Gaskell by Celebrated Contemporaries," *Bulletin of the John Rylands University Library of Manchester* 19 (1935): 43; W. R. Greg, "False Morality of Lady Novelists," in his *Literary and Social Judgments* (New York: Henry Holt and Company, 1876), pp. 110–11.

Chapter 9

1. Ganz, *Elizabeth Gaskell*, p. 109 n. 116.

2. A. Cobden Smith, "Mrs. Gaskell and Lower Mosley Street, a Centenary Address," *Sunday School Quarterly* (January 1911): 156.

3. For example, Chadwick, *Mrs. Gaskell*, p. 245.

4. Louis Cazamian, *The Social Novel in England, 1830–50: Dickens, Disraeli, Mrs. Gaskell, Kingsley*, trans. Martin Fido (1903; rpt. London: Routledge & Kegan Paul, 1973), p. 217 n. 10.

5. For a brief but good discussion of Unitarian economics in Gaskell's circle in Manchester, see Webb, *Harriet Martineau*, ch. 4.

6. W. R. Greg, "Mary Barton," in his *Essays on Political and Social Science, Contributed Chiefly to The Edinburgh Review*, 2 vols. (London: Longman, Brown, Green, and Longmans, 1853), 1:361.

7. Lansbury, *The Novel of Social Crisis*, p. 187.

8. On Gaskell's political ambivalence, see also Phillippa Walsh Colella, "Elizabeth Gaskell as Social Commentator: Radical Liberal or Bourgeois Apologist?" *Studi dell'Instituto Linguistico* 4 (1981): 69–83.

9. Cazamian, *The Social Novel in England,* pp. 221–22.

10. Greg, "Mary Barton," p. 377.

11. Gaskell may actually have written two pieces on the Camorra, but the second, which was supposedly called "La Camorra" and which seems to have been scheduled for publication in the *Cornhill Magazine* in June of 1863 (see *L* 523a), appears never to have been published.

12. Gaskell's Preface was written for the English translation by L. and M. Ellis of C. Augusto Vecchj's *Garibaldi at Caprera* (Cambridge and London: Macmillan and Co., 1862).

13. Tillotson, *Novels of the Eighteen-Forties,* p. 211.

Chapter 10

1. Different readers take different views of the female world of *Cranford.* See especially Nina Auerbach, *Communities of Women,* and Pauline Nestor, *Female Friendships and Communities: Charlotte Brontë, George Eliot, Elizabeth Gaskell* (Oxford: Oxford University Press, 1985).

2. Ganz, *Elizabeth Gaskell,* p. 143.

3. See Martin Dodsworth, "Women without Men at Cranford," *Essays in Criticism* 13 (1963): 132–45.

4. Sanders, *Elizabeth Gaskell,* p. 7 n. 1.

5. Chadwick, *Mrs. Gaskell,* p. 94.

6. Both Sharps and Gérin refer to this letter from John Stevenson (*Mrs. Gaskell's Observation and Invention,* p. 21 n. 29, and *Elizabeth Gaskell,* p. 34). The original seems lost. I quote, with his very kind permission, from a typescript in the possession of J. G. Sharps.

Chapter 11

1. See also Nina Auerbach's general discussion of women wishing for wings in *Woman and the Demon,* ch. 4.

2. Cecil, *Victorian Novelists*, p. 204; Elizabeth Haldane, *Mrs. Gaskell and Her Friends* (London: Hodder and Stoughton, 1930), p. 282.

3. See also Gilbert and Gubar's comments on women being imprisoned in *The Madwoman in the Attic* (listed under "Prisons" in the Index).

4. Virginia Woolf, "Professions for Women," in her *The Death of the Moth and Other Essays* (1942; rpt. New York: Harcourt Brace Jovanovich, 1970), pp. 236–38.

Chapter 12

1. Ganz, *Elizabeth Gaskell,* p. 78.

2. The paragraph in which this passage appears was added by Gaskell to the second edition of the publication of *North and South* in volume form. It is not reprinted in the Knutsford edition of the novel, but Dorothy Collin (shrewdly) includes it in her edition for Penguin Books (Harmondsworth, Middlesex: Penguin Books 1970), p. 502.

3. Sanders is, as far as I know, the only reader who has mentioned the theme of

lying in Gaskell's fiction. See, in *Elizabeth Gaskell,* his discussion of the subject in *Ruth* (ch. 6) and *North and South* (ch. 8).

Chapter 13

1. Gérin, *Elizabeth Gaskell,* p. 44; Pollard, *Mrs. Gaskell,* p. 62; A. B. Hopkins, *Elizabeth Gaskell: Her Life and Work* (1952; rpt. New York: Octagon Books, 1971), p. 111; Ganz, *Elizabeth Gaskell,* p. 41.
2. Easson is right to say that, geographically, Hollingford is not precisely Knutsford (*Elizabeth Gaskell,* p. 187). But it is Knutsford metaphorically.
3. Arnold Kettle, "The Early Victorian Social-Problem Novel," in *From Dickens to Hardy,* vol. 6 of The Pelican Guide to English Literature, ed. Boris Ford (1958; rpt. Baltimore: Penguin Books, 1963), p. 181; Hopkins, *Elizabeth Gaskell,* 139; but see Miriam Allott, who rightly points out that in *North and South* the lovers do not look back, like Elizabeth and Darcy, but forward, like Esther Lyon and Felix Holt in George Eliot's *Felix Holt.* Allott considers the contentious lovers of D. H. Lawrence, in fact, as their true descendants (*Elizabeth Gaskell,* p. 19).
4. Ritchie, Preface to *Cranford,* p. x.

Chapter 14

1. For a literary rather than a biographical analysis of Gaskell's use of the sea as a metaphor, see Stephen Lee Schwartz, "Sea and Land Symbolism in Mrs. Gaskell's *Sylvia's Lovers,*" *Estudos Anglo-Americanos* 7–8 (1983–84): 1–15.
2. For a discussion of the relationship in *Sylvia's Lovers* between sexuality and social repression, see Missy Kubitschek, "Defying the Old Limits of Possibility: Unconventional Aspects of Two Gaskell Novels," *University of Mississippi Studies in English* 4 (1983): 101–11.
3. Easson, *Elizabeth Gaskell,* p. 169.
4. Others have also noted this similarity. See for example, Lansbury, *The Novel of Social Crisis,* pp. 157, 159.

Chapter 15

1. This, another of the letters in the possession of J. G. Sharps, is cited here by his kind permission. Winifred Gérin also alludes to this letter in her biography (*Elizabeth Gaskell,* p. 16 n. 8).
2. See, for example, Ganz, *Elizabeth Gaskell,* p. 136.
3. Gérin, *Elizabeth Gaskell,* p. 119.
4. Easson, *Elizabeth Gaskell,* pp. 201–2.
5. Lansbury, *The Novel of Social Crisis,* p. 61.
6. Lansbury, *The Novel of Social Crisis,* pp. 76–77, 211–12.
7. Adrienne Rich, "It Is the Lesbian in Us . . . ," in her *On Lies, Secrets, and Silence: Selected Prose, 1966–1976* (New York: W. W. Norton & Company, 1979), p. 200. (The essay was first delivered as an address to a session cosponsored by the Women's Commission and the Gay Caucus at the annual meeting of the Modern Language Association on December 28, 1976.)

8. And see Reddy, who argues also that Amante is meant as a "masculine" type ("Gaskell's 'The Grey Woman,'" p. 190).

Chapter 16

1. Greg, "Why Are Women Redundant?" pp. 302, 276, 303.
2. Many have commented on Gaskell's lack of interest in the theoretics of fiction. See, for example, Allott, *Elizabeth Gaskell,* p. 14; Gérin, *Elizabeth Gaskell,* p. 80; Edward Wagenknecht, *Cavalcade of the English Novel: From Elizabeth to George VI* (New York: Henry Holt and Company, 1943), p. 254; and Ernest A. Baker, *From the Brontës to Meredith: Romanticism in the English Novel* (London: H. F. & G. Witherby, 1937), p. 85.
3. The development of Gaskell's skill as a writer is one of Easson's central themes in his *Elizabeth Gaskell.*
4. McVeagh, *Elizabeth Gaskell,* p. 85.
5. Miss Mat. Hompes, "Mrs. E. C. Gaskell," *Gentleman's Magazine* 279 (1895): 130–31.

Chapter 17

1. Sanders, *Elizabeth Gaskell,* p. 87.
2. Edgar Wright, *Mrs. Gaskell: The Basis for Reassessment* (London: Oxford University Press, 1965). See especially ch. 10.
3. And Heger did not. The letters were only brought to light in 1913, when the Heger family donated them to the British Museum.
4. Masson, "Mrs. Gaskell," p. 154.
5. T. J. Wise and J. A. Symington, eds., *The Brontës: Their Lives, Friendships, and Correspondence,* 4 vols. (Oxford: Shakespeare Head Press, 1932), 3:40.
6. Margaret J. Shaen, ed., *Memorials of Two Sisters, Susanna and Catherine Winkworth* (New York: Longmans, Green, and Co., 1908), p. 24.
7. See A. B. Hopkins, "Dickens and Mrs. Gaskell," *Huntington Library Quarterly* 9 (1946): 357–85.
8. G. B. Smith, "Mrs. Gaskell and Her Novels," pp. 192–93; Shaen, *Memorials of Two Sisters,* p. 24; Marianne Gaskell quoted in Lyall, "Mrs. Gaskell," pp. 142–43.
9. Gérin, *Elizabeth Gaskell,* pp. 146–49.
10. Gérin, *Elizabeth Gaskell,* pp. 146–49.
11. Wise and Symington, *The Brontës,* 4:116.

Chapter 18

1. See A. W. Ward's discussion of the date (*The Knutsford Edition of the Works of Mrs. Gaskell,* 1:502–3).
2. The letter, dated February 1, 1863, is also quoted by A. B. Hopkins (*Elizabeth Gaskell,* p. 152). I am grateful to the Huntington Library, San Marino, California, where the original is to be found (HM 18338), for permission to quote from it.

3. Gilbert and Gubar speak throughout *The Madwoman in the Attic* of women having things to hide.

4. For a more literal assessment of Gaskell's sense of the Mediterranean, see Jean-Pierre Garces, "La Méditerranée; ou, L'Autre Sud dans *North and South,*" in *L'Angleterre et le monde méditerranéen,* ed. N.-J. Rigaud (Aix-en-Provence: Université de Provence, 1987), pp. 53–77.

5. Norton and Howe, *Letters of Charles Eliot Norton,* 1:1.

6. Norton and Howe, *Letters of Charles Eliot Norton,* 1:xix.

7. Lucy Stebbins, "Elizabeth Gaskell," in her *A Victorian Album: Some Lady Novelists of the Period* (New York: Columbia University Press, 1946), p. 106; Gérin, *Elizabeth Gaskell,* p. 229.

8. This is another letter of which the original seems lost. Gérin, who quotes from it in her book (*Elizabeth Gaskell,* p. 47), is using the copy to be found in The Brotherton Collection, Leeds University Library, from which, with its kind permission, I am also quoting here.

9. This letter too is quoted by Gérin (*Elizabeth Gaskell,* p. 50). The original is extant in The Brotherton Collection, Leeds University Library, with the kind permission of which I am quoting from it here.

10. Shaen, *Memorials of Two Sisters,* p. 114.

11. Mrs. Alexander Ireland, ed., *Selections From the Letters of Geraldine Endsor Jewsbury to Jane Welsh Carlyle* (London: Longmans, Green, and Co., 1892), p. 383.

12. I am grateful to the Trustees of the National Library of Scotland for allowing me to quote from this letter in their possession. Shaen, it might be added, was right. Haldane must not have wished to deal with the implications of this letter, for she does not even mention it. Hardly anyone, indeed, ever questions William's conduct. J. G. Sharps alone, in fact, quotes from and comments on Shaen's letter (*Mrs. Gaskell's Observation and Invention,* p. 409 n. 208).

13. Sharps again is the only one who takes notice of this letter (*Mrs. Gaskell's Observation and Invention,* p. 409 n. 208), the original of which is in the National Library of Scotland, to whose Trustees I am greatly indebted for permission to quote from it.

14. For example, Gérin, *Elizabeth Gaskell,* p. 69; Rubenius, *The Woman Question,* p. 18 n. 2; Haldane, *Mrs. Gaskell and Her Friends,* p. 301.

15. Hopkins, *Elizabeth Gaskell,* pp. 240–441.

Chapter 19

1. See Easson, *Elizabeth Gaskell,* p. 181.

2. For example, Gérin, *Elizabeth Gaskell,* chs. 22, 23; Pollard, *Mrs. Gaskell,* p. 29; Hopkins, *Elizabeth Gaskell,* pp. 310–18.

3. Gérin, *Elizabeth Gaskell,* p. 291.

4. Gérin is particularly sensitive to Gaskell's morbid streak, especially as it is seen in the "Diary" (*Elizabeth Gaskell,* p. 54).

A Select Bibliography

Abalain, Hervé. "Le Refus de la marginalité: Le Combat d'Elizabeth Gaskell pour la réisertion et la réhabilitation de la *femme déchue* dans la société." In *La Marginalité dans la litérature et la pensé anglaises,* ed. N.-J. Rigaud, pp. 105–23. Aix-en-Provence: Université de Provence, 1983.

Allen, Walter. *The English Novel: A Short Critical History.* New York: E. P. Dutton & Co., 1958.

Allott, Miriam. *Elizabeth Gaskell.* London: Longmans, Green & Co., 1960.

Auerbach, Nina. *Communities of Women: An Idea In Fiction.* Cambridge, Mass.: Harvard University Press, 1978.

———. *Woman and the Demon: The Life of a Victorian Myth.* Cambridge, Mass.: Harvard University Press, 1982.

Baker, Ernest A. B. *From the Brontës to Meredith: Romanticism in the English Novel.* London: H. F. & G. Witherby, 1937.

Basch, Françoise. *Relative Creatures: Victorian Women in Society and the Novel,* trans. Anthony Rudolf. New York: Schocken Books, 1974.

Bick, Suzann. "'Take Her Up Tenderly': Elizabeth Gaskell's Treatment of the Fallen Woman." *Essays in Arts and Sciences* 18 (1989): 17–27.

Brill, Barbara. "'My Dear Mr. Norton.'" *Gaskell Society Journal* 1 (1987): 30–40.

Butler, Marilyn. "The Uniqueness of Cynthia Kirkpatrick: Elizabeth Gaskell's *Wives and Daughters* and Maria Edgeworth's *Helen.*" *Review of English Studies* 23 (1972): 278–90.

Calder, Jenni. *Women and Marriage in Victorian Fiction.* London: Thomas & Hudson, 1976.

Cazamian, Louis. *The Social Novel in England, 1830–50: Dickens, Disraeli, Mrs. Gaskell, Kingsley,* trans. Martin Fido. 1903; rpt. London: Routledge & Kegan Paul, 1973.

Cecil, Sir David. *Victorian Novelists: Essays in Revaluation.* 1935; rpt. Chicago: University of Chicago Press, 1958.

Chadwick, Mrs. Ellis H. *Mrs. Gaskell: Haunts, Homes, and Stories.* London: Sir Isaac Pitman and Sons, 1910.

Chapple, J. A. V. *Elizabeth Gaskell: A Portrait in Letters,* assisted by John Geoffrey Sharps. Manchester: Manchester University Press, 1980.

———. "William Stevenson and Elizabeth Gaskell." *Gaskell Studies Journal* 1 (1987): 1–9.

———, and Arthur Pollard, eds. *The Letters of Mrs. Gaskell.* Cambridge, Mass.: Harvard University Press, 1967.

Colella, Phillippa Walsh. "Elizabeth Gaskell as Social Commentator: Radical Liberal or Bourgeois Apologist?" *Studi dell'Instituto Linguistico* 4 (1981): 69–83.

Collins, H. P. "The Naked Sensibility: Elizabeth Gaskell." *Essays in Criticism* 3 (1953): 60–72.

David, Deirdre. *Fictions of Resolution in Three Victorian Novels: North and South, Our Mutual Friend, Daniel Deronda.* New York: Columbia University Press, 1981.

Dodsworth, Martin. "Women without Men at Cranford." *Essays in Criticism* 13 (1963): 132–45.

Duthie, Enid. "Echoes of the French Revolution in the Work of Elizabeth Gaskell." *Gaskell Studies Journal* 2 (198): 34–40.

Easson, Angus. *Elizabeth Gaskell.* London: Routledge & Kegan Paul, 1979.

Eve, Jeanette. "A Misdated Gaskell Letter and the Background Story to *Ruth.*" *Notes & Queries* 34 (1987): 36–39.

ffrench, Yvonne. *Mrs. Gaskell.* London: Home & Van Thal, 1949.

Freud, Sigmund. *The Interpretation of Dreams,* trans. and ed. James Strachey. New York: Avon Books, 1965.

Fryckstedt, Monica Correa. "The Early Industrial Novel: *Mary Barton* and Its Predecessors." *Bulletin of the John Rylands University Library of Manchester* 63 (1980): 11–30.

Ganz, Margaret. *Elizabeth Gaskell: The Artist in Conflict.* New York: Twayne, 1969.

Garces, Jean-Pierre. "La Méditerranée; ou, L'Autre Sud dans *North and South.*" In *L'Angleterre et le monde méditerranéen,* ed. N.-J. Rigaud, pp. 53–77. Aix-en-Provence: Université de Provence, 1987.

Gaskell, Elizabeth. *The Knutsford Edition of the Works of Mrs. Gaskell,* ed A. W. Ward. 8 vols. 1906; rpt. New York: AMS Press, 1972.

———. *The Life of Charlotte Brontë.* 1857; rpt. New York: Doubleday & Company, n.d.

———. "My Diary: The Early Years of My Daughter Marianne." London: privately printed by Clement Shorter, 1923.

———. *North and South,* ed. Dorothy Collin. Harmondsworth, Middlesex: Penguin Books, 1970.

———. Preface to C. Augusto Vecchj, *Garibaldi at Caprera,* trans. L. and M. Ellis. Cambridge and London: Macmillan and Co., 1862.

Gérin, Winifred. *Elizabeth Gaskell: A Biography.* Oxford: At the Clarendon Press, 1976.

Gilbert, Sandra M., and Susan Gubar. *The Madwoman in the Attic: The Woman Writer and the Nineteenth-Century Literary Imagination.* New Haven: Yale University Press, 1979.

Greg, W. R. "False Morality of Lady Novelists." In his *Literary and Social Judgments,* pp. 85–114. New York: Henry Holt and Company, 1876.

———. "Mary Barton." In his *Essays on Political and Social Science, Contributed Chiefly to The Edinburgh Review.* 2 vols. London: Longman, Brown, Green, and Longmans, 1853. 1:344–88.

———. "Why Are Women Redundant?" In his *Literary and Social Judgments,* pp. 274–308. New York: Henry Holt and Company, 1876.

Haldane, Elizabeth. *Mrs. Gaskell and Her Friends.* London: Hodder and Stoughton, 1930.

Handley, Graham, "The Chronology of Sylvia's Lovers." *Notes & Queries,* n.s. 12 (1965): 302–3.

Hompes, Miss Mat. "Mrs. E. C. Gaskell." *Gentleman's Magazine* 279 (1895): 130–31.

Hopkins, A. B. "Dickens and Mrs. Gaskell." *Huntington Library Quarterly* 9 (1946): 357–85.

———. *Elizabeth Gaskell: Her Life and Work.* 1952; rpt. New York: Octagon Books, 1971.

Ireland, Mrs. Alexander, ed. *Selections from the Letters of Geraldine Endsor Jewsbury to Jane Welsh Carlyle.* London: Longmans, Green, and Co., 1892.

Kettle, Arnold. "The Early Victorian Social-Problem Novel." In *From Dickens to Hardy,* vol. 6 of The Pelican Guide to English Literature, ed. Boris Ford, pp. 169–87. 1958; rpt. Baltimore: Penguin Books, 1963.

Kubitschek, Missy. "Defying the Old Limits of Possibility: Unconventional Aspects of Two Gaskell Novels." *University of Mississippi Studies in English* 4 (1983): 101–11.

Lansbury, Coral. *Elizabeth Gaskell: The Novel of Social Crisis.* New York: Barnes & Noble, 1975.

———. *Elizabeth Gaskell.* Boston: Twayne Publishers, 1984.

Laun, Ellen M. "A Missing Gaskell Tale Found." *Studies in Short Fiction* 15 (1978): 177–83.

Lyall, Edna. "Mrs. Gaskell." In *Women Novelists of Queen Victoria's Reign. A Book of Appreciations by Mrs. Oliphant et al.,* pp. 117–45. London: Hurst & Blackett, 1897.

McVeagh, John. *Elizabeth Gaskell.* New York: Humanities Press, 1970.

Martin, Carol A. "Gaskell's Ghosts: Truths in Disguise." *Studies in the Novel* 21 (1989): 27–40.

Masson, David. "Mrs. Gaskell." *Macmillan's Magazine* 74 (1865): 154.

Moers, Ellen. *Literary Women: The Great Writers.* Garden City, N.Y.: Doubleday: Anchor Press, 1977.

Montgomery, K. L. "Elizabeth Cleghorn Gaskell." *Fortnightly Review,* n.s. 75 (1910): 450–63.

Nadel, Ira Bruce. *Biography: Fiction, Fact, and Form.* New York: St. Martin's Press, 1984.

Nestor, Pauline. *Female Friendships and Communities: Charlotte Brontë, George Eliot, Elizabeth Gaskell.* Oxford: Oxford University Press, 1985.

Norton, Sara, and M. H. DeWolfe Howe, eds. *Letters of Charles Eliot Norton.* 2 vols. Boston: Houghton Mifflin, 1913.

Payne, G. A. *Mrs. Gaskell: A Brief Biography.* Manchester: Sherratt & Hughes, 1929.

Pollard, Arthur. *Mrs. Gaskell: Novelist and Biographer.* Cambridge, Mass.: Harvard University Press, 1965.

Reddy, Maureen. "Gaskell's 'The Grey Woman': A Feminist Palimpsest." *Journal of Narrative Technique* 15 (1985): 183–93.

Rich, Adrienne. "It Is the Lesbian in Us . . ." In her *On Lies, Secrets, and Silence: Selected Prose, 1966–1976,* pp. 199–202. New York: W. W. Norton & Company, 1979. The essay was first delivered as an address to a session cosponsored by the Women's Commission and the Gay Caucus at the annual meeting of the Modern Language Association on December 28, 1976.

Ritchie, Anne Thackeray. Preface to *Cranford.* London: Macmillan and Co., 1891.

————. "Mrs. Gaskell." In her *Blackstick Papers,* pp. 209–32. London: Smith, Elder, & Co., 1908.

Rubenius, Aina. *The Woman Question in Mrs. Gaskell's Life and Works.* The English Institute in the University of Upsala: Essays and Studies on English Language and Literature. Upsala: Almqvist & Wiksells Boktryckeri Ab, 1950.

Sanders, Gerald DeWitt. *Elizabeth Gaskell.* 1929; rpt. New York: Russell & Russell, 1971.

Schwartz, Stephen Lee. "Sea and Land Symbolism in Mrs. Gaskell's *Sylvia's Lovers.*" *Estudos Anglo-Americanos* 7–8 (1983–84): 1–15.

Sewall, Richard B. *The Life of Emily Dickinson.* 2 vols. New York: Farrar, Straus and Giroux, 1974.

Shaen, Margaret J., ed. *Memorials of Two Sisters, Susanna and Catherine Winkworth.* New York: Longmans, Green, and Co., 1908.

Sharps, J. G. *Mrs. Gaskell's Observation and Invention: A Study of Her Non-Biographic Works.* London: Linden Press, 1970.

Shelston, Alan. "Elizabeth Gaskell's Manchester, I." *Gaskell Studies Journal* 3 (1989): 46–67.

Shelston, A. J. "*Ruth:* Mrs. Gaskell's Neglected Novel." *Bulletin of the John Rylands University Library of Manchester* 58 (1975): 173–92.

Showalter, Elaine. *A Literature of Their Own: British Women Novelists from Brontë to Lessing.* Princeton, N.J.: Princeton University Press, 1977.

Smith, A. Cobden. "Mrs. Gaskell and Lower Mosley Street, a Centenary Address." *Sunday School Quarterly* (January 1911): 156–61.

Smith, G. B. "Mrs. Gaskell and Her Novels." *Cornhill Magazine* 29 (1874): 191–212.

Stebbins, Lucy. "Elizabeth Gaskell," In her *A Victorian Album: Some Lady Novelists of the Period,* pp. 95–128. New York: Columbia University Press, 1946.

Stoneman, Patsy. *Elizabeth Gaskell.* Brighton, Sussex: Harvester Press, 1987.

Storey, Graham, and Kathleen Tillotson, eds. *The Pilgrim Edition of the Letters of Charles Dickens,* Vol. 6. Oxford: At the Clarendon Press, 1988.

Swinburne, Charles Algernon. *A Note on Charlotte Brontë.* London: Chatto & Windus, 1877.

Tillotson, Kathleen. *Novels of the Eighteen-Forties.* 1954; rpt. London: Oxford University Press, 1962.

Wagenknecht, Edward. *Cavalcade of the English Novel: From Elizabeth to George VI.* New York: Henry Holt and Company, 1943.

Waller, R. D., ed. "Letters Addressed to Mrs. Gaskell By Celebrated Contemporaries." *Bulletin of the John Rylands University Library of Manchester* 19 (1935): 43.

Webb, R. K. *Harriet Martineau: A Radical Victorian.* New York: Columbia University Press, 1960.

Welch, Jeffrey. *Elizabeth Gaskell: An Annotated Bibliography: 1929–1975.* New York: Garland Publishing, 1977.

Wheatley, Vera. *The Life and Work of Harriet Martineau.* Fair Lawn, N.J.: Essential Books, 1957.

Wheeler, Michael D. "The Sinner as Heroine: A Study of Mrs. Gaskell's *Ruth* and the Bible." *Durham University Journal* 37 (1976): 148–61.

Whitfield, A. Stanton. *Mrs. Gaskell: Her Life and Work*. London: George Routledge & Sons, 1929.

Wise, T. J., and J. A. Symington, eds. *The Brontës: Their Lives, Friendships, and Correspondence*. 4 vols. Oxford: Shakespeare Head Press, 1932.

Woolf, Virginia, "Professions for Women." In her *The Death of the Moth and Other Essays*, pp. 235–42. 1942; rpt. New York: Harcourt Brace Jovanovich, 1970.

Wright, Edgar. *Mrs. Gaskell: The Basis for Reassessment*. London: Oxford University Press, 1965.

Index

Crime: as image, 48, 177–78, 255–57; in "The Crooked Branch," 33; in "Crowley Castle," 165; in "A Dark Night's Work," 255–56; in "The Grey Woman," 216; in *Mary Barton*, 151, 180, 181; in "The Moorland Cottage," 73, 177; in *North and South*, 170–71; in "Right at Last," 274; in *Ruth*, 47–48; in "The Squire's Story," 51–52; in *Sylvia's Lovers*, 199

"Crooked Branch, The" (short story; alternate title: "The Ghost in the Garden Room"), 33, 178

"Crowley Castle" (short story; first published as "How the First Floor Went to Crowley Castle"), 18, 70, 72, 163–65

"Curious if True" (short story), 31, 89, 114–15

Daemonic double: as image, 47–54, 74, 83, 284–85; in "Crowley Castle," 164; in "The Half-Brothers," 76; in *The Life of Charlotte Brontë*, 238–40; in "Lois the Witch," 113, 131; in "The Moorland Cottage," 73; in *North and South*, 175; in "The Poor Clare," 94–95, 113; in *Ruth*, 94–95, 121, 123–27, 131–32, 165; in *Wives and Daughters*, 65, 70, 74

Darkness, as image, 122–23

"Dark Night's Work, A" (short story), 4, 255–57, 258–59

Daughter: as image, in *The Life of Charlotte Brontë*, 238–39; in "Lizzie Leigh," 125; in *Mary Barton*, 152, 179; in *Wives and Daughters*, 55–76

Death: EG's, 37, 279, 285; as image, 279–85; of members of EG's family, 15–19, 28–31; in "The Half-Brothers," 75–76; in *The Life of Charlotte Brontë*, 252–53; in "Lois the Witch," 116–17, 119; in *Ruth*, 89, 91, 122, 123, 130–32; in "Sketch of Clopton House," 254; in *Sylvia's Lovers*, 201–2; in *Wives and Daughters*, 63, 76

Demon, as image, 47–53, 143–52, 284–85

Dickens, Charles: as image, in *Cranford*, 157–58, 223

Disappearance: of EG's brother, 29, 160–61; as image, 29, 182; in *Cranford*, 160–61, 182; in "The Manchester Marriage," 196; in *Sylvia's Lovers*, 198

"Disappearances" (essay/story), 29

"Doom of the Griffiths" (short story), 9, 60–61, 64

Dreams, 7, 15; as image, 272, 273, 283; in "Curious if True," 114–15; in "Half a Lifetime Ago," 283; in *Ruth*, 129–32, 195, 227

England: as image, 70–72, 263–64; in "A Dark Night's Work," 255, 257; in *The Life of Charlotte Brontë*, 237–38; in "Lois the Witch," 112–13, 116; in "The Moorland Cottage," 71–72; in *North and South*, 175; in *Sylvia's Lovers*, 208; in *Wives and Daughters*, 71–72

Esau: as image, 32; in "Modern Greek Songs," 32; in "The Moorland Cottage," 32

Exile: EG's to Knutsford, 15, 27, 31, 46; as image, in *Wives and Daughters*, 58, 67

Experience: power of on EG's mind, 86, 105; in *Ruth*, 88; in *Wives and Daughters*, 105

Eyes: as image, 96, 167; in "Lois the Witch," 96, 112–13; in "Right at Last," 274; in *Ruth*, 97, 118, 119

Fallen/falling woman: as image, 133, 150, 221; in *The Life of Charlotte Brontë*, 237, 239, 242; in *Mary Barton*, 180; in "The Poor Clare," 52–53; in *Ruth*, 77–95

Family, as image, 43–46, 109, 218, 276

Father: as image, in *Mary Barton*, 143, 179–80; in "The Poor Clare," 49, 117; in "Right at Last," 32; in *Ruth*, 47–48, 124, 134–35; in *Sylvia's Lovers*, 198–99; in *Wives and Daughters*, 56–63, 66, 67, 142. See also Stevenson, William (EG's father)

Female: circle in EG's life, 156; as image, 32–46; place of, 162, 184; in *Cranford*, 153–61; in *Mary Barton*,

DATE DUE